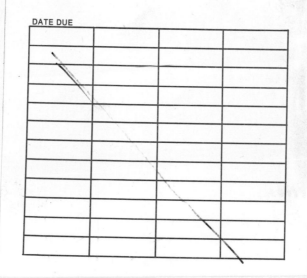

ALSO BY WERNER KELLER

The Bible as History
East Minus West = Zero
Diaspora

The Etruscans

WERNER KELLER

The Etruscans

**Translated from the German by
Alexander and Elizabeth Henderson**

ALFRED A. KNOPF NEW YORK 1974

THIS IS A BORZOI BOOK
PUBLISHED BY ALFRED A. KNOPF, INC.

First American Edition

Translation copyright © 1974 by Alfred A. Knopf, Inc.

The lines on page 224 are
from Pindar's *Pythian Ode I,* from
Richard Lattimore's translation,
Some Odes of Pindar. Copyright 1942
by New Directions Publishing Corporation.
Reprinted by permission of New Directions
Publishing Corporation.

Library of Congress Cataloging in Publication Data

Keller, Werner, (Date)   The Etruscans.

Translation of Denn sie entzündeten das Licht.
Bibliography: p.
1. Etruria—History.   I. Title.
DG223.K4313 1974   913.37′5   73–16473
ISBN 0–394–47301–9

Manufactured in the United States of America

*To my daughters
Christiane, Dorothee, and Angela,
in memory of unforgettable days
in ancient Etruria*

Contents

List of Illustrations

ILLUSTRATIONS

x

Foreword

No other European people has been as neglected as the Etruscans, and the legacy of no other group has been so systematically destroyed. It is as though posterity had conspired to erase every trace of a nation whose pioneer activity constituted the first major chapter in the history of the West. There has been no real change in this attitude even though excavations have, since the last century, brought to light an amazing quantity of discoveries. If one inquires when Rome was founded, the answer generally given is a date—753 B.C.—that is wrong and long superseded, but nevertheless still recorded in every work of reference and school book. The question of who founded the city is also given an incorrect answer, namely, Romulus, just as Roman schoolboys learned two thousand years ago.

And yet it is now reasonably certain that it was an Etruscan king called Tarquinius Priscus who founded Rome in about 575 B.C. This historical fact has remained largely unknown to the public. And it is not the only one, for the Etruscan foundation and development of the city on the Tiber that subsequently became Rome is only one of the many admirable achievements of this remarkable people. Long before Rome existed, they had already established an empire on Italian soil, with big cities, industry, arts and crafts, and world-wide trade. But of all this the general public has been told almost nothing. Anyone who wants to find out about this people is in for a disappointment.

Go into a bookshop or library, in Europe or the United States, and ask for a history of the Etruscans. Or check out the history books and similar works. To no avail. Certainly there are many treatises on the mysterious origins and language of the Etruscans, and on excavations and the secrets of their religion. And in recent years whole stacks of illustrated volumes on their art. But on Etruscan history?

The past of Europe is always taken to mean Greece and Rome. It is only the ancient Greeks and the ancient Romans who are considered the great peoples of antiquity, and the founders of Western civilization. They alone have been admired, praised, revered, and investigated. The works of historians and other specialists are full of them. And cultured people proudly speak of the Periclean Age, or the Augustan. The Etruscans are excluded from this view of the past. It is as though they had never existed, even though they lived and worked on European soil for seven centuries. As Will Durant once said, it is a provincialism in traditional history-writing that makes Europe begin with Greece.

Thus from the Middle Ages down to recent times, a picture was built up that was biased, incomplete, and hence erroneous. There was a huge gap in it. One great chapter of European history, the earliest and most exciting—that of the Etruscans—remained unwritten.

For centuries there was good reason for this since there was a lack of authentic, detailed records. Nothing has survived of what the Etruscans themselves wrote about their history. Their own chronicles were destroyed. And even the twenty volumes of the emperor Claudius's *Tyrrhenica* were lost. Thus the only sources were the brief observations and comments of a few ancient Greek and Roman authors. The names of rulers and outstanding personalities were unknown, there were no accounts of their deeds, no stories or episodes; in short, everything that helps to bring to life the history of a people was missing.

And the places where evidence of the greatness of Etruria lay buried had systematically been destroyed. For nearly two thousand years, from Roman times down to those of the aristocratic big landowners and grave robbers in the nineteenth century, the vast cemeteries were despoiled of their fabulous treasures. Just for the sake of gain the ancient tombs were barbarously broken open by the tens of thousands. The precious gold, silver, and bronze work, the luxury articles, and the beautiful pottery were greedily snatched, what appeared to be uninteresting was smashed, and the graves were filled in, so that even their position can no longer be traced.

In the last century, when scientific interest was at last aroused and careful excavations began, it was a rarity to find an untouched grave. However, over the decades down to the present day, archeologists have painstakingly unearthed a mass of astonishing finds, some really sensational.

An image of ancient Etruria has gradually emerged in the same way that that of the ancient Near East has been built up from excavations in Asia Minor and Egypt. Out of innumerable documents and relics the general outline of this mysterious people's life has been put together. We still lack systematic investigations into the Etruscan cities themselves, but what has so far been discovered and ascertained provides a view of a past which was hitherto barely suspected, and which obliges us to revise the familiar historical picture.

On the frontiers of prehistoric times and the beginnings of history it was the Etruscans who, long before the Romans, created a sophisticated civilization in the heart of Italy, and thereby laid the foundations for the subsequent rise of Europe. It was they who transmitted the heritage of the ancient East with its highly developed civilizations and domesticated it in western Europe.

As a writer interested in modern research, I was tempted by the task of putting together the fascinating discoveries and new knowledge in the context of history. To coordinate the material took more effort and time than I had foreseen. I write this foreword after a long journey of more than a decade which became, for me, an unforgettable experience. It took me to all the places where Etruscan antiquities are to be found, to innumerable excavation sites, ruins, and cemeteries all over Italy, from the once famous Spina on the Adriatic to the marvelous old Tuscan country between the Arno and the Tiber, down to once Etruscan Pompeii in Campania; through all the museums with important Etruscan collections in

Europe and the United States; to the countries where once the friends and foes of the Etruscans lived, to ancient Carthage, as well as to Greece and the Near East.

My thanks are due to Dr. Ambros Josef Pfiffig, lecturer in Etruscology and Italian Antiquities at the University of Perugia, for reading through my manuscript and for valuable suggestions. I am most grateful too to my wife Helga, who once again gave me her unwearying help.

WERNER KELLER

PART ONE

Before Western History Began

Asia claims the Tuscans as her own.

Seneca, 1st century B.C.

It is evident . . . that the Etruscans
were the first people in Italy
to adopt Greek and Oriental cultures
and to spread them to other Italic peoples.

Axel Boëthius, 1960

I

Light from the East

BEGAN LATE IN EUROPE, LESS than a millennium before the Christian era. It was the Near East which, early in the ninth century B.C., stirred Europe from its prehistoric sleep, and set Ereb, "the land of darkness" as the Phoenicians called it, on the way to creating a civilization which had a more profound influence than any of its predecessors in shaping the destinies of mankind.

At that time the Mediterranean came alive with a great westward movement of peoples. Where Asia and Europe almost meet at the Hellespont, in the ports of Asia Minor, along the coast of Greece and among the islands in between, fleets of sailing ships and oar-manned galleys set forth on the daring journey into an as yet unknown, distant, and dangerous world. Following the setting sun they crossed the Ionian Sea toward the Italian peninsula and Sicily, its bridge to Africa.

3

They were the heralds of change. Wherever the alien newcomers landed, the native peoples of the West found their lives much altered by this contact with a new, highly civilized world. Nowhere else was the impact as powerful as in the very heart of Italy. In response to the influences from the eastern Mediterranean, Europe's first culture and civilization began to appear in the lands between the the Tiber and the Arno.

At the time when Europe's future was barely a promise, the Near East already had a long, eventful, and glorious past behind it. Great civilizations had long ago arisen in the vast semicircle reaching from the Persian Gulf across Mesopotamia, Syria, and Palestine to the deserts of Arabia and the banks of the Nile.

For two thousand years past, the countries of the Tigris and Euphrates had witnessed the ascendancy and decline of powerful empires. The Sumerians, poets of the Epic of Gilgamesh and builders of the first ziggurats, had been followed by the empires of the Babylonians and Assyrians and, farther west, by the Hittites. On the Nile, the origins of political organization are almost as old, for the first pharaohs began to rule around 3000 B.C.

It is to the ancient Near East that the whole world, and the peoples of Europe first and foremost, are indebted for every stimulus which, beginning in the Stone Age, slowly led them out of their backward, primitive ways. Numberless discoveries, inventions, innovations, and pioneering achievements in every field of endeavor are the Fertile Crescent's gift to the world.

It was here that urban life began, that the first great cities were built. Triumphs of architecture were achieved in the great palaces and colonnaded temples with their sculptured reliefs and painted walls. Miners dug valuable metals out of the earth—copper from the mines in Sinai and silver from the Taurus Mountains. There was a vast development in the skill and output of craftsmen, of goldsmiths, ivory carvers, bronze casters, joiners, and weavers.

The calendar and the clock were long since known, together with the division of the year into 360 days and of the day into twenty-four hours. So too were letters of credit and contracts duly sealed. Hammurabi, king of Babylonia, laid down the first comprehensive code of law. In the valleys of the Nile, the Euphrates and the Tigris, farms and large-scale plantations with elaborate irrigation and drainage systems produced rich crops of grain, vegetables of all kinds, and the choicest fruits. An astonishingly high level was reached in the arts, in sculpture, painting, literature, and music, and in the sciences, in astronomy, medicine, geometry, mathematics, and philology. Thanks to the invention of hieroglyphic and cuneiform scripts, to the use of ink and papyrus, reading and writing were well established, and there were books, libraries, and schools.

It was at the beginning of the second millennium B.C. that the earliest vigorous stimulus from the East reached the Aegean and gave rise to a unique civilization. Remote legends carried a memory of the event, and in those legends the name of the continent in the West occurred for the first time. On the coast of Phoenicia, we are told, lived a wondrously beautiful princess, white of complexion, who was called Europa. She was the daughter of King Agenor. When Zeus, the greatest of the gods of the Greeks, saw her, he at once fell passionately in love. In the form of a milk-white bull he approached the girl as she was playing with her companions on the seashore. The god won her trust and, unsuspecting, she seated herself on the animal's back. Whereupon Zeus plunged with her into the waves and swam from the shore of Asia to Crete, where he changed into an eagle and fathered three sons upon Europa. The firstborn was called Minos. The great island upon which the divine bull settled with his captured princess was to become the first great fertilizing force in the West.

Influences from Egypt, northern Mesopotamia, and Syria met in Crete, and a sophisticated civilization developed. Here, early in the second millennium B.C., appeared the empire of the kings who built the magnificent frescoed palaces of Knossos, the capital, of Phaistos, Mallia, and Kato Zakro, and established the first sea power known to history. Their fleets were soon masters of the Aegean and the eastern Mediterranean, and they traded from the Bosporus to the Nile. The Cretans seem, too, to have been the first to risk crossing the Ionian Sea in a westerly direction, for well into classical times the Greeks still remembered a second Minos, perhaps the grandson of the founder, who was killed on a voyage to Sicily.

A detailed picture of the Cretan civilization and economy gradually emerged from the excavations of the British archeologist Sir Arthur Evans, which began in 1899. Crete's agriculture had advanced from simple cultivation of the land to profitable exploitation of olive groves. Its artisans had mastered very complex procedures in metal working and pottery making. They possessed molds and furnaces for casting tools, weapons, and jewelry. There was large-scale production for domestic consumption and export. Trade and business used standard weights and a currency of gold and copper bars. There was a decimal system of numeration and a syllabary, either scratched on clay tablets or written with ink.

Economic prosperity and the profits from overseas trade led to remarkable refinements in the Cretan way of life. The palaces had a system of baths, water conduits, and drainage. Such sports as boxing and bull-jumping provided both physical training and entertainment. Worship had its magical and religious ceremonies, in which women too participated. The double axe was a sacred symbol. At an early stage the dead were buried in great *tholos* tombs, domed giant beehives made of overlapping rings of stone slabs.

Crete, an offspring and an outpost of the ancient Near East in the Aegean, became the great intermediary between Asia and Europe. From 1700 B.C. onward, Cretan trade delegations, intent on opening up new markets, seem to have arrived with increasing frequency on the coasts of nearby Hellas. The inhabitants they encountered, the original Achaeans, were descendants of the first wave of peoples speaking an Indo-European language, who came down from the north soon after 1900 B.C., and conquered the land. They were barbaric warriors, rough and primitive in their way of life and habits, like all the other tribes of Europe at that time.

> **But all unsuspecting the Cretans had set in train a sequence of events that was to result in their own downfall.**

However, these Achaeans proved themselves surprisingly apt pupils of the traders from the highly civilized Minoan empire. In emulation of the Cretans they built ships and became seafarers and traders in their turn. On the Greek mainland Indo-European speaking peoples developed their first civilization under Cretan inspiration and influence. Thanks to the profits of its traders, Mycenae, the Achaean capital, became a city whose wealth of gold still found mention in Homer. Palaces—the first on European soil—were built in the Minoan style. The dead were buried in vaulted tombs made of massive stone blocks like the *tholos* graves in southern Crete. The Mycenaeans became the first Indo-European speaking people to learn to read and write. They took over the Cretan syllabary.

But all unsuspecting the Cretans had set in train a sequence of

6

events that was to result in their own downfall. Mycenae became the center of a mighty movement of expansion. Not long after 1500 B.C. the Achaeans, with a powerfully armed force of men and ships, set out to enlarge their dominion. A vast earthquake brought terrible destruction to Crete, and soon afterward the Achaeans landed on the beach of Knossos and occupied the island. The Minoan empire came swiftly to an end.

Mycenae inherited Crete's position in trade, shipping, and command of the sea and developed into a powerful economic empire. Its ships were seen off all the islands and coasts of the eastern Mediterranean. Its merchants established depots at Miletus and at the old Phoenician seaport Ugarit. Westward they crossed the Ionian Sea. Shards of Mycenaean pottery have been found in Ischia and the Lipari islands, in Sicily and southern Italy, in especially large quantities at Taranto.

The lines of Mycenae's trade radiated across the whole continent, reaching even such distant places as Jutland and the Baltic, Scandinavia, and the farthest west. This is the message of the amber beads in the shaft graves and *tholos* tombs in the Peloponnese, of the Mycenaean spiral patterns on Danish sword hilts, and of the double axes in chieftains' graves on the river Saale in Germany. Gold from central Europe and even tin from faraway Britain traveled overland to Greece.

For the inhabitants of the lands to the north and west, Mycenae became the great example and stimulus to economic development. Articles of daily use and luxury goods from the workshops and foundries on the Aegean arrived via the trading routes. And along them too spread knowledge of the metal worker's craft. Thus the Bronze Age began in northern Germany. But this promising beginning came to nothing before the end of the millennium.

Around 1200 B.C. the Sea Peoples burst into the Aegean and wrought havoc and destruction. A migration got under way which swept like a hurricane over whole countries from Asia Minor through Syria to Palestine. It brought about the collapse of the Hittite empire. Miletus and Ugarit were destroyed; the whole of Cyprus was devastated. It was only at the borders of Egypt that the invaders were halted in two battles, by sea and on land.

Greece too suffered destruction. A wave of even more barbarous Indo-European speaking tribes, the Dorians, invaded the Balkan peninsula from the north, as the Achaeans had once done. After the invasion, the thriving civilization in the southeast tip of Europe, the first of its kind, lay in ruins. The eruption of the Sea Peoples and of the Dorians wrecked the economy of Mycenae and its shipping, and thus ended Greek command of the sea. But Mycenae's place did not remain vacant. On the opposite shores of the eastern Mediterranean, from a base in the Levant, shipping began to flourish again as Phoenicians from Lebanon succeeded the Mycenaeans.

One city above all enjoyed an extraordinary rise to dominance as a sea power and trader. This was Tyre, famous in Old Testament times, of which Ezekiel said, "Tyrus, O thou that art situate at the entry of the sea, which art a merchant of the people for many isles." With Tyre a new and stirring chapter in the history of seafaring begins.

For more than two thousand years everything that mattered had taken place in the eastern part of the Mediterranean. Beyond the Ionian Sea the known world came to an end; there seemed to be a frontier which no one dared to cross. Men of Tyre broke the spell by their intrepid explorations. Tyre equipped ships which for the first time dared to sail out of the familiar inner sea into the waters of the West.

The Phoenicians, says the Greek historian Thucydides, were among the first to set up their trading stations on the headlands and islands all around Sicily. In their hunt for new treasures and new goods for their widespread markets, the Phoenicians explored far beyond Sicily. They sailed along the coast of Africa until one day their ships reached the farthest limits of the Mediterranean.

At the entry to the Atlantic Ocean they discovered the legendary kingdom of Tartessus in Andalusia. This was a kind of El Dorado to the ancient world, rich in agricultural products, rich especially in silver obtained from Spanish mines and in tin which came over ancient trading routes from the mysterious Cassiterite Islands in the northern seas. At Gades, the modern Cadiz, the hospitable kings of the country allowed the Phoenicians to set up a trading post. And on the opposite African shore they established their base, Lixus. Melkart, their god, became the guardian of the straits, over which strict control was maintained. No foreign ship was allowed past the Pillars of Hercules.

A chain of moles, depots, and landing places was established along the African coast for the defense and supply of the shipping lines to the new bases. Utica, a new city with a safe harbor, was built at the point where in present-day Tunisia the Medjerda River flows through the foothills of the Atlas Mountains into the sea. According to Pliny, it was founded in 1101 B.C.; it still exists and is now called Utique.

For centuries the Phoenicians were the only people to navigate the great western sea, and no one disputed their monopoly of trade with Tartessus, the Land of Silver. They had no competitors, for Greek shipping was still confined to the Aegean. Their dominating position was further strengthened when Assyrian conquests drove emigrants from Tyre to found another city in North Africa. Led by Princess Dido they left their homeland, and in 814 B.C., not far from Utica, they laid the foundations of Carthage at the foot of the two-hundred-foot-high hill called Byrsa, which became the citadel.

Barely a century later, however, the situation in the western Mediterranean was decisively altered. Carthage and the Phoenicians were unexpectedly faced with a dangerous rival to their commercial empire beyond the Ionian Sea. Not long after Tyre had founded its Carthaginian base, another migration across the sea had started. This one came from Hellas.

For more than four centuries after the invasions of the Sea Peoples and the Dorians into the Aegean, little had been heard of the Greeks. After the onslaught of the northern barbarians, everything relapsed into primitive darkness; nothing remained of the sophisticated civilization of Mycenaean times, not even in Attica where the Ionians survived the Dorian invasion. No more palaces or monumental stone buildings were erected. People lived in mud huts once again, and big workshops were a thing of the past. Even writing fell into oblivion. As in earliest times, a rudimentary subsistence economy prevailed; people lived on the produce of the land, on arable farming and animal husbandry. Their art was as plain and simple as their way of life. An austere geometric style of decoration became characteristic of their pottery.

It was not in the homeland of the Greeks, but on the opposite shores of the Aegean, in Asia Minor, that signs of a hopeful new beginning first appeared. And the stimulus for a rebirth in Hellas came again from the ancient Near East, this time from Anatolia and Phoenicia, as the first stimulus, nearly a thousand years earlier, had come from the ancient culture of the Minoans.

On the sites of such ruined cities as Miletus, where the Greeks had possessed trading posts in Mycenaean times, new settlements, cities, and ports gradually appeared. They were founded mainly by Ionian-speaking emigrants who had left their homeland in large numbers after the Dorian whirlwind had passed away.

As early as the ninth century a chain of colonies sprang up and soon flourished along the coast, from Smyrna to the neighborhood of Halicarnassus. Ionians settled likewise on the islands of Chios and Samos. Trade brought growth and prosperity. In Asia Minor and in Syria were the terminals of the great caravan routes. Along them came merchandise from the countries of Hither Asia, chiefly from Mesopotamia. From Miletus and Phocaea, at the mouths of the two biggest rivers of the peninsula, the Meander and the Hermus, the two most important trading routes led from the Aegean Sea up into the tableland of Anatolia. While time stood still in the Greek homeland and even Athens led a shadowy existence, Ionia became the scene of initiatives which opened the way to the future. The cities of Ionia became great and rich. From its ports merchantmen began again to traffic in the Aegean. Industrial crafts developed, especially metal working and pottery; there was a steady production for export.

> **The whole of Hellas seemed suddenly seized by restlessness, gripped by a spirit of change and renewal.**

Homer was an Ionian Greek. His incomparable epics were created around 750 B.C. on the soil of Asia Minor. His *Iliad* conjured up the battles for Troy, the memory of a heroic past, of a world of knights to whom war meant everything. But in the *Odyssey* a quite different, more topical theme is heard. It celebrates the bold seafarer who endures the most extraordinary perils, as though the poem were meant to inspire enthusiasm for further daring ventures at sea. The century in which the great poet composed his verses was the beginning of an age of expansion.

The whole of Hellas seemed suddenly seized by restlessness, gripped by a spirit of change and renewal. From the colonies in Asia Minor, from the homeland, and from the islands, ships set out, alone and in convoys. Some were seeking new and profitable trade, others new land to colonize with new homes. Behind it all lay overpopulation, social crises, and the urge to find new markets. Around the Aegean there was no more unoccupied land; access to Syria and Lebanon was barred by the Assyrians and Phoenicians. Only in Italy, beyond the Ionian Sea, were there still thinly populated areas. These were the emigrants' goal.

The ships of the land-hungry Greeks appeared off the coasts of southern Italy and Sicily, singly at first, scouting out the land, and then in whole swarms. One of the first flotillas passed through the Strait of Messina, reached the island of Ischia, and founded a settlement there. Twenty years later, about 750 B.C., the new-comers settled to the north of Vesuvius on the coast opposite the island and founded Kyme, which the Romans later called Cumae. Within a few decades wave after wave of immigrants arrived in southern Italy and Sicily. All the Hellenic peoples, Ionians, Dorians, and Achaeans, took part in the colonization.

In 735 B.C. Ionian settlers from Chalcis on Euboea landed at the foot of Mount Etna in Sicily. The following year Dorians from Corinth settled on the island of Ortygia and laid the foundations for Syracuse, which later, under the rule of its tyrants, became so power-ful and famous. In 729 B.C. Leontini and Catane, the present Ca-tania, were founded. As in Sicily, so too in the "instep" of Italy, in Apulia and Calabria, one city after another was established—by the Achaeans at Sybaris in about 720 B.C., and at Croton in 710 B.C., and by the Spartans at Tarentum (Taranto) in about 708 B.C.

In the course of little more than a century, Greek colonies sprang up all along the Italian and Sicilian coasts of the Ionian Sea, from the Gulf of Taranto in the east to the Strait of Messina and beyond, along the eastern and southern coasts of Sicily, from Cape Pelorus (Punta del Faro) to Cape Lilybaeum (Capo Boeo). A whole region was occupied which in extent was barely smaller than the mother-land south of Thermopylae.

Only when it was already too late did Carthage realize what dangerous rivalry its trading empire in the western Mediterranean now had to face from the Greek colonies. But then the Carthaginians swiftly went to work to save what could still be saved of their gravely threatened positions, so as to safeguard their command of the sea, as yet intact, along the North African coast as far as Tharsis. They boldly occupied Sardinia. They stationed troops on the Balearic Islands, which were an important stepping-stone on the way to

Spain. In Sicily, where the Greeks were already established on the eastern and southern coasts, they prepared for counterattack from the western tip of the island where they had bases at Motya, Lilybaeum, Panormus, and Soloeis.

These moves and countermoves were part of a wide-ranging struggle between Greeks and Carthaginians for trading posts, settlements, and raw materials, for colonies and vital markets in the western Mediterranean, southern Italy, and Sicily. And amid them all occurred perhaps the most significant event, as far as Europe was concerned, of the first half of the first millennium B.C. It was an event that was to influence profoundly the future of the whole continent. For it is to this period that we can date the beginnings of Etruscan history. In the heart of the Italian peninsula appeared the first tangible evidence of a famous people that was long believed to be an enigma and a mystery, a people that was as much admired as it was feared and maligned.

II

Italy—The "Land of Calves"

ITALY, THE "LAND OF CALVES," AS THE Greeks called it, had for thousands of years remained a forgotten corner of the world. Although brilliant civilizations had flourished on other shores of the Mediterranean in the east, Italy seemed untouched by what happened elsewhere. Archeologists who searched its soil for evidence of prehistoric times were not rewarded by a single lucky discovery. No palace came to light, no citadel, no temple or treasury. Not even the foundations of a city were found, or any remains of brick-built houses. There was no trace of building in stone.

The glass cases of the prehistoric collections at Perugia, Bologna, and elsewhere contain what the archeologist's spade has uncovered. Room after room packed with the yield of long and laborious efforts by innumerable scholars—fragments from habitations and graves, vessels and ornaments, implements and weapons. There seems to be an almost uncountable quantity of objects, evidence of millenniums reaching back into the remotest times when stones served as tools and weapons. A monotonous fog lies over the vast span of man's past which they represent. These relics have little to say to us. As like as not they offer a riddle rather than a solution. They contain no writing or image that might evoke the appearance of those who made them. The life of the people to which they testify must have been as dull and plain as the shards of their pots, as primitive as their implements. A life sluggish, uneventful, monotonously dragging along, generation after generation.

It is hardly surprising that the prehistory of Italy presents many a problem, has led to many a dispute over the interpretation and dating of the evidence. It remains obscure and full of unanswered questions, and it has barely revealed more than a preliminary uncertain outline.

Among the oldest inhabitants were the Ligurians, who lived in the region of Genoa and in the Po valley. They belonged to a primitive Mediterranean race, related to the Iberians. In the east of the peninsula, in Picenum, Apulia, and in eastern Sicily, were tribes which some authors include among the Pelasgians, a people who in the earliest times inhabited the Aegean and Asia Minor. These prehistoric folk lived in caves and buried their dead in a contracted position. With the dead they placed weapons made of roughly chipped stone, implements of horn and bone, ornaments made of shells or animals' teeth. Tilling the soil became common only in Neolithic times. Simple, crude vessels made of clay came into use; they were shaped by hand, for the potter's wheel, which had been in use in Egypt and Mesopotamia for several centuries, was still unknown. Belatedly, the use of metal was introduced from the East. The first bronze objects date from about 1800 B.C.

To the north, at the foot of the Alps, a hitherto unknown culture appeared not long after. Into the Po valley as far as the slopes of the Apennines near Bologna came newcomers who built their settlements on palisades and cremated their dead. Known as the Terremare people, they put an embankment or a ditch around their villages and also enclosed the cemeteries in which they buried urns containing the ashes of the dead. They raised livestock and tilled the soil and were skilled potters and metal workers.

But many more centuries were to pass before life quickened in Italy. It is not till after 1200 B.C., when the Bronze Age was beginning to pass away, that the archeological evidence clearly shows the presence of a new people who must have arrived from elsewhere. The experts declare them to be the first definitely identifiable Indo-European speaking peoples. They came in a series of waves, and left an imprint on large parts of the Italian peninsula that was to prove crucial for the future. Among them were the ancestors of the Italian peoples whose names are known to history.

Some of the earliest of the new arrivals were the Latin tribes who settled on the Tiber, and their neighbors, the Faliscans. They appeared about the year 1000 B.C., not long after the Mycenaean empire in Greece collapsed under the Dorian attack. Somewhat later came other peoples, Umbrian and Sabellic. They gradually took possession of the mountainous backbone of Italy. From the Tiber northward were Umbrians; in central Italy, Sabellic tribes; and in the south, Oscans and Samnites.

Soon after their arrival there is evidence of major changes in habits and ways of life. An artistic impulse began to show itself. The hitherto primitive pottery vessels in which the ashes of the dead were buried assumed more pleasing forms. Large urns came into use, of conical shape above and below, and often lidded with an inverted bowl or helmet. Most important of all, a new metal age opened in Italy with the use of iron. The new culture is known as Villanovan, after the village Villanova near Bologna, where archeologists found the first evidence of it in an extensive cemetery. This Villanovan culture can be traced from northern Italy through Tuscany as far as Latium, and there is some evidence of it farther south in the province of Salerno.

Since time immemorial the inhabitants of Apennine Italy—both the herdsmen and those who tilled the soil—had led a nomadic existence.

The fullest cultural flowering of these Indo-European speaking invaders occurred along the Tuscan coast of the Tyrrhenian Sea. Everywhere in this region archeologists have discovered evidence of significant progress, traces of crucial changes. An abundance of pottery and bronze objects has come to light. The concurrent artistic fashion was one of severe geometric patterns. Vessels were decorated with straight or zigzag lines, triangles, and swastikas.

Since time immemorial the inhabitants of Apennine Italy—both the herdsmen and those who tilled the soil—had led a nomadic existence. They never settled for long in any one place. Then a change came about. The Villanovans became sedentary. As early as the ninth century B.C. the beginnings of permanent dwelling places appear in Latium and Tuscany. The position and shape of settlements were determined by the natural defenses of the site. Preference was given to high plateaux surrounded by deeply cut watercourses or ravines with steep, unscalable cliffs, or else to high knolls, difficult of access, or hills set amid swamps, such as the Palatine hill on the Tiber. Close to the dwellings of the living— clusters of wattle and daub huts—extensive cemeteries developed as the generations succeeded each other. In them two types of graves are found side by side. These are the pit graves in which the ashes, contained in an urn, were placed, and the trench graves in which the body was laid.

Weapons were put into the men's graves—lances with bronze or iron tips, bronze helmets, long daggers and knives or iron swords. Women's graves contained ornaments such as pins to fasten garments, combs cut from bone or sometimes ivory, and other trinkets. The vessels which the dead person had used were also placed in the grave. These vessels were either of clay—the pots were still shaped by hand, not thrown—or of bronze. Together with indigenous products there were occasional articles of foreign origin, gifts such as scarabs and figurines from the Aegean, Egypt, and the Near East. These are a certain indication that travelers from other countries, Phoenicians and Greeks for instance, must by then have visited the coast.

In Latium, and also north of the Tiber, the ossuaries often imitated the dwellings of the living. These are the so-called hut urns found in large numbers in the Alban hills and in Rome. From these hut urns and from the foundations and fragments of walls that have been discovered it is possible to construct quite a vivid picture of what the settlements looked like. The huts were built on the bare ground to a plan that was sometimes square, sometimes rectangular, and sometimes round. The walls were of wattle and daub, and the roofs of straw or reed. On the outside the hut walls were decorated with incised geometric patterns picked out with white paint. There was a portable cooking stand and a triangular opening over the door to let out smoke. "The land of the Villanova people," says the Swedish scholar Axel Boëthius, "like the rest of Italy must have seemed a barbarous coast to the seafarers from the East. Every-

*Terra-cotta cinerary urn from Chiusi;
second half of seventh century B.C.*

where they met 'savages,' of which there is perhaps a reminiscence in the legendary name 'Agrios' which Hesiod gives one of them in his *Theogony*. Like Odysseus on Circe's island, they took their spears and swords to the 'nearest commanding height' to look out for signs of human activity or smoke from the dense woods.

Bronze helmet, probably the lid of a cinerary urn; Villanovan period, eighth century B.C.

**Bronze cinerary urn in the form of a hut,
Italic; late eighth century B.C.**

"Tilling the land and animal husbandry were the main occupations. We get the impression of a simple rural life, such as Roman poets lauded in the reign of Augustus and longed for amid the deafening hubbub of the capital, as they dreamed of simple huts on silent hillsides, where nearby brooks rippled through the green coverts, and sacrifices to shapeless gods were offered on open-air altars.

"In imperial Rome the hut of Romulus on the Palatine recalled that past. Dionysius of Halicarnassus describes it just as Iron Age dwellings looked, and says that it was always rebuilt in the same shape if destroyed by fire. All this recalls a cultural stage in Rome's own prehistory, the traces of which can be definitely shown only in the Villanovan age."

19

But it is easy to be misled. Simple though their life may have been, the new settlers were not mere primitive herdsmen and tillers of the soil. They were highly gifted craftsmen, and in metal working displayed remarkable technical skill, as is shown by the household implements and weapons they made. They wore bronze cuirasses and high, pointed, and crested helmets, and carried round shields.

The Villanovans seem also to have known how to obtain in their own territory the raw material needed for this extensive consumption of metal. Can it have been pure chance that this peasant culture reached its highest development in southern Tuscany, and in particular at the place where Tarquinii, the Etruscans' cardinal city, was later built? Only a day's march away lie the Tolfa Mountains, rich in the metalliferous ores that were so prized and sought after at that time. Archeological investigations have shown beyond doubt that the earliest mining there took place in Villanovan times.

But despite the changes and advances that had come with the immigrants, Italy remained sunk in its ancient lethargy and uneventfulness. Some more powerful stimulus from outside was needed to carry the inhabitants of Italy out of their primitive darkness. For that the time was ripe. And the new stimulus was at hand.

PART TWO

The Advent of the Etruscans

The Tyrrhenian nation
is found to . . . agree with no other either in its language
or in its manner of living.

Dionysius of Halicarnassus,
1st century B.C.

Careful study of the archeological documents
in our possession is sufficient to persuade us that
both the predominant role
and absolute chronological priority
in the formation of the civilization
of ancient Italy belong to Etruria.

Massimo Pallottino, 1955

III

The First Giant Tombs

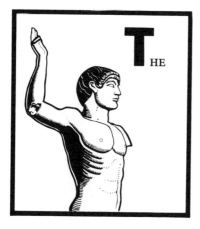

NINTH CENTURY B.C. WAS STILL prehistory in Italy. But a mere century later a great upheaval was taking place, and the way of life, the customs and language of the Indo-European speaking inhabitants were changing. Even the landscape began to look different in places.

The scene of this transformation was the land in the heart of Italy that corresponds to the Tuscany of today. Between the Arno, the Tiber, and the Tyrrhenian Sea, within the curve of the Apennines, lies the rolling country of the famous red earth. Bordering the olive groves and vineyards grow wild myrtle, mastic, rosemary, lavender, and cistus; eucalyptus, pines, cypresses, and cork oaks are the predominant trees. The contours of the hills, formed of sedimentary deposits, are gentle, and the streams and rivers are turbid with the soil they carry down the valleys. A plowed field gleams bright brick-red in the sun and a newly barked cork oak has a rusty glow. Despite the swarming holidaymakers on the beaches and the lines of motor vehicles on the roads, it is a region that still keeps much of its ancient charm.

Farther south, beginning at Orvieto and continuing into Latium, the picture changes. Swift torrents have cut the countryside into deep ravines with abrupt cliffs of tufa rock. There are many hot and cold springs that supply the baths of spa towns and mineral waters for the table. All this is volcanic country, scattered with extinct craters now filled by lakes, large ones such as Trasimene and Bolsena, and small ones like Lake Vico in the Ciminian forest, and Lake Bracciano. Some of these volcanoes are believed to have been still active at the time when the great changes were taking place in the country.

Archeological evidence makes it possible to fix the date fairly exactly. It was about 750 B.C. that signs of a highly developed civilization first appeared in the midst of the still primitive Villanovan settlements. The earliest change shows in the treatment of the dead. Alongside the cremation graves there is a noticeable increase in inhumation graves. At Tarquinia fifty-eight out of eighty-six known burials of the period are inhumations. The graves, which originally were covered only with stone slabs, sometimes arranged in a gable as though to imitate house roofs, were replaced by solidly built sepulchers. Chamber tombs, four-sided like rooms, came into use. They were excavated underground out of the soft tufa rock, and conceived as houses for the dead. They were approached by a corridor or stairway leading down. Sometimes when a number of chambers were close together, they were grouped around a common anteroom.

Such underground tombs had hitherto been unknown in Italy or in any other country in the West. But even they were only a prelude. About 700 B.C. the picture changed again. The sepulchers became huge. The chambers cut out of the rock developed into great halls of the dead. A monumental tomb architecture came into being. Sepulchral monuments, visible far and wide, of a size and form at

These great tombs appeared at first singly, and then in groups, amid the inconspicuous Iron Age cemeteries with their simple burial customs.

that time unknown elsewhere in the Mediterranean, appeared in the domain of the Indo-European speaking peoples north of the Tiber, within sight of their settlements along the coast as far as Elba.

These great tombs appeared at first singly, and then in groups, amid the inconspicuous Iron Age cemeteries with their simple burial customs. Gradually the huge tumuli, like cathedral domes, spread from the tufa plateaux near the sea far into the countryside, toward the Apennines; the piled-up masses of earth were often of vast dimensions, like hills. Built when the prehistoric was passing into the historic, these strange constructions mark, as it were, the boundary of that change. After two and a half millenniums many of them still survive. Deep within them are the stone rooms designed as last resting places of the dead.

At Cerveteri, little more than twenty-five miles from Rome, the famous Banditaccia necropolis has a gloomy aspect. The tumuli are of varying size, with diameters ranging up to 130 feet. The base is a tufa drum, ornamented with moldings; it is carved out of the living rock or built of blocks of stone. Grass covers the knolls on which cypresses grow. Under the great mound of earth lie one or more tombs, approached through a descending corridor. They are built to imitate the inside of houses, with doors, feigned windows and

Etruscan tumuli, Cerveteri

ceilings, columns and pilasters, and furnished with thronelike chairs and funerary couches.

Between the tumuli is the Funeral Way, marked by the enduring ruts cut into the ground by the heavy hearses. Along this road for centuries the dead were taken in solemn ceremonial to their graves. Carved stones—little houses for a woman and phallus-like shapes for a man—lie scattered about near the tomb entrances. They denote the sex of the dead persons buried deep within the tumulus. To walk amid the silence of this strange, ancient necropolis is an unforgettable experience.

In the quiet bay of Porto Baratti near Populonia, opposite the island of Elba, are the remains of other huge cupolalike structures. They also date from the seventh century B.C. They have a circular wall constructed, without cement, of blocks and slabs and closely fitted flat pieces of stone. The largest of them is some ninety feet in circumference. A broad, paved path surrounds the mausoleum. Overhead, limestone slabs project from the perpendicular walls and carry off the rainwater from the mound of earth that lids the whole like a round buckler. Within is a square room over which a false dome is built from overlapping stone blocks. The method of building recalls the *tholos* tombs of the Mycenaean civilization which were constructed in the second millennium B.C., or the tomb known as the Treasury of Atreus near Mycenae, or the towerlike *nuraghi* of Sardinia.

During excavations in the last century on the slopes of the hills around Vetulonia, Populonia's neighbor near present-day Grosseto, sepulchral monuments of another kind were discovered. These were tombs marked by huge circles of hewn stone slabs set upright in the ground. Some of the circles are more than 150 feet in circumference. In the midst of them the body was buried in a trench under a great mound of earth. Tombs of this kind were also found at nearby Marsiliana d'Albegna.

The ruins of yet another great structure, the Tomba della Pietrera, as it is popularly known, are widely visible from the plain at the foot of Vetulonia where the old Roman military road, the Via Aurelia, passes. Only fragments remain of the original construction which enclosed a square tomb chamber with a domelike vault. For centuries people from all around treated the place as a cheap and handy quarry. The structure was some two hundred feet in diameter and consisted of a retaining wall the height of a man, above which was raised an earthen tumulus. This has long since disappeared. Investigation of the surviving fragments showed that the tomb was built twice over. The first collapsed soon after it was completed, burying the funerary couches. The stone used for the vault had been too soft and cracked under the great weight of the covering material. The second time the builders were successful. They used a harder stone, known as *sasso fortino,* which was brought from a distance.

The Tomba della Pietrera at Vetulonia and the Populonia tombs show what fantastic efforts were made to build a true dome. In the tombs, at both places, says the French Etruscologist Raymond Bloch, "we note elements of construction characteristic of the Aegean region but unknown to the Greeks, such as the vault and the cupola. These are still in an initial stage of development and achieved by the superposition of blocks leaning gradually toward the axis of the tomb rather than by means of the wedge-shaped voussoir. Even so they constitute an advance toward more rational forms of construction, and the appearance of such architectural techniques on Italian soil was of extreme significance for the future."

"La Montagnola," interior of the tomb; seventh century B.C. Discovered at Quinto

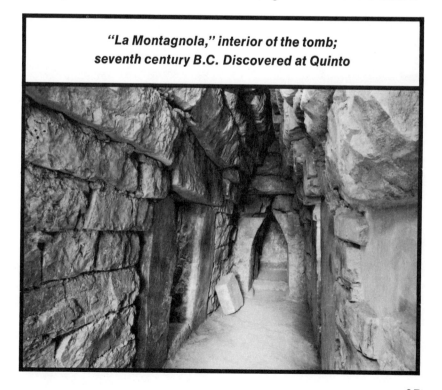

The monumental sepulchral architecture that appears in the seventh century B.C. was an importation. It shows influences coming from the East. The great mortuary tumuli of central Italy bear a striking resemblance to the tumulus fields of Anatolia, especially those at Gordion and Sardis, the ancient capitals of the Phrygian and Lydian kingdoms.

Domed tomb at Casale Marittimo, Volterra; sixth century B.C.

These tumuli still stand at a number of places widely scattered over Tuscany and northern Latium—the Melone di Camucia near Cortona on Lake Trasimene, the Doganaccia mounds near Tarquinia, the Monte Calvario near Castellina in Chianti with its arrangement of tombs pointing to the four cardinal points of the heavens. Near Vulci there are two giants of this kind known as Cucumella and Cucumelletta, and another seven similar ones close to Veii. They are the last that still remain, a mere handful. Many hundreds have long since vanished, carried away, leveled out by nature and the hand of man. They all bore witness to the powerful new conception of the meaning of life, to the hitherto unknown creative urge that found expression in the seventh century B.C. in the country north of the Tiber. For western Europe they announced the beginning of a new age.

PRINCESS LARTHIA'S LUXURY TOMB

FROM IMMEMORIAL TIMES THE high, rounded mounds tempted treasure seekers and tomb robbers. They were too regular in shape to be a natural formation. They proclaimed man's handiwork and were bound to suggest buried treasure. As a result they were ransacked again and again. For centuries, tunnels and shafts were repeatedly driven into them. It is no wonder that when scientific archeology at last took a serious interest in them, they were for the most part found to have been plundered long before.

However, the last century saw some unexpected pieces of luck. A few hitherto untouched burial mounds were discovered and made to yield their secrets. One of the earliest excavations indeed was to exceed all expectation. It became a sensation and attracted attention from far outside the narrow world of learning.

In 1836 two Italians interested in antiquities, Alessandro Regolini, a priest, and General Vicenzo Galassi, decided to excavate in the Sorbo necropolis to the southwest of Caere (Cerveteri). They started on a large hill planted with vines, but at first were disappointed. Others had successfully burrowed in the hillside long before them, for the five tombs they found were already empty. However, Regolini and Galassi were not discouraged and pushed on with their search. Their efforts were to be rewarded in a way they had scarcely dreamed. A shaft which they had driven as far as the center of the great mound met another grave. This time it was untouched.

When the workmen had carefully cleared the opening and Regolini and Galassi expectantly entered, they could hardly believe their eyes. The narrow corridorlike tomb, built of stone blocks, was full of precious furnishings and ornamental objects. On the stone floor of the steeply gabled room lay the skeleton of a woman covered with rich jewelry. This and the quantity of valuable gifts interred with her indicated that she must have been a person of high rank, a princess or a priestess.

In the forepart of the whole sepulcher, separated from the princess, were two other tombs. One, a rounded niche, contained a cremation burial. In an urn were the ashes of a man. The second was in the entrance passage to the main tomb chamber. Here there stood a bronze couch, on which lay the bones of a warrior surrounded by his weapons.

The two excavators made repeated visits to the tomb, and it was only after several days that they grasped the full extent of their remarkable discovery. (The furnishings and gifts which so fascinated them may be seen today in the Regolini–Galassi room of the Museo Gregoriano at the Vatican in Rome. Unfortunately they are badly labeled and inadequately lit.)

The robe of the princess must have been heavily embroidered with gold, and she wore a large gold breastplate or pectoral, covered with repoussé ornamentation of plant and animal motifs that has the appearance of delicate, precious embroidery. A breastplate of this kind was a mark of the highest rank. Only privileged persons could wear it. It was a symbol of power and authority, and originated in the ancient Near East. On a bronze bowl from Nimrud (Calah) on the Tigris, one of the capitals of Assyria, a winged sphinx wears a similar pectoral. It is also found on a statuette showing the Assyrian king Assur-nasir-pal II as a royal priest. The Old Testament describes similar articles. In the Bible, the breastplate of office—called *hoshen* in Hebrew—was worn over the vestment known as an ephod. "And he made the breastplate of cunning work, like the work of the ephod," says *Exodus,* "of gold, blue, and purple, and scarlet, and fine twined linen." These are the "holy garments" made for Aaron, "as the Lord commanded Moses."

A gold disk fibula, one of the most superb pieces of ancient goldsmiths' art, held the princess's robe in place. Its center shows five lions on a three-quarter moon-shaped field bordered by linked palmettes. Within a narrow, smooth margin a second border of palmettes surrounds the whole. Two hinged, semicylindrical cross-bars connect the disk with an oval gold plate covering the pin

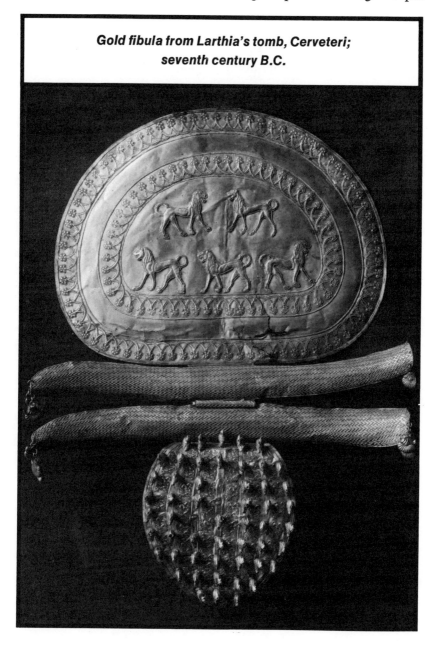

Gold fibula from Larthia's tomb, Cerveteri; seventh century B.C.

mounting. The slightly convex surface of the plate is decorated with seven rows of tiny ducks, some fifty minute, three-dimensional figures. Only a magnifying glass reveals all the infinite delicacy and remarkable skill of this masterpiece of the goldsmith's craft. Everywhere the wonderful repoussé work is enriched with long rows of the finest granulation, the infinitesimal golden balls of which are barely recognizable to the naked eye. They outline the animals and plants, and are attached with such skill that they seem barely to touch each other or the background.

Merely to melt the gold into these minute globules requires profound technological knowledge, the utmost skill, and endless patience. And then to solder them together so that the heat of the process does not distort their shape or displace them seems not far short of magic. Granulation, the apex of the goldsmith's art, comes from the Near East where it has a long history. But the technique was forgotten. For centuries the greatest goldsmiths in the West, including Benvenuto Cellini, the great sixteenth-century Florentine artist, strove in vain to find the right procedure. Only in our day did the Cologne woman goldsmith E. Treskow succeed in producing work of similar delicacy and precision.

> *Near it, against the walls, leaned large, round shields, on some of which were molded panthers' heads with gaping jaws and staring enamel eyes.*

Two wide cufflike bracelets that the princess was wearing are in the same gold repoussé and granulation technique and show the Mistress of Animals in front of a group of palm trees between two rampant lions. Like the Egyptian goddess Hathor she wears her hair in drooping locks. Three women stand near the goddess, clapping their hands. In the treasure were also necklaces, one of large incised gold beads and another with pendants of gold and amber, as well as earrings, spiral-shaped rings, and pins. All the jewelry was as light as a feather, because the goldsmiths worked the metal to an extreme fineness.

The gifts buried with the dead woman were as princely as was her jewelry. Splendid, precious, and exotic, they had a touch of the East, like something out of a fairy tale, such as had never before been found in a tomb in Italy. The grave furnishings of the Villanovan cemeteries seemed barbarous and primitive in comparison.

The bronze couch or bier found in the entrance to the main tomb was made of latticework, with a headrest and six legs. Near it, against the walls, leaned large, round shields, on some of which were molded panthers' heads with gaping jaws and staring enamel eyes. Wonderfully worked bronze cauldrons, from which the heads of griffins and lions projected, stood on pedestals. All around lay quantities of glossy black pottery, the famous *bucchero* ware. Bowls, jugs, beakers, and pots were all decorated with a multitude of fantastic animal designs. In addition there were magnificent drinking vessels made of pure silver and dishes of thin, gilded bronze. Winged bulls and lions covered the sides of bronze bowls, birds' heads decorated metal firedogs, a railing of lotus flowers encircled an incense burner in the shape of a four-wheeled wagon.

Two carriages had also been put in the tomb. One was the four-wheeled hearse on which the dead lady was taken to her last resting place. Its high, narrow fellies are set with broad nailheads and bands of palmettes ornament each side. The other vehicle was a *biga,* a two-wheeled chariot built for use at festivals and in war. Drawn by two horses, it carried the driver into battle or in solemn procession to religious ceremonies. Nearby stood a throne, the symbol of dignity and power; it was entirely plated with bronze richly embossed with pacing lions, leaping stags, and plants.

In brief, every kind of luxury article and valuable equipment, such as was needed in a royal household of the utmost elegance, was included in the tomb. Nor were amusements left out. There was the apparatus for the game of *kottabos*—stands with balanced and attached disks—and dice which, according to Herodotus, were invented by the Lydians to distract them during the famine which made them migrate to Italy. Food supplies were not forgotten. Large earthenware vessels contained wheat, oil, honey, and even eggs.

It took some time to remove all the treasures. And it was only as they were being examined one by one that a final surprising discovery was made. At the feet of the princess was a silver table service of eleven pieces, each engraved with her name, Larthia.

No inscriptions were ever found in Villanovan graves. The Indo-European speaking inhabitants of the country were illiterate. But in the circles to which Larthia belonged, reading and writing were normal accomplishments. Her tomb dates from the seventh century B.C.

The material recovered from the Regolini–Galassi tomb was a uniquely sensational discovery. Nowhere else was such a quantity of the choicest treasures found in a single sepulcher. Yet the hoard unearthed at Caere was not unique in kind. Other similar material of the seventh century B.C. was found elsewhere in central Italy— ornaments, furniture, and objects of daily use. It all testified to an extraordinary progress and wealth that had nothing in common with the bare simplicity of the preceding peasant culture.

At Tarquinia a tomb was discovered and opened in April, 1895. Its contents were in great disorder, and evidently the tomb had been robbed earlier. But what remained was enough to show the luxury with which it had been furnished. Here too a lady of high rank had been buried, and she too wore a gold breastplate. Her robe, which had long since crumbled away, seemed to have been sewn with little round and rectangular gold plaques. The remains of her other gold ornaments were strewn about; among them were fibulae decorated with tiny horses ridden by monkeys. There were also fragments of a bronze amphora with handles shaped like lotus flowers, and jugs in bizarre shapes. The lady's necklace consisted of ninety-one green faience figurines of Egyptian gods, while two figurines, covered in silver, of the Egyptian deity Bes

Sarcophagus of Larthia Scianti; sixth century B.C.

Blue-glaze Egyptian vase, from a tomb at Tarquinia; c. 730 B.C.

seemed to have been worn as earrings. These faience articles were imported.

But the most spectacular and beautiful imported article, one which caused a sensation, was a large balsam vase of greenish blue faience. On it an upper band of pictures shows an Egyptian ruler in the company of the gods, with below him a row of palm trees, chained Negroes, and apes. From the name inscribed on the vase, experts deduced the age of the tomb. The name was that of the pharaoh Bokhenranf, called Bocchoris by the Greeks, who founded the twenty-fourth dynasty (consisting only of himself) and reigned for only six years, from 734 to 728 B.C. He died fighting the Ethiopians. The faience jar, made during the pharaoh's lifetime, must have been placed in the tomb at Tarquinia not long after his death, probably about 700 B.C.

Gold, silver, bronze, and ivory gifts were found in several other sepulchers, such as the Barberini and Bernardini tombs at Palestrina, the Warrior's Grave at Tarquinia, and the great stone-circle graves of Vetulonia and Marsiliana d'Albegna. In all of them there were, besides native products, jewelry, luxury articles, and utilitarian objects from abroad— from the countries of the eastern Mediterranean and Asia. Some came from Egypt and Syria, Cyprus, Rhodes, and Greece, others from even farther afield, from Mesopotamia and Urartu, the kingdom of Van, near the biblical Mount Ararat, in present-day Turkey.

> **Who were the builders of the great tombs? Who were the unknown persons buried in them with all the pomp of royalty?**

At this time images and motifs from the East made their appearance in central Italy. Figures of wild beasts and exotic plants became fashionable, the like of which did not exist in Italy or elsewhere in Europe, and which their inhabitants had never seen. These were the first representations in the West of lions, panthers, leopards, and cheetahs, of ostriches and monkeys, stylized palms and lotus flowers. Along with them appeared weird creatures of the imagination, all of them inventions of the Near East, such as griffins, sphinxes, chimeras, winged bulls, and man-headed lions. It was a new kind of exciting picture book that was brightly painted on the walls of tombs and on pottery or molded on bronze vessels,

36

a book of animals, plants, and fabulous creatures such as were known to the Bible.

A progressive civilization of an Eastern type had penetrated all aspects of life and begun to imprint its style on a whole landscape. It was to strike deep roots and leave an indelible mark throughout the West. What brought about this sudden change, this unparalleled development? Who were the builders of the great tombs? Who were the unknown persons buried in them with all the pomp of royalty? Had swarms of foreigners from the Near East invaded the country and conquered it?

Whatever revolutionary upheaval may have occurred in that part of Italy, beginning in the eighth century B.C., has remained obscure. But one thing is certain. The people who built the huge tumuli and buried their leaders in them amid fabulous treasures, these people who spread a new, Orientalizing culture in central Italy, did not speak an Indo-European language. In this they differed from the native Villanovans. Unlike the Italic peoples, the Latins, Oscans, and Umbrians, who used Indo-European idioms, they spoke and wrote a tongue that had no relation or resemblance to the former, and has remained mysterious to this day. They were the Tyrsenoi, as the Greeks called them, otherwise the Etrusci or Tusci, in the Roman version of their name, or the Rasenna as they called themselves.

It was this people, and not the Greeks, who did most to develop the Italian lands. Their contribution, which has not hitherto been rightly appreciated, was to transmit an advanced Eastern civilization to the West, to teach the Romans and prepare the way for their empire.

IV

The First Economic Miracle in the West

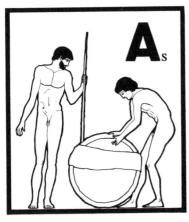

As A PEOPLE, THE ETRUSCANS WERE noted for their energy and courage, according to Diodorus Siculus, the Greek historian who lived in Rome in the first century B.C. "In ancient times," he adds, "they possessed great territory and founded many notable cities." From their first appearance in the ancient world, the Etruscans are described as a rich and powerful nation. Hesiod, with Homer the oldest Greek poet, is the first to refer to them by name. In his *Theogony,* written about 700 B.C., he speaks of the sons Circe bore to Odysseus and who, far away in the holy islands, ruled over all the famous Tyrsenoi. His wording indicates the respect in which the Etruscans were held by the Greeks at that time.

It is the same in the traditions transmitted by later writers such as Cato and Livy. The Etruscans suddenly make their appearance on Italian soil, like a deus ex machina, already strong and feared, simultaneously admired and maligned.

Systematic excavations were begun in the last century, and from their innumerable discoveries there has now at last been built up a picture of the Etruscans, at least in general outline. As though in a documentary film, we get a flashback over 2,700 years to an extraordinary event, the successful transplanting of an advanced foreign civilization into western Europe.

The country between the Arno and the Tiber, between the Tyrrhenian Sea and the Apennines, seems suddenly to have been aroused from sleep in the decades following 700 B.C. and to have taken on a different look. A countryside which, from time immemorial, had remained more or less as nature made it, changed into a cultivated landscape. Fruitful fields, groves, and gardens replaced impenetrable thickets of bushes and trees. Where the forests were cleared and the swamps drained, plows furrowed the soil. Into the formerly silent valleys came the clanging of bronze picks and axes. Mines were cut into the mountainsides, the ore was extracted and carried off in long lines of wagons.

In many a place fires burned day and night as the charcoal stacks smoldered and the smelting furnaces worked the ores to get copper and what, at that time, was the most sought-after of all metals—iron. The smoke and flames of the new industry were visible too over the island of Elba. Shipping moved busily up and down the coast. Traders came from far and near with their foreign cargoes. A motley crowd thronged the ports whose warehouses were stacked with goods from everywhere.

In all directions a transformation was taking place. An economic miracle, the first in Europe, was in progress. There was a complete change in housing. A modern style of building came in that replaced the former primitive settlements of straw and reed huts. The first towns, a precondition of any higher civilization, were founded. They were the most northerly in Europe, and they were to remain foreign to the peoples beyond the Alps for close to another thousand years, that is, until Etruria's pupils, the Romans, built them there. As late as the time of Tacitus, the Germans still lived in villages.

Most of the new towns lay within sight of the sea, but a few miles inland. The danger of piratical raids from the sea was known only too well. So the towns were built where nature provided a good defense, on plateaux or hilltops surrounded by steep gorges where streams flowed. Only easily accessible places were protected by walls made of brick on stone foundations, by ramparts and ditches.

It was not until later that the Etruscans built the great cyclopean walls of massive stone blocks. As yet, they feared no enemy anywhere in the country. They were the undisputed masters, for Rome, their great and mortal foe of the future, did not yet exist. Only unknown hut dwellers occupied the hills among the swamps along the Tiber.

On the coast the landscape was dominated by a chain of great citadels. The adjoining hinterland was rich in copper and iron—at La Tolfa in the south and in the Colline Metallifere (metalliferous hills) farther to the northwest. In addition there was the island of Elba with its abundant ores. These natural resources attracted the Etruscans. In this neighborhood they settled first, here they built their first towns. These already bore names that were later to become famous, though often preserved for posterity only in Latin, in the accounts of Rome's wars.

Situated some twenty miles from the mouth of the Tiber, on a plateau inland from the coast, Caere (modern Cerveteri), which the Etruscans called Chaire or Cisra, grew and prospered. It was among the greatest cities of the Mediterranean. Its three ports, Alsium (near Palo), Punicum (S. Marinella), and Pyrgi (S. Severa), were used by international shipping. Cargo boats, propelled by sail and oar, made their rendezvous in these harbors. They came from Tartessus, the Land of Silver, from Africa, Egypt, Asia Minor, and from Greece. Phoenician, Carthaginian, and Greek traders swarmed into the Etruscan ports.

Twenty-five miles to the north on a plateau high above the Marta River was Tarquinii, the legendary founding city of ancient Etruria. Its modern descendant, called Tarquinia, after the Roman form of the name, is now a unique tourist attraction. The famous wall paintings in the tombs cut out of the tufa of its necropolis are the oldest in Europe. Farther to the northwest, on the banks of the Fiora, lay Vulci. Nothing remains but ruins and innumerable wrecked graves close by the ancient Ponte della Badia to recall the city which was once the home of a world-famous bronze industry. At Vulci was born Servius Tullius, the second Etruscan king to rule the Romans, and a great reformer.

On a hill above a lagoon with access to the sea the Etruscans built the powerful city of Vetluna (called Vetulonia by the Ro-

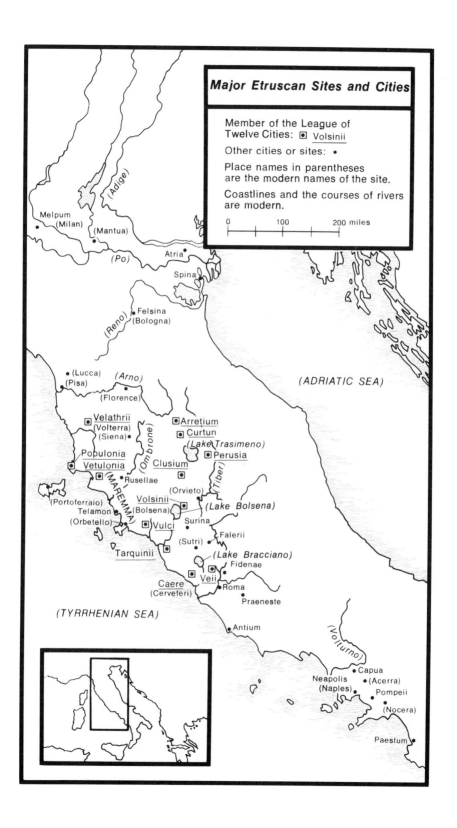

Major Etruscan Sites and Cities

Member of the League of
Twelve Cities: ⊡ Volsinii

Other cities or sites: •

Place names in parentheses
are the modern names of the site.

Coastlines and the courses of rivers
are modern.

0   100   200 miles

Melpum
(Milan)
(Mantua)
(Adige)
(Po)
Atria
Spina
(Reno)
Felsina
(Bologna)
(Lucca)
(Pisa)
(Arno)
(Florence)
(ADRIATIC SEA)
⊡ Velathrii
(Voltera)
(Siena)
⊡ Arretium
⊡ Curtun
(Lake Trasimeno)
⊡ Perusia
Populonia
Vetulonia
⊡ Clusium
(Ombrone)
Rusellae
(Tiber)
(Portoferraio)
Telamon
(Orbetello)
(MAREMMA)
(Orvieto)
Volsinii
(Bolsena)
⊡ Vulci
(Lake Bolsena)
Surina
(Sutri)
Falerii
Tarquinii
(Lake Bracciano)
Fidenae
⊡ Veii
Caere
(Cerveteri)
Roma
Praeneste
(TYRRHENIAN SEA)
Antium
(Volturno)
Capua
Neapolis
(Acerra)
(Naples)
Pompeii
(Nocera)
Paestum

mans). Beyond the river Bruna and farther inland in the hills was the stronghold of Rusellae, the modern Roselle. To the northwest of Vetulonia, on a promontory opposite the island of Elba, lay Populonia, called Pupluna or Fufluna in Etruscan. To the northeast of Populonia, on a high hill in the valley of the Cecina, stood Velathri (Roman Volaterrae and modern Volterra). The Porta all' Arco, partly Etruscan, leads into the medieval part of the town, where the streets are white with stone dust, because craftsmen still work the local alabaster from which the city's sculptors in Etruscan times fashioned splendid, richly carved cinerary urns.

Still farther inland important new cities were founded as early as the seventh century B.C. Among the biggest was Camars, the modern Chiusi, which the Romans called Clusium, built on a hill overlooking the valley of the Chiana, southwest of Lake Trasimene. It is said to have been the birthplace of the famous king Porsena who captured Rome. Other towns were Volsinii, probably on Lake Bolsena, later the sanctuary and meeting place of the Etruscan league, and away to the south, Veii, on the river Cremera (Valchetta), a tributary of the Tiber. Other foundations, over toward the slopes of

Funeral Way from the city to the necropolis, passing under aqueduct of later date, Tarquinia

the Apennines, were Arretium, Curtun, and Perusia, the modern Arezzo, Cortona, and Perugia, and Orvieto (whose Etruscan name is unknown), on a conical platform of tufa in the middle Tiber valley.

A network of new roads spread out over the countryside. They were the first in western Europe, and they provided the model for Rome's great military highways. Processional roads were built from city gates to the cemeteries, and cross-country roads connected one town with another, and led to the coastal ports. In many places archeologists have found traces of the ancient, carefully laid paving. The road running east of Tarquinii later became the route of the important Roman military way, the Via Claudia.

But all these towns were only the starting point for the great expansion that was to come. Others were to follow, first, up in the foothills of the Apennines and as far as the Arno, and a century later well beyond the heart of Etruria—as far as the Po valley and the Adriatic coast in the north, and in Campania down to the Gulf of Salerno in the south. As yet, Etruria had not become a great power, its golden age had not begun.

Every city had three gates and later reckoned among its most splendid ornaments three sacred buildings, that is, temples, the first in Italy. The Etruscan temple was a special kind of building. It was massive and squat, in fact almost square. There were religious reasons for this. The temple was often consecrated to a triad of divinities and therefore contained three cellae. Along the front were columns similar to the Doric type, but standing on a base. Vitruvius, the architect and engineer of the time of Augustus, says that Etruscan temples looked grave and heavy, and had a projecting roof with a gable supported on solid columns.

They looked very different from Greek temples. In Etruria, the temple was raised on a platform, to which there were steps only in front. It was not, as in Greece, a sanctuary surrounded by steps on all sides. Its architecture and decoration were accordingly designed to correspond with the single approach. The effect must have been striking, as Raymond Bloch suggests. "The facade of the temple," he says, "was its most important side and introduced an essential shift in perspective. In Greek architecture the building was conceived as a whole with no particular emphasis on any of its components. In Etruria and later in Rome the overall structure and its proportions were considered less important than the impression produced on the approaching devotee or visitor by the front part, an essential characteristic of Italic art with its tendency toward an immediate, direct, decorative effect."

> **The temples were populated by figures from a strange, mythic world, painted in strident colors—red, white, blue, brown, and violet—with glaring eyes, gnashing teeth, wild grimaces, and threatening gestures.**

Subsequently the exotic effect of Etruscan temple buildings was intensified by brilliantly colored, extravagant decoration of a kind that had little in common with the harmony of classical Greece. Life-size colored statues of the gods and relief plaques made of terra-cotta decorated the pediment, the ridgepole, and the cornice of the deep-eaved roof. Lotus and palmette motifs were used in the roof decorations, while the walls carried gay friezes showing grotesque, fabulous creatures, fighting warriors, or dancing and embracing Sileni and nymphs. In the terra-cotta antefixes on the eaves, faces of maenads and gorgons, spirits and demons looked down. The temples were populated by figures from a strange, mythic world, painted in strident colors— red, white, blue, brown, and violet—with glaring eyes, gnashing teeth, wild grimaces, and threatening gestures. An unbridled imagination combined images of terror and the uncanny with the grotesque in an orgy of form and color.

These Etruscan sanctuaries provided a pattern for all Italy. Such a temple, brilliantly colored and decorated, built by Etruscans, was later to adorn Rome itself with its first great and famous sanctuary, that of Jupiter Capitolinus. And after more than another five hundred years, when Etruria's power and glory had long faded away, the surviving examples of this rich and splendid religious architecture still aroused admiration. In the first century A.D., Pliny the Elder recorded that the finest temple statues of gods were made of terra-cotta and added, "Statues of this kind are still to be found in various places, while at Rome and in the municipal towns there are many temples whose roofs are still adorned with terra-cotta figures remarkable for their modeling and artistic quality as well as their durability   more deserving of respect than gold, certainly more innocent."

Public buildings and the villas of the nobility were also brightly painted and decorated with reliefs and terra-cotta plaques, like the temples. Architecturally they too were unlike those of Greece. A completely new type of dwelling came into use, the famous atrium house, the ancestor of the Roman house. The visitor first entered a covered hall, lit from above, which also received the rainwater from the roof in a basin sunk in the floor. This hall was the atrium. Opposite the entrance to it was another large room containing a hearth and cistern. To the left and right were two further rooms. The gabled roof was supported on columns. Diodorus Siculus, writing during the reign of Augustus, says that the Etruscans added a peristyle to the atrium in their houses, and that this was a "useful device for avoiding the confusion connected with the attending throngs." The design of Etruscan houses, like that of the temples, goes back to Near Eastern models in Asia Minor and Syria.

The Latin expression *atrium tuscanicum* is a reference to the inventors in Italy of the Etruscan type of house. The word *atrium* itself comes from the Etruscan language. It is assumed to mean courtyard or sometimes harbor, and occurs in place names. A town founded by the Etruscans near the mouth of the river Po was called Hatria, and this gave its name to the sea on whose shores it lay, in English the Adriatic.

The highest political and religious authority in each city was a priest-king. Then came an aristocratic upper class. Monarchic government too was an innovation in western Europe. The sovereign embodied in his person the supreme judge, military leader, and priest. In the earliest times it seems that his office was hereditary. Later there is mention of kings ruling for one year. The monarch, known as *lauchme* in Etruscan, or *lucumo* in Latin, was chosen from among the oldest and most distinguished families.

At his appearance in public, and when dealing with official business, the sovereign was the center of magnificent ceremonial intended to express his majesty and power. The Etruscans, says Diodorus Siculus, "were the authors of that dignity which surrounds rulers." It was they who brought to the West from the ancient Near East the insignia of supreme power that Rome was later to adopt, and which afterward spread throughout Europe—the golden diadem and the scepter, the purple robe that the Romans called the *toga palmata,* and the ivory throne, the *sella curulis.*

In Etruria the calendar was based on the phases of the moon, as it was later in Rome. The moon determined the festival days and the king's official activities. After every eight days came market day, which was also the day when the king held public audience and pronounced his decision on matters submitted to him. The symbol of his authority over his subjects, an axe in a bundle of rods—the *fasces,* as it was later called—was carried before him or held by an official stationed at his side.

The double axe had been a sacred symbol to the Cretans long before. The lictor's rods, however, originated with the Etruscans. Roman writers of imperial times, Silius Italicus and Florus, explicitly attribute this symbol to them. The former in fact dots the i and says it originated in Vetulonia. Doubts had often been expressed about this statement, but archeology gave it some support by two remarkable discoveries, both dated to the seventh century B.C. In 1898 excavators in the necropolis at Vetulonia found a model of a bundle of iron rods with a double axe in the middle of them. By pure chance there came to light at the same place the stele of an Etruscan warrior, Avele Feluske, depicted with a double axe in his hand. Thus it appeared that the double axe was at that period both a weapon and, enclosed in a bundle of rods, an emblem or cult object.

Later on, Rome took over from the Etruscans the bundle of lictor's rods as a symbol of political and religious power, of the imperium. In the twentieth century Mussolini gave this ancient Etruscan symbol a dubious political significance, in choosing the *fasces,* after which the Fascist party was named, as the badge of his Blackshirts.

Etruscan costume underwent a big change. A new fashion appeared, exotic and colorful. The women of the leading families were elegantly dressed, carefully coiffured, and adorned with valuable jewelry. They wore a close-fitting gown, belted at the waist, that came down to the ground. Over this they wore a sort of cloak reaching to the knees. The material, dyed in beautifully harmonious tints, was either the finest linen or byssus from Miletus in Ionia, at that time the chief source of supplies to the world of fashion. The dresses were often richly embroidered and edged with fringes or braids. The hair was drawn back except for two plaits that hung down over the breast. On their head the women wore a round or pointed cap called *tutulus.* Similar hats were popular centuries ear-

46

lier with Hittite ladies in Asia Minor. The men wore a belted jerkin, the *tunica,* and a cloak thrown over the shoulder, the *tebenna.* This garment, characteristic of the Etruscans, was later to acquire world fame. It was the predecessor of the Roman toga.

The Etruscans used a variety of footwear such as was unknown to the Greeks, who often went barefoot; footwear, too, of a kind far more luxurious than that of any other Mediterranean people. Etruscan shoemakers produced a range of boots and shoes, from light sandals with gilded straps to laced boots for everyday and festive wear. They even made overshoes for rainy weather, covered on the outside with the sheerest bronze. Shoes with pointed, turned-up toes were considered particularly smart by men and women alike. These too are reminiscent of Hittite models.

The new cities pulsed with life. The streets and squares where traders offered an abundance of goods, native and foreign, were full of noise and bustle. Imports from all over the Mediterranean flooded in through the ports of Caere, brought by Phoenician and Greek traders. In their ships came ivory, scarabs, and ostrich eggs from Africa, incense from Arabia, great cauldrons from Anatolia, oil in red terra-cotta jars from Athens, perfumes and pottery, including beautiful Corinthian vases painted with decorative animals, gold and silver articles ornamented in relief from Phoenicia, gold jewelry from Rhodes and the East.

The Etruscans' own economy boomed. New workshops started up and made ready to displace primitive, homemade subsistence production. Many workshops and factories produced both for the domestic market and for export.

Pottery kilns turned out not only earthenware of all kinds, including copies of foreign types, but also the beautiful glossy black pottery known as *bucchero* that is typical of Etruria. Foreign craftsmen, too, were employed, especially at Caere. A talented master potter from Greece was responsible for the production of the so-called Caeretan *hydriae,* big, painted water jars, mostly decorated with scenes from Greek myths. Demaratus, an artist from Corinth, settled at Tarquinii, bringing three other artists with him.

The stiff, geometrical style of decoration became a thing of the past and was replaced by ornament based on plant forms, animals, and figures from myth and fable taken from Anatolia, Mesopotamia, and Egypt. Oriental motifs and patterns dominated Etruscan taste,

47

as they did that of the Greeks, from the fountainhead in the Ionian cities of Asia Minor.

The foundries turned out bronze vessels and utensils of all kinds, including engraved and modeled mirrors, boxes, and chests. Bronze plate was hammered out for the decoration of furniture and carriages. Most remarkable of all was the goldsmiths' work, especially

Italiote crater: Admetus and Alcestis flanked by demons

the jewelry with its miraculously fine filigree and granulation. Like the work of the ivory carvers and silversmiths, this jewelry was in no way inferior in beauty and technical virtuosity to the products of the Near East. The goldsmiths' workshops were, incidentally, often visited by medical practitioners and their patients, for the Etruscans were expert at dentistry. In tombs at Vetulonia and elsewhere, artificial teeth, gold bands to fasten loose teeth, and even complete dentures have been found.

With the noise and bustle was mingled the sound of musical instruments. In Etruria music was unusually important; indeed the

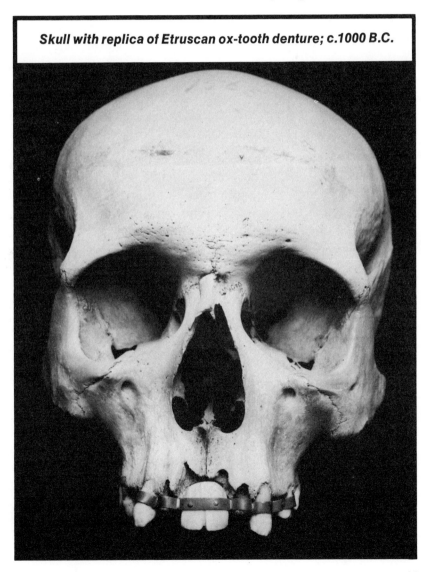

Skull with replica of Etruscan ox-tooth denture; c.1000 B.C.

whole of life was dominated by it, on weekdays as well as on holidays, in religious ceremonies and at sports meetings, at work and even during punishments.

The Etruscans, says Diodorus Siculus, "were the inventors of the *salpinx* . . . a discovery of the greatest usefulness for war and named after them the 'Tyrrhenian trumpet.'" But the trumpet's sound not only accompanied the Etruscan troops, it could also have a quite different, profound significance, as a presage of fate. The gods, it was believed, proclaimed their inexorable will by the sound of a trumpet. Heard in the sky, the trumpet was considered an infallible sign that a *saeculum* in the life of the Etruscan people had come to an end and that a new *saeculum* had begun.

> **The gods,
> it was believed,
> proclaimed their
> inexorable will by the
> sound of a trumpet.**

The Romans adopted the Etruscan trumpet and called it *tuba;* it became the most important instrument in their military bands, accompanying their expeditions for centuries. There were other wind instruments in Etruria: a short, slightly curved horn—a kind of hunting horn, and a long trumpet with a curved end. There were also a seven-stringed cithara, like the lyre on which King David played, and castanets for dancing. But the Etruscans' favorite, most popular instrument was the flute. Aristotle records that the Etruscans boxed, whipped their slaves, and kneaded dough to the sound of flutes. They had all kinds, from the single and double flutes to what would now be called clarinets and oboes. The flute was not an Etruscan invention; it originated in Asia Minor where it had always played an important role. But Etruscan musicians became phenomenal virtuosos of the instrument. Their flute-playing was world-famous. It was from Etruria that Rome hired the *subulones,* who performed on the flute as a prelude to ritual sacrifices. And even in later times when the Etruscan nation had long since died out, the hypnotic power of the Etruscan flute was well known.

Aelian, the sophist, writing in the third century A.D., relates how the Etruscans used music in hunting: "There is an Etruscan story current which says that the wild boars and the stags in that country are caught by using nets and hounds, as is the usual manner of hunting, but that music plays a part, and even the larger part, in

*Flute player, detail of fresco
from the Tomb of the Leopards, Tarquinia; c.470 B.C.*

the struggle . . . They set the nets and other hunting gear that en-
snare the animals in a circle, and a man proficient on the pipes
stands there and tries his utmost to play a rather soft tune, avoiding
any shriller note, but playing the sweetest melodies possible. The
quiet and the stillness easily carry the sound abroad; the music
streams up to the heights and into ravines and thickets—in a word
into every lair and resting place of these animals. Now at first when
the sound penetrates to their ears it strikes them with terror and
fills them with dread, and then an unalloyed and irresistible delight
in the music takes hold of them . . . and beneath the wizardry of the
music they come and fall into the snares, overpowered by the
melody."

In southern Italy too, and in Sicily, the first towns, founded by
Greek immigrants, sprang up during the eighth century B.C. "Almost without exception," says Professor Alfred Heuss, "they were
situated along the coast, and occupied as much territory as they
needed for their food supply, but primarily they looked to the sea
and maritime trade. They were not organized among themselves,
for they had no intention of subjugating the hinterland. Such expansion as did take place was restricted to the founding of daughter
cities of the same littoral type. For the rest they were happy not to
meet with any resistance from the indigenous inhabitants and left
them alone. Such Greek influence as the latter experienced came
from peaceful intercourse. But the result was not at first very impressive; the disparity between ways of life was too great."

The development in central Italy was very different. There the
whole country and its inhabitants were affected. The Etruscans,
though hardly more numerous than the Greeks were in the south,
pushed far inland from the coast. And the native population fell in
with their ways and welcomed their completely foreign civilization.
This did not remain a mere veneer, but penetrated deeply. The
Italic peoples not only learned from the Etruscans to live in cities,
they also began to speak the latter's language and to write it. They
shared in the tremendous progress that came with the arrival of the
Etruscans. While other peoples and tribes in the rest of Italy continued their primitive way of life unchanged, just as it had been for
centuries, in the region north of the Tiber a great revolution took
place.

Thanks to the planning and management of Etruscan experts,
central Italy became a model country of highly developed agricul-

ture. Rome's pride, its peasantry, so often extolled in later times at the zenith of the empire's power, never accomplished anything comparable. The Indo-European speaking Latins continued to till the soil and raise livestock in a primitive way. They contributed nothing progressive to the world's agriculture.

The new masters brought a development program and technical assistance to central Italy. They started a large-scale experiment in soil improvement and land reclamation, such as the Greeks never undertook. With this treatment the land flourished and began to produce an abundance of high-quality foodstuffs to the benefit of the entire population. The secret of this remarkable success lay in the expert knowledge and ability of Etruscan agronomists. They brought a long-established body of experience to the problems of agricultural engineering.

**Northern end of the
"Tagliata Etrusca" channel cutting, Cosa (Ansedonia)**

They had at their command all the proven techniques of the ancient Near East and successfully applied them to European soil; it was the first time that this had been done. They knew the methods of digging channels and building dams, by which the Babylonians had irrigated extensive areas along the Euphrates and turned the desert into a fertile paradise. They knew the Phoenician system of land drainage, of removing water from marshes, of installing elaborate networks of underground tunnels—technically known as cuniculation—to withdraw water. Their engineers knew how to drive galleries and shafts into the sides of hills, as had already been done in the Holy Land at the royal command.

Surviving hydraulic installations from later days suggest that Etruscan engineering skills were drawn on by the Romans for works which still command admiration today. Near Ansedonia, where the Roman colony Cosa was established in 273 B.C., there is the so-called *Tagliata Etrusca,* an ingenious system of channels cut through the rock and combined with a breakwater to prevent the Roman harbor from silting up.

Another impressive coastal installation survived until recent times near Porto Clementino, once the site of the Roman colony Graviscae in Tarquinian territory. This was an artificial watercourse covered with a stone barrel-vault thirty feet high. The construction was unfortunately destroyed during the Second World War.

The draining arrangements at Lake Nemi near Rome have also apparently revealed the master hand of Etruscan hydraulic experts. At the bottom of the lake lay two Roman ceremonial ships; over the centuries many attempts had been made to raise them, but in vain. Finally they were recovered in 1928 when a way was found to lower the water of the lake. This was done by pumping it through the ancient outlets—technically known as emissaries—which had been rediscovered.

Roman writers, among them Varro and Pliny, repeatedly refer to the quality and abundance of Etruscan crops. And Diodorus Siculus says: "The land the Tyrrhenians inhabit bears every crop, and from the intensive cultivation of it they enjoy no lack of fruits, not only sufficient for their sustenance but contributing to abundant enjoyment and luxury." But there is never a word about the fact that it was Etruscan agricultural technology which made such rich harvests possible. And even today, scholars have little to say about it. The historian M. Rostovtzeff rightly remarks that the economic history of the Etruscan league still remains to be written. Yet, as Otto-Wilhelm von Vacano observes, what little scientific observation has been devoted to the water control constructions makes it clear that without them the dense settlement of Tuscany at that time would have been impossible. Large areas of swamps and marshes along rivers, in valley bottoms and plains, especially near the sea, were drained, while inland districts and hill slopes, which previously were too dry to cultivate, were artificially irrigated.

Mario Lopes Pegna, the Italian Etruscologist, says: "The Etruscans were the first to tackle and solve the problem of land improvement, and did so by a series of technical operations so ingenious as to arouse admiration even in our days. A complicated, skillfully constructed network of canals collected surplus and stagnant water throughout Etruria and Latium. These waters were then channeled to wherever they were needed for farming purposes, and any excess still remaining was carried in big drains down to the sea. The Romans in North Africa adopted and improved the technique of intercepting river water and collecting night dews. But it was the Etruscans who first developed the technique of what is now called dry farming and applied it to the arid soils of the Maremma hills."

The largely ruined remains of the system used by the Etruscans to make the most of every precipitation are still to be found in the Maremma. The rain, which fell chiefly in winter, was collected and stored, and then distributed to the fields in the hot, dry summer months when the fruit and grain crops were ripening. Lopes Pegna says that "at suitable places on their holdings the farmers built one or two small artificial lakes. Their bottom and sides were plastered with carefully cleaned clay mixed with just a little slaked lime, thus making a practically impermeable layer. Outlets were set at different heights, from which terra-cotta pipes carried the water through clay gullies to the vineyards." This method of irrigation, he says, which is coming back into fashion in Tuscany, produced splendid results.

> In the Chianti district, grape seeds have been found in graves, indicating that it was the Etruscans who introduced the grape to Italy and established it there.

Remains of rural buildings dating from the seventh century B.C. have been found in the Maremma and the valleys of the Arno and Chiana. These are all regions which owed the fertility that ancient writers so often admired to the hydraulic techniques of Etruscan agricultural engineers. Agriculture, horticulture, and animal husbandry flourished on the land reclaimed and made fertile, whether by draining fens or irrigating arid soil.

The cultivation of the wheat species *Triticum dicoccum,* emmer, was characteristic of the Chiana valley, which was crisscrossed by innumerable water channels, both subterranean and on the surface. The Latin name of this cereal was *far,* from which the Italian word for flour, *farina,* is derived. The Etruscans, and after them the Romans, used this grain to prepare a sort of porridge, called *puls,* a predecessor of bread. Millet, rye, and oats were also grown, and flax for linen.

The vine, for which Tuscany is still celebrated, began to be cultivated. In the Chianti district, grape seeds have been found in graves, indicating that it was the Etruscans who introduced the grape to Italy and established it there. Some seven centuries later, the Romans carried it to Gaul and Germany. The Etruscan vines sometimes grew to be small trees; Pliny reports that at Populonia there was "a statue of Jupiter formed of the trunk of a single vine."

Etruria's harvests were so abundant that it was able to export not only large quantities of grain, but also linen, wine, and cheese. One Etruscan product was still much liked in Roman times. This was the pecorino cheese, made of ewes' milk at Luni, on the border of Liguria, in pieces of enormous size, sometimes weighing as much as a thousand Roman *librae,* equal to 720 pounds. A single *caseus Lunensis,* says Martial, was big enough to provide a thousand meals for the slaves in one family.

The Etruscans' stock breeding was famous. They raised a breed of horse that was exactly like the typical sinewy, narrow-headed, pure-bred Arab. Being first-class race horses, they were ridden, or harnessed to the two-wheeled *biga* in the extremely popular racing contests.

Sheep were raised, and great herds of pigs were driven out into the oak forests in autumn to feed on the acorns. They were trained, says Polybius, the Greek historian, to obey the trumpet signals blown by the herdsmen. The Mediterranean was at that time still rich in fish, and tuna were caught in large quantities. Special wooden towers were built on the seacoast from which lookout men watched for the shoals of tuna fish. The Etruscans were as much addicted to hunting game as the modern Italians, in particular hare, birds, deer, and, to judge by many Etruscan reliefs, the big, husky, black boar. There was plenty to eat for everyone. Indeed there was an abundance such as the other peoples of Italy and those north of the Alps could hardly imagine. "Twice each day," says Diodorus Siculus, "they spread costly tables and upon them everything that is appropriate to excessive luxury."

The hydraulic engineering that was of such value to agriculture was also applied in the towns, each of which had its water supply and storage system. Wells and clay pipes supplied drinking water to the inhabitants. Shafts were driven into the ground to divert small watercourses and bring them nearer the cities or to drain the subsoil and dispose of stagnant water. Many of these tunnels, which sometimes formed part of a truly labyrinthine underground network, still survive after two and a half millenniums. They have been found during excavations and when prospecting the sites where Etruscan cities once stood.

"The narrow tunnels, not quite the height of a man," says Professor von Vacano, "are of ogival section, and they intersect and are sometimes connected by vertical shafts with a similar system at a lower level. They are now more or less filled up or ruinous, and are found below many of the ancient city areas, often enlarged by later Roman, medieval, or modern digging, and so changed that the original installation is hard to identify."

The Etruscans even knew how to overcome differences of height by means of underground piping systems with pressure boxes and siphons, by which water was brought over great distances into the cities. "At Populonia," says Mario Lopes Pegna, "water was carried to the top of the hill by means of such a system, traces of which I have found."

The Etruscan constructions can stand comparison with the much later Roman aqueducts, which became so famous. With their spectacular giant arches, the aqueducts, built at vast expense in men and materials, aroused the admiration of the world and are still admired today. The much more complicated underground systems built by the Etruscans to provide their cities with drinking water fell into decay and were completely forgotten.

At Viterbo, where the church of S. Lorenzo stands above the

remains of Etruscan Surina, the underlying rock is perforated by innumerable channels, devised to drain the ground. Their construction shows that the builders had an astonishingly good knowledge of the local geology. Below the topsoil lie volcanic formations of tufa, with, below that, a deeply fissured layer. "The deep layer is saturated with moisture from the subterranean outflow of the crater lakes," says a modern report. "The topsoil absorbs all the rainwater. The surplus from the two layers passes into the middle layer from which it cannot evaporate and which remains permanently wet. The land was only dry and healthy so long as water was removed from the absorbent layer of tufa." Investigation has shown that it was precisely through this tufa layer that the Etruscans drove their *cuniculi*, as the drainage tunnels are called.

Similar drainage channels, often widely ramified throughout the rocky hills, have been found at many other places, for instance at Chiusi, Vetulonia, Bomarzo, Orbetello, and Bieda (ancient Blera). Their existence is usually the surest indication that the site must have been Etruscan. They are all masterly achievements, worthy of the utmost admiration.

It was thanks to the initiative of Etruscan experts that the experience and sophisticated techniques hitherto known only to peoples of the ancient Near East were transmitted to the West and first put into practice there on a large scale. But posterity never thanked them for it. It paid no attention to the remarkable civilizing work which they carried out on Italian soil in a world that was still prehistoric. This was forgotten, as was also the historical fact that Etruria provided a pattern that was later carried all over the world. As Mario Lopes Pegna rightly points out: "The system of irrigation and drainage applied to agriculture in which the Etruscans were masters was gradually spread by the Romans and their successors not only throughout the Mediterranean but also in continental Europe as far as the Baltic."

There are whole shelves of volumes packed with learned controversy about the sources of Etruscan art. But where is the expert work dealing thoroughly with the incredible technical achievements of this people? Its theme could only be that Europe's first economic miracle took place in Etruria.

V

Etruscan Industry

PORTO BARATTI IS A SMALL, CIRCULAR BAY OF the Tyrrhenian Sea. It lies opposite the island of Elba and only a few miles from Piombino whence a steady stream of tourists pours onto the island. A hill, picturesquely reflected in the waves, shelters a tiny village with only a handful of people. But its name is a famous one: Populonia. It is the site of Etruscan Pupluna, a town often mentioned by ancient writers and the only one the Etruscans ever built right on the coast. On coins its name appears together with the town's emblem, the hammer and tongs. The town itself shared the fate of all other Etruscan cities and disappeared from the face of the earth. Only the graves of a nearby extensive necropolis attest its existence.

It was only recently, after more than two and a half thousand years, that the great part Populonia once played was rediscovered, and in a truly extraordinary fashion. At the same time, a long-forgotten economic achievement of the Etruscans was recalled to attention.

For ages the land around the bay had been covered with *macchia*, scrub. Among the sprawling bushes the earth shows rusty brown. In Tuscany red earth is part of the usual scene, especially on newly turned plowland and in vineyards. But near Populonia the color was different, it was darker and browner. The reason why became clear when one day the earth was examined more carefully. It was rust. All around the hill far and wide, wherever it was dug, the site was covered with masses of slag.

It was known that in Roman times iron had been smelted at Populonia. The Roman historian and geographer Strabo, who visited the place in the first century A.D., said: "And in looking down from the city you can see, albeit from afar and with difficulty, the island of Sardo [Sardinia], and, nearer, the island of Cyrnus [Corsica], and much better than these, the island of Aethalia [Elba] . . . And I also saw the people who work the iron that is brought over from Aethalia."

Sample soundings proved that the slag heaps were immense. Pottery shards found in them showed that they must date back to pre-Roman times. The belief that the slag heaps must be a relic of Etruscan enterprise was to be confirmed some years later by discoveries of a unique kind.

> It is strange to think that in 1917, when the fierce battles on the Isonzo flared up, the Italian artillery and the shells they fired at the Austrian troops contained iron smelted from ore that Etruscan miners had dug.

During the First World War, the Italian government was faced with grave difficulties due to the shortage of iron. An ingenious suggestion was made which, however absurd it might sound, did in fact help to solve the problem. The suggestion was to exploit the slag heaps at Populonia. This was done, and with more success than anyone could have hoped. For the vast extent of the deposits around the hill was only discovered as exploitation proceeded. And resmelting the ancient slag proved thoroughly worthwhile, for it was found to contain as much as 35 or 40 percent iron.

Thus modern industry was able to take advantage of what the producers in an early epoch had discarded as waste. And the help came at a difficult time, when arms were urgently needed. It is strange to think that in 1917, when the fierce battles on the Isonzo flared up, the Italian artillery and the shells they fired at the Austrian troops contained iron smelted from ore that Etruscan miners had dug.

Even after 1918 the slag continued to be used. For decades power shovels and bulldozers have carved away at the slag heaps. And the end is not in sight.

The clearance yielded unexpected discoveries to archeology. The biggest surprise came when the shovels in some places got down to the natural soil. They unearthed the remains of huge tombs, which at some remote period must have collapsed under the enormous weight of the slag heaps. How this had come about was a puzzle.

Further researches produced an answer. What occurred can probably be reconstructed as follows. About 400 B.C. iron smelting, previously done only on the island of Elba, began on a big scale at Populonia, which rapidly grew into one of the largest industrial towns of the ancient world. Over the centuries the slag accumulated until it eventually reached San Cerbone, Populonia's oldest necropolis, lying right at the foot of the hill on which the town was built. Finally the slag heaps buried the cemetery and with it part of one of the earliest chapters of Etruscan history.

The buried tombs date from the seventh century B.C. This was proved by the votive gifts found in them which included numerous articles of everyday use and apparel such as spirals, pendants, fibulae, as well as many imported articles. Other material indicated that Populonia must at the time have been the center of a big, highly developed copper and bronze industry. Its workshops produced bronzes in large quantities, in particular, wonderful plaques for ornamental purposes. The rise and prosperity of the city were based on the possession and exploitation of the copper mines on Elba and at Campiglia Marittima in the nearby hinterland. Copper metallurgy made Populonia a thriving, rich industrial town.

About two centuries earlier there had been a similar, amazing development in the eastern Mediterranean, that of the Jewish kingdom under King Solomon after the opening of copper mines and refineries. Within a generation the predominantly peasant state of King David became a leading economic power. The production of iron in Etruria began at the same time as that of copper. At Populonia, iron occurs in grave furnishings of the beginning of the seventh century B.C. In the great Tumulo dei Carri it was found applied to the decorative bronze plaques of war chariots. The plates are inlaid with animal and hunting scenes made of iron. They indicate that at first iron was considered a precious metal in Italy, just as it had been centuries earlier in the Near East.

The history of what is now the commonest metal goes back a long way and is still not fully known. But one thing is certain: in the beginning it was not used for weapons or tools, but for jewelry. Tutankhamen's knife with an iron blade, which dates from about 1360 B.C., has become famous. This Egyptian king considered it so precious that he ordered it to be included among the few treasures placed within his inner golden coffin. The metal was so rare at that time that rulers corresponded among themselves at length about it. "As for the good iron which you wrote about to me," says a letter from the Hittite king Hattusilis III to another monarch, probably the king of Assyria, "good iron is not available in my seal-house in Kizzuwatna. That it is a bad time for producing iron I have written. They will produce good iron, but as yet they will not have finished. When they have finished I shall send it to you. Today now I am dispatching an iron dagger-blade to you."

It was about the beginning of the first millennium B.C. that the breakthrough in metallurgy was made. A way was found to raise the necessary temperature from about 1,000°C., the melting point of copper, to about 1,500°C., the melting point of iron. The smelting was done with charcoal. Thus it became possible to treat iron ore, and a new age began.

The Bronze Age was followed by the Iron Age, as Hesiod wrote in about 700 B.C. But before the new invention could become of general utility, the devastating Aegean migrations cut short any further progress. In Asia Minor the Hittite empire collapsed. Its conquerors thereby learned the manufacturing secret, and the Bible story tells what subsequently happened to it. The Philistines built the first iron-smelting works on the coastal plain of the country that was later named Palestine after them. This was south of Gaza at the foot of the mountains of Judah. Armed with the new metal, they conquered a large part of Judah. But by the time of King David the Philistines no longer had the monopoly of iron smelting; the Israelites also possessed iron weapons and drove out the invaders.

Nevertheless no further progress was made until about the ninth century B.C. Then substantial production of iron at last got under way, chiefly in Asia Minor. Iron began to appear on the world market and to supersede bronze. The changeover was of course slow at first, for the great demand far exceeded the supply. It was still the most expensive of all metals, more precious than gold.

And so it was to remain for a long time. After 800 B.C. a new wave of great political upheavals and wars swept over the ancient Near East. The rise of the Assyrian empire had begun. King Tiglath-pileser III advanced into neighboring kingdoms, took Damascus and occupied Syria and the land east of the Jordan. In 721 B.C. Samaria, the Israelite capital, fell. In Anatolia Sargon II made Midas, the last king of Phrygia, his vassal. About the same time the kingdom of Urartu (Ararat), with its rich Caucasian mines, came under Assyrian control. Under Esar-haddon, Phoenicia became a province and Lower Egypt was conquered. In 663 Assur-bani-pal with his victorious army entered Thebes.

By about 650 B.C. the world of the Near East, from Asia Minor to Egypt, lay in ruins. The ancient states were destroyed and Assyria had become the sole ruler. Nineveh gave the orders which decided the fate of every man, woman, and child in the vast Assyrian empire. But the former brisk trade and shipping of the East was interrupted, the flow of goods ceased. And access was barred to the mining areas of Anatolia, the source of iron.

New markets had to be found, and new sources of ore. The great search for copper and iron deposits began. This was Etruria's opportunity. The occasion could not have been more favorable. There were no metals in Sicily. But between the Tiber and the Arno were hills containing masses of the sought-after raw materials. Apart from the Sardinian mines, the resources of Etruria were in fact the vastest in the whole of the central Mediterranean. Moreover they all lay near the coast, thus making sea transport easy.

The sailor coming up from the south can see the hills from far off. After monotonous miles along the low shores of Latium, the Tolfa hills, with their characteristic profile, stand out after the mouth of the Tiber is passed. In their middle rises the peak of

Monte le Grazie. Here farther inland lies another area of mineral resources, the most southerly deposits in Etruria and the earliest to be exploited. Iron pyrites and chalcopyrite, lead and zinc are found there, as well as antimony and, in small quantities, mercury.

A few more hours' sailing and, after rounding the steep cliffs of Monte Argentario, a peninsula projecting far into the sea, the island of Elba appears. Besides copper it contains iron, as the name of its principal harbor Portoferraio still proclaims. Virgil, in the *Aeneid,* called it *"insula inexhaustis chalybum generosa metallis,"* the island rich in mines of inexhaustible iron. Opposite Elba, on the mainland, lie the Colline Metallifere, the metal-bearing mountains dominated by the volcanic cone of Monte Amiata. These mountains contain copper, iron, lead, and silver. They belonged to the rulers of Populonia, Vetulonia, and Volterra, which lies farther north in the Cecina valley.

It was in these mountainous areas of Etruria that the first heavy industry in Italy, and indeed in western Europe, was established in the seventh century B.C. The mines provided the basis for the economic development of Etruria and its almost fabulous wealth. That astonishing industrial boom left its mark upon the countryside, and evidence may still be found of the intensive exploitation of the ore deposits and their refining. Great heaps of slag lie on the soil of Elba, just as at Porto Baratti, and they are found at Luni (Monte Fortino) too.

Near Tolfa and neighboring Allumiere, an area of iron, lead, and zinc deposits, scholars have found the oldest traces of mining. They discovered many workings, in the neighborhood of which the remains of the extracted ore still lay. "The Etruscan method of mining metal," writes the German author Sibylle von Cles-Reden, "was very wasteful by modern standards. Given the state of technology at the time, only the ore-bearing rock that lay near the surface could be exploited. Where the pick could not be used, fires were lit. Then the hot rock was cracked by drenching it with cold water. All the same, the Etruscan mining industry was of astonishing size, as is attested by the smelting furnaces still scattered about the countryside and the many expertly cut galleries in the mountains along the coast of Tuscany."

Round about the little Lago dell'Accesa near Massa Marittima in the province of Grosseto, the mountain slopes are riddled with mine workings. More than two hundred dating from Etruscan times have been identified. Heaps of broken ore were still lying about the ruined furnaces, and pieces of pickaxes and shards of little oil lamps had been found in the galleries, when the city fathers of Massa Marittima in 1830 again bethought themselves of the riches still buried in the earth. So mining was resumed on the hillsides surrounding the little town with its thirteenth-century cathedral, precisely in the places where it had been discontinued so long before.

The region around Campiglia Marittima, some eight miles northeast of Populonia, is similarly strewn with old mine workings. Here the Etruscans obtained not only copper and iron ore, but also lead and, as has recently been discovered with some surprise, tin. Thus Etruria's metal industry became independent of imports of this essential metal, of which the Phoenicians had long had a monopoly. Henceforth the industry had supplies of tin sufficient to meet all the needs of its bronze foundries. This has been proved by analyses of the slag and bronze scrap found near Campiglia Marittima at Campo delle Bucche, Cento Camerelle, Cavina, and on Elba.

Traces of old mines and smelteries have been found as far north as Volterra, in the shape of bits of iron ore dropped during transport in carts and baskets, of copper ingots and fragments of crude iron which at that time was cast in loaf-shaped ingots. Silver residues also have been found. Near Larderello, where the hot vapor from the boric acid deposits jets from the ground, another important mining district was discovered at Gerfalco, on the headwaters of the river Cecina.

The shafts that once were driven by gangs of miners into the lodes have fallen in and lie in ruins. In the Campigliese, notably in the Val di Fucinaia, the "Valley of the Forge," a multitude of mines and smelteries has come to light, with trenches and shafts and communicating galleries. Some of the miners' lamps even have been found, made of solid earthenware with two holes for cords to hang them up by.

Rows of furnaces have been discovered, some of them so well preserved that the details of their construction can be made out. "They have the form of a truncated cone," says the French Etruscologist Jacques Heurgon, "about 1.80 m. in diameter, the interiors lined with refractory bricks and divided into two chambers, one above the other, by a partition pierced with holes. This partition was supported by a column of local porphyry. A square door opened in the base to ventilate the furnace and regulate combustion. The upper chamber was filled with copper pyrites and charcoal. A fire was lit in the lower chamber."

> The pieces of wood made into charcoal invariably show twenty annual rings, indicating that the forests were logged systematically in a twenty-year rotation.

Even the location of the furnaces was masterly. They were built near the mines on slopes where the upwind and fall wind would act as a natural bellows. The vast quantities of charcoal required for smelting were provided by the Etruscan forests, which would seem to have been managed on modern lines. The pieces of wood made into charcoal invariably show twenty annual rings, indicating that the forests were logged systematically in a twenty-year rotation.

King Solomon's rediscovered copper mines in Israel have rightly been considered sensational, and swarms of tourists have visited them for years. But the no less remarkable Etruscan mines, among the oldest and most important in Europe, have remained disregarded and in fact unknown. No one visits them, and modern guidebooks never mention them.

"Their industry," says G. Maggi, the Italian scholar, "made the Etruscans rich at a stroke, and the zenith of their wealth and power coincides with the moment when bronze was most widely used and when the trade in iron began; they were responsible for the spread of its trade in Europe."

"Etruscan metal exports," says Mario Lopes Pegna, "moved through two channels—by sea and by land over the old routes through the easiest passes of the eastern and western Alps. The exports by land were handled by Etruscan traders, though they did not actually cross the Alps before the seventh century B.C. Exports by sea were shipped by Phoenician traders, later by Carthaginians and Greeks."

The Etruscans became great by peaceful development. The application of technical methods and the skill of their engineers laid the foundations for the growth of their brilliant culture. From their first appearance on Italian soil their interests were economic. Their fortunes prospered by production and trade, not by war and conquest, or by the subjection and pillage of other peoples. And this remained characteristic of them. Wherever they penetrated, even far beyond their original base, remarkable progress was made. They must have exercised an extraordinary fascination, or the old-established, still primitive peoples would not have been induced to adopt the Etruscans' customs and culture, and to collaborate gladly in the complex activities of a sophisticated civilization which the Etruscans would have been too few to achieve by themselves.

THEY RULED THE SEA

THE SEA IS PART OF ETRUSCAN history from the beginning. It was as a seafaring people that the Etruscans made their appearance in Italy. The first daring moves to conquer and control the sea routes around the peninsula were based in Tuscany. Quite early they must have built a merchant navy for shipping their imports and exports, and also have maintained a powerful fleet of warships for the defense of their harbors, coasts, and trading empire.

Early accounts of the Tyrrhenians often spoke of their "thalassocracy," their domination of the sea. "Etruria, indeed," says Livy, "had at this time both by sea and land filled the whole length of Italy from the Alps to the Sicilian strait with the noise of her name." It was not by chance that the Sardinian sea was named after its new neighbors. "Because they had powerful naval forces," says Diodorus Siculus, "and were masters of the sea over a long period, they caused the sea along Italy to be named Tyrrhenian after them."

Ancient writers depict the Etruscans as bold and awe-inspiring seafarers. Legends, episodes, and incidents of derring-do gathered about them. To the Greeks they were pirates whose audacious raids and pillaging expeditions were feared throughout the Mediterranean. The Homeric hymn to Dionysus tells of them, relating how one day the god was captured by Tyrrhenian pirates, and managed to escape only by changing his captors into a shoal of dolphins.

Tyrrhenians, it was said, stole the famous statue of Hera on the island of Samos and were responsible for the rape of the women of Brauron in Attica. They were accused of the conquest and sack of Athens, and were said to have been a standing threat to shipping in the Tyrrhenian and Ionian seas and off the coast of Sicily. Diodorus Siculus speaks of an Etruscan occupation of Corsica, and Strabo of their possession of Sardinia. Other authors refer to Etruscan colonies on the Balearic Islands and the coast of Spain. There is even a story, narrated by Diodorus Siculus, about a conflict between the Carthaginians and the Etruscans over the possession of an island far out in the Atlantic, which it is thought may have been Madeira.

Dionysius speaks of the Etruscans' proficiency in seamanship, and Theophrastus says that they felled trees whose trunks were long enough to form the keel of a big ship. Pliny quotes a Greek source to the effect that a Tyrrhenian from Pisae (the modern Pisa) invented the beak, or *rostrum*, with which a ship could ram an enemy vessel. In the harbor of Rhodes the *rostra* of captured Tyrrhenian ships were exhibited as tokens of victory. The anchor too is said to have been an Etruscan invention.

The sources testifying to Etruscan naval skill and experience are too numerous and varied for their accounts to be dismissed as mere imagination, as was at one time done all too readily. There is a historical basis, and many discoveries have confirmed it.

A painted scene on a vase from Caere shows what a naval battle was like in the middle seventh century B.C. Two hostile ships are in the midst of the struggle. One, a longboat propelled by oars, is rushing at the enemy. It is manned by warriors and provided with a long, powerful ram. The other is a high-prowed sailing vessel, its warriors standing at the ready. In both ships the fighting men have the same weapons and armor. They wear helmets with high, decorative crests, carry javelins and round shields. The only difference is in the emblems on the shields. Those of the attackers are decorated in the geometrical style common in Etruria at an early date. Those of the men in the sailing ship are decorated with a bull's head, a constellation, and a crab. Does the picture show a battle between Etruscans and Greeks? We do not know. Both types of ships occurred in the Tyrrhenian Sea at that time and must have been used by the Etruscans.

At Vetulonia excavators found a little bronze ship with animals on board. This has been identified as a Sardinian import; but elsewhere clay models of boats have been found in Etruscan graves, and pictures of the journey of the dead over the water on funerary urns and gravestones. Such material points to maritime activity, but little is known about it. The quantity and wide dispersal of imported and exported articles that have been discovered suggest that the Etruscans must have had a very considerable merchant navy. Massimo Pallottino says: "Even without taking into consideration the very large, almost incalculable, number of foreign objects and motifs (Eastern, Sardinian, Punic, Hellenic) that have been found in archaic Etruscan tombs, denoting intense maritime activity that cannot wholly be due to Phoenician and Greek shipping, there is no lack of evidence pointing to the spread of the Etruscan civilization along the shores of Italy, Sardinia, Corsica, North Africa, as well as in Greece, southern France, and Iberia. This consists of *bucchero* vases, of wrought bronzes, and even of inscriptions in Etruscan (e.g., an ivory tablet bearing the effigy of a lion found at Carthage)."

Common to all the ancient accounts is the admiration and respect, not to mention the fear, which the Etruscan mariners evidently inspired in the Greeks. Such a tradition can only grow up on the basis of events, of very concrete, personal experiences. But the fact that the Etruscans were so often accused of piracy may perhaps be put down to deliberate economic propaganda, to defamation of a rival in the struggle for raw materials and markets that was doubtless a tough one, with no holds barred.

In archaic times conditions at sea were as lawless as on land. There was nothing dishonorable about piracy, any more than about cattle rustling or the pillaging of settlements. Such activities were admissible under common law. And the Greeks were in no position to complain about the Etruscans on this score. Even Solon, the wise law-giver, declined to take action against pirates. Polycrates of Samos was in the habit of capturing foreign ships and presenting a

69

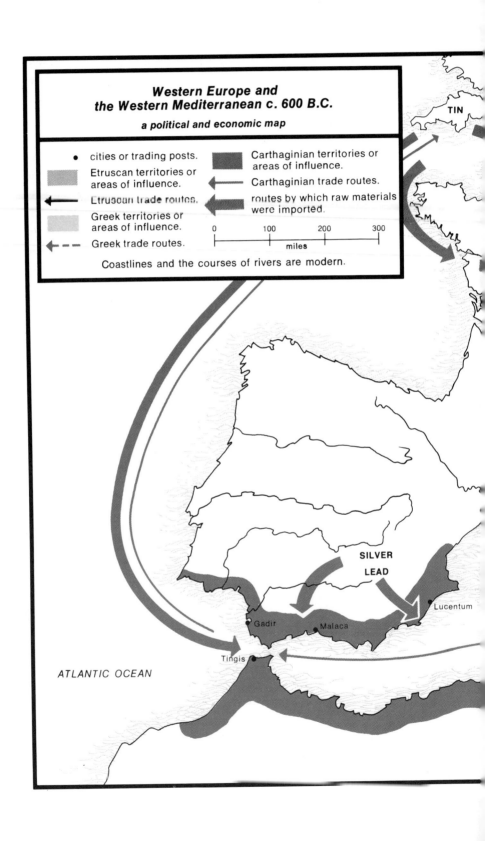

Western Europe and the Western Mediterranean c. 600 B.C.

a political and economic map

- • cities or trading posts.
- Etruscan territories or areas of influence.
- ← Etruscan trade routes.
- Greek territories or areas of influence.
- ←-- Greek trade routes.
- Carthaginian territories or areas of influence.
- ← Carthaginian trade routes.
- ← routes by which raw materials were imported.

0   100   200   300
miles

Coastlines and the courses of rivers are modern.

TIN

SILVER
LEAD

Lucentum

Gadir
Malaca

Tingis

ATLANTIC OCEAN

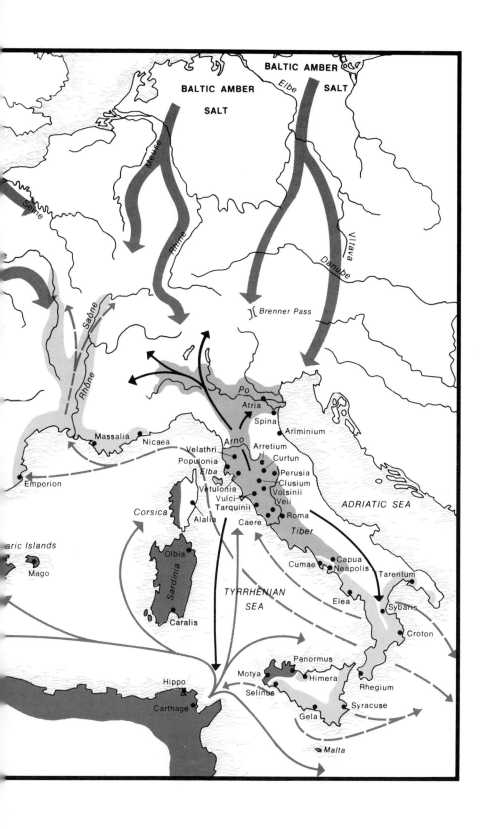

BALTIC AMBER
SALT

BALTIC AMBER
SALT

Elbe

Meuse

Seine

Rhine

Saône

Rhône

Vltava

Danube

Brenner Pass

Po

Atria

Spina

Ariminium

Massalia

Nicaea

Velathri

Arretium

Curtun

Arno

Emporion

Populonia

Elba

Perusia

Clusium

Volsinii

Veii

Vetulonia

Vulci

Tarquinii

ADRIATIC SEA

Corsica

Alalia

Caere

Roma

Tiber

aric Islands

Olbia

Sardinia

Cumae

Capua

Neapolis

Tarentum

Mago

TYRRHENIAN
SEA

Elea

Sybaris

Caralis

Croton

Hippo

Panormus

Motya

Himera

Rhegium

Carthage

Selinus

Syracuse

Gela

Malta

tenth of the plunder to sanctuaries. And Thucydides indicates that even in his day, around 400 B.C., there was still the risk of piracy and armed robbery in parts of Hellas.

For the Greeks of Asia Minor, too, piracy was a profession. When the Ionians were defeated after their rising against the Persian king Darius, says Herodotus, "The Phocaean commander Dionysius, who had captured three enemy vessels in the course of the engagement . . . set his course . . . for Phoenicia, where he sank a number of cargo-vessels and took from them property of considerable value; he then sailed for Sicily, which he made his base for piratical raids against Carthaginian and Tyrrhenian shipping."

We do not know what battles may have taken place between Greeks and Etruscans for domination of the waters between Sicily and the coast of Tuscany and for the possession of the ore-bearing mountains north of the Tiber. The brief references in ancient authors are no more than a distant echo of that conflict, a faded recollection of the fierce struggle for raw materials, markets, and monopolies in a remote past.

In very early times Greek traders already had an advance post in Tyrrhenian waters. Somewhere about 770 B.C. Chalcidians from Euboea landed on the island of Pithecusae, the modern Ischia, and established a base. Greek ambitions had, however, wider aims than the Gulf of Salerno. The Greeks knew their way about the seas farther north, as is shown by the names they gave to the islands of the Tuscan archipelago that lie off the coast of Etruria. Montecristo they called Oxasia, Giannutri was Artemisia, the island of Gorgona was Gurgon, while Capraia and Giglio were, respectively, Aigilion megas and Aigilion mikros.

These islands lie on the northern and southern approaches to Elba, with its coveted deposits of copper and iron ore. By the Greeks it was called Aethaleia, meaning "black with smoke," because of the dark clouds of smoke that constantly lay over it from the charcoal kilns and smelting furnaces. The Greeks never succeeded in acquiring the precious island for themselves. They were accepted only as traders, as welcome intermediaries for the Etruscans' rapidly developing world export business. The shores and islands of central Italy were protected by the Etruscan fleet, which made forays far to the south. Strabo in his *Geography* quotes a report by Ephorus to this effect. Referring to the foundation of the oldest Greek cities at the

Sicilian straits, he says that they date from the fifteenth generation after the Trojan War, and that before this the Greeks were so afraid of the Etruscans' piratical attacks that they would not venture into these seas, even for the sake of trade. Yet the Etruscans' attempts at obstruction were in vain. They could not prevent the Greeks from establishing themselves in the west and east of Sicily and in southern Italy.

But to the north of Sicily, beyond the Strait of Messina, the Etruscans remained the masters. The Greek migrants who had settled on Ischia did manage to found Cumae on the nearby mainland in about 750 B.C., but this remained their most northerly city, isolated from the other colonies much farther south. They never got beyond this point, which thus marked the limits of the respective zones of influence in the Tyrrhenian Sea.

Hostilities were followed in the seventh century B.C. by a period of peaceful trading. The Greeks were, along with the Carthaginians, the Etruscans' most active trading partners. Etruria's relations seem to have been especially close with Syracuse, whose merchants handled the imports from Corinth, the great port of transshipment for the Ionian cities. Greek merchants as well as artists and craftsmen settled in Etruscan towns. There was a colony of them at the port of Pyrgi. But conflict between the two peoples was only postponed. By the end of the sixth century B.C. it was to flare up again with the utmost violence.

Without its strong fleet and its citadel towns defended by powerful forces, the course of Etruria's history would have been different. The country would have been exploited by foreign trading peoples and would have become a colonial territory. The respect which it was able from the earliest times to command in the Tyrrhenian Sea made a decisive contribution to its unparalleled economic progress. It was the safe, unobstructed sea communications with the coast of Etruria that made possible the transport of the most precious of all exports, the heavy cargoes of copper and iron. These goods could never have been moved in such quantities over the land routes, and it was these exports which brought the Etruscans their vast wealth.

VI

The Spell of Magic

THE CEMETERIES OF ETRURIA, WITH their uncounted graves, cover large areas of a countryside from which the cities of the inhabitants buried in the tombs have long since vanished. Only the burial places remain, thousands and thousands of them, spread over lonely plateaux, in ravines and on the cliffs of silent, scrub-covered valleys. But even they are only a last surviving remnant of what once existed, which man and nature have for the most part long since destroyed or made unidentifiable. Within sight of the dwelling places of the living, vast boroughs, crossed by processional roads, housed the dead.

Generation by generation they grew. For centuries the area of land given over to the dead increased until it exceeded that of the towns. Ancient Caere covered about seventy acres. But the hills occupied by its innumerable, great and small tombs eventually covered twice as much, almost 140 acres. From the coastal plain to the hills stretched one single silent town. No other people cherished and guarded its dead as the Etruscans did, no other provided such overwhelming, vast cemeteries of massive stone and hewn rock.

For many a year the cemeteries, unique in Europe, remained undisturbed. They were considered sacred land, whose peace no one dared to trouble. But once the Etruscans had died out, once their history was forgotten, the impieties began. Treasure seekers and tomb robbers, clandestine and official, were tempted by the prodigious riches hidden in the tombs, by the quantity of precious gold and silver jewelry, bronze and ivory objects, and superb vases, the famous black-figure and red-figure ceramics of Attica.

The Romans of imperial times were keen collectors of Etruscan treasures. And it was not only Etruscan bronzes that were much sought after. What the Romans began was continued by posterity for a millennium and a half, from the invading Teutonic tribes down to the clandestine grave robbers of today. Did not Theodoric the Great himself give the order to plunder?

Etruscan tombs, Cerveteri

The instructions of the Ostrogothic king are preserved in a document which says: "It is a traditional and sound custom to restore to the use of men treasures buried in the earth, and not to leave with the dead things that can help the living. For there is no kind of profit in what lies buried. For this reason We order that wherever our command to this effect is published, you shall at once undertake the search for gold and silver in order to bring it to light without hesitation. You are to respect whatever serves the dead—the ashes preserved in tombs, the columns and marbles that adorn them. But the treasure buried in them belongs to the government of the living. It is proper to remove gold from graves which are no longer in anyone's possession."

> **Today the tombs lie empty; the masonry is broken, the contents long since rifled.**

Today the tombs lie empty; the masonry is broken, the contents long since rifled. Only a tiny fraction of what they once contained has been preserved. Broken and patched together it fills the glass cases of museums and private collections all over the world. It is exceptional for archeologists to come upon an intact, unviolated tomb. Yet the great cemeteries are still charged with the sense of a strange, uncanny world, their dark graves and chambers still keep the mystery of a remote, archaic age.

Nowhere else is the strange, enigmatic quality of the Etruscan people so oppressive as in its burial places, nowhere else do we come so close to its soul, its thinking and feeling. The cemeteries are the last remaining evidence of a secret, magic world that once held in its spell every human activity.

"The Etruscan communities," says Livy, "deeply learned as they were in sacred lore of all kinds, were more concerned than any other nation with religious matters." All ancient writers describe them as deeply religious. This impression is confirmed by what the Etruscans left behind them, by what has been uncovered by excavations. Innumerable objects show how deeply rooted in worship and ritual their life was.

The evidence is found in the scenes engraved on bronze mirrors, in stone and terra-cotta reliefs, in mausoleums, gems, and vases. They are populated by gods and heroes, demons and spirits, winged beings like angels, and by diabolical fabulous creatures and exotic animals. They all seem to be ubiquitous, can appear indoors or out-doors, at work as well as at play, in life as in death. Whatever happened, whatever the Etruscans did, was all controlled by their religion. Nothing reflects it more vividly than their dances in honor of the dead.

"Fragments of people at banquets, limbs that dance without dancers, birds that fly in nowhere, lions whose devouring heads are devoured away!" Thus writes D. H. Lawrence, describing the tombs at Tarquinia with their damaged frescoes. "Once it was all bright and dancing; the delight of the underworld; honouring the dead with wine, and flutes playing for a dance, and limbs whirling and pressing . . . As the pagan old writer says: 'For no part of us nor of our bodies shall be, which doth not feel religion: and let there be no lack of singing for the soul, no lack of leaping and dancing for the knees and the heart; for all these know the gods.' Which is very evident in the Etruscan dancers. They know the gods in their very finger-tips. The wonderful fragments of limbs and bodies that dance on in a field of obliteration still know the gods, and make it evident to us."

The Etruscans were the last representatives in Europe of an archaic world. They were a versatile people, highly gifted, bursting with energy, pioneers in practical achievements, by which they lifted a whole country and its inhabitants out of prehistory. Yet at the same time they were themselves still held in thrall by the magical conceptions of primitive beliefs, of an all-pervasive religion, the roots of which went back to a remote and nebulous past. The Etruscans never got away from those conceptions which determined their culture and knowledge, accompanied their entire history, and, in the end, became a sort of destiny that inexorably and irrevocably led to their decline.

The religious writings of the Etruscans have been destroyed like most of their cemeteries, have disappeared like their cities and harbors. With them has been lost the knowledge of the origin and meaning of many cults and rites which became the heritage of many centuries, in some cases down to our own times. "Etruscan traditions were of very great importance to the Romans of the imperial age," says Massimo Pallottino, "not only because Etruria gave the first and most important contribution to the definition of those Italic religious forms among which the religion of Rome developed from its very beginnings, but also because religion was that portion of the Etruscan inheritance acknowledged with the least reserve by Rome and most vigorous in its resistance to the overwhelming impact of Hellenic culture." And Sibylle von Cles-Reden adds: "Far too little research has yet been done on the significance of Etruscan religion in the spiritual structure of the Roman state and the shaping of the Roman outlook and its effect on the whole of Italy, which persisted well into the Middle Ages. But one thing is certain, namely that Tarquinii, the center of the Etruscans' spiritual life, was once the source of spiritual currents that influenced decisively the development of the Italic peoples and of the West as a whole."

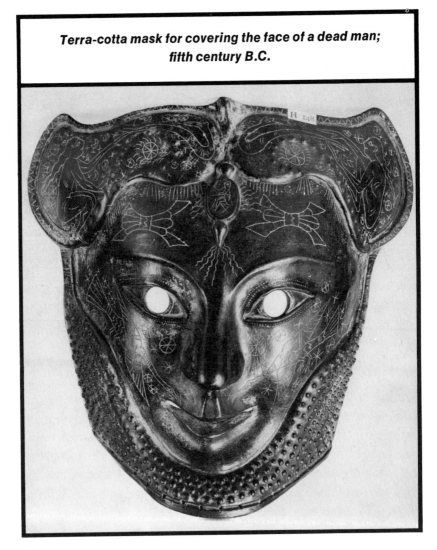

Terra-cotta mask for covering the face of a dead man; fifth century B.C.

There is little in the way of source material on the subject. Etruscan religious writings were still known in Roman times, and translations into Latin existed. In 63 B.C., when a flash of lightning struck the bronze sculpture of the famous she-wolf which had been made by an Etruscan and is now preserved in the Capitoline Museum, Cicero commented on the event: "Then what diviner, in turning the records and tomes of the augurs, failed to relate the mournful forecasts the Etruscans had written?"

And did not the emperor Claudius, who wrote a twenty-volume history of the Etruscans, personally insist that the "oldest Italian art" should not die out? In a speech to the senate in A.D. 47, of which fragments have survived, he proposed the establishment of a college of Etruscan soothsayers (*haruspices*). He recalled that "Leading Etruscans, on their own initiative—or the Roman senate's —have kept up the art and handed it down from father to son."

But what still existed in imperial times was subsequently lost. Not a single document has survived, either in the original Etruscan or in Latin translation. It is hard to believe that this was the result of pure chance. It seems highly likely that what was considered a dangerous inheritance from "pagan" times was the victim of deliberate, systematic destruction. With the emergence of Christianity there began a ruthless war on all the ancient religions and cults. And well before Constantine gave Christianity official support, Etruria was condemned by Arnobius in his defense of Christianity as the originator and mother of superstitions.

What we know of Etruscan religion resembles a broken mosaic. Like Judaism and Christianity it was a revealed religion. An account of the revelation as the Romans received it from the Etruscans is given by Cicero. One day, says the legend, in a field near the river Marta in Etruria a strange event occurred. A divine being rose up from the newly plowed furrow, a being with the appearance of a child, but the wisdom of an old man. The startled cries of the plowman brought *lucumones,* the priest kings of Etruria, hurrying to the spot. To them the wise child chanted the sacred doctrine, which they reverently listened to and wrote down, so that this most precious possession could be passed on to their successors. Immediately after the revelation the miraculous being fell dead and disappeared into the plowed field. His name was Tages, and he was believed to be the son of Genius and grandson of the highest god, Tinia, that is, Jupiter.

The field on which the child appeared to the plowing farmer became the site on which the first city of the Etruscans was built. The farmer's name is said to have been Tarchon, and in antiquity he was credited with being the founder of the city named Tarquinii after him, and indeed the founding father of all the Etruscan city-states which were later associated in the League of Twelve, and which all kept strictly to the doctrine revealed by Tages. This doctrine was embodied in the so-called *disciplina etrusca,* a collection of sacred writings. The ancient peoples of the Near East had possessed similar sacred books, but the Greeks never had.

Images of the myth of Tages occur on engraved gems found in tombs at Tarquinia in the nineteenth century. They show a head rising from the ground and about it, in attitudes of reverence, countryfolk and priests holding writing tablets. Rings with gems of this kind may have been worn by members of the Tarquinian order of sixty *haruspices* known to have existed at a later period.

Another discovery testifies to the deep roots in the Etruscan memory of the mythical event in the plowed field and to the central significance it always held. In the nineties of the last century a superb bronze mirror was found at Tuscania, a little town by the Marta, not far from Tarquinia. The picture engraved on the back of the mirror brings before us one of the esoteric rituals of the Etruscans, the scrutiny of the liver.

In the picture a beardless young man is bent slightly forward looking at a sacrificed animal's liver which he holds in his left hand. His costume shows him to be a *haruspex.* Over a short-sleeved undergarment closed at the neck he wears a pleated cloak falling to below the knee. On his curly hair he has the characteristic headdress of Etruscan priests, a hat with a tall, conical crown. Beside him stands a bearded man, also in priestly robes, holding a staff. He also has a pointed hat, but has pushed it to the back of his neck where it is held by a string under the chin. To the right stands a naked man, his cloak slung behind him, and in his right hand a spear. He is watching the inspection of the liver.

Around the border of the mirror some words in Etruscan are engraved. They held a surprise for the scholars who interpreted them. Over the young *haruspex* is written *pavatarchies,* the second half of which resembles the Etruscan form of Tages. The bearded priest is *Tarchunus,* otherwise Tarchon, and the man with the spear represents *Veltune,* otherwise Vertumnus or Voltumna, the chief god of the Etruscans. At his shrine, the Fanum Voltumnae, near Volsinii, the Etruscans annually met in a great religious celebration of the tutelary god of the league of the twelve cities.

The bronze mirror from Tuscania was made in the third century B.C. Its engraving and inscription reveal the close connection between Tarchon, the legendary founder of Tarquinii, and the god of the federal sanctuary, and the fundamental importance in the life of the Etruscan people of the doctrine propounded by Tages at Tarquinii.

> **The disciplina etrusca reflects a sense of close union with the cosmos, the Etruscan belief in the profound interconnection of all elements, in the mystic unity that joined the celestial and terrestrial worlds with the underworld.**

It is no longer possible to say in detail what was the doctrine of Tages. His prophecies filled a large part of the sacred books, which also circumscribed and determined the fate of the Etruscan nation on this earth. The *disciplina etrusca* reflects a sense of close union with the cosmos, the Etruscan belief in the profound interconnection of all elements, in the mystic unity that joined the celestial and terrestrial worlds with the underworld. Everything on earth, the life of the individual as well as that of the nation, is integrated in the unalterable rhythm of creation. Nothing is due to chance. Every event is preordained. The individual and the people are at the mercy of the gods, ineluctably subject to the will of unfathomable powers. This was something unknown to the Greeks, even in regard to Moira, the awe-inspiring power of fate. It was as though the human ego had surrendered, was resigned to the divine will, and set its sole hope in a belief in the magical efficacy of ritual.

An intricate system of rules and commands prescribed in the smallest detail every word and deed, determined every action, private and public. Man's whole care seems to have been to find out the will of the deity from the signs it gave, to use every imaginable method to secure its benevolence and to avert all evil, all dangers and threats. There was no such thing as freedom of will or action. In Etruscan life the ritual laws were omnipresent with their admonitions and requirements, were a perpetual burden to the spirit. "In all these practices and conceptions," says Pallottino, "as in all Etruscan ritual manifestations generally, one receives the impression of surrender, almost of abdication, of all human spiritual activities before the divine will."

The *disciplina etrusca* seems to have comprised three categories of books of fate. The first was that of the *libri haruspicini,* which dealt with divination from the livers of sacrificed animals; the second, the *libri fulgurales,* on the interpretation of thunder and lightning; the third, the *libri rituales,* which covered a variety of matters. They contained, as Festus says, "prescriptions concerning the founding of cities, the consecration of altars and temples, the inviolability of ramparts, the laws relating to city gates, the division into tribes, curiae and centuriae, the constitution and organization of armies, and all other things of this nature concerning war and peace."

Among the *libri rituales* were also three further categories: the *libri fatales,* on the division of time and the life-span of individuals and peoples; the *libri Acherontici,* on the world beyond the grave and the rituals for salvation; and finally, the *ostentaria,* which gave rules for interpreting signs and portents and laid down the propitiatory and expiatory acts needed to obviate disaster and to placate the gods.

So complex and all-embracing a doctrine naturally required long and laborious study. For this, the Etruscans had special training institutes, among which that at Tarquinii early enjoyed the highest repute. These institutes were much more than priests' seminaries in the modern sense. To judge by their range of studies they were a kind of university with several faculties. For their curricula included not only religious laws and theology, but also the encyclopedic knowledge required by the priests, which ranged from astronomy and meteorology through zoology, ornithology, and botany to geology and hydraulics. The last subject was the specialty of the *aquilices* who advised the city-states on all their hydraulic engineering projects. They were expert diviners who knew how to find subterranean water and how to bore wells, how to dig water channels, supply drinking water in the towns, and install irrigation and drainage systems in the fields. In addition they could create artificial reservoirs, sometimes underground, and lower the water of natural lakes. On these jobs they collaborated with other priests who specialized in constructing subterranean corridors and tunneling mountains.

In Etruria, as in the ancient East, theological and secular knowledge were not separated. Whatever man set himself to do on earth must be in consonance with the cosmos. Thus all the efforts of the priests were directed upon the heavens when it was necessary to discover the will of the gods in accordance with the sacred doctrine. The orientation and division of space were of crucial importance, as much in divination from an animal's liver as in laying the foundation of a temple, in interpreting a shooting star as in surveying land and marking out a garden and field.

Heaven and earth were imagined as being quartered by a great invisible cross consisting of a north-south axis called *cardo* and an east-west line called *decumanus,* to use the Latin terms. All ritual and religious observance was based on this division of celestial and terrestrial space. It alone enabled the priests to decipher and understand the signs emanating from the gods. And every sacral and secular undertaking on earth had to be coordinated with it. For the Etruscans believed that auspicious and inauspicious powers were irrevocably and for all eternity located in the four quarters of the sky, in accordance with the cosmic stations of the gods.

The east was considered of good augury, because there the highest deities, those favorable to man, had chosen to dwell. The northeast was the most auspicious and promised good fortune. In the south the gods of earth and nature ruled. The terrible and merciless gods of the underworld and of fate dwelt, it was believed, in the drear regions of the west, especially in the quarter between north and west, which was the most inauspicious.

The Etruscans even evolved a system of town planning based on these religious concepts, which were likewise reflected in the elaborate ritual prescribed for the foundation of a new city. In Etruria the town laid out in accordance with the sacred rules was considered a minute portion of the cosmos, harmoniously integrated with an all-embracing order governed by the gods.

The priest, after fixing the north-south and east-west lines by the sky, turned to the south and pronounced the words: "This be my front, and this my back, this my left and this my right." Then he took his *lituus,* his staff of office, a crook in shape like the crozier which has come down through the Romans to the bishops of the Roman Catholic and Anglican churches and to the Swedish Lutherans, and solemnly marked out the *cardo* and the *decumanus.*

At the central point of the new town, where the axes crossed, was dug a deep shaft. This connected the living with the dead, with the powers of the underworld. It was sealed with great stone slabs, and was called *mundus,* the same word as that used for the vault of the heavens, to which it was considered a subterranean counterpart. Varro says that it was held to be the gateway to the gods of the underworld. The boundaries of the city were then traced in a great circle around this point, in accordance with a solemn ceremonial.

Varro and other writers describe the Etruscan ceremony, which had to be performed on a day that the auguries showed favorable. The founder must wear his toga girt up in the ceremonial fashion and must yoke a white bull and a white cow to a plow, the bull on the right and the cow on the left. The plowshare must be of bronze. Then he plows a furrow, the cow being led on the inside while he holds the plow so that the clods fall inward. These clods of earth indicate the future city wall, and the furrow indicates the ditch. At places where a gate is to be, the plow is lifted up, for the gates are not sacred, though the wall is, and the whole area delimited by the furrow, which constitutes the city as *templum,* is a consecrated space.

> **The Romans learned the rites for the foundation of a city from the Etruscans and adopted them.**

The *cardo* and *decumanus,* which fixed the position of the *mundus,* also determined the position of gates and streets, altars, temples, and the citadel. "On the acropolis too," says Raymond Bloch, "the temples faced in a north-south direction so that the gods from their inner sanctum might extend protection over the city whose fate was entrusted to them." According to Roman sources, an Etruscan city was not considered as a true city unless it had three temples, three streets, and three gates.

Some seventeen miles from Bologna, near the village of Marzabotto, is the site of an Etruscan city of the sixth century B.C., the name of which may have been Misa. It is the only purely Etruscan

84

city which has been systematically excavated. And it shows a street plan laid out according to the Etruscan ritual. A *mundus* in front of a temple has also been discovered.

The Romans learned the rites for the foundation of a city from the Etruscans and adopted them. Their recollection of the procedure according to the Etruscan custom, *more etrusco,* is preserved in the legend of the founding of Rome by Romulus. Plutarch says that for this event Romulus "sent for men out of Tuscany, who directed him by sacred usages and written rules in all the ceremonies to be observed, as in a religious rite."

The Etruscan model, which is supposed to have been followed in the foundation of the legendary *Roma quadrata* (quartered Rome) on the Palatine, is reflected, too, in the layout of Roman military camps and in the procedures of pitching camp when the legions were on the march. This, Polybius says, is "one of those things really worth studying and worth knowing," and he goes on to describe it at some length.

When a suitable site for the camp has been found, one of the tribunes plants a white ensign at the spot "giving the best general view and most suitable for issuing orders," where the general's tent, the *praetorium,* is to stand. At this point, two straight roads cross at right angles; one of them, the *via praetoria,* runs east-west and connects two of the gates, the *porta praetoria* facing east and the *porta decumana* facing west. This street corresponds to the *decumanus* of Etruscan cities. The north-south street crossing it in front of the general's tent connected the main gates and was called *via principalis,* corresponding to the *cardo,* and another, parallel to it five blocks away, the *via quintana.*

The cosmic conceptions embodied in Etruscan ritual left their mark too on the significance which was attributed to the gates of the Roman camp. The *porta praetoria,* facing sunrise in the east, whence the favorable auguries came, had the reputation of being a lucky gate, and the legionaries marched out through it to battle. But the *porta decumana,* which opened to the sunset in the west, was counted unlucky. Through this gate those sentenced to death were taken out to execution.

The trench surrounding the camp was also dug according to the Etruscan ritual. The excavated earth was piled up on the inner side to make a rampart which was completed by a palisade. Subsequently many frontier towns of the Roman empire developed on the pattern of such camps, with stone or brick walls replacing the earth rampart. Classic examples of such geometrical, rectangular layouts are Turin, and Timgad in Algeria, on the edge of the Sahara, which was founded by the emperor Trajan in A.D. 100.

The estates, farms, and plantations of Etruria were all subject to sacred laws. Two legends narrate how these were made known. Tages himself, it was said in Tarquinii, taught Tarchon the rules of *limitatio,* land surveying. They had been handed down in a codex, the Latin title of which was *Liber qui inscribitur terrae iuris Etruriae,* the land law of Etruria.

According to another version of the legend, from Chiusi, a prophetess Vegoia communicated to a certain Arruns, prince of Chiusi, "the decisions of Jupiter and of justice." This version is better known because the revelations of Vegoia were translated into Latin by Tarquitius Priscus, a *haruspex,* during Cicero's lifetime and were preserved in the temple of Apollo on the Palatine.

A fragment of this Latin text has survived in a later collection of documents, where it is entitled: "Extract from the books of Vegoia for Arruns Veltumnus." It reads: "Know that the sea was separated from the sky. When Jupiter had claimed for himself the land of Etruria, he determined and ordered that the plains should be measured and the fields marked out. Knowing the greed of men and their desire for land, he wished everything to be established with boundaries . . . Whoever shall touch or displace them in order to extend his property and diminish that of others shall for this crime be condemned by the gods. If such men be slaves, they shall be brought into an even lower state of servitude. If the master is guilty of the same, his family shall be extirpated and his whole race shall perish."

The Etruscan Jupiter, who was called Tinia, held boundaries sacred, watched over them, and ensured their inviolability. "Etruscan civilization," says Jacques Heurgon, "defines itself here, among all Italic civilizations, as a civilization of peasant farmers passionately attached to the Etruscan land law, the *ius terrae Etruriae.* They proudly defended the sanctity of their boundaries, and this attitude went right back to the origins of their race, when Jupiter had established his reign."

Thus the famous and universally admired Roman law of property, which is still taught in law schools and is fundamental to European legislation, may be traced back to pre-Roman origins. The principle of *dominium,* the inalienable right of property, goes back to the sacred land law of the Etruscans.

The Etruscan priests later found the Romans apt pupils of their art of surveying. This was something that appealed to the practical, sober-minded Latins, and over the centuries they never lacked opportunities to practice it. The endless wars of conquest provided ever more foreign soil for the purpose.

On the other hand many of the Etruscans' other religious practices seem to have remained a mystery to the Romans. This was especially so when it was a question of discovering and interpreting the will of the gods, something to which the Romans attached great importance. Diodorus Siculus says plainly of the Etruscans: "The teaching about nature and the gods they also brought to greater perfection, and they elaborated the art of divination by thunder and lightning more than all other men."

Perhaps it was merely an oversight of this historian that he failed to mention another religious practice, hepatoscopy. For this, the Romans down to imperial times relied on Etruscans. Divination from the liver of sacrificed animals was a most complicated business. To get the interpretation right required a sound knowledge not only of astronomy but also of anatomy and pathology.

In 1877 at Piacenza a bronze model of a liver was found. It was evidently a model used in a priests' school for teaching the art of haruspicy, and of a fairly late period. On the upper surface are marked sixteen divisions in which are inscribed the names of some thirty gods, some more than once. Each of the sixteen divisions corresponded to a section of the heavens, for the Etruscans regarded the liver as an image of the cosmos, as a microcosm of the universe. The liver, it was believed, exactly reproduced the heavenly firmament with its sacred laws and controlling divinities and its division, first into four, by the intersecting axes and then into sixteen subdivisions.

The liver was taken from a sacrificed animal, usually a sheep, and the job of the *haruspex* was to recognize the warning and prophetic signs and to interpret them. From the diagnosis, as it were, the priest could tell which god was speaking through the signs. A diseased liver indicated disaster and a healthy liver good fortune.

Scrutiny of the liver was an art derived from the ancient East. From time immemorial it had been practiced in Mesopotamia and Asia Minor. It originated with the Babylonians and was later adopted by the Hittites. Excavations have turned up inscribed, baked clay livers. They have confirmed what we learn from the Old

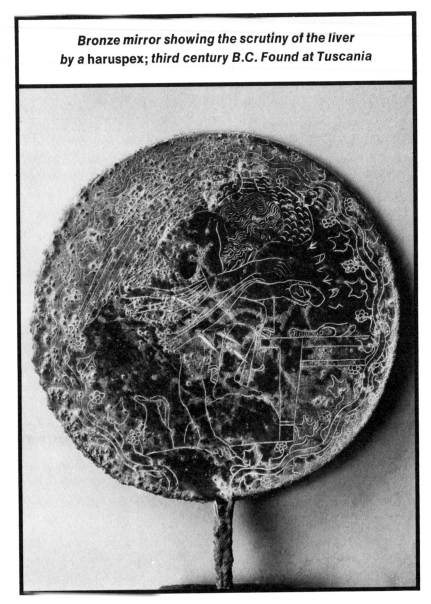

Bronze mirror showing the scrutiny of the liver by a haruspex; *third century B.C. Found at Tuscania*

Testament, when Ezekiel says: "For the king of Babylon stood at the parting of the way, at the head of the two ways, to use divination: . . . he looked in the liver."

Hepatoscopy was first brought to Europe by the Etruscans, and became firmly established in Italy. The Romans attributed great importance to it, and regarded the *haruspices* with respect, as is shown by many incidents. Until late imperial times, Etruscan liver diviners were in great demand. The senate sought their counsel, they belonged to the general staff of the Roman armies, and accompanied generals on their campaigns. This continued even when Etruria had long ceased to be independent and had been absorbed into the empire. For instance, so Pliny relates, "when the later Emperor Augustus was sacrificing at Spoletum, upon the first day of his entering on the imperial dignity, in six different victims the liver was found rolled over within itself, from the very lowest lobe; and the answer that was given by the diviners was to the effect that, in the course of the year, he would gain a twofold sway."

It seems probable that hepatoscopy reached Greece from Etruria via Syracuse in Sicily. It was already known to the Greeks, in a form closely corresponding to the Etruscan, at the time of the Persian wars. Aeschylus makes Prometheus explain what shape and color the liver must have to please the gods.

Another method of discovering the will of the gods was the interpretation of lightning and unusual celestial or terrestrial phenomena and occurrences. According to the Etruscan theory there were eleven different types of lightning, just as there were in ancient Mesopotamia among the Chaldeans. What the lightning signified depended not only on which of the sixteen subdivisions of the heavens it came from, but also on the season of the year, the day or month, and on its shape, color, and effect. Some of the Etruscan rules of interpretation are strikingly similar to those laid down in minute detail in ancient Babylonian texts.

The place where lightning struck was considered to be of significance. It was called *fulmen regale,* a royal thunderbolt, if it struck the place of popular assemblies or a government building. In this case it presaged civil war or the decline of the state. If it struck the *praetorium* in a camp it meant the latter's capture and the death of the commander.

Every thunderbolt required expiation. It was the duty of the *fulguriator,* as the officiating priest was called in this case, to purify the spot where the lightning had struck. He collected the marks of its passage, such as damaged objects, dead people, or animals, and interred them. This grave was then tabu and no one must walk on it. The Romans adopted this ritual, and only Etruscan experts were entrusted with the burial and the expiation of thunderbolts.

The Etruscans believed in predestination. Although a slight postponement is sometimes possible by means of prayer and sacrifice, the end is certain.

According to the Etruscan ritual books as described by Censorinus, man had allotted to him a cycle of seven times twelve years. At eighty-four years, his life was fulfilled. Anyone who lived longer lost the ability to understand the signs of the gods. Staseas of Naples, the Peripatetic philosopher, said he was like a runner in a race, or a racing vehicle, running outside the marked track.

A similar belief in destiny is expressed in the Etruscan system of reckoning time. As a man passed through the stages of his life toward certain death, so, the Etruscans believed, the existence of their people was also limited to a time-span fixed by the gods. According to the doctrine, ten *saecula* were allotted to the *nomen etruscum,* the Etruscan name. Each had its own particular length which could not be calculated in advance, nor established by counting years, as is now done. Rather, it was a matter of recognizing and understanding the signs given by the gods. The end of one *saeculum* and the beginning of another might be indicated by natural disasters such as earthquakes and other extraordinary events, a plague, or the birth of a freak, a thunderbolt, a shower of stones, or the appearance of a comet.

> As a man passed through the stages of his life toward certain death, so, the Etruscans believed, the existence of their people was also limited to a time-span fixed by the gods.

Historical reality has been given to the Etruscans' time theories, which seem so strange to us, by some fragmentary writings transmitting earlier traditions. In his *De die natali* of A.D. 238, Censorinus, explicitly basing himself on older information about Etruscan historical records provided by the grammarian Varro, says: "It is written that the first four *saecula* each lasted 100 years, the fifth 123, and the sixth 119, the seventh the same and the records were set down in the course of the eighth. A ninth and a tenth were still to run and when these had expired the end of the 'Etruscan Name' would have come."

Historians who unearthed this text had no difficulty in establishing that the final year of the eighth *saeculum,* still in progress, as Censorinus said, was 88 B.C. In that year interpreters of omens summoned from Etruria to Rome had announced the beginning of a new age. But when attempts were made to calculate the birth date of the Etruscans from the available data, the result was too far back, namely, 968 B.C. That is to say, Etruscan memory put the beginning of Etruscan history a long time before that of Rome, which, according to tradition, was founded in 753 B.C.

The figures for the fifth, sixth, and seventh *saecula* seem credible. They take the reckoning back to 568 B.C., to the century when Etruria was at the height of its power. The figures may derive from the temple of the goddess Nortia at Volsinii where a nail, it is said, was driven into the wall at the close of each year. But on the other hand the figures of one hundred years for each of the first four *saecula* seem much too regular. Probably they were inserted later when knowledge of the earliest period was already lost. Against their credibility stands the fact that there is no archeological proof of the presence of the Etruscans in Italy in the tenth and ninth centuries B.C. The earliest date for which such proof has been found is the eighth century.

The beginnings of Etruscan history within the traditional ten *saecula* may be obscure and perhaps will always remain so. But something else, however strange it may seem, did in fact happen, and can be verified, in historical times. The Etruscans, whose existence as a nation had been shaped by the sacred teaching of the legendary Tages, duly vanished from the earth when the portents showed, in accordance with that teaching, that the time had come. They were submerged and, as a people, disappeared as mysteriously as their ancestors had once made their first appearance.

After the murder of Caesar in 44 B.C., when "the sheeted dead did squeak and gibber in the Roman streets" and the living were terrified by a brilliant comet in the night sky, the Etruscan seer Vulcatius, according to Augustus, proclaimed the end of the ninth *saeculum,* and the beginning of the tenth and last. In A.D. 54, on the death of the emperor Claudius—the emperor who was the historian of the Etruscans and perhaps the last Roman to command their language—another comet appeared and lightning struck his father's tomb. Was the prophecy now fulfilled and the end come?

It may seem an improbable story. But there is in fact no archeological evidence of the existence of the Etruscans later than the middle of the first century A.D.

VII

Mysterious Origin, Mysterious Language

WHO WERE THESE ETRUSCANS WHOSE appearance in central Italy was followed by such a tremendous upheaval? Where did they come from and where did their language originate? All these questions have been asked for more than a couple of thousand years. There has been no lack of answers, but so far none has been truly satisfactory.

The oldest answer on the origin of this people is that given by Herodotus, the Greek historian of the fifth century B.C. According to him, they came from Lydia, the kingdom in Asia Minor whose capital was Sardis and whose rulers included two who have become famous in story, Gyges, with his ring, and Croesus. The Lydians, says Herodotus, remembered the time "when they sent a colony to settle in Tyrrhenia." His account of that event reads: "In the reign of Atys, the son of Manes, the whole of Lydia suffered from a severe famine. For a time the

93

people lingered on as patiently as they could, but later, when there was no improvement, they began to look for something to alleviate their misery. Various expedients were devised . . . They managed to live like this for eighteen years. There was still no remission of their suffering—indeed it grew worse; so the king divided the population into two groups and determined by drawing lots which should emigrate and which should remain at home. He appointed himself to rule the section whose lot determined that they should remain, and his son Tyrrhenus to command the emigrants. The lots were drawn, and one section went down to the coast at Smyrna, where they built vessels, put aboard all their household effects, and sailed in search of a livelihood elsewhere. They passed many countries and finally reached Umbria in the north of Italy, where they settled and still live to this day. Here they changed their name from Lydians to Tyrrhenians, after the king's son Tyrrhenus, who was their leader."

Herodotus's account, which puts the emigration in the time of the Trojan War, was generally believed in Roman times, when the Etruscan language was still a living one. There are innumerable instances. Horace addresses as a Lydian his patron Maecenas, the emperor Augustus's counselor, who came of an old Etruscan family. Virgil, himself born in Mantua, in his *Aeneid* apostrophizes the Etruscans as the "elect manhood of Lydia." Conversely, the inhabitants of Sardis, the ancient Lydian capital, in imperial times referred to their relationship with the Etruscan royal house of the Tarquins.

Ancient writers never had any doubts about the origin in Asia Minor of the Etruscans, with one single exception, Dionysius of Halicarnassus. Greek by birth, but Roman by inclination, he asserted that the Tyrrhenians were indigenous, were a people long settled in Italy. They were, he said, a very ancient nation that "is found . . . to agree with no other either in its language or in its manner of living."

The account given by Herodotus has long been the subject of controversy. The whole Near East has been raked over in the search for the Etruscans' forebears. More than once it seemed that a clue had been found, for instance in the Egyptian word *Turusa,* occurring in hieroglyphic texts of the thirteenth century B.C., as in the name of a palace official Iun-Tursa, who lived about 1300 B.C. Or the Lydian place name Tursa or Tyrrha, or the Lydian word for prince, *turannos.* And there was no doubt about the similarity between the tumulus fields at Sardis and those in Etruria, as also between the great bronze cauldrons from Gordion, the Phrygian capital, and those found in Etruscan tombs.

But the search yielded no result. Nowhere outside Italy, neither in the Aegean nor in the Near East, was there any demonstrable

Small bucchero jug in the form of a cock, with the Etruscan alphabet incised on it; seventh or sixth century B.C. Found at Viterbo

Etruscan site or place of origin of the Etruscan people. It was the same with the language. The look of Etruscan script is known from many sources. The earliest inscriptions were found in the splendid, spacious royal tombs; they were the names of the dead scratched on vases and bowls. The oldest alphabets that have so far been found likewise date from the seventh century B.C. In a necropolis at Marsiliana d'Albegna, near the lagoon of Orbetello, a little ivory tablet was discovered. It measures only 3½ inches by 2 inches, and on its surface were still traces of wax and of writing which appeared to have been done with a stylus. Along one edge an alphabet of twenty-six letters, reading from right to left, had been engraved. Clearly it was there as a reminder to help the owner in his use of the neat little device. A hole in the knob suggests that the owner kept it always with him, hanging from a ribbon, perhaps. This ivory tablet is dated to about the first half of the seventh century B.C.

Another object looks as though it may have been used as an ink pot. It is a thin-walled *bucchero* figure of a cockerel, found at Viterbo. The bird's head forms the lid. Around its breast the same alphabet is inscribed. Similar finds, all of the seventh century, have been made at Formello, near Veii, at Cerveteri and other places. Taken together with numerous inscriptions, they indicate how widespread in Etruria the art of writing was at that period.

In one respect there is no difficulty about these alphabets. They can be read without trouble, because the letters are those of the west Greek alphabet, which derives from the Phoenician. First developed by Semites in Sinai, the alphabet had been in use for centuries in the Phoenician trading cities, especially in ancient Ugarit. It was one of the many cultural achievements which the Greeks

> **We even know what Etruscan sounded like. But with few exceptions the words remain incomprehensible.**

acquired from the Near East around 800 B.C. What is still disputed is from whom the Etruscans received their alphabet. Some scholars believe that they learned it from the peoples of the Asia Minor coast. Others assume that it reached them from the Greek colony at Cumae in Campania.

The real problem lies in the inscriptions, in the texts. They can be read, letter by letter, like the alphabet. We even know what

Etruscan sounded like. But with few exceptions the words remain incomprehensible.

So far, all attempts to decipher the Etruscan language have failed. More than ten thousand inscriptions are known, but most of them are brief; nine tenths consist of funerary and votive inscriptions, containing the name and family relationships or official title of the dead person, and few verbs or nouns. Their content is minimal. Nonetheless, by dint of great efforts, scholars have managed to interpret some three hundred words of Etruscan. *Aska mi eleivana, mini mulvanike mamarce velchana* inscribed on a little flask, means: "I am an oil bottle and Mamarce Velchana donated me."

But this does not go very far toward translating and understanding the longer inscriptions that have been discovered. It does not help with the famous text of 1,185 legible words written on the linen wrapping of an Egyptian mummy, which is now in the National Museum at Zagreb, Yugoslavia. Nor with the tile found at Capua containing some six hundred words, of which about half are legible, that is now in Berlin.

But even if these texts were translated, there would still be a long way to go. They would tell us little. For their content, it is clear, does not go beyond liturgical formulas connected with the cult of the dead, like those in funerary and votive inscriptions. The mummy wrapping contains prescriptions connected with public ceremonies regulated by a calendar; the Capua tile likewise contains formulas connected with funerary rites.

No bilingual or trilingual inscription, no Rosetta Stone for Etruscan, has so far come to light. But something approaching it has been found at Pyrgi (Santa Severa). On July 8, 1964, three rectangular sheets of thin gold were disovered between the foundations of two temples. One is inscribed in Punic and two in Etruscan. They are dated to about 500 B.C. Two years later, a bronze tablet, also in Etruscan, was found. The holes in the gold tablets show that they must once have been nailed to temple walls or doors. The Punic inscription has been translated and says that Thefarie Velianas, ruler of Caere, had given a sacred place dedicated to Astarte within the temple. The Punic is not a translation of the associated Etruscan tablets, but the general sense is similar. Thus this find has considerably enriched the knowledge of the Etruscan language. Together with other material from the excavation, the gold sheets are now in the Villa Giulia Museum in Rome. The possibility of further such discoveries is not to be excluded. After all, not a single ancient Etruscan city has yet been systematically and completely excavated.

It is known that Etruscan was not an Indo-European language. Nor was it Semitic or related to any known living or dead language. It seems to have certain grammatical features which occur in dialects of western Asia Minor, such as Lycian, Carian, and Lydian. But so far only one discovery outside Italy has suggested any definite clue. This is a grave stele of the sixth century B.C. found on the island of Lemnos in the Aegean. It contains two inscriptions in a language which has several remarkable similarities with Etruscan.

Thucydides speaks of "the Tyrrhenian race that once lived in Lemnos," and Herodotus says that they "passed many countries" before they reached Umbria. Did they perhaps stop at Lemnos on the way and leave some of their race behind there? It is conceivable, but cannot be proved.

The truth is that the origin and language of the Etruscans are still a mystery. But one thing seems undeniable—their close, direct dependence on the East, by which they were profoundly influenced. Many discoveries point to this conclusion. They suggest that Herodotus's account of a migration from the East, even if his date for it is much too early, contains a core of historical truth, and that Seneca was quite right when he said: *"Tuscos Asia sibi vindicat"* ("Asia claims the Tuscans as her own"). As we now know, the times were ripe for large-scale migrations. With the end of the eighth century B.C. a period of grave disorders set in for the Near East. How else are we to explain the development attested by the archeological discoveries?

From the seventh century B.C., central Italy under the Etruscans was like an oasis transplanted from the East; it was like a piece of the ancient Near East. Everything about it was new to Italy, its whole civilization and culture, its technology and architecture, its farming methods and mines, its crafts and industries, its customs, fashions, and way of life, and its religion and language. All these had hitherto been unknown to the predominantly Indo-European speaking inhabitants.

Such far-reaching changes cannot be introduced and established by mere trade, by the occasional arrival of foreigners or the import of goods. Much more continuous and stronger stimuli must have been at work, deriving from an influx of a people of superior capacity who enthralled the old inhabitants and even induced them to adopt a language unknown to them.

THE GREAT EXPANSION BEGINS

REMARKABLE THOUGH THE ADvances were that the Etruscans had brought about, they did not rest on their oars. With unbounded energy and enterprise they pushed on to yet further achievements. As early as the seventh century B.C. they set their course for new goals, and their civilization began its triumphant progress through the Italic lands. Thanks to innumerable archeological discoveries it is possible to plot on the map the routes of the Etruscans' advance. "A careful study of the archeological documents in our possession," says Pallottino, "is sufficient to persuade us that both the predominant role and absolute chronological priority in the formation of the civilization of ancient Italy belong to Etruria."

There are no ash layers along the Etruscans' route; there is no tradition of campaigns of extermination against the indigenous peoples, who were still semibarbarous. The Etruscans' aims were peaceful. They went out to other peoples with the object of opening up new regions to civilization and trade. They wanted new markets for the products of their crafts and industry. They founded many new cities.

In the north and east, Volterra from the seventh century B.C. thrust into the valleys of the left-bank tributaries of the Arno, the Era, and the Elsa. A memorial to this expansion is the great tumulus tomb of Castellina amid the vineyards and olive groves of the Chianti district on the road from Florence to Siena. Another foundation was Faesulae, modern Fiesole, which itself later became the parent city of Florence.

In the south, there was a push across the Tolfa hills eastward beyond Lakes Vico and Bracciano, as far as the Tiber. The Faliscans, an Italic people, came under Etruscan influence. One of their old settlements was replaced by the town of Falerii. Its cemeteries cover the valley bottom near Civita Castellana. Farther south, within the curve of the Tiber, the same thing happened with the Capenates.

Exterior face of Porta Del Arco, Volterra; second century B.C. Arch restored at a later date

The new urban foundation in their territory was given the Etruscan-sounding name of Capena. The many tunnels and channels dug into the hills still attest the hydraulic skill of the new masters.

As the Etruscans advanced into new lands, so too did their language and writing. It was from them that the illiterate Italic peoples first learned to read and write.

Gradually, the Etruscan influence spread farther to the south, beyond the Tiber into Latium. Here the Indo-European speaking peoples, the Latins, Sabines, Volscians, and others, just like the Umbrians, Faliscans, and Capenates, were still at a rather backward stage of development. They kept to themselves and had little contact with the outside world, either farther afield or even on the nearby sea coast with its international shipping. They inhabited scattered villages of primitive, unadorned huts. They lived on the produce of their herds and their simple agriculture. Their village craftsmen turned out rough, unpolished wares. More highly developed techniques and arts were unknown to them, as were reading and writing.

What happened in this backward part of Italy when the Etruscan colonists arrived and what tremendous progress they brought with them were long unknown. Roman tradition with good reason kept silent on the point. It was only in the nineteenth century that excavations brought the facts to light. Discoveries which aroused widespread amazement revealed the first important successes of Etruscan development aid to the land beyond the Tiber.

At the southern end of the Sabine hills, on the slopes of Monte Ginestro, lies Palestrina, a little town beneath whose houses are buried the remains of an ancient city, the Roman Praeneste. It was famous for the huge temple of Fortuna Primigenia, the first-born daughter of Jupiter, built by Sulla at the site of a spring much visited on account of its oracle. No one suspected that in the soil that covered the vast ruins of the temple there lay the evidence of a much older past, of monuments that went back to pre-Roman times.

In 1855–6 a great discovery was made. Members of the old-established Barberini family set to work to search for hidden treasure in the land around their home town. The search was so successful that they decided to continue, and in 1859 and 1866 more gangs of workmen dug in various places near Palestrina. Their finds exceeded all expectations. They uncovered an untouched royal tomb, henceforth known as the Tomba Barberini. It contained a superb treasure of precious jewels and luxury articles: ornaments, cups, and a table service of gold and silver; pins and clasps in the gold granulation technique; carved ivory boxes; craters, beakers, bowls; bronze mountings and incense burners.

Ten years later, in the spring of 1876, it happened again. This time the luck was with some poor peasants. They uncovered a second splendid tomb, in the plain some six hundred yards from the little town, close to the church of S. Rocco.

"It was not only a virgin tomb," says George Dennis, who visited it soon after the discovery, "but, fortunately for its discoverers, it was the last resting-place of some nameless chieftain or high-priest, whose wealth had been buried with him, and was thus preserved intact through nearly 3,000 years. Its contents bear a close analogy to those of the Regolini tomb at Cerveteri, but the tomb itself was even of a more primitive construction . . . It was a mere pit, sunk two yards below the surface, surrounded by rude masonry, inclosing a space some six yards by four, within which, in a cavity sunk in the floor, was deposited the body, in all its panoply of rich vestments and gorgeous ornaments, which surpass in their elaborate beauty even those of the Regolini sepulchre. By its side lay also weapons and armour, and around the walls of the pit were deposited various articles for the toilet or for domestic use, in the precious metals and in bronze . . .

> *"The most striking object . . . and the most elaborate piece of jewellery perhaps ever rescued from an Italian sepulchre, is an oblong plate of gold, eight inches by five, studded all over with minute figures of beasts and chimaeras, not in relief, but standing up bodily from the plate, and numbering not less than 131 in that limited space."*

"To specify all the wonders of this tomb would occupy too much space, yet some of its contents are so novel and curious as not to be passed over lightly . . . The most striking object . . . and the most elaborate piece of jewellery perhaps ever rescued from an Italian sepulchre, is an oblong plate of gold, eight inches by five, studded all over with minute figures of beasts and chimaeras, not in relief, but standing up bodily from the plate, and numbering not less than

131 in that limited space. There are five rows of tiny lions, arranged longitudinally, some standing with their tails curved over their backs, some couchant, others sitting on their haunches, two rows of chimaeras, and two of sirens, flanked transversely at each end by a row of exquisitely formed little horses, full of life and spirit . . . But of pure gold, bright as if newly polished, is a little plain *skyphos,* or two-handled cup, about four inches high, with two Egyptian sphinxes at the setting-on of each handle. By its side stands a bowl full of fragments of gold leaf, the relics of the vestments of the priest or warrior, which were found mingled with his dust. There are fragments also of a fringe of pure silver thread, which may have adorned his robes . . ."

What Dennis described with such gusto is now preserved as the contents of the Bernardini tomb, along with the material from the Barberini tomb, in the glass cases of a Roman museum, the Villa Giulia. But only part of this material is at present—the fall of 1973—on view to the public. The rest was taken over by the Villa Giulia recently from the Pigorini prehistoric and ethnographic collection on the latter's move to the Museo Preistorico ed Etnografico in the EUR quarter of Rome, but is not yet on display.

Progress in archeology has made it possible to clear up much about the tombs that long remained controversial or doubtful. It is now known that both tombs date from the middle of the seventh century B.C. Their sumptuous contents are typical of the orientalizing style then dominating Etruscan art.

Neither at that time nor for centuries to come were there in Latium itself any native goldsmiths or other artists and craftsmen of such skill and refinement. All articles of display and luxury, jewelry ornamented with animals, fabulous beings and minute granulation, carved ivory, and objects of repoussé or cast bronze, and other such things were imported.

Where they came from is no longer in doubt. "The funeral furnishings of the Praeneste tombs fit into the general picture of Etruscan work of the seventh century B.C.," says Luisa Banti. "The splendid furnishings of the Barberini and Bernardini tombs are not of local origin, for which there is no supporting evidence. They came from southern Etruria, where, especially at Caere, we find in both native work and imports the same characteristics as in the material from Praeneste."

In the view of the Swedish scholar Axel Boëthius, the Praeneste tombs, which display the same splendor as the archaic tumuli tombs north of the Tiber, confirm that the Etruscans, when they spread out to the south, brought their advanced civilization to the Latin-speaking areas. Furthermore, as Lopes Pegna points out, "soil tests have shown that in the course of the seventh century B.C. more and more land in Latium was cleared and drained. The direct and immediate result was agricultural output of such size as to constitute the counterpart for imports of expensive luxuries."

The Praeneste tombs are the earliest evidence of the period when Etruria was putting out feelers toward the south. That was only the beginning. Later the land beyond the Tiber came more and more under Etruscan influence.

This colonizing movement into Latium was to have unforeseen effects, not only for the Etruscans, but for all the other peoples of Italy, and ultimately for the West as a whole. For it was this movement which started on their road to power the inhabitants of seven insignificant hills rising out of the swampy valley of the Tiber.

PART THREE

The Etruscan Empire

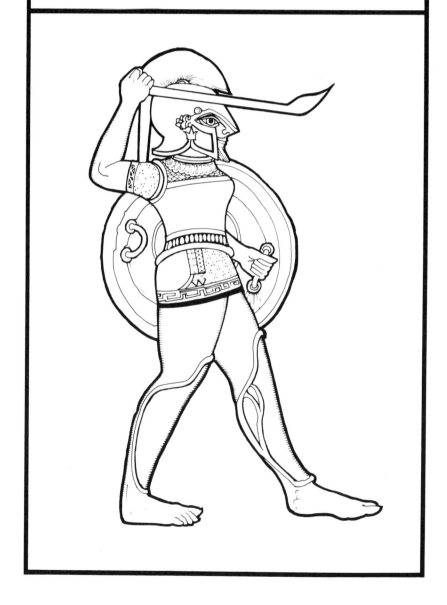

*Nearly the whole of Italy
had been under Etruscan domination.*

Cato, 2nd century B.C.

*Before the days of Roman domination
Etruscan influence, both by land and sea,
stretched over a wide area:
how great their power was
on the upper and lower seas
(which make Italy a peninsula)
is proved by the names of those seas,
one being known by all Italian peoples
as the Tuscan—the inclusive designation of the race—
and the other as the Hadriatic,
from the Etruscan settlement of Hatria.
The Greeks know them
as the Tyrrhenian and Adriatic seas.*

Livy, 1st century B.C.

VIII

The Romulus Legend Exploded

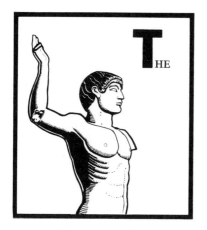

THE ANCIENT WORLD WAS FULL OF unrest at the turn of the seventh and sixth centuries B.C. From Mesopotamia to Africa, from the Aegean to the farthest west of the Mediterranean there was hardly a region unaffected by upheavals and shifts of power, by innovations and discoveries.

In Mesopotamia the empire that had for so long dominated Asia collapsed. Assyria, the great conquering state which had made tributary all the peoples from the Black Sea to the Red, succumbed to the attack of the allied armies of the Medes and the Chaldeans from southern Babylonia. The ancient capital Assur fell in 614 B.C.; two years later Nineveh itself was destroyed, and the prophecy of the Old Testament prophet Jonah, "Nineveh shall be overthrown," was fulfilled.

But the rejoicing in Judah was to be short-lived. For the Babylonian kings in their turn strove for world domination, and Palestine once again experienced the terrors of foreign invasion. Barely a generation later, in 586 B.C., came the country's darkest hour, when Jerusalem was conquered after three years of siege by the troops of Nebuchadnezzar II. The city and the temple were destroyed, and the long lines of prisoners set out on the road to exile.

Babylon, to which they were taken, became a metropolis whose greatness and splendor eclipsed that of all its predecessors. Nebuchadnezzar lavished wealth on its buildings. The famous Tower of Babel, the new temple to the city's god Marduk, was some 280 feet high. The Ishtar Gate of the city glowed with colored glazed bricks patterned with bulls and dragons. In the great palace on the waterside were the Hanging Gardens, one of the wonders of the ancient world.

In Asia Minor, too, at almost the same time, a major conflict was in progress. On May 28, 585 B.C. in Anatolia the troops of the Lydian king Alyattes defeated the Medes in the battle of the river Halys. The battle had an unusual feature which at the time was without precedent. This was the use of scientific calculation on the Lydian side to gain an advantage over the enemy.

King Alyattes's adviser was the Greek philosopher Thales of Miletus. According to Herodotus, he predicted the date of an eclipse of the sun, and at the time fixed by Thales the Lydian king ordered a surprise attack on the Medes. The latter, terrified and thrown into confusion by the sudden darkening of the sun, were driven from the field. The defeat of the Medes was such that they abandoned their plans of conquest and made peace with Lydia. The river Halys became the frontier between the two nations.

Barely half a century later, the Ionian Greeks were to experience the consequences of the Lydian victory. For the kings of Lydia now had their hands free for a drive to the sea coast and its rich ports. As yet the Greeks had no inkling of the threat hanging over them. Their cities were enjoying a boom such as they had never before experienced; the economy, trade, and shipping were flourishing; exports and imports were rising.

In the seventh century, when the Etruscan kings were carrying out their great civilizing work in central Italy, the Greeks of Ionia had made remarkable progress. The Ionians were enjoying the fruits of their long-established close contacts with the great empires of the East. Adventurous and enterprising as they were, they had become known all over the Near East as traders and as mercenaries who fought in the armies of Egypt and, later, of Babylon.

For the Ionians it was a time of learning, a preparation for the future. What had happened earlier in the Mycenaean Age was repeated on a large scale. While Attica was still primitive and insignificant, the Greeks of Asia Minor traveled all over the countries of the ancient East, acquiring knowledge, learning the skills and accomplishments of its inhabitants. No other people, perhaps, if we except in modern times the Japanese and the Russians, has ever so thoroughly drawn on foreign sources, copied so much, adopted and absorbed so much from others. In the Fertile Crescent and in Egypt, they made their first acquaintance with vast temples, columned halls, and large-scale sculpture in stone, an experience which was to provide so vital a stimulus to their own architecture and sculpture. There, too, they learned the fundamental ideas without which their own swift progress in scientific thinking would scarcely have been possible, in particular the foundations of mathematics and geometry, knowledge of the heavens and astronomic calculation.

It was hardly surprising if they themselves were at first fascinated by the East. The pottery and textiles which the Ionian towns produced were, to begin with, copied from Eastern models. These provided the ornamental motifs, the fabulous creatures, the wild animals and the plants, the sphinxes, lions, and lotus blossoms. The Oriental style was eagerly adopted, became the fashion. Exported by Ionia, it was welcomed in the motherland and in the colonies.

Around 600 B.C. Miletus was the queen of the Asia Minor coast, a city richer and more powerful than all the others. The founder of scores of colonies, it was famous for its incomparable textiles. In second place came the important commercial center Phocaea. And at a time when the literature of Asia, written in cuneiform, hieroglyphs, and the Phoenician alphabet, already filled whole libraries, poetry made its appearance on the island of Lesbos. Here, beside the famous Sappho, were her countrymen Arion and Alcaeus, likewise composing poetry. The first love songs in Greek were sung, like the songs of King David, to the accompaniment of that old Oriental instrument, the lyre.

In Hellas, Corinth, in close contact with Ionia, had risen to be a first-class sea power, and was thriving as an important trading center and port of transshipment. There was a great demand for

Corinthian pottery. But already competition was threatening. Master potters in neighboring Attica began to produce clay vessels—the superb black-figure vases—which soon were to excel all others. In Athens the revival of art was accompanied in the political and social field by Solon's constitutional reforms.

Greek merchant ships had a lion's share of the trade and shipping in the Black Sea, the Aegean, and the Mediterranean as far as Sicily and southern Italy. Greek merchants established their own trading stations and depots on the coast of Syria and Phoenicia. But still their thirst for adventure was unslaked; they were driven to explore yet more distant lands and to conquer yet more markets.

For a good many years, in fact since about 650 B.C., when the Egyptian Pharaoh Psamtik I sent for Greek mercenaries, Greek merchants had been in Egypt organizing trade. In the following century King Amasis granted them the privilege of setting up their own trading center at Naucratis, near the mouth of the western branch of the Nile. Somewhat earlier, King Necho, whose reign straddles the end of the seventh century and beginning of the sixth, began the construction of a canal to the Arabian Gulf—the first "Suez Canal," as it were—and a Phoenician ship set out from Egypt and circumnavigated Africa.

While these developments were going on in Egypt, other Greeks ventured into the distant western waters of the Mediterranean. A group from Phocaea reached southern France and, in about 600 B.C., founded the colony of Massalia, the Roman Massilia and modern Marseilles, at the mouth of the river Rhone, right in the hitherto uncontested Carthaginian zone of influence. Thus they secured a base for a move into Spain.

Just about this time occurred the event which history books seldom evaluate correctly. This was the action taken by kings from Etruria to found a city that was later to eclipse all other cities of the Mediterranean, that was to become the capital of the world.

Just about this time occurred the event which history books seldom evaluate correctly. This was the action taken by kings from Etruria to found a city that was later to eclipse all other cities of the Mediterranean, that was to become the capital of the world.

"There can be no doubt," says Mommsen in his *Römische Geschichte,* completed in 1856, "that the period of the kings not merely laid the foundations of Rome as a state, but also founded Rome's power in the outer world. Its glory lights up the royal house of the Tarquins like a rich sunset in which outlines are blurred." He goes on to add, in regard to the oldest period of Rome, "Of course there is no question of an actual foundation of the city as the legend supposes . . . The story of the establishment of Rome by . . . Romulus and Remus is nothing but a naïve invention of ancient pseudo-history . . . It is essential for historians to clear away all such fables purporting to be history."

This was a bold statement. It called in question the trustworthiness of the most ancient Roman tradition. True, it was made by a highly regarded expert on Roman history. But all the same—was Mommsen really right? Where was the proof? Nobody, not even the great historian himself, could produce it. In the middle of the nineteenth century scientifically secure knowledge of that early period was precisely nil. And thus it was to remain until the first decades of the twentieth.

Knowledge of Rome's early history was, in fact, limited to the traditions recorded by a few ancient authors. The most famous source was the vast work of Livy, written in the time of Augustus, in 142 books, of which thirty-five are extant. It narrated the story of the city and the empire up to the death of Drusus in 9 B.C., beginning *ab urbe condita,* with the foundation of the city.

Livy was considered an authority and his writings enjoyed a wide circulation. In antiquity his work was celebrated as the acme of historiography. Generations of Romans swallowed his imaginative story, decked out with rhetorical trimmings, of how Romulus was supposed to have founded the Eternal City on the Palatine hill, and later it was eagerly received by millions throughout Europe. The date 753 B.C. for the founding by Romulus, calculated by Livy's fellow countryman, the scholar Varro, was accepted by everyone as authentic. It got into all histories and school books. And so things remained until now.

For centuries no one dared to question the account of the primitive city and its origins given by Livy and other ancient historians. It was not until the last century that doubts began to be raised. It was recognized that Livy was anything but a trained historian in the modern sense. He simply collected a great mass of information and stories of all kinds without any critical analysis. He himself made no bones about it. In the preface to his history he admitted that: "Events before Rome was born or thought of have come to us in old tales with more of the charm of poetry than of a sound historical record, and such traditions I propose neither to affirm nor refute. There is no reason, I feel, to object when antiquity draws no hard line between the human and the supernatural: it adds dignity to the past, and, if any nation deserves the privilege of claiming divine ancestry, that nation is our own."

And so he dug out everything he could in the way of legends and stories about the alleged first four kings of Rome—Romulus, Numa, Tullus Hostilius and Ancus Marcius, and wrote it all down, embellished with completely invented dialogues of his own. It was no wonder that this part of his work was more a collection of old tales than a history.

Livy was inspired by enthusiasm for Rome's greatness, for the ancient Romans whose deeds and virtues he lauded to the skies. He never made any fact-finding tours, though to Herodotus, centuries earlier, such travel was a self-evident necessity. And in Livy's day the scenes of ancient Roman history had already vanished from the earth. They were buried deep beneath rubble and later buildings.

So how much was romance and legend, how much authentic tradition and a correct historical account? Scholars who were impatient for an answer had to wait more than half a century.

The fate of the West and its peoples was more closely bound up with Rome, and for a longer period, than with any other city. No other played so decisive a part in the history of western European civilization. But it was precisely Rome which was most neglected by archeology. No other metropolis of antiquity had to wait so long for a serious attempt to discover its early history with the spade. It almost seemed as though the descendants of the early inhabitants on the Tiber were afraid of lifting the veil and revealing the distant past, as though they were afraid of destroying a familiar and treasured historical picture.

In the last century, scores of archeologists descended on the Near East. In Egypt, Mesopotamia, Asia Minor, Palestine, a whole series of exciting discoveries was made. The histories of the ancient peoples and empires, which hitherto had been known only in general outline, at last really began to take shape.

In 1843 Paul Emile Botta brought to light the remains of Khorsabad, on the Tigris, the residence of Sargon, king of Assyria. Two years later Austen Henry Layard started to excavate Nimrud, and in 1853–5 Henry Creswicke Rawlinson excavated the Assyrian metropolis Nineveh. In the meanwhile Jean François Champollion had deciphered the Egyptian hieroglyphs, and Rawlinson and others had translated scripts in three ancient languages written in the cuneiform script. In 1870 Heinrich Schliemann began excavating the nine strata of Troy, discovering the "treasure of Priam" in 1873. Three years later, at Mycenae, he excavated the royal graves with their rich furnishings. In a few decades archeologists had opened up a view over millenniums of history.

But while the countryside of the Near East was being dug up and long-vanished worlds were being recovered, nothing stirred on the Tiber. Let us recall the appearance even a hundred years ago of the ancient Forum Romanum, the heart of the Roman empire for so many centuries. It looked like the setting for a dreamy idyll among the ruins. On the Palatine vegetation ran riot in gardens amid which stood monasteries. Here time had stood still. Since the tenth century the hill had belonged to private individuals who planted vineyards there and pastured their herds and flocks on its slopes. At the beginning of the sixteenth century, Marliani said sarcastically, "It is not merely abandoned to sheep, but also to horses and goats, so that there is every reason to call it 'Belatino,' the bleating hill."

Thus it remained. And as it was on the Palatine, the hill of Romulus, so it was too in the dip at its foot. Here, between the Capitol and the Esquiline, cattle peacefully grazed amid the scattered blocks of marble, and broken columns and ruins.

In his *A Description of the Antiquities and other Curiosities of Rome, from personal observation during a visit to Italy in the years 1818–1819,* published in London in 1828, the Reverend E. Burton gives a good picture of the scene: "But standing upon the hill of the Capitol and looking down upon the Roman Forum, we contemplate a scene with which we fancy ourselves familiar, and we seem suddenly to have quitted the habitations of living men. Not only is its former grandeur utterly annihilated, but the ground has not been applied to any other purpose. When we descend into it we find that many of the ancient buildings are buried under irregular heaps of soil; and a warm imagination might fancy that some spell hung over the spot, forbidding it to be profaned by the ordinary occupations of inhabited cities . . . Where the Roman people saw temples erected to perpetuate their exploits, and where the Roman nobles vied with each other in the magnificence of their dwellings, we now see a few insulated pillars standing amidst some broken arches . . . Where the Comitia were held, where Cicero harangued, and where the triumphal processions passed, we have now no animated beings, except strangers attracted by curiosity, the convicts, who are employed in excavating, as a punishment, and those more harmless animals already alluded to, who find a scanty pasture and a shelter from the sun under a grove of trees. The Roman Forum is now called the Campo Vaccino."

The site of Rome's power center had literally disappeared into the ground, had vanished under masses of rubble. And even that concealed only fragments of the former palaces and temples. For many of the buildings which had survived wind and weather for more than a millennium and a half in the end fell victim to vandals. In the fifteenth and sixteenth centuries the still extant buildings of ancient Rome were used as convenient stone quarries, and marble was carted away in tons to the lime kilns.

Scholars were uncertain even about the precise location of the Forum. There had been isolated attempts at excavation, the first in 1803, near the arch of Septimius Severus and the arch of Constantine. Others were made later at the temple of Castor and Pollux and the temple of Concordia. But it was all rather scrappy.

It was not until 1870, when Rome became the capital of the new Kingdom of Italy, that things changed. There seemed to be a desire in the new state to make a systematic attack at last on investigating the sites of Rome's ancient glory. Everything that once belonged to the central area of the city was officially declared an "archeological zone." It included the Forum, Palatine, and Capitoline, and extended as far as the foot of the Quirinal and the valley of the Circus Maximus, and from the Colosseum to the Via Appia Antica.

So a systematic excavation by modern methods was begun. By the end of the century, layers of rubble, sometimes as much as forty feet deep, had been cleared away and the foundations and remains of buildings thus exposed were restored. But what was uncovered was predominantly the relics of a late period, the monuments of the Imperial Age. Beyond that the discoveries did not go, because at that point, to the annoyance of the impatiently waiting historians, the authorities stopped the excavators. Rodolfo Lanciani, in his *New Tales of Old Rome*, recounts what happened: "As soon as a paving-stone, or a brick or marble floor was found, whether imperial, or Byzantine, or medieval, it did not matter, we were made to stop without trying to ascertain whether older and more important relics were concealed in the lower strata."

> It was only in the present century that the exciting opportunity occurred to confirm on the spot the statements of the ancient writers, something that historians and archeologists had been awaiting for decades, something that Livy and his colleagues would doubtless never have imagined.

But it was precisely in those lower strata that the evidence of the origins of Rome must lie hidden. Even in Cicero's time there had been a spot called *doliola* on the Forum, where spitting and loud talking were forbidden as sacrilegious because there sacred objects had been buried in little casks (doliola). Tradition had it that these were urns containing the ashes of the earliest inhabitants.

It was only in the present century that the exciting opportunity occurred to confirm on the spot the statements of the ancient writers, something that historians and archeologists had been awaiting for decades, something that Livy and his colleagues would doubtless never have imagined.

Credit for this goes to Giacomo Boni, a gifted and energetic Roman architect. In his capacity as Director of Antiquities he managed to break down official obstructionism and obtain a permit to carry out deep excavations—but even then only in places where no pavement or floor had yet been discovered.

In April, 1902, when Boni began his new excavations, he had luck right from the start. At the edge of the Forum, near the ancient Via Sacra, the Sacred Way, at a depth of some fifteen to eighteen feet he came upon an archaic cemetery. Here he found both cremation graves, in the shape of hut-like urns, that contained ashes, and inhumation graves. These discoveries showed that there must have been a human settlement at this place in Rome as early as the eighth century B.C. Boni's finds created quite a stir. The scientific investigation of the legendary foundation of Rome had truly begun.

Some years later, after traces of inhumation graves had been found in 1907 in hitherto untouched levels on the Quirinal, Boni decided to explore in depth the place that was traditionally more sacred than any other, the Palatine. This was the hill where Romulus was said to have founded the famous *Roma quadrata*. This was where, in Cicero's time, an old wattle-and-daub hut with a straw roof, situated on the west side of the Palatine where it slopes down toward the Tiber, was proudly pointed out as Romulus's hut.

Boni began his excavations near the ruins of the palace that the emperor Domitian built in the first century A.D. Once again he was lucky. Many feet below the superimposed layers of buildings the Palatine yielded up part of its great secret. At the bottom of a deep shaft Boni came upon the post-holes of primitive huts. And from the same level came shards which made accurate dating possible. They belonged to the same period as the cremation graves in the Forum cemetery. They were relics of a settlement that dated back to the middle of the eighth century B.C. In fact precisely to the time when the city was traditionally said to have been founded, in 753 B.C.

It was not long before further deep excavations found traces of settlements and cemeteries at other points. Earlier uncertainty hardened into certainty. From a number of finds it was possible to put together a consistent picture of the oldest settlements on the Tiber. It was one that reached much farther back into prehistory than had been supposed.

As early as the first half of the second millennium B.C., at a time, that is, when in Mesopotamia the third dynasty of Ur ended and, in the biblical story, Abraham came to Canaan, men had settled on the hills by the Tiber. Their implements, primitive tools, and weapons of flint and copper were found in the lowest strata of the Esquiline. Through stratum upon stratum the monotonously similar traces of early inhabitants of Rome can be followed for a thousand years. Then suddenly a new phase began.

In the eighth century, that of the legendary Romulus, newly arrived tribes all at once settled on the hills. These were the Latins. Some time later yet other settlers arrived, probably the Sabines. Along with new arrivals, the archeological evidence of post-holes points to groups of dwellings. They were huts roofed with straw or reed, with walls made of wattle and daub. These huts were built on the Palatine, the Esquiline, and the Quirinal, in little villages, each distinct from the others.

The Capitol hill was left unoccupied. Excavations down to the bedrock by Professor A. M. Colini have shown that at that period no one lived on this steep hill with its two summits. The valleys between the hills were likewise uninhabited.

The early settlers lived a simple life, looking after their sheep and tilling the soil. They did not even stay permanently in one place, but from time to time moved in groups to new sites. They buried their dead on the slopes. It seems that by the early seventh century B.C. the hilltops were no longer big enough, and huts were built on the slopes that hitherto had been used only for cemeteries. Thus things remained until the last quarter of the century.

Then, about 625 B.C., the settlements spread yet farther out. For the first time remains of dwellings and traces of post-holes are found in the valleys, too, in places where previously the nature of the site had prevented habitation. For the low ground was unhealthy and in places impassable. Between the Capitol and the little hill that was later called Velia was nothing but a swamp. At the time of the spring thaw or after heavy rain, the water of the Tiber rose, and where its bed narrows as the river bends at the Vatican hill and flows alongside the Janiculum, it overflowed its banks. It flooded the flat region later called the Campus Martius, as well as the valleys. Livy himself admits it, without realizing what he thus gave away. Referring to the childhood of Romulus, he says: "The Tiber had overflowed its banks; because of the flooded ground it was impossible to get to the actual river . . . In those days the country thereabouts was all wild and uncultivated."

And when the floods retreated, there came fever—that is, malaria.

Settlement of the low-lying ground would never have been possible without action to drain and dry the land. But that needed experienced experts, hydraulic engineers in short, and these were not available among the still primitive inhabitants. For land drainage was a technique unknown in Europe. Who then could have assisted the hut dwellers on the Tiber to drain the valleys?

The answer to this question was provided by other finds datable to the same period, namely, shards of black pottery. There could be no doubt about its origin. This was *bucchero* ware, the national ceramic of the Etruscans. A grave on the Esquiline contained a particularly fine example, a two-handled glossy black drinking cup, a kantharos. Like the rich tombs of the ladies in Caere and Praeneste, it dates from the seventh century B.C.

This discovery was followed, in 1963, by a truly sensational one. In the ground below the Forum Boarium, the ancient cattle market near the Tiber, was found a shard of an impasto vessel on which were engraved archaic letters reading UQNUS. The shard is dated to about 700 B.C., and is not only one of the earliest Etruscan inscriptions, but is the earliest inscription of any kind ever found in Rome.

From that period on, Etruscan products such as clay and metal articles of daily use appear frequently in the settlements on the

Mounted bowman, detail from the lid of a bronze urn

Tiber. Caere and Veii, the nearest big Etruscan cities, supplied chiefly pottery from their own workshops and imported from Greece. Fragments of terra-cotta revetments suggest the master hand of artists from Veii. The simple settlements had come under the influence of the great neighboring people beyond the Tiber.

When the first Etruscans, probably traders, crossed the Tiber in the eighth century B.C., the settlers and shepherds on the hills could scarcely have imagined that these strangers were to be their great teachers in the future. The fact that anyone was interested in them at all they owed to an accident of nature. At the point in the Tiber where a little island rose above the muddy gray waters, there was a ford. For the powerful city-states of Etruria this ford provided a convenient crossing of the river on the way to the south, to Latium and Campania.

The archeologists' discoveries in the ground below the city destroyed the credibility of the oldest Roman tradition. After two thousand years it collapsed like a house of cards. Rome's historians had created a historical fable, had ingeniously combined fact and fancy. And posterity had fallen for it. Now, for the first time, there was scientific proof that Rome did not exist as a city either in the eighth century or the seventh. Where it was later built, there was, until about 625 B.C., only an uninhabitable, untamed wilderness.

> **Romulus, if a person of that name ever existed, could therefore have been no more than the headman of an insignificant settlement.**

On the Palatine, the traditional site of the foundation of Rome, and on the neighboring hills, there existed at that date only modest groups of primitive huts, i.e., villages. But villages are not a city. Romulus, if a person of that name ever existed, could therefore have been no more than the headman of an insignificant settlement. There could be no question of a kingdom for him and his legendary successors, Numa Pompilius, Tullus Hostilius, and Ancus Marcius. In short, the traditional first four kings of Rome never existed. Mommsen had guessed right.

The evidence of the archeologists confirmed what philologists, ancient historians, and Etruscologists had already concluded, namely that a great deal of invented material had later been worked into the tradition of Rome's origins for the sake of Rome's glory, and that the Romans had dressed up their early history in borrowed plumes, chiefly Etruscan ones.

Even the proud name of Rome is not native to the soil of the hill settlers. The origin of the name and of that of the supposed founder is now reasonably certain. "Romulus, the legendary first ruler of Rome," says Lopes Pegna, "never existed. Contrary to what Livy says, 'the newly built city' was not 'called by its founder's name'; rather, the Etruscan toponym 'Rumlua' became the Latin Roma, and from this the adjective 'Romulus' was derived."

"Even the hills of the oldest Rome have Etruscan names, and names formed on the Etruscan model," says Franz Altheim, who adds: "The oldest organization of Rome divided the community into three tribes and each tribe into ten *curiae*. The tribes were named Tities, Ramnes, and Luceres. Just as Rome's name was Etruscan, corresponding to that of the *gens* Ruma, so too were the tribal names. All three go back to Etruscan gentilitial names, and the same is true of some of the names of curiae."

Up to the fourth "king," Rome's early history turns out to be fiction. It is only with the fifth ruler, a sovereign from Etruria, that we are on the firm ground of historical fact.

IX

Tarquinius Priscus, the Etruscan Founder of Rome

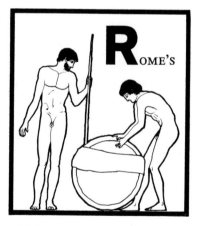

FIRST KING DID NOT COME INTO the world in a hut on a hill by the Tiber. He came from abroad, from Etruria, and was the son of a wealthy family. The accounts of Livy and Dionysius provide full details of his family, his origin, and the time of his immigration.

"A man named Lucumo . . . ambitious and wealthy," says Livy, left his native Tarquinii, which as Dionysius makes clear, was "a large and flourishing city at that time." Having inherited the whole of his father's huge fortune, Livy continues, he "became in time as proud as he was wealthy," not least in consequence of his marriage to Tanaquil, an equally ambitious young woman of aristocratic birth. The couple decided to leave Tarquinii; for their ambitious plans, Rome seemed the most suitable place. "Rome was a young and rising community; there would be opportunities for an active and courageous man in a place where all advancement came swiftly and depended on ability . . . So they packed their belongings and left for Rome."

A most promising omen greeted them on their arrival, Livy goes on to relate. "The pair had reached Janiculum and were sitting together in their carriage, when an eagle dropped gently down and snatched off the cap which Lucumo was wearing. Up went the bird with a great clangor of wings until, a minute later, it swooped down again and, as if it had been sent by heaven for that very purpose, neatly replaced the cap on Lucumo's head, and then vanished into the blue." As was to be expected of an Etruscan lady, Tanaquil knew what to make of celestial portents. She "joyfully accepted the omen. Flinging her arms round her husband's neck, she told him that no fortune was too high to hope for . . . Thus dreaming upon future greatness, Lucumo and Tanaquil drove on into Rome, where they bought a house, and Lucumo took the name of Lucius Tarquinius Priscus."

There could, of course, be no question of a "city" of Rome, as the traditional story claims. Lucumo, the foreigner from Tarquinii, was, to be precise, the man who was to build it. As yet there existed only a few villages of huts inhabited by illiterate tribesmen. The wealthy couple had come to the backwoods where conditions were still prehistoric.

The city-states of Etruria and the poor settlements on the Tiber were as different as day and night. The former at a peak of civilization, the latter still backward, stuck in the past. It was not surprising that "In Rome Lucumo soon began to attract attention as a wealthy stranger."

It is clear from Dionysius's account that the distinguished foreigner from the powerful neighboring empire was welcomed by the tribesmen with admiration and regard. "On campaigns he fought most bravely of all, whether of the infantry or of the cavalry, and wherever there was need of good judgment he was counted among the shrewdest counselors . . . he gained the affections of the populace by his cordial greetings, his agreeable conversation, his dispensing of money and his friendliness in other ways . . . This was the character of Tarquinius."

"Tarquinius took over the sovereignty about the second year of the forty-first Olympiad," says Dionysius. This would be about 607 B.C. About this time a new phase began in the rise of the Etruscans, in the growth of their power, as they spread out over Italy from their original centers. It was a century of historic events in which they laid the foundations for the future rise of Rome to world dominion.

Under Tarquinius Priscus the hilly place on the river crossing came under the influence of its highly civilized neighbors. They gave it a stimulus which in a few decades was to shape it anew, to inspire it with a modern outlook hitherto unknown to this insignificant corner of Italy, remote as it was from great events. The Etruscans' mission, to be the great teacher of the Romans, pursued its course. It was a unique enterprise of successful technical assistance and development, which has hitherto remained unknown.

In a series of campaigns Tarquinius succeeded in imposing respect for his rule and for the inhabitants of the Tiber villages. The neighboring Latin peoples were the first to be taught that a new spirit was abroad, and that an Etruscan was now in command. When "the Apiolani and all the rest of the Latins . . . were laying waste the Roman territory by plundering and pillaging," says Dionysius, "Tarquinius . . . set out with a large force and ravaged the most fruitful part of their country; then, when important reinforcements came to the Apiolani from their Latin neighbors, he fought two battles with them and, having gained the victory in both, proceeded to besiege the city," which was taken by storm, the walls being razed to the foundations.

After Tarquinius had captured the Latin city of Corniculum, says Dionysius, "The Latins . . . voted to lead a joint army against the Romans; and having raised a numerous force, they made an irruption into the most fruitful part of their country." But again Tarquinius was victorious, as he was also against an alliance of Latins and Sabines.

After the successful completion of his campaigns Tarquinius applied his energies to works of peace. "It was peace with a difference," says Livy, "for the king set his people with such enthusiasm to various civic undertakings that they had even less leisure than they had had during the wars." Among the public works ordered by Tarquinius was the draining of the swampy land among the hills. "The low-lying areas of the town around the Forum, and the valleys between the hills, where flood-water usually collected, were drained by sewers leading down into the Tiber." And this, adds Dionysius, was "a wonderful work exceeding all description."

Tradition makes it clear that under Lucius Tarquinius Priscus valuable new land was recovered in the heart of Rome. Thanks to the drainage technique of Etruscan experts, what had been a swamp at the base of the Capitol and Palatine was permanently dried out. A whole network of drainage channels was dug through the marshy ground, and at the same time the stream that separated the two hills with their village settlements was regulated, its embankments were strengthened, and finally it was covered over. The newly recovered land, as we learn from Livy, was made available for the use of the inhabitants, for "Tarquin also made grants of land round the Forum to be used as private building sites."

> **Its historians hid from posterity, either through ignorance or deliberately from national pride, another brilliant enterprise of the Etruscan king, perhaps the most important in the whole of Roman history.**

This corresponds to the facts. It was then that huts were built in the valley, the remains of which Boni found by his excavations. This was about 625 B.C., according to the archeological evidence, that is, before Tarquinius was king, at the time, no doubt, when he "was counted among the shrewdest counselors." However, it is now established that the Roman tradition is incomplete and inexact. Its historians hid from posterity, either through ignorance or deliberately from national pride, another brilliant enterprise of the Etruscan king, perhaps the most important in the whole of Roman history.

The development program started by Tarquinius Priscus in fact went far beyond the land drainage mentioned above. That was only the overture. The archeological explorations deep in the soil of Rome that helped to destroy the legends about Romulus and his alleged three regal successors also led to what was perhaps the most astonishing reversal of existing historical belief. The efforts of many scholars over decades, often hindered by the Italian authorities' lack of understanding, and their prohibitions, at last revealed what was still completely unknown at the beginning of this century. A whole jigsaw puzzle of relics of different kinds, such as innumerable stone fragments, pottery shards, pieces of metal, and minute traces of wooden constructions, has been assembled according to

124

the most modern dating methods, and leads us back to the birth of Rome.

There was worldwide interest when Babylon was brought to light, when Nineveh, the Valley of the Kings, and the ruins of Memphis were discovered, when Troy, Mycenae, and Knossos were excavated. But curiously enough, when Rome was the subject, there was no international sensation. The general public paid little heed to the discoveries among the Tiber hills, epoch-making though they were. What the scholars discovered reduced to wastepaper whole libraries about the early regal period. Yet it was scarcely noticed or appreciated. And to this day no sightseeing tour of Rome conducts visitors to the sites where the Etruscan evidence was found, as though nobody wanted to damage the millennial, carefully cherished image of national pride.

But what precisely was discovered?

About 575 B.C. the familiar picture of primitive settlements among the hills suddenly changes. The straw- and reed-roofed wattle huts at the foot of the Palatine, Esquiline, and Quirinal disappear from the ground. This was not due to destruction by war or fire. This much is clear from the investigations. The rude dwellings were removed in accordance with a carefully planned building program.

It began with demolition. Hut after hut was pulled down, and the resulting mass of rubble, clay, and posts was carefully leveled out. On top of this, pebbles were beaten in, and a big open space was created, forming a public market and a common civic center for the hitherto separate settlements. The most famous of all public squares in history thus came into being, for this was the later Forum Romanum.

Modern stratigraphic research dates this event to around 575 B.C. "There is no doubt," states Einar Gjerstad, "that this date is epoch-making in the history of Rome, marking the transition from a primitive and rustic type of habitation to a monumental and urbanistic form of culture. This transformation from *pagi* into *urbs* is the real foundation of Rome, inasmuch as Urbs and Roma are synonymous."

The creation of the big public square, the Forum, was in effect the birth of the future world metropolis, the future center of the Imperium Romanum. With that, and not, as traditionally stated and so long believed, in 753 B.C., began the history of Rome. We shall have to relearn our history in the future, and correct all the historical tables. It was not Romulus, but the Etruscan Lucius Tarquinius Priscus who founded Rome.

The pebbling of the Forum was only the first decisive step in a construction enterprise that now went ahead at an astonishing pace. The new king did not seem disposed merely to rule over a market-place surrounded by little villages. Under his direction there began a large-scale program of town planning, modeled on the Etruscan cities and carried out with the assistance of technical experts brought from Etruria. Within a few decades the rural appearance of the place had vastly changed. The new square was like a big, rapidly growing building site. Progress radiated from it with astonishing speed. What had happened in the eighth century in Etruria on the sites of earlier settlements was now repeated.

The old way of building gave way to a new, urban architecture, for private and public buildings alike. The dwellings were no longer, as they had been in the past, set directly on the bare ground. They were given a stone foundation. Their walls were no longer made of wattle and daub. Instead they were built of sun-dried bricks. The ground plan, too, changed. The round or oval shape was replaced by rectangular buildings. The first regular dwelling houses went up, built around a courtyard. The roofs were no longer straw or reed but hollow tiles. The brick walls were covered with stucco painted in colored designs.

The traces of the first regular streets can be clearly made out. They begin in the center. Part of the most important, the Via Sacra, the Sacred Way, has been excavated in the Forum. Its earliest road-bed dates from about 575 B.C. Public buildings and temples were erected. At the foot of the Palatine stood the Regia, the sanctuary of the king and the high priest, and also the round temple of Vesta. They were built of wood and decorated with gaily painted terra-cotta revetments with reliefs of animals and other ornaments. Toward the river, near a mooring place for boats, a second big square was laid out. Here too the old huts were demolished and the site leveled. On it a cattle market, the Forum Boarium, was established.

This amazing revolution, this transformation of prehistoric village settlements into what was unmistakably a town, was accomplished within a single generation. Etruscan influence began to shape the face of Rome for all time. These are the facts revealed by the excavations.

Tradition records other important buildings with which the Etruscan king embellished his new city. On Tarquinius's return to Rome after a victory to be celebrated by public games, the Circus Maximus was planned, says Livy. "On the ground marked out for it, special places were assigned to senators and knights to erect their stands in—or 'decks' as they were called. These stands were supported on props and raised twelve feet from the ground." Thus began the world-renowned Circus Maximus, for more than a thousand years the scene of the most popular entertainments in Rome, a vast arena that was subsequently made more and more magnificent. Not until A.D. 549 were the last races held there, under Totila the Goth.

The Murcia valley, the site chosen by the Etruscan king, was as though made by nature for the purpose. It lay between the Palatine and the Aventine hills, was some 650 yards long and 162 yards wide; one lap all around was a Roman mile, or rather less than a British and American mile. Down to the Imperial Age it remained the most imposing racetrack in western Europe.

> **It lay between the Palatine and the Aventine hills, was some 650 yards long and 162 yards wide; one lap all around was a Roman mile, or rather less than a British and American mile.**

After Tarquinius's first campaign against the Latins, he returned to Rome "with more plunder than what report had led people to expect," says Livy. He consecrated the stadium and "celebrated public games on a scale more elaborate and opulent than any of his predecessors."

As was the custom in Etruria the games opened with a solemn ceremony. For they were considered a religious festival, a rite intended to propitiate the city's gods. To the music of flutes, trumpets, and tambourines, priests and athletes marched around the long track in a colorful procession. Animal sacrifices were offered. Only after these preliminaries did the games begin. The varied program included horse racing and chariot racing, athletics such as track events, and wrestling and boxing. Sporting contests, which had long been highly popular in the city-states of Etruria, were something quite novel to the Tiber settlers. For this reason, as Livy says: "Horses and boxers, mostly from Etruria, provided the entertainment."

There can be no doubt about the truth of this statement. We can still get an idea of the contests, even now, after twenty-five hundred years, by looking at the various representations which have survived from the Etruria of the sixth century B.C. The superb wall paintings in the chamber tombs of Tarquinia and Chiusi have preserved a panorama of Etruscan sport, as have the cinerary urns (though mostly of a later period) from Volterra.

The ancient pictorial representations show the various sports in detail. Some of them record a dramatic moment in the contest. They convey all the excitement of great sporting events with their athletes, prizes, and thrilled spectators.

In the Tomba delle Bighe (Tomb of the Chariots) at Tarquinia, Tarquinius Priscus's native city, a brightly colored wall painting shows men getting horses and chariots ready for a race. It is the

Wrestlers, detail of fresco from the Tomb of the Augurs; c.530 B.C. The walls of this tomb are painted with scenes depicting various games held in honor of the deceased

moment just before the start. Riders for a flat race have already mounted their horses. Wreaths await the victor and his mount. Heralds and referees stand around, in expectation of the start. On the same ground there is a crowd of athletes. A youth, discus in hand, is tensed for the throw. Nearby another competitor is taking great strides as he runs up for his javelin throw. Boxers lift their fists in greeting before beginning their match. Wrestlers try their strength. A referee, recognizable by the *lituus* (crook) he holds, is talking to a sportsman, while other competitors are resting or massaging their muscles.

To the right and left of the sports ground are the spectators, talking excitedly with lively gestures. They are members of patrician families, both men and women, for Etruria was different from Greece, where women were not allowed at sporting contests. The spectators are seated on two wooden platforms, raised, as Livy says, "on props"; the rows of benches are clearly visible. There is a canopy over them on a scaffolding, as protection against the sun and rain. Down below, in the pit, competitors are lying about and squatting between the posts under the raised seats.

The Tomb of the Olympic Games, at Tarquinia, discovered by C. M. Lerici in 1958, carries us right into the exciting atmosphere of a sporting contest such as Rome enjoyed under its new· king. The painter, like a modern sports photographer, has captured the discus throwers, the jumpers, the boxers at the most gripping moment, when they are tense with concentration and effort. Three runners, naked but for a narrow loincloth, are putting their last ounce into their sprint, a few yards from the finishing line. Nearby a chariot race is in full swing. Four *bigae* (two-horse chariots) are whirling along the track. The drivers have tied the reins around their waists and are lashing the horses on with whips. The leader, in sight of victory, throws a swift glance over his shoulder. Behind him, the fight for second place is being decided. One chariot, driven at a furious pace, is overtaking its immediate opponent. A fourth driver is out of the race. His chariot has overturned with a broken axle. One horse rears, the other, which has fallen, lies on the ground, its legs sticking up. The driver is hurled through the air. Three seated women spectators cover their faces with their hands in fright.

According to tradition, Tarquinius Priscus was responsible for a third great "civic undertaking." This was a temple on which a start was made during his reign. "Finally," says Livy, "the foundations of the temple of Jupiter on the Capitol were laid . . . One cannot but feel that in some way he already foresaw the future splendor of that famous place."

Dionysius describes the difficulties that had to be overcome in constructing a solid foundation. "Having, therefore, surrounded the hill on which he proposed to build the temple with high retaining walls in many places, since it required much preparation (for it was neither easy of access nor level, but steep, and terminated in a sharp peak), he filled the space between the retaining walls and the summit with great quantities of earth and, by leveling it, made the place most suitable for receiving temples."

But Tarquinius did not see more than the preliminary work. Four years after it was begun he is reported to have been assassinated. It was the third Etruscan king, his son or grandson, Tarquinius Superbus, who completed the building.

Repeated excavations carried out since 1919 on the Capitol hill have revealed the remains of the sanctuary. After the Palazzo Caffarelli was demolished, the excavators found, deep under the Palazzo dei Conservatori on the Campidoglio, some carefully aligned great blocks of *cappellaccio,* a local gray tufa of volcanic origin. They were the foundations of the Capitoline temple, and they date from the sixth century B.C.

Under Tarquinius Priscus, Etruscan insignia and ceremonies also came to Rome. With them came pomp and circumstance of ancient Oriental origin, which was in sharp contrast to the extremely simple and unceremonious appearance of Greek magistrates and the Spartan kings. But it was precisely what the Indo-European speaking settlers on the Tiber appreciated. It became something deeply characteristic of their state and later empire and remained so to the end.

From Rome the ceremoniousness spread out all over western Europe, in symbols, insignia of sovereignty, badges of office of the highest representatives of ecclesiastical and secular power, among emperors and kings, popes, cardinals, and bishops. We still see the last surviving vestiges of ancient Oriental modes of expressing sovereign dignity in the pomp and regalia of coronation ceremonies, and in the vestments of a clerical hierarchy whose center is that Eternal City which an Etruscan monarch once made his home.

"The oldest and most respected men from each city" in Etruria, says Dionysius, came to Tarquinius, "bringing the insignia of sovereignty with which they used to decorate their own kings. These were a crown of gold, an ivory throne, a scepter with an eagle perched on its head, a purple tunic decorated with gold, and an embroidered purple robe like those the kings of Lydia and Persia used to wear, except that it was not rectangular in shape like theirs, but semicircular. This kind of robe is called *toga* by the Romans and *tebenna* by the Greeks . . . And according to some historians they also brought to Tarquinius the twelve axes, taking one from each city. For it seems to have been a Tyrrhenian custom for each king of the several cities to be preceded by a lictor bearing an axe together with the bundle of rods, and whenever the twelve cities undertook any joint military expedition, for the twelve axes to be handed over to the one man who was invested with absolute power. . . .

"Tarquinius . . . from that time till he died always wore a crown of gold and an embroidered purple robe and sat on a throne of ivory holding an ivory scepter in his hand, and the twelve lictors, bearing the axes and rods, attended him when he sat in judgment and preceded him when he went abroad. All these ornaments were retained by the kings who succeeded him, and, after the expulsion of the kings, by the annual consuls—all except the crown and the embroidered robe; these alone were taken from them, being looked upon as vulgar and invidious. Yet whenever they return victorious from a war and are honored with a triumph by the senate, they then not only wear gold but are also clad in embroidered purple robes."

> **For a thousand years, this procession, the famous "triumph," was among the most splendid and solemn of Roman shows.**

A new custom introduced by the sovereign from Etruria was the religious procession which was observed in Rome down to the Imperial Age. For a thousand years, this procession, the famous "triumph," was among the most splendid and solemn of Roman shows.

Its purpose after a victorious campaign was to give thanks to the supreme gods for their protection, and it was an outstanding occasion in Etruscan religious ritual. The *triumphator* himself wore the vestments of the god, a purple, gold-embroidered tunic, the *tunica palmata,* a purple toga, also decorated with gold, the *toga picta,* and gilded shoes. He carried an ivory scepter surmounted by an eagle, and was crowned with a laurel wreath. His face and arms were painted with minium, as appears in Etruscan statues.

At the head of the procession walked the lictors, also in purple tunics. Behind them a body of men carried the booty captured during the campaign, the weapons, standards, and treasures of the enemy. Next came priests leading the sacrificial animals—beautiful white oxen with gilded horns and ribbons around the neck. After them came the principal prisoners, then the triumphant general, standing in a two-wheeled ceremonial chariot drawn by four white horses and preceded by acolytes swinging censers. Alongside the chariot went a group of harpists and pipers, "in imitation of an Etruscan procession, wearing belts and golden crowns," notes Appian, who continues: "They are called Lydi because, as I think, the Etruscans were a Lydian colony. One of these, in the middle of the procession, wearing a purple cloak reaching to the feet and golden bracelets and necklace, caused laughter by making various gesticulations, as though he were dancing in triumph over the enemy."

The procession ended with the soldiers of the victorious army singing songs about the general and their officers, some ribaldly satirical, some in their praise, "for in a triumph," says Appian, "everybody is free, and is allowed to say what he pleases."

According to the tradition, Tarquinius Priscus reigned for not quite forty years. These decades, as the archeological evidence shows, saw an extraordinary development in the little Latin and Sabine place on the Tiber. Under his rule it became a town that was typically Etruscan in its architecture, economy, customs, and way of life. The work that he began was to be completed by two other Etruscan kings.

X

The Reforms
of Servius Tullius

ONE OF THE FIRST THINGS A VISITOR to Rome sees on arrival is an impressive section of the oldest fortifications. On stepping out of the train at Rome's ultramodern Stazione Termini or out of the coach from Fiumicino airport, his eye is caught by the remains of a massive structure. Close to the entrance hall of the gleaming marble station stands a fragment of the famous Servian walls. Once these fortifications were nearly fifty feet high and almost a hundred feet wide, forming a ring around the seven hills to protect the Romans from their foes. Their first builder, says tradition, was Servius Tullius, who succeeded Tarquinius Priscus on the throne of Rome.

During his reign the number of citizens is said to have grown to eighty thousand. "The population of Rome was by now so great," Livy tells us, "that Servius decided to extend the city boundaries.

He took in, accordingly, two more hills, the Quirinal and the Viminal, and subsequently added to the area of the Esquiline . . . The city defenses he strengthened by constructing trenches, earthworks, and a wall. This involved extending the 'pomerium.' "

The pomerium, Livy explains, is the strip of ground which "the ancient Etruscans used to consecrate with augural ceremonies when a new town was to be founded." Inside and outside the wall a strip of ground was marked off by stones. "Its purpose was to keep the walls, on their inner side, clear of all buildings . . . and at the same time to leave, on the outer side of the walls, an area unpolluted by the use of man." Thus in Rome, faithful to Etruscan precedent, "whenever, with the growth of the city, it was proposed to increase the area enclosed within the walls, this strip of consecrated ground was pushed outward accordingly."

Livy's statement is supported by Dionysius, who confirms that Tullius enlarged the city by adding two hills to the original five and "surrounded the seven hills with one wall."

Nevertheless the credibility of this tradition was for a long time hotly disputed. The objections to it seemed to be serious. In Rome's long history the Servian wall, as was known, had constituted the supreme defensive bastion. It had, certainly, been repeatedly repaired, strengthened, or restored, but its circumference and course supposedly remained unchanged throughout the centuries of the republic and well into the Christian era.

Under the empire the city's population and the adjoining settlements grew so much that the wall was no longer capacious enough. In the later part of the third century A.D., a second, more extensive ring of walls was built outside the first. It was known as the Aurelian wall, after the emperor who ordered its erection. Throughout the whole of the Middle Ages it constituted the city's chief line of defense.

It seemed hard to believe that the famous Servian wall, which did duty for more than three quarters of a millennium, had been set up, to its full extent, as early as the sixth century B.C. Was it really possible that Rome owed the construction of that mighty fortification to the foresight and enterprise of one of its kings, the earliest rulers in its history? The only hope of getting an answer to these questions lay in looking at what was hidden underground.

The opportunity for this came after 1870, when a start was made on carrying out plans for the modernization of the new capital of united Italy. In the course of ground clearances, workmen found in a number of places remains of ancient fortifications which in fact had once girdled all the seven hills. Nowadays they lie right in the midst of the noise and bustle of the modern metropolis. One stretch of some ninety feet can be seen on the Aventine; two other pieces emerge from the facade of a house in the Via Giosuè Carducci. The oldest remains of the wall, so famous in history, had been discovered.

But what period do they belong to? Close examination of the masonry did not yield an unambiguous answer. The fortifications were, in fact, by no means uniform. Every one of the fragments found displayed two distinct methods of building. One, carried out with great care, makes use of the variety of tufa stone known as *cappellaccio;* the other, evidently executed in great haste and hence somewhat carelessly, contains blocks of *grotta oscura* tufa.

The discovery that two kinds of building stone were used provided an important clue. *Grotta oscura* tufa is known to come only from quarries on the right bank of the Tiber at Prima Porta, north of Rome. Rome could have obtained access to these quarries only after its conquest of the Etruscan city-state of Veii in 396 B.C. Thus this part of the wall must date from a later period, from the time of the republic. It was built about 378 B.C., after the Gauls under Brennus had occupied and burned the city. The *cappellaccio* stone, on the other hand, did not have to be imported, nor did it involve conquering a neighboring Etruscan state. It was a tufa of which there was plenty on the spot. It could be dug out of the slopes of the Capitoline hill without much trouble. The fragments of wall built of local *cappellaccio* were the oldest evidence of the fortifications. Fragments of archaic roof tiles and of earthenware vessels found among the building material made dating possible. They pointed to the sixth century B.C.

> **Roman traditions preserved a whole series of remarkable and legendary stories about his birth, parentage, and youth, beginning from the moment of his conception.**

The tradition was thus confirmed. The Servian wall was built when Rome was still ruled by kings. It was to the enterprise of its ruler Servius Tullius that the city owed its most ancient and most famous fortifications. But just who that king was likewise remained unclear for a long time. Roman traditions preserved a whole series of remarkable and legendary stories about his birth, parentage, and youth, beginning from the moment of his conception.

"In the reign of Tarquinius Priscus, it is said," relates Pliny the Elder, "there appeared upon his hearth a resemblance of the male generative organ in the midst of the ashes. The captive Ocrisia, a servant of Queen Tanaquil, who happened to be sitting there, arose from her seat in a state of pregnancy." The son born to Ocrisia was called Servius Tullius. This remarkable event, by no means an everyday occurrence after all, had been almost forgotten when one day, according to Livy, "a very odd thing" happened to the boy. As he was "lying asleep . . . his head burst into flames. Many people saw it happen. The noise and excitement caused by such an extraordinary event came to the ears of the king and queen, and brought them hurrying to the spot. A servant ran for water and was about to throw it on the flames, when the queen stopped him, declaring, as soon as she could make herself heard, that the child must on no account be disturbed, but allowed to sleep till he awoke of his own accord. A few moments later he opened his eyes, and the fire went out. Tanaquil took her husband aside . . . 'Listen,' she said, 'this child . . . will one day prove a light in our darkness, a prop to our house in the day of its affliction. We must see that he is taught and tended from now onward with every care, as one through whom will come great glory to our family and to Rome.' "

Tanaquil's advice was followed. From that moment on, the boy was treated as though he were the royal couple's own son and was educated like a prince. "It was the will of heaven and all went well: he grew in time to be a man of truly royal nature, and when Tarquin was looking for a son-in-law, he could find no one in Rome comparable in any way to young Servius; so to Servius he betrothed his daughter." This was despite the fact that Servius was supposed to be the son of a slave.

Livy does not conceal his doubts about that story. "However we may try to account for this singular honor, the fact of it does, at least, make it impossible to believe that either Servius or his mother was ever a slave."

Livy evidently felt that it was hardly flattering to Roman national pride to have to include in the royal genealogy a person of such lowly birth. So in an attempt to establish a better family tree, he adds a different, more patrician version, to wit, that Ocrisia may have been the wife, already pregnant, of a certain Tullius who reigned in Corniculum, and later died in battle. What the truth was, and whether indeed Livy knew it or had made any effort to find out, is something the reader never learns.

Today we know the factual background to this obscure Roman account. Two discoveries contributed to the explanation. The places where they were made lay far apart, as did the times from which they date, and at first sight there seemed little reason to connect them. Both provided highly interesting information about Tarquinius Priscus's successor as king.

In 1524 an inscribed bronze tablet was found at Lyons. Its Latin text is part of a speech that the emperor Claudius made to the assembled senate in A.D. 48. What it says is remarkable.

"Servius Tullius," begins Claudius, "was, if we follow our Roman sources, the son of Ocrisia, a prisoner of war." But then the emperor goes on: "If we follow Etruscan sources, he was a loyal friend of Caelius Vibenna and his companion in all his ventures." Claudius then gives the Etruscan version, according to which Servius Tullius came from Etruria with the remains of Caelius's army, and occupied a hill in Rome henceforth named accordingly the Caelian. He then changed his name—it was Mastarna in Etruscan—to Servius Tullius and became king of Rome, "to its great advantage."

> **This statement, coming from an emperor, created something of a sensation.**

This statement, coming from an emperor, created something of a sensation. There could be no doubt about the expert authority of the speaker. For Claudius was a historian who knew his subject inside out. Long before he became emperor in A.D. 41 (much against the wishes of his family, who tried to stop him doing anything of the kind), he had devoted himself with passionate enthusiasm to learning. He was above all interested in a subject which Roman authors had always studiously neglected, even though it was closely connected with Rome's own history, namely the past of the Etruscans. The result of his labors was a great and unique work.

For twenty-one years he researched and wrote and produced a twenty-volume history of the Etruscans, the *Tyrrhenica,* a work now lost.

What Livy and other historians never mentioned, or as much as hinted at, Claudius proclaimed openly to the highest body in the empire. His revelations are highly significant in more than one respect. Not only did the emperor admit that alongside the official Roman tradition there was also an Etruscan one, recorded, in the words of the bronze tablet, by *auctores Tusci,* by Etruscan authors. He also revealed that this Etruscan tradition contradicted the Roman account of a crucial historical event with an entirely different version, the accuracy of which he explicitly confirmed. He conceded that Servius Tullius, the king who ruled Rome "to its great advantage," was not a slave, but an Etruscan. And before adopting his royal name he was known in his mother tongue as Mastarna.

What Claudius said was true. But his statement to the senate, as we now know, was incomplete. He disclosed only part of the facts known to him from his historical studies. An understandable reverence for the official Roman tradition inhibited him from revealing what the Etruscan tradition had to say about this Mastarna and his fellow warriors, about their origin, and about the circumstances in which Servius Tullius succeeded in making himself king on the Tiber.

It was left to an exceptional stroke of luck to recover this knowledge from the soil of ancient Etruria. In the middle of the last century, Prince Torlonia, the owner of broad acres near Vulci—a few miles north of the Via Aurelia and halfway between Tarquinia and Ansedonia—decided to undertake some new excavations. The landed nobility in that region had long realized what priceless treasures were still hidden in the rubbish-strewn Etruscan cemeteries and what excellent business could be done with objects dug out of the ground.

There was one example to make all the big landlords envious. This was Napoleon's own brother, Lucien Bonaparte, ennobled by the Pope as Prince of Canino. His rifling of the tombs in the region had yielded thousands of valuable Greek vases which he sold all over the world, thus making a fortune. As early as 1787, Goethe, while on his Italian journey, had noted that "Large sums are now paid for Etruscan vases, and there are certainly some beautiful ones

138

among them. There is not a traveler who doesn't want to possess a sample . . . I am afraid of being tempted myself." But Prince Torlonia, unlike the Bonaparte parvenu, went to work systematically. He sent for experts—the French historian A. Noël des Vergers and Alessandro François, a man well known for his lucky finds, who knew the Etruscan soil better than anyone and had an infallible

The François vase (restored)

flair for where to dig successfully. He had become famous for the vase named after him, which he discovered near Chiusi in 1845. This François vase, a superb painted Attic *crater,* or mixing bowl, is now in the Florence Archeological Museum.

Torlonia was well advised. Once again the flair of this unusually gifted excavator proved its worth. In 1857, François made yet another discovery which has remained linked with his name. In the overgrown, lonely gorge which the river Fiora has hollowed out of the volcanic rock near the necropolis of Vulci, François began his search at the point where the ancient Ponte della Badia spans the stream at a height of some one hundred feet. Its foundations date from Etruscan days. Once upon a time it linked the living city with its cemetery. For days François and des Vergers prowled through the dense thicket that was higher than their heads. Then, on a cliff-side, hidden under moss-covered scree, François came upon an opening filled with rubble. After careful examination, he felt certain that this must be the entrance to a subterranean sepulcher of some size.

A gang of workmen was summoned and the excavation started. No sooner had the removal of the rubble begun than a burial cippus, a pointed column, was discovered. It showed that they were on the right track to a tomb. But then, as the diggers pressed forward, difficulties appeared which threatened to bring everything to nought.

"One evening," says François, "I went back to the excavations. I found the overseer greatly worried. He said right away that everything was going wrong. He thought that the tomb had caved in and that, owing to its depth, it was not possible to enter it. The work which had been going on for a fortnight would have to be called off. This was a terrible blow to me, for I had set the greatest hopes on this hypogeum. I was taken to the spot and did in fact see a heap of debris which seemed to point to complete destruction."

But François did not give up. The next day: "I had a hole bored in the middle of the debris. Then I lay down full length on the ground and worked my way through the opening. After I had gone about ten feet I was able to lift my head and I lit the torch I had brought with me . . . I saw, at a distance of some twenty feet, another opening through which I crawled. Soon I found myself in an underground room hewn out of the travertine rock, and about eleven to thirteen feet high . . . The Etruscans had constructed this large subterranean chamber in order to protect the hypogeum below it from collapse and damp."

Delighted, François fumbled his way back to daylight. He ordered the opening to be enlarged, and then, together with des Vergers and some workmen, he went back into the bowels of the earth. The unforgettable moment of his great discovery came when, wrote des Vergers, "at the last stroke of the pick the stone that closed the entrance to the crypt yielded, and the torchlight shone upon vaults whose darkness and silence had remained undisturbed for more than twenty centuries."

> **As though time had stood still, the world of the Etruscans, unchanged, untouched, appeared before them.**

As though time had stood still, the world of the Etruscans, unchanged, untouched, appeared before them. Des Vergers describes the scene thus: "Everything was in the same state as on the day when the entrance was walled up. Ancient Etruria appeared before us as it was in the days of its glory. The warriors lying in full armor on their biers seemed to be resting from the battles they had fought against the Romans and Gauls. For a few minutes their shapes, clothes, stuffs, colors were visible. Then everything vanished as the outside air penetrated into the crypt, threatening to extinguish our flickering torches. It was an evocation of the past that was briefer than a dream and then faded away, as if to punish us for our reckless curiosity."

Spellbound, the two men lingered, stirred by the magic of this bygone world. Then, as after a little while their eyes became accustomed to the gloom and they began to gaze around the sepulchral chamber, there came the second surprise, no less exciting than the first.

All around, the walls of the tomb were covered with frescoes. They depicted scenes of bloodshed and cruelty, scenes of furiously fighting men and of slaughter. To the left of the entrance was the fratricidal struggle of Eteocles and Polynices, then Ajax seizing Cassandra at the altar, and in between, the killing of the Trojan prisoners, the human sacrifice offered to the soul of the dead Patroclus. Achilles was shown in the act of carrying it out. He had plunged his sword deep into the neck of a youth whose eyes seemed frozen with terror and pain. All these were scenes from Greek legends and the subject matter was nothing new.

But the frescoes continued on the right of the entrance. And here, suddenly, were pictures of a totally unknown subject matter. Amazed, François and his companions looked at the faded paintings. They too depicted a scene of carnage. Ten warriors, some bearded, others clean-shaven, were fighting, eight of them in a murderous hand-to-hand struggle. Here too men fell dead under the sword. But what exactly was this event that the artist had recorded? What was the meaning of this picture in an Etruscan tomb?

François did not know the answer. Excited as he was by the events of the day, he could not at that moment suspect what an important and unique discovery he had made, that it was these very wall paintings which threw light on the most obscure period of Rome under the kings.

It was only later, when the inscriptions on the frescoes had been deciphered, that the meaning of the scenes became known. The artist who long ago had painted the burial chamber had put these inscriptions over the heads of the combatants—in Etruscan lettering. The vault contained the only depiction of an event in Etruscan history that was already known at the time. Here were the clearly outlined figures of a long-forgotten past. To the great surprise of scholars, two of them were identified by the very names which the emperor Claudius had mentioned in his speech, namely, Caelius Vibenna and Mastarna. But, surprising or not, the name Mastarna could only mean that the fresco portrayed Servius Tullius, the Roman king.

The Etruscan artist had captured a moment of high drama. He shows a group of armed warriors, led by Mastarna, who have just brought off a surprise attack. They have burst into the sleeping enemy camp where one of their own leaders, Caelius Vibenna, is held prisoner. None of his captors has had time to seize a weapon, and thus the attackers succeed in rescuing their comrade.

The fresco depicts Caelius Vibenna holding out his bound hands to Mastarna, who has tucked his sword under his left arm and with a dagger in his right hand is cutting the prisoner's bonds. Alongside these two tall, bearded figures, a furious melee is going on. The enemy is being ruthlessly slaughtered. Slashed and stabbed, they are sinking to the ground in streams of blood. Among them are both Romans, recognizable by their clean-shaven faces, and bearded Etruscans. The name of each and the town he comes from are carefully written above victims and aggressors alike.

Aulus Vibenna, brother of the liberated Caelius, thrusts his dagger into the chest of a warrior whose home town is indecipherable. Two of his comrades are killing Etruscans from the towns of Sovana and Volsinii. A third is shown plunging his sword into a man bearded like himself. The inscription identifies the victim as Cneve Tarchunies Rumach, that is to say, Gnaeus Tarquinius of Rome, presumably a relative of the king.

Thus the inscribed frescoes in the Vulci tomb depict the victory of the brothers Vibenna and of Mastarna over a hostile coalition in which such important Etruscan towns as Volsinii and Sovana were joined with Rome. There must previously have been a battle in which Caelius Vibenna—here shown at the moment of liberation —had been defeated and taken prisoner. But did the event recorded in the fresco actually occur during the lifetime of Servius in just this way? The historicity of the Vulci frescoes continued to be disputed until one day another discovery was made.

During the excavation of a sanctuary at Veii, a fragment of a *bucchero* vase with an Etruscan inscription was found. It was a votive offering. The text, in archaic Etruscan, contained the name of the donor: Avele Vipiiennas, that is, Aulus Vibenna. The inscription dates from the middle of the sixth century B.C. It shows that a certain Aulus Vibenna had deposited a votive offering in the Veii temple during the lifetime of Servius Tullius.

This discovery, together with the paintings in the François tomb, made credible an old, often doubted tradition. According to that tradition, a group of Etruscans led by Caelius Vibenna and his brother Aulus had settled on the Caelian hill in Rome. Tacitus and Festus say that the Vibenna brothers had come to Rome under a King Tarquinius. Tacitus in fact adds that the hill was originally called Querquetulanus, because of its dense growth of oak trees, and was later named Caelian, after Caelius Vibenna, the Etruscan chief who brought help to Rome and was granted the hill as a residence.

Both brothers appear in the François tomb frescoes as comrades-in-arms of Mastarna. They cannot, admittedly, be portraits from life, because these frescoes were not painted until the third century B.C. or possibly even later. In them the artist immortalized an episode from the history of his own people, the Etruscans, an episode which Roman tradition deliberately tried to suppress. The painting records the antecedents of a revolution which overthrew the Tarquinian dynasty and brought the Etruscan Servius Tullius to power. And this happened not as the result of an assassination of Tarquinius Priscus, as Livy and other Roman historians would make posterity believe, but of a military expedition by Etruscan troops.

> **In them the artist immortalized an episode from the history of his own people, the Etruscans, an episode which Roman tradition deliberately tried to suppress.**

The battles of that time had nothing to do with Roman history as such. They were a struggle for power among Etruscan city-states, a struggle of the Tarquin dynasty on the Tiber and its allied towns to preserve the old order against a rebellion in the Etruscan lands. Mastarna and the Vibenna brothers, young noblemen from Vulci, had set out to overthrow the established tyranny of an absolute monarchy. They wanted a new, freer order of things. The idea was in the air. In Athens oligarchic power had been restricted by Solon's reforms of 594 B.C., and in Etruria too the new idea had found enthusiastic supporters. Scores of them joined the young revolutionaries whose armed bands soon caused serious unrest in the towns of the Etruscan league.

Reactionaries saw the threat to the orderly calm of their world, based on sacred traditions, and they hit back. Tarquinius Priscus in Rome, allied with friendly city-states, formed an army and went into action against the rebels. Our sources are silent about the course of the war. All we know is that Tarquinius Priscus and his allies lost. They were defeated by Mastarna and Aulus Vibenna in a legendary "battle of the kings." This victory brought the new movement to power and overthrew Tarquinius. During the fighting the Vibenna brothers seem to have been killed.

In Rome their companion-in-arms Mastarna assumed power. He remained loyal to the new ideas. This Etruscan, now officially known as Servius Tullius, became the second founder of Rome, a modern reformer of the stature of Solon, the great Athenian, and an outstanding statesman whose farsighted plans shaped the affairs of his Latin and Sabine subjects well into the future. His accession to the throne was quickly followed by a thorough reorganization of existing public institutions, for which posterity was to remember him. Livy is full of praise for his innovations: "The political reputation of Servius Tullius rests upon his organization of society according to a fixed scale of rank and wealth. He originated the census, a measure of the highest utility to a state destined, as Rome was, to future preeminence; for by means of it public service, in peace as well as in war, could thenceforward be regularly organized on the basis of property; every man's contribution could be in proportion to his means."

According to Dionysius, Servius Tullius justified the measure in a speech in which he said: "In order to lighten for the future the burden also of the war taxes you pay to the public treasury, by which the poor are oppressed and obliged to borrow, I will order all the citizens to submit a valuation of their property and everyone to pay his share of the taxes according to that valuation . . . for I regard it as both just and advantageous to the public that those who possess much should pay much in taxes and those who have little should pay little."

The assessment of property was an ancient custom of the East; it is mentioned as early as about 1800 B.C. in the clay tablet archives of the royal palace of Mari on the Euphrates. At that time already its purpose was to provide a basis for the collection of taxes and for military service. From Mari it was taken over by the Babylonians and Assyrians. The children of Israel more than once in their history were made to feel this kind of official imposition, the first time under Moses after the flight from Egypt, and then again under King David. And the Greeks of Ionia followed the precedent set by the East.

Though nothing new to the old civilizations of the Near East, the census was a novelty in the West. Servius Tullius, says Dionysius, "ordered all the Romans to register their names and give in a monetary valuation of their property . . . This law continued in force among the Romans for a long time."

There is a reference to this legislation in the Nativity story according to St. Luke's Gospel: "In those days a decree was issued by the emperor Augustus for a general registration throughout the Roman World." Censuses for purposes of taxation and military service still exist. But not many know that it was an Etruscan king who first legally established such a registration in Rome, from whence, with the rise of the Roman empire, it spread throughout Europe.

"After all had given in their valuations," continues Dionysius, "Tullius took the registers and determining both the number of the citizens and the size of their estates, introduced the wisest of all measures, and one which has been the source of the greatest advantages to the Romans, as the results have shown." What this measure was is stated by Livy thus: "The population was divided into classes and 'centuries' according to a scale based on the census, and suitable for both peace and war."

The reforms of Servius Tullius were animated by a new and modern spirit.

The reforms of Servius Tullius were animated by a new and modern spirit. In Etruria the social system consisted of an aristocratic governing class based on families and clans, below which was the subject population with few rights. Servius abolished this and organized society on a new basis. He restricted the absolute rule of the aristocracy and their privileges and power, but that was not all. For the first time all free residents were made liable to military service and were granted political rights. At a time when Etruria was governed by an absolute monarchy this was a great and revolutionary change.

The essential feature of the new system was the centuriate organization by which the division of the people into classes was linked with a reform of the army. Residents were divided into six classes, from the richest in the first class to the poorest in the sixth, who were exempt from military service. The classes were divided into centuries or companies with specifically defined military equipment and obligations.

The richest citizens, in the first class, were required to provide the centuries of cavalry. They were wealthy enough to buy and maintain their own warhorses. The main fighting force of infantry was provided by the first, second, and third classes, who equipped themselves with varying grades of arms and armor, from the full panoply of the first class (that is, helmets, bucklers, corselets, greaves, swords, and spears), down to the soldiers of the third class, who had no corselets or greaves, and long shields instead of round bucklers. The fourth class was armed only with spear and javelin, and the fifth with nothing but slings and stones. In addition, the reorganization provided for specialized units, namely, two centuries

Bronze situala *with armed warriors; sixth century B.C.*

of engineers with armorers and carpenters, and two of "trumpeters and horn-blowers and such as sounded the various calls with any other instruments." The famous Certosa bronze *situla* (bucket) found in a cemetery near Bologna and dating from about 500 B.C. depicts in relief soldiers so equipped. Two horsemen are followed by infantrymen, some with heavy armor and some with light.

Raymond Bloch considers that the procession corresponds to the formation of Etruscan army units and that it may perhaps be a prototype of the primitive Roman legion as organized by Servius Tullius in the three lines of *hastati, principes,* and *triarii.*

When the census was completed, says Dionysius, "Tullius . . . commanded all the citizens to assemble in arms in the largest field before the city; and having drawn up the horse in their respective squadrons and the foot in their massed ranks, and placed the light-armed troops each in their own centuries, he performed an expiatory sacrifice for them with a bull, a ram and a boar. These victims he ordered to be led three times round the army and then sacrificed them to Mars, to whom the field is consecrated." It was on this Field of Mars that Rome's youth was later to be trained in arms, and this, the first parade ground in Europe, was where the legions were to be mustered for the campaigns that destroyed the Etruscan people.

The nation in arms was promised a share in government proportionate to each man's means. "This constitution," says the German scholar Karl Otfried Müller, "abolished the whole organization of the state as it had been since time immemorial. In place of a system based on belief and opinion, on prestige and authority, it established a purely dynamic principle by which each man ranked according to his property . . . Never, so far as we know, did the Greeks divide up the classes and orders into centuries or companies of the army and home guard even for the purpose of voting. And never did the Greeks make the highest representative of the national will so military an organization as that assembled on the Field of Mars, the *exercitus urbanus.*"

All power lay with the upper classes, those who provided the mounted centuries and those bearing full armor. In elections the decisive vote rested with them. Those who could afford to provide themselves with the expensive equipment were granted in return political rights. But everyone was free to get into a higher class if he could.

148

The centuriate organization persisted not only till the end of the Roman republic, but outlasted even the Imperial Age. In Ranke's view, it created "the military and popular institutions which made Rome what it was." For the power of the Roman state had a military basis beyond that of any other state. Together with the plow it was only the sword that counted. The constitution of Servius Tullius made the Roman armed forces a peasant army, a nation in arms.

> *Rome, on the other hand, thanks to the system of centuries introduced by Tullius, acquired a fighting power that was to make possible unrivaled conquests and to lead it to world dominion.*

Sparta, with a society based on serfdom, was never able to turn the strength of its rural population to account and came to grief as a result. Rome, on the other hand, thanks to the system of centuries introduced by Tullius, acquired a fighting power that was to make possible unrivaled conquests and to lead it to world dominion.

But in its day the revolutionary new system aroused opposition among the aristocratic ruling classes whose power had previously been unrestricted, and who supported the old institutions. Reactionaries created trouble, both on the Tiber and in the city-states beyond the river.

"After the death of Tarquinius," says Dionysius, "those cities which had yielded the sovereignty to him refused to observe the terms of their treaties any longer . . . anticipating great advantages for themselves from the discord that had arisen between the patricians and their ruler" (i.e., Tullius). A revolt broke out in Veii, followed by others in Caere and Tarquinii, until "at last all Tyrrhenia was in arms." But Tullius was successful in all battles, "both against the several cities and against the whole nation."

The protagonists of the old order failed on the battlefield to achieve their aim—the removal of the revolutionary ruler on the Tiber. But his enemies in Rome succeeded. Lucius Tarquinius, son or grandson of Tarquinius Priscus, says Dionysius, "sent some of his servants against Tullius armed with swords and they overtook Tullius when he was already near his house and slew him" in the Vicus Cyprius.

Servius Tullius reigned for forty-four years. "It was a good reign," says Livy, "and even the best and most moderate successor would not easily have emulated it." The Romans, though they went out of their way to conceal the fact that he was Etruscan, cherished the memory of his rule. "The Romans," notes Dionysius, "say that this man was the first who altered the ancestral customs and laws by receiving the sovereignty, not from the senate and the people jointly, like all the former kings, but from the people alone." The Romans were rightly grateful to this Etruscan—since it was he who laid the foundations of their future freedom and power.

With the accession of a member of the powerful Tarquin family who seized the throne by force and who became known as Tarquinius Superbus, the rule of Etruscan kings in Rome was to reach a last period of glory. In the meantime the power and prestige of the Etruscans had greatly increased in places other than Rome, and they had gained in reputation both on land in Italy and at sea.

XI

The Campanian League

ETRURIA, INDEED," SAYS LIVY, "HAD AT this time both by sea and land filled the whole length of Italy from the Alps to the Sicilian strait with the noise of her name." Even when Tarquinius Priscus became king of the city on the Tiber, Etruscan city-states were already on the point of greatly extending their rule to the south, to Campania, by way of Latium.

Since the seventh century B.C., Etruscan influence in the country south of the Tiber had steadily grown. The tombs at Praeneste with their rich furnishings from Etruscan workshops show what importance this place on the edge of the Sabine hills had already acquired. In the meantime the backward Latin peoples had come more and more within the zone of influence of the pioneering Etruscans and had become associated with them in both the political and the religious spheres.

Tarquinius Priscus, as the Roman tradition says, became ruler of all the Latins. Under his successor, Servius Tullius, there was peace, and the bonds became yet closer. "Servius deliberately cultivated personal friendship with the Latin nobles and good public relations with their country," says Livy. "He at last carried his point, and a temple of Diana was built in Rome by the Latin peoples in association with the Romans. This was an admission that the long struggle for supremacy was over: Rome, by common consent, was the capital city." Under his successor, Tarquinius Superbus, Rome was actually to become the leading power in the Latin league.

Progress came with the swarms of merchants, artisans, and engineers who streamed into Latium from Etruria. The economy prospered. The fields, hitherto tilled in archaic ways, began to yield more plentiful crops as the local farmers learned modern techniques from the foreign agronomists. New methods in animal husbandry were introduced.

The artificial improvement of the land, something unknown to the indigenous population, was successfully taken in hand. As in Etruria, an extensive system of channels was constructed, by means of which superfluous water was collected and drained away or directed to arid areas. Many of the regions then cultivated later became derelict and waste. Among these probably belonged the great plain along the sea near Antium, the modern Anzio, where the Volscians lived. Once upon a time it was renowned for its fertility and abundant harvests, which it owed to an elaborate drainage system. Under the Romans the old drainage channels were more and more neglected, and in the end they no longer worked. The land became a marsh, malaria arrived, and the whole district was deserted. Thus the ill-famed Pontine marshes came into being.

It was only in the twenties of the present century that this uninhabitable region was, after more than two thousand years, once more drained and returned to cultivation. It was done in the same way that the Etruscans did it, by means of an extensive network of ditches and big drainage channels.

Large tracts of Latium were at that time measured by Etruscan surveyors, who for the first time worked outside their own country. The land was marked out in units suitable for intensive cultivation, "in accordance with ancient principles of land division," says Raymond Bloch, "in the form of allotments, marked off into skillfully and regularly defined squares. The Etruscans had, in fact, an extensive knowledge of surveying and mensuration, and the Roman surveyors, some of whose writings have come down to us, in their turn learnt to apply the principles that lay behind this ancient technique."

Bloch points out the remarkable fact that: "The division of Italy and the Roman provinces into squares with sides of 710 m. —which, in various areas and in particular in North Africa, is revealed to us by aerial photography and astonishes by its extraordinary extent and perfect geometry—thus goes back to the Tuscan heritage."

> "The division of Italy and the Roman provinces into squares with sides of 710 m.—which, in various areas and in particular in North Africa, is revealed to us by aerial photography and astonishes by its extraordinary extent and perfect geometry— thus goes back to the Tuscan heritage."

The results of this development aid by outsiders soon began to show in the advent and spread of prosperity. Thanks to the increased yield of the soil, purchasing power grew, and the hitherto really poor and frugal population began to want a number of goods. More and more products of Etruscan workshops and industry came in. With these material goods came art. "The whole civilization of Latium and Campania from the seventh to the sixth century B.C. was frankly Etruscan," says Massimo Pallottino. "We only need think of the type and form of the temple, and of its decorations in painted terra-cotta."

Ancient Latium has hardly been explored by archeologists so far. But what little evidence has come to light clearly reflects the change and progress that set in during the seventh and sixth centuries. The finds of that period, whether from Satricum (modern Conca), Lanuvium (Lanuvio), or Velitrae (Velletri) point clearly to facts that the Roman sources pass over in silence. At Satricum, once a Volscian town northeast of modern Nettuno, the remains of a temple of purely Etruscan character were discovered in 1896 by the French archeologist F. Graillot. It had been erected in the sixth century B.C. over an older sanctuary set amid primitive huts.

Quantities of fragments dating from the same period were also found, fragments of tiles molded in relief and of figures, all made of painted terra-cotta, that once decorated the roof, gable, and walls. Among them were the head of a bearded god, a gorgon mask, a horse's head, reliefs of battle scenes, maenads and satyrs. Along with votive statues and bronze figurines the mass of rubble contained shards of *bucchero* vases of all kinds, bronze tripods and—an unmistakable testimony to Etruscan dentistry—a gold tooth fitting. These finds at Satricum proved that the Etruscans, with their more advanced culture, exercised the predominant influence in Latium at that time.

When the temple at Satricum was built, a further advance had long been under way. Etruscan colonizers had already pushed south as far as the plain at the foot of Vesuvius. Along the southern shore of the Tyrrhenian Sea they had established a new dominion. South of Naples and the rocky Sorrento peninsula with its famous bathing resorts Amalfi and Positano, a green plain stretches along the Gulf of Salerno. Where the road approaches the coast, almost within a stone's throw of the waves, immense monuments of a remote past greet the traveler—the ruins of the Greek city Paestum. Surrounded by a city wall of some three miles circumference, with gates and towers, three magnificent temples of honey-colored stone stand out against the sky.

Ponte della Badia over the river Fiora, Vulci

This is an entirely new experience for the traveler coming from the north. Here for the first time he encounters on Italian soil the art of Magna Graecia. Goethe, who visited Paestum on his way to Sicily, felt it strongly. "The first impression was one of astonishment. I found myself in an utterly strange world," he says in his *Italienische Reise*. At first sight he felt that "there is something oppressive, even terrible about these thronging masses of stocky, tapered columns."

The Etruscans pressed on to within sight of the Greek colony. Their territory extended as far as the little river that still bears their name, the Tuscana, the waters of which are carried down to the sea by the Sele. The banks of the latter formed the boundary. Campania was a big stride toward southern Italy, at that time consisting of the flourishing Greek colonies of Magna Graecia. In Campania the Etruscans found vast tracts of underdeveloped land in a diversified countryside of hills, mountains, and plains.

It is about 175 miles by air from the mouth of the Tiber to the southern tip of the Gulf of Salerno. It is a long drive, too, leaving Rome at the Porta San Sebastiano where the Via Appia Antica begins, over the ancient Roman paving, then along the gently rising slopes of the Alban hills, southward to the coast at Terracina, and then following it until Vesuvius is passed. The journey by sea from Ostia to Naples is about the same as that from Caere north to Populonia and Elba.

Campania felix, happy Campania, as the Romans later called it, was already well known to the Etruscans in the sixth century B.C. Many generations earlier, people from Etruria seem to have settled there—the first of them, according to the Roman historian Velleius Paterculus, in Capua and Nola as early as about 800 B.C.

Even at that time Etruscan warships and pirates ruled the sea to beyond the Strait of Messina. Naval operations at such a distance to the south, far from the ports of Etruria as such, presuppose local land bases. In addition there must have been depots, warehouses, and fortified camps on the shores of Campania, as there were in Latium, possibly at Terracina, the name of which is reminiscent of Tarchon.

We have, luckily, an eyewitness report on Campania from a man who himself saw and admired the fertility of Campanian fields under Etruscan management. He was the Greek Polybius, a cavalry commander who, along with a thousand other eminent hostages of the Achaean Confederation, was brought to Rome in 167 B.C.

In the forty books of his world history, which he wrote after extensive journeys through Italy, Sicily, Gaul, and Spain, he observes: "The Etruscans were the oldest inhabitants of this [the Po] plain at the same period that they possessed also that Phlegraean plain in the neighborhood of Capua and Nola, which, accessible and well known as it is to many, has such a reputation for fertility. Those therefore who would know something of the dominion of the Etruscans should not look at the country they now inhabit, but at these plains and the resources they drew thence." When Polybius penned this commendation, the Etruscans had long been driven out of the south. Their rule over Campania ended when Capua fell around 425 B.C.

The Phlegraean fields, then as now a center of volcanic activity, lie in the heart of Campania. Here, within sight of Vesuvius, says the legend, the Giants, savage sons of the Earth goddess Gaia, fought against the gods and were defeated by them. The *autostrada* crosses this country, as rich in legends as in history, a few miles before the traveler from Rome reaches Naples.

When the Etruscans were establishing their southern league, Greek Cumae remained a constant source of anxiety to them. They were never able to defeat this trading city, and their colonists spread out around it, to the north and southeast, among the long-established Oscans, a peasant people. The most important foundation of the new Etruscan dominion was Capua, near the river Volturnus (modern Volturno). The modern town Capua originated much later in Roman times, as a port directly on the river. Nevertheless it is worth a visit, since the local Museo Campano contains an interesting collection of architectural terra-cottas, bronzes, and votive figures in the Etruscan style.

In the last century the archeological remains were still so scanty that many scholars doubted whether the Etruscans had in fact ever been in Campania, despite the references to be found in ancient authors and traditions. However, material and inscriptions found in recent decades have provided the proof. The most important of the latter is an Etruscan inscription on a tile which contains more than three hundred legible words. The tile was found during excavations near the ancient city of Capua and is now in Berlin.

"From the historical point of view," says Pallottino, "Etruscan rule in Campania, which was once doubted by modern scholars, now presents at the most only secondary problems."

156

Etruscan Capua, which, according to Livy, was originally named Volturnum after the nearby river, was some three miles farther east.

> **If the mute remains from the ancient cemeteries could speak they would tell how rich and great Capua once was.**

A modern-looking town at the foot of Mount Tifata, in a rich, well-farmed district, conceals in its soil the remains of the former powerful metropolis. Its modern name, Santa Maria Capua Vetere, preserves the memory of the Etruscan age. But the fragments of a triumphal arch and of an amphitheater almost as big as the Colosseum date from Roman imperial times, when the Etruscans had long been expelled.

Nothing remains of the original city whose inhabitants opened the gates to the victorious Hannibal after the battle of Cannae in 216 B.C. His soldiers grew indolent after spending a winter in the town, and the luxurious living of Capua soon became proverbial. Etruscan viniculture was famous in the south, and the fiery Falernian wine, which is still produced in the district, got top marks from Roman drinkers. It had such a high alcoholic content that it was drunk mixed with honey.

If the mute remains from the ancient cemeteries could speak they would tell how rich and great Capua once was, in part thanks to the high fertility of the volcanic soil around Vesuvius. But even more important were the industry, crafts, and trade which its founders set going and vigorously developed. Their workshops and manufactories gave employment to the indigenous inhabitants. And thus the city grew and became so populous that at a later date, as Cicero said, it alone, next to Rome, Corinth, and Carthage, "could support the dignity and name of an imperial city." That sort of magnitude and population could never have come from the peasant Oscans in early times nor later from the Samnite mountaineers. It was Etruscan entrepreneurs who attracted people in large numbers to Capua and accustomed them to urban life.

The name of the second settlement in Campania mentioned by Polybius still survives in Nola, northeast of Vesuvius. But what historians have to say about the little town has nothing to do with its Etruscan origin and past. They tell us that the emperor Augustus died there in A.D. 14, and that about A.D. 400 the local bishop invented the church bell, called in Latin *campana* or *nola*.

Near Naples two other places recall former Etruscan towns—Acerra, and Nocera on the river Sarno, not far from a township still called Cava de' Tirreni. Other Etruscan foundations have been forgotten. Excavations in Campania have turned up coins bearing the names of Etruscan places, such as Velcha, Velsu, and Irnthi, but where they were is not yet known. However, in the case of two other towns belonging to the southern Etruscan league, namely Herculaneum and Pompeii, archeology did, of course, score a success.

In the eighteenth and nineteenth centuries the question whether the Etruscans were ever the rulers of Pompeii was much disputed by scholars. As was so often the case, people did not believe the admittedly meager statements of ancient authors. And yet the geographer Strabo, who wrote during the first century A.D., who had visited Etruria, and who drew on the best extant literature, expressly declared that Pompeii had once been an Etruscan possession. But although excavation followed excavation, no typically Etruscan material came to light, and thus doubts continued.

Today the uncertainty has at last been ended, thanks to the untiring labors of Professor Amedeo Maiuri, who for a generation conducted the research on the spot. He succeeded in proving that Pompeii did in fact belong to the twelve cities of Etruscan Campania.

With the exception of Herculaneum, no archeological investigation has ever been so long drawn out as that of Pompeii. Chance finds led, in 1748, to the first exploration of the soil, in the course of which wall paintings, articles of bronze and silver, and the lava-encased dead were found. A series of discoveries began which excited the world.

Encouraged by one sensational find after another, the search went on all through the nineteenth century. The astonishment at the rediscovery of this town, buried for almost two thousand years, completely distracted attention from its history. It was not until about 1900 that the excavators began to direct their attention to that also. At last the opportunity to settle the Etruscan question occurred.

Maiuri, who was director of excavations since 1924, went systematically to work to investigate the subsoil. During excavations under the temple of Apollo near the Forum he made a conclusive

158

discovery. This was a deposit of votive gifts in which, in addition to fragments of black-figure Attic ceramics, shards of *bucchero* vases with Etruscan inscriptions were found. These fragments of gifts to the sanctuary were easily dated to the period 550 to 470 B.C. Strabo was thus proved right—there had been an Etruscan occupation of Pompeii. Neighboring Herculaneum also belonged to the southern league of cities, for Strabo and Theophrastus both mention the Etruscans as being there.

Farther to the south, tradition and archeological discoveries likewise confirm Etruscan dominion. On the peak high above Sorrento was once a statue of Minerva which, says Statius, was called "the Etruscan." In the neighborhood of Salerno began the region known as the *ager Picentinus,* which, according to Pliny, was Etruscan. There, as Strabo reports, lay "Marcina, a city founded by the Tyrrheni." In this district, archeological material with Oriental motifs was found at Pontecagnano, and at Fratte di Salerno graves yielded pottery with incised Etruscan inscriptions.

Trading and other economic contacts with Etruria proper were close, and Campania, whose indigenous Oscan inhabitants were simple peasants, throve and prospered under Etruscan rule, which changed the face of the region. From the Tiber to the Vesuvius plain, a new, flourishing Etruscan bastion against southern Italy was established. It barred the way to further Greek penetration by the land route.

This southern dominion was of great importance to Etruria as such, because of road connections through Calabria to the Greek colonies of southern Italy. Close commercial links and friendly relations were forged in particular with Sybaris, the great rival of Croton. Through Sybaris went a steady stream of goods, of exports and imports to and from Asia Minor. The city's most important trading partner was Miletus, the biggest commercial center of Ionia.

A vast area of Italy, now for the first time unified under one predominant language, had been welded into a great economic empire under Etruscan inspiration and control. But the zenith of Etruscan power had not yet been reached. Around the middle of the sixth century events occurred which were to make Etruria's name and greatness known and respected throughout the world. This time the decision lay at sea.

| **THE ALLIANCE WITH CARTHAGE** | Somewhere about 545 b.c. Etruria and Carthage made their great alliance. It was clearly directed against the third up-and-coming trading power in the |

West, the Greeks. Since the beginning of the century, the tension between the three great maritime peoples had steadily increased. Long past were the times when, despite a good deal of piracy, they had remained friendly rivals. The first warning signal of the approaching clash had come some fifty years earlier.

About 600 b.c., news reached Carthage of an event that threatened to undermine Punic supremacy in the western Mediterranean and confine the great metropolis to the African coast. The news was that Greek colonists, Phocaeans from Ionia, had landed from their warships at the mouth of the Rhone in southern Gaul and established a base, Massalia, modern Marseilles. To the Carthaginians, who had hitherto been the undisputed masters of the sea in the western Mediterranean, this meant the arrival of their Greek competitors right in the midst of their own trading area.

Thanks to their swift warships, the fifty-oared galleys, the Phocaeans had outmaneuvered and defeated the Carthaginians and secured a key position which threatened to bar the Carthaginian merchantmen from the coastal traffic between Liguria in Italy, the shores of Provence, and Catalonia in Spain. Worse still, Massalia could block access to one of the most important trading routes to the north, the roads up the Rhone valley and across Gaul. Over this route tin, that rare metal indispensable for bronze making, had long traveled from the mines of Britain.

What the Carthaginians feared did in fact happen. The Phocaeans made their new settlement, Massalia, a center for further advances. Expanding eastward they set up new bases at the sites of modern Nice and Antibes. And before long, their warships appeared off the coast of Spain.

The Carthaginians did not sit idly by. They knew what was at stake. They knew that rivalry for commercial supremacy and spheres of interest had reached the point where Carthage had no option but to prepare for war with the Greeks, unless they wanted to surrender their position for all time. Throughout their widespread settlements and possessions, the Carthaginians accordingly set to work to mobilize their forces.

Etruria's interests were even more seriously menaced. The Phocaeans were in a position to control access of shipping to Etruria and threatened to seal off the Tyrrhenian Sea from southern Gaul to Sicily. The waters which had been wide open to the Etruscans as long as anyone could remember, which bore their name, were suddenly in danger of becoming a Greek sea. That would mean that Italy would be cut off from Africa, Carthage, and even the Aegean lands.

> **The waters which had been wide open to the Etruscans as long as anyone could remember, which bore their name, were suddenly in danger of becoming a Greek sea.**

Only two large islands shielded the Etruscan coast. Access to the West was still open through Sardinia, occupied by friendly Carthage, and Corsica. Here, on the island's east coast, the Etruscans had long since established bases and through them exploited the island economically. They exacted from the natives a tribute of resin, wax, and honey.

But Etruria's coastal cities seemed unable to make up their minds, to pull themselves together. In any case, what were they to do? Prepare a naval expedition to Massalia? So they marked time until one day rumors were confirmed, and the alarming news broke: Greek colonists, Phocaeans, had landed on Corsica and settled at Alalia on the east coast of the island. This invasion of Etruria's territory took place about 545 B.C.

What led up to this event was reported in some detail by Herodotus. It happened in the Phocaeans' homeland on the shores of Asia Minor. There, on a promontory near Smyrna, they were forced to abandon their city Phocaea, the modern Turkish Foca, to Persian besiegers under the command of Harpagus, the Median general who helped to put Cyrus on the throne of Persia.

"Harpagus brought his troops to Phocaea," says Herodotus, "and began a siege, proclaiming to the Phocaeans that he would be satisfied if they consented to pull down a single tower in the fortifications and set apart one house for the service of the king. The Phocaeans, however, dreading the thought of slavery, were very angry at the proposal, and promised to answer on the following day, when they had had time to consider the matter, stipulating at the same time that Harpagus should withdraw his forces during their deliberations. This Harpagus consented to do . . . so the troops were withdrawn, and the Phocaeans at once launched their galleys, put aboard their women and children and movable property, including the statues and other sacred objects from their temples . . . and sailed for Chios. So the Persians on their return took possession of an empty town."

The Phocaeans then tried to buy a group of islands on which to settle, but the Chians refused to sell, says Herodotus, because they were afraid of trading competition with their own island. "So the Phocaeans prepared to sail to Corsica, where twenty years previously on the advice of an oracle they had founded a city called Alalia . . . For five years they lived at Alalia with the former settlers and built temples in the town; but during that period they caused so much annoyance to their neighbors by plunder and pillage that the Tyrrhenians and Carthaginians agreed to attack them with a fleet of sixty ships apiece."

The time for action had come. The Etruscans and the Carthaginians realized that only by acting in concert against any further move by their Greek rivals could they hope to save the situation. So an alliance was made, which is referred to by Aristotle in his *Politics:* "A state is also something more than a pact of mutual protection or an agreement to exchange goods and services; for in that case Etruscans and Carthaginians, and all others with contractual obligations to each other, would be taken as citizens of a single state."

The testing time for the alliance came a few years later, in about 535 B.C. Phocaean ships were observed in Sardinian waters. Swiftly the Etruscan and Carthaginian vessels were manned and the combined fleet of 120 ships went out to meet the invaders. "The Phocaeans replied by manning their own vessels, also sixty in number, and sailed to meet the enemy off Sardinia," says Herodotus.

In the battle the outnumbered Phocaeans suffered heavy losses, "for forty of their vessels were destroyed and the remaining twenty had their rams so badly wrenched as to render them unfit for service."

There was nothing for it but flight. "The survivors returned to Alalia, took aboard their women and children and such of their property as there was room for, and sailed from Corsica to Rhegium." From there, in the toe of Italy, near the Strait of Messina (modern Reggio di Calabria), "they afterwards sent men to found

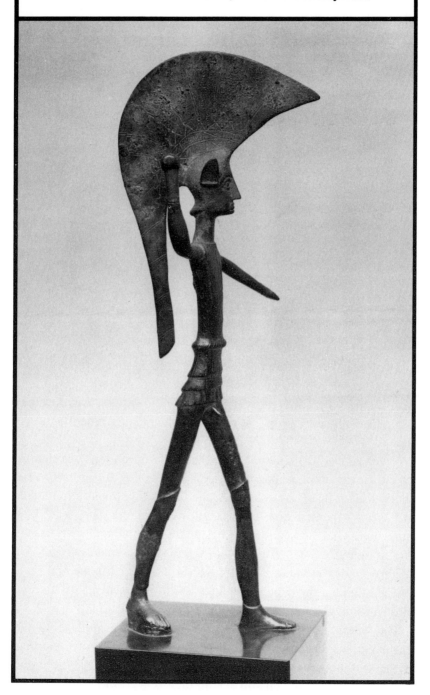

Bronze statuette of warrior; late sixth century B.C.

a new city in Oenotria." This was at Elea, or Velia, modern Castella-
mare di Bruca, in Lucania, about twenty-five miles south of
Paestum.

A cruel act of retaliation marred the victory of the two allies.
"The Carthaginians and Tyrrhenians drew lots for the possession of
the prisoners from the ships which were sunk. Of the Tyrrhenians,
the people of Agylla [Caere] got by far the largest number, and they
took them all ashore and stoned them to death." As a result, there
was a curse on the spot where the murdered Phocaeans lay, which
haunted the people of Caere. So, says Herodotus, they "sent to
Delphi, and were told by the priestess to begin the custom, which
they still observe today, of honoring the dead men with a grand
funeral ceremony and the holding of athletic and equestrian contests."

Alalia was a tremendous victory and it made a worldwide impression. The ancients understood very well the great significance of
this naval battle to the Etruscans and Carthaginians, and rightly
considered it an event of international importance. Apart from the
victory of Pharaoh Rameses III in about 1200 B.C. over the Sea
Peoples in a battle off the mouth of the Nile, it was the first great
naval battle in history.

The Persian wars were not yet on the horizon and neither Athens
nor Syracuse yet counted as a naval power. The only other important
naval battle on record, as we learn from Thucydides, was that between Corinth and Corfu. But this was only an engagement between
Greeks.

Never before had so great an armada of "barbarians" as that of
the Etruscans and Carthaginians engaged the Greeks in battle and
utterly routed them. At one stroke the Greek threat was eliminated,
and the Tyrrhenian Sea, or at least its northern part, was once
more free. The Etruscan city-states could breathe again.

The treaty between Etruria and Carthage was renewed and the
alliance made yet closer. The treaty also covered commercial matters and divided the western Mediterranean into spheres of interest,
with Sardinia going to Carthage and Corsica to Etruria.

The victory of Alalia was of great long-term advantage to the
Carthaginians, because it once more gave them undisputed mastery
of the seas between Sardinia, Africa, and Spain. They seized the
opportunity to strengthen and extend their power. In about 530 B.C.

they conquered the former kingdom of Tartessus in Spain, and they established a blockade of the Straits of Gibraltar through which foreign ships were not allowed to pass. Thus the Greeks were locked in the Mediterranean and had no access to the sea route to the tin mines of Britain.

For Etruria the sea to the west was again open, and they made good use of it. There is archeological evidence of Etruscan merchants visiting Carthage. However, the Etruscans were soon to encounter the Greeks again in another quarter, the southern Tyrrhenian. The reason was that the Greeks of Cumae, incited by the Phocaeans, constructed a harbor of their own in the sheltered bay of Naples at Dicaearchia, the site of what later became Puteoli, modern Pozzuoli. (This was the port where St. Paul first stepped onto Italian soil, as a prisoner, on his way to Rome.) With the building of this harbor, an active rival to Etruria was introduced into its own dominion of Campania. Before long, Greek goods were to flood into the country through this port and compete with the Etruscans' own production.

This was the port where St. Paul first stepped onto Italian soil, as a prisoner, on his way to Rome.

Etruscan control of the seas, that famous thalassocracy which the Greeks so feared, reached its zenith with the battle of Alalia. From then on, its days were numbered.

But who at the time could have foreseen as much? For the moment the gods seemed still favorably disposed, and fortune smiled on the Etruscans. It was just at this time that they were extending and strengthening their empire by their great thrust in the north, where they were to achieve yet further triumphs.

XII

Etruscan Pioneers in the Po Valley

THE NEWS OF THE CARTHAGINIAN and Etruscan naval victory at Alalia was being talked of in all the colonies and ports of the Mediterranean, another great enterprise of the Etruscans was under way. Advancing beyond the Apennines, they were opening up yet additional underdeveloped regions of Italy. It was a daring venture of which history has yet to take the full measure, for in effect it gave the Etruscans access to the lands beyond the Alps, to France and the Rhineland, Switzerland and Hungary. Through a widespread trading network the Etruscans were soon to establish contacts with the peoples of northern Europe, at that time unknown to the rest of the world. More than five centuries before the Romans appeared on the scene, conquering by force of arms, setting up military colonies and building fortifications, the Etruscans' peaceful penetration got under way. They exported their goods and their civilization to the northern lands, introduced to the Celts and Teutons and their neighbors the products and achievements of the Mediterranean world, in particular, those of Etruria and Greece.

"On each side of the Apennines," says Livy of the Etruscans, "they built twelve towns, the first twelve on the southern side toward the Lower Sea, and later the second twelve north of the range, thus possessing themselves of all the country beyond the Po as far as the Alps with the exception of the little corner where the Venetians live around the shores of their gulf."

Livy's account describes an accomplished fact. The ancient sources are silent on the actual Etruscan advance into the Po valley and on its colonization in the sixth century B.C. Only legends preserve a memory of the event.

One of them has survived in fragmentary accounts of the Etruscan history by Aulus Caecina, a cultivated Etruscan noble and friend of Cicero. He ascribes to Tarchon, the legendary hero of Tarquinii, the conquest of the Po valley and the founding of twelve cities in the north. Tarchon is supposed to have crossed the Apennines at the head of a great army. Mantua is said to have been the first city founded by him, in accordance with the sacred ritual, and named after the Etruscan god of death, Mantus. Later Tarchon is said to have founded another eleven cities and united them in a league.

According to another legend the first advance was made from one of the northern city-states of ancient Etruria. An expedition led by Ocnus set out from Perugia, crossed the Arno and the Apennines and, to the north of the mountains, founded the town of Felsina.

Beneath the houses, the streets and squares of Bologna, lies buried the evidence of the activities of the enterprising settlers from Tuscany who built a new city center here twenty-five centuries ago.

Strong forces of Etruscan cavalry and chariot-borne warriors descended into the broad plain of the Po valley. The occupation of this territory seems to have been peaceful and bloodless. "The vast territories to the north of the Apennines," says Raymond Bloch, "were . . . occupied only by scattered tribes, ill equipped to oppose the entry of a regular army into the Po valley. Etruscan merchants must earlier have reconnoitered this fertile valley, beyond which they could trade with the Alpine populations and establish contact with the tribes of Germany and Gaul."

Felsina, modern Bologna, which rapidly developed into an important town, was to become the center of the new Etruscan dominion in the north. Its power reached its peak when the Etruscans

Head of a warrior

one day arrived on the Adriatic and established trading stations on the coast.

Beneath the houses, the streets and squares of Bologna, lies buried the evidence of the activities of the enterprising settlers from Tuscany who built a new city center here twenty-five centuries ago. It is true that they were not the first on the spot. Others had dwelt here before them, including some of their own countrymen who came as merchants. But it remained just a moderately big settlement. Only with the newcomers of the sixth century B.C. did it grow into a city planned and built according to the well-proven Etruscan ritual and methods.

It was not until the last century that the cemeteries of Etruscan Felsina were discovered. In 1869 Antonio Zannoni, chief engineer and architect to the municipality of Bologna, began systematically to explore the ground. He found *stelae* carved in relief, Etruscan bronzes, and inscriptions. In the following decades, further excavation campaigns brought to light a quantity of other objects, among them the famous Certosa *situla,* a magnificent bronze bucket with fine figural reliefs. These discoveries proved the antiquity of the Etruscan city. The earliest burials with Greek vases and funeral texts in Etruscan writing go back to the end of the sixth century B.C. However, all efforts to find the city itself were unsuccessful.

Since 1909 there have been no further systematic excavations in the Etruscan cemeteries. The city fathers of modern, busy Bologna had more urgent and topical problems to deal with. And by now there is little hope left of ever finding sites of Etruscan times, whether of dwellings or of the acropolis. Even in the outer districts, the claims of archeologists face insuperable difficulties because of the rapid growth of new residential quarters. And yet every time the power shovels rip open the ground, fragments of the past come to light, such as the groups of *stelae* found when the new stadium was being built in 1950, the Etruscan structures near the Faculty of Engineering, or the remains of masonry near the Palazzo Albergati.

Fortunately there is, not far from the prosperous chief city of Emilia, a solitary spot that richly rewards the visitor with everything that Bologna denies him. Leaving the town by the Porta Saragozza, one takes the Porrettana road, national highway number 64. It follows the ancient Etruscan route along the valley of the

Reno, gradually rises to the Porretta pass (Passo della Collina) at 3,029 feet, and then, down the Ombrone valley, winds along the Apennines to Pistoia, near Florence. Some sixteen miles from Bologna the road reaches the village of Marzabotto. A few paces, and the visitor stands where the stony skeleton of a city emerges from a field of thistles. This is the site of an Etruscan foundation of about 500 B.C., whose name is believed to have been Misa.

Its discovery in the last century aroused immense excitement among scholars of antiquity, and it is still of unique value for the study of Etruscan history. It was in 1865 that Count Gozzadini, digging for treasure in what he hoped would turn out to be a necropolis in the upper Reno valley, was surprised to find that the site hid much more than the graves he first came upon. What he found was the ruins of an Etruscan city, the first which ever came to light in all its complexity and, until recently, almost the only one of its kind.

The scale and systematic planning of the site are astonishing. They reveal the hand of builders who carried out their work in ac-

**Remains of street plan of Misa (?)
near Marzabotto; c. 500 B.C.**

cordance with the sacred rules and ritual enjoined by the Etruscan priesthood. This Etruscan center, says Massimo Pallottino, "is particularly important for its characteristic chessboard pattern (the 'gridiron' system), with straight streets rigorously laid at right angles to one another in the direction of the four cardinal points, thus following the rules for the planning of Etruscan cities later handed down to the Romans."

The city of Misa has a circuit of some two and one half miles; about sixty-seven acres were occupied by houses, factories, and shops. The main street runs due north and south and is some fifty feet wide. It is crossed at right angles by three streets running east and west. Narrower lanes divide the whole area into blocks of individual dwellings. The most northerly of the east-west streets leads to the sacred area, to the acropolis, where the sacred buildings are likewise oriented by the cardinal points. The characteristic high podium of one of these temples still remains; made of travertine, it is reckoned the earliest monument of Etruscan architecture north of the Apennines.

Another temple shows clearly the outline of three cellae. Part of its foundation, and indeed all the southeastern part of the acropolis, rest on a man-made terrace. The ground was artificially leveled so that the prescribed orientation could be strictly applied. Nearby, one of the oldest water systems in the whole of Italy has been discovered. There is an elaborate network of drainage and distribution channels connected with a central cistern.

The Etruscan architects and town planners took into account all the practical requirements of a city, its economic aspects and interests. Recent excavations have revealed that ancient Misa had its own industrial quarter. Along the broad main north-south street were numerous workshops, and small factories operated in the center of the town. There is evidence that the production of metal goods must have been on a considerable scale and that trade was important. Buildings were suitably equipped for their purposes. A long corridor led through each house to the workshop in the inner courtyard. It was provided with a well, washing facilities, and covered drains for carrying away the industrial effluent. In front of the houses, on the main street, were pavements as much as fifteen feet wide, on which the finished goods could be displayed for sale.

The skill of the artists and craftsmen of Misa is shown in the pottery and terra-cotta objects that have been found, including painted antefixes with palmettes, as well as parts of a mold and whole series of votive objects. The most impressive specimen of local work is a terrifying gorgon's head.

Misa's commercial connections were far-reaching. Gold jewelry, with filigree and granulation, came from all over the motherland, bronze figures and utensils from Chiusi, and painted Greek pottery via Felsina (Bologna) from Spina on the Adriatic.

The excavators were also able to establish that vines must have been grown on the neighboring hillsides, and that the huntsmen of Misa found plenty of game in the thickly wooded slopes and valleys of the Apennines. Quantities of bones of wild boar and deer have been found on hearth sites.

The ancient stories of Etruscan city foundations in north Italy, so often rejected as mere fancy, acquired substance with the discoveries of the cemeteries and wall foundations at Bologna, and with the identification of the "gridiron" of Misa. After twenty-five hundred years, the evidence of the Etruscan past in those regions began to speak. But which were the other cities of the legendary league of the Po valley? Where were the towns north of the Apennines which Livy calls "the second twelve"?

> After twenty-five hundred years, the evidence of the Etruscan past in those regions began to speak.

It is difficult to give a precise answer to this question. "In the direction of the Adriatic," says Pallottino, "the Etruscans founded and occupied the cities of Caesena (Cesena), Ravenna, Ariminium (Rimini), and Spina. . . . Inland, there were the cities of Parma, Placentia (Piacenza), Mutina (Modena), and Melpum, perhaps in the vicinity of Milan." But, he says, apart from historical sources, the evidence consists only of a limited amount of archeological and epigraphic material and indications from place names. Thus we have: "Ariminium (Rimini, probably from an Etruscan *Arimna-*), Caesena (Cesena, probably cognate to the Etruscan *Keisna,* a family name found in Bologna), Mantua (Mantova, in Etruscan *Mandva-?*), Mutina (Modena), Parma and the city which the Romans rechristened Placentia (Piacenza)."

There is no hope now of recovering the ancient chessboard layout in Piacenza, Modena, Mantua, or Ravenna. These are densely inhabited towns whose buildings conceal forever what is buried under them. It is only in places where the sequence of generations has been interrupted, where there is no layer on layer of masonry, that the lucky find may yet reward the excavator.

Spina was to be such a place. Its name had never been entirely forgotten. Over the centuries the belief lingered on that here had been a great, wealthy, powerful commercial city that dominated the mouth of the Po and the shores of the Adriatic, a city of luxury and splendor, a kind of ancestor and predecessor of Venice, founded more than a thousand years later.

Classical scholars also knew about Spina, for ancient literary sources indicated that there must once have existed a thriving maritime trading settlement of great economic importance, until the Celtic invasion of the Po valley destroyed it. Pliny the Elder refers to Spina in his *Natural History*. Strabo, the Greek geographer who lived in Rome at the beginning of the Christian era and wrote the seventeen books of his *Geography,* had seen with his own eyes the "village" which in his time was all that remained of the "anciently celebrated" city.

In the Renaissance, Flavio Biondo, the archeologist and historian from Forlì, was the first to look for the lost city, and since then the question of its history and whereabouts has more than once intrigued scholars and whetted their scientific curiosity. They knew, in a general way, where to search. Somewhere in the region where the Po over the centuries has pushed its deposits of sediment farther and farther into the shallow sea, in the desolate, strange wilderness of lagoons that stretches along the coast as far as Ravenna, somewhere under the sand and mud, under the brackish water or the barren marshes, Spina must lie. But the great question remained—where exactly along this extensive stretch of coast should the search begin?

It was only in this century, in the quite recent past, that a somewhat unusual clue was found. At the beginning of the twenties, museum officials and antique dealers were driven to a surprising deduction. They realized that there must be people who had somehow managed to tap a rich source in ancient Spina, because otherwise it was impossible to explain how Greek vases and Etruscan bronzes kept turning up on the black market for antiques. An army of snoopers was set in motion, the police and customs officials were roped in to help. But the result was nil; nothing was discovered about the source. Nobody suspected how the illegal diggers pursued their clandestine and highly profitable trade within range of numbers of official observers, and under the eyes of the police. As it later turned out, the diggers were in fact fishers. They lived at Comacchio, an ancient little town on a wide lagoon, some nineteen miles north of Ravenna. The shallow waters of the famous *valli*, with their marshes and seabirds, which stretch far and wide all round the little fishing town, provided a bountiful "hunting ground."

Eels are the principal catch, and the fishermen quite openly and officially went out to fish for eels in the traditional way. In their shallow-draft flat boats they glided slowly over the wide waters, armed with their traditional harpoonlike lance. This, they discovered, could be used to fish up not only eels, but also the much more lucrative, indeed highly valuable painted vases. Just one of these would bring in more than months of laborious fishing of the ordinary sort. Thus, in complete secrecy, a profitable vase fishing went on, and no outsider noticed anything. After all, why should anyone see anything unusual in eel fishers going out at night?

It was by chance, as the result of an administrative measure for quite different purposes, that one day the authorities got on the track of the Comacchio fisher folk. The government had decided on the draining and reclamation of the troublesome flooded areas. No sooner had the work begun in 1922 than there was a surprise discovery in the Valle Trebba, about four miles west of Comacchio. The workmen came upon a vast necropolis, and what they dug out—the first legal archeological finds—revealed the site of ancient Spina.

Under the supervision of Enrico Arias, director of the Museo Archeologico Nazionale of Ferrara, the contents of the first graves were dug out. When scores upon scores of magnificent vases were found, it suddenly became clear why the people of Comacchio had so vigorously opposed the land reclamation scheme. They feared that it would rob them of their main source of income, the vase-fishing grounds which had proved so profitable.

Soon Professor Arias's assistant, the young archeologist N. Alfieri, was put in charge of the excavations, and he quickly recognized that these burials differed from those in Tuscany. He found no imposing

174

stone tomb chambers, no sarcophagi or stone funerary urns. And instead of grave *stelae,* the sand yielded only smooth slabs of rock.

For all that, the grave goods were rich and splendid. The votive gifts of 1,213 graves were recovered before the campaign was interrupted in 1935. They included native work—Etruscan bronzes and gold jewelry—and imported Attic vases dating from the sixth to fourth century B.C. The glass cases of the Ferrara archeological museum rapidly filled up with the unexpected treasures from the Valle Trebba.

It seemed that the great goal, Spina itself, could not be far away. So large a necropolis, with such richly furnished graves, could not be all that distant from the city whose inhabitants had been buried there for centuries. But this assumption was not confirmed until work on the land reclamation scheme was resumed after an interval of eighteen years.

In an area hitherto submerged under the waters of the Valle Pega, a second and equally large necropolis was discovered in 1954. A further 1,810 graves yielded up their treasures of pottery and bronze, all the various articles of luxury and daily use which reflect the life of the Etruscans.

It seemed certain that Spina must lie somewhere between the two cemeteries. The final key to its ultimate discovery came from aerial photography. Some of the photographs taken for the purposes of land cultivation schemes solved the centuries-old puzzle. This bird's-eye view of the northeastern edge of the Valli di Comacchio showed something unusual. Underneath the white lines of the modern drainage channels of the reclaimed area appeared a ghostly network of dark lines and light rectangles.

> **Alfieri realized at a glance that the spectral dark lines indicated vegetation growing taller on the site of ancient canals and thus revealed the layout of the buried city.**

Alfieri realized at a glance that the spectral dark lines indicated vegetation growing taller on the site of ancient canals and thus revealed the layout of the buried city. Not only the precise topographical situation was clear; even before the soil was touched by a spade, the town plan could be studied. The *insulae,* the blocks of houses, the roads and canals could be pinpointed. The densely inhabited town center lay around the harbor quarter, on a sixty-foot-wide canal leading to the sea. All this could be clearly made out. And smaller settlements were visible on the periphery. The whole city had once covered an area of about 870 acres.

As the archeologists got to work with the help of the aerial photographs their expectations were confirmed. A line of wooden piles was discovered; they had once supported the bank of the main canal. Clearly this was the *Canal Grande* of Spina, the great waterway up which ships from all over the Mediterranean had come with their cargoes, above all with the precious vases from Athens, first the black-figured ones and then the red-figured. Wedged in the wooden piles was an insignificant handle of a *skyphos,* or cup; it dated to the fourth century B.C. and silenced any remaining doubts. The excavators had hit upon the heart of the ancient port.

The construction of the Grand Canal revealed the experienced hand of Etruscan technicians. "The harbor canal," emphasizes Alfieri, "bears witness to a trading settlement in country where the Etruscans applied their hydraulic engineering skill to keep open the waterway between Spina and the sea. The Etruscans' ability to adapt themselves to a region geographically so different from their Etruscan motherland shows in the simple layout of the residential areas of Spina (and of Adria) as well as in the ingenious system applied by them to ensure the continuous functioning of the sea port of Etruria Padana."

The rediscovered harbor installations were only a fraction of pioneering works that extended far beyond Spina. They once formed part of a unique large-scale canalization system that served both to regulate the Po and to provide numerous waterways for transport. Some idea of the size and capacity of the system developed by the Etruscans on the Adriatic coast may be gathered from the accounts of ancient authors. They make clear how perfectly the experts of the time succeeded in taming unpredictable nature over a whole countryside so that it served men's needs.

The emperor Claudius, on the way to Rome to celebrate his triumph over Britain, sailed out of the Po into the Adriatic, "in what was a vast palace rather than a ship," as Pliny says. He sailed from the mouth of the Po nearest Ravenna, at the point where the river Vatrenus (modern Santerno) joins the Po and formed a large basin, says Pliny, who notes: "This mouth was formerly called . . . the Spineticus from the city of Spina that formerly stood near it." Nearby, to the north, was another Po river mouth, the Ostium Caprasiae, at modern Comacchio. Deposits of silt and sand from the Po over half a millennium had pushed the coast forward, and Spina, like Ravenna to the south, was no longer on the sea. When Strabo wrote his *Geography* in the first century A.D., Spina was already "ninety stadia," some ten miles, distant from the coast.

From the main channel of the Po the ramifications of a system of waterways spread out over the countryside. Pliny, who, as the commander of a fleet, may be presumed knowledgeable on such matters, says that this system was "first made by the Tuscans, thus discharging the flow of the river across the marshes of the Atriani called the Seven Seas, with the famous harbor of the Tuscan town of Atria which formerly gave the name of Atriatic to the sea now called the Adriatic." The "Seven Seas" mentioned by Pliny were lagoons, separated from the open sea by sandbanks.

Amid this chain of lagoons the Etruscans made new canals to act as auxiliary branches of the Po. They constructed cross-connections between the individual lagoons, and then further connections between the former. The most northerly of these canals, the "Philistina," led to Atria. Thus an extensive system of inland waterways was constructed along the coast. As late as the time of the emperor Vespasian, says Pliny, galleys could still travel from Ravenna to Atria.

Etruscan hydraulic experts contrived to do what seemed impossible, namely, to confine the wide river at Spina to its continually rising bed. They did this by means of the artificially constructed auxiliary branches of the river and the canals. Even when "the melting of the snows at the rising of the Dogstar causes it to swell in volume," as Pliny puts it, this system carried the annual floods away into the lagoons and the sea. By this means they mastered the terrible inundations, with their dangers to land and people, which even now still occur in the region.

"The masterpiece of their hydraulic know-how," says Mario Lopes Pegna, "was their abolition of the periodic scourge of floods in the lower reaches of the Po. This was a gigantic undertaking accomplished by digging a whole network of coordinated canals, and at the same time damming the river with caissons or brushwood.

Special schools, the forerunners of our technical institutes, gave training for a profession which evidently required the knowledge and skills of the hydraulic engineer and the agronomist."

These Etruscan experts had carried out a project which was not only remarkable for its time, but was something hitherto unknown in western Europe. This was the first time that the techniques of irrigation and drainage, which had long been practiced in Mesopotamia and the Nile valley, were applied on such a large scale in the West.

Under Etruscan control of the river and associated waterways, the plain of the Po in its lower reaches was transformed from a region of recurring floods, inhabited only by nomadic shepherds, into fertile farmland, yielding grain, vegetables, and good pasture. Polybius, Strabo, Virgil, and other ancient writers again and again extol the abundant harvests of this region, the vast fields of grain and the vineyards whose output required casks "larger than houses."

From this angle it is easy to understand the statement by Polybius that: "The Celts, being close neighbors of the Etruscans and associating much with them, cast covetous eyes on their beautiful country, and on a small pretext, suddenly attacked them with a large army and, expelling them from the plain of the Po, occupied it themselves." But all that came much later, after a long period of close commercial relations between the two peoples. For the Etruscans, long accustomed to trading with foreign peoples, lost no time in making contacts in countries far to the north.

Beyond the Alps, Etruscan merchants established an extensive network of foreign trade which introduced the finest products of the Mediterranean, in particular of Italy and Greece, to the principal countries and peoples of Europe, and kept them supplied with these goods. It was the Etruscans who first opened up the markets of central Europe extensively.

"Situated at the center of the peninsula, Etruria was in fact the only beacon to radiate its civilization from early times upon generally backward peoples."

"If the political rule and direct colonization of the Etruscans only extended over part of continental Italy," Pallottino points out, "their commercial activities and their cultural influence reached much further afield. Situated at the center of the peninsula, Etruria was in fact the only beacon to radiate its civilization from early times upon generally backward peoples."

From the Etruscan towns in the Po valley a copious flow of goods was sent over the Alps long before the Romans had even heard the recipient countries' names. The traces of that traffic are scattered all over Europe, though it is only in recent decades that they have gradually come to light. They are evidence of the first common market at the dawn of western European history, all knowledge of which had been lost, and whose very existence was barely suspected until recently. Goods exported by Etruscan merchants have been discovered in Austria, France, Hungary, and Poland. They have been found in Switzerland and the Rhineland, and even in Scandinavia. At Hassle, in Sweden, a regular little "treasury" of Etruscan bronzes represents the most northerly find.

It seems that Etruria made its first trading contacts with the lands north of the Alps at a very early date, before the migrating Phocaeans in about 600 B.C. founded Massalia. The earliest discoveries north of the Alps that point to Etruscan influence and contacts date from the seventh century B.C. It was the period when another great nation, the Celts, appeared as such on the scene in the southwestern part of central Europe, when the Celtic tribes coalesced into an identifiable community with a common cultural and linguistic heritage.

In the middle of the seventh century B.C. wagon graves beneath a barrow appear for the first time. Warriors are buried in wooden mortuary houses, laid on wagons with their weapons, their iron swords and spears. The graves often contain horse-bits and pottery vessels, as well as joints of beef and pork. As in the Etruscan royal graves at Caere and Praeneste, the wagon wheels stand leaning against the walls. The oldest of such burials are in Bohemia, upper Austria, and Bavaria. Later, in the sixth century B.C., as the result of Celtic expansion and migration, these graves appear farther to the west, and their furnishings or contents become more and more splendid with imported, foreign articles. These later graves are found first around the source of the Danube, then on the middle Rhine and in eastern France, in Burgundy, near the source of the Seine.

The warriors or chieftains in the wagon burials represent the ancestors of an emerging Celtic unity. From their predecessors the Illyrians they took over the exploitation of salt and iron ore. Their culture is known as the Hallstatt culture, from the place of that name where it was first discovered in the Salzkammergut, Austria. Near an ancient salt mine there, a great cemetery was excavated in the last century. It yielded, along with iron swords and daggers, magnificent bronzes, some of them from Italy. The people who included in the grave furnishings such valuable foreign articles owed their wealth to the export of salt, which at that time had a high value.

The use of iron, inhumation instead of cremation, burial with wagons or carts and horse-bits—all this was new. It indicates imports and influences from other countries and peoples. But from which? This is a question on which the experts still do not agree. "The wood-built burial chamber under a barrow," says T. G. E. Powell, the great expert on the Celts, "seems to point either to an eastern source . . . or to reflect influence stemming ultimately from the Etruscans whose burial pomps, with funerary cars and inhumation, had reached their height at this time."

One thing, however, is undisputed. From the sixth century B.C. Etruscan influence is clearly noticeable. Goods of all kinds began to cross the Alps from the Po valley. Etruscan traders exported the products of native industry, bronzes and pottery, and also wine. Furthermore the Etruscans offered objects in great demand among themselves, namely Greek products, chiefly Attic vases, which seem also to have delighted the rough northern warriors.

Soon, however, the Etruscans came up against keen competition from the Greeks in the west. From Massalia, up the valleys of the Rhone and the Saône, Greek traders had become active as far as the Swiss lakes and Württemberg on the upper Danube. Greek imports have been found in Celtic wagon graves at Vilsingen near Sigmaringen, at Kappel on the Rhine, at Lahr in Baden. They date from between 560 and 520 B.C. At that period a chieftain's hill-fort of a unique kind was built in Württemberg and occupied for several generations. Excavations of this fort, known as the Heuneburg, revealed a curious fact. Part of the wall was built of unbaked clay bricks. This was something entirely new at that date among the peoples north of the Alps.

It is highly unlikely that the barbaric chieftain had thought out for himself this method of construction. He had doubtless sent for foreign builders. But who were they? Speculation turned first to the Greeks, because the pottery found on the site was Greek. Some scholars thought that the builders might have come from Massalia. Maybe so, but geographically much nearer to Württemberg than the Rhone delta was the Po valley ruled by Etruscans. Building with clay bricks, introduced by the Etruscans, had long been common in Italy as far south as Campania. Even the backward settlers on the Tiber had learned it and had given up their straw huts. And Etruscans also traded in Greek vases such as were found in the Heuneburg fort. They could order such vases at any time from the Greek merchants settled at Spina.

The influence of Etruria's foreign trade was at first strongest among the Celtic peoples on the upper course of the Danube, and then on the middle Rhine and in Burgundy. Soon wine took first place among imports from the south. It was much appreciated and became a serious competitor of native Celtic beer. The warrior chieftains were heavy drinkers, and once they had got a taste for wine, they ordered it in ever-increasing quantities. Its introduction opened up a vast new market for it north of the Alps, as well as one for the necessary drinking services. Along with the wine, all kinds of containers, mixing bowls, and other vessels were supplied—flagons, amphorae, cups, both Etruscan and Greek. The transport of these goods, laborious and long though it often was, brought a good return.

Other articles of Etruscan provenance that were in great demand were bronze flagons, cauldrons, bowls, and incense burners. But it seems that before long the northern purchasers expressed their own very definite wishes. What they wanted most of all were large articles.

In the burial mound of a Celtic princess at Vix near Châtillon-sur-Seine was found a big bronze *crater,* a mixing bowl. It stood nearly five feet six inches high, and weighed over 457 pounds. Fragments of another *crater* unearthed at the Heuneburg fort belonged to a vessel of similar dimensions. It was a bowl painted with scenes from the Theseus legend. At Stuttgart a large *kylix* or goblet was discovered. It was evidently considered most precious, because a Celtic craftsman had mended it with gold bands. The Etruscan craftsmen, in their turn, could not escape the northern taste for bulk, and even their beautiful beaked flagons were produced in unusually large sizes.

The finds at Spina indicate how great the demand for vases from Athens must have been, in addition to that for Etruscan jugs, tripod candelabras, and flagons. The number of Greek vases runs into thousands, many of extra-large size.

To the Etruscans, Spina was not only a center for their own production, where they also made imitation Greek goods, but a pottery market as well, the place where purchasers found a wide selection. Many Greek traders had set up there, and orders could be placed with them for goods which the Etruscans then sold to their Celtic customers. At the same time they offered for sale to the Greek merchants articles of Etruscan production.

Along with their towns, their agricultural and industrial know-how, the Etruscans brought many other valuable cultural gifts to the Po valley, in the shape of their art, religion, language, and above all, their script.

The famous bronze liver discovered at Piacenza is believed to be a model used in the training of *haruspices*. The *disciplina etrusca* was a key element in Etruscan life and thought in the Po valley as elsewhere. And much of it seems to have penetrated beyond the Alps. Powell speaks of the potent, exotic influence of the Etruscans on Celtic cult art. "This is manifest in a few surviving sculptures mainly from the Middle Rhenish zone. Here, individual motifs of Etruscan origin are found in sculpture . . . The relief-carved, four-sided pillar from Pfalzfeld, in the Hunsrück, is the most outstanding of the existing monuments."

The Middle-Rhenish Celts, Powell adds, received from the Etruscans not only the practice of raising sculptured stone monuments, but probably also "the idea of portraying two-headed, or two-faced, Janus-like, images. The finest surviving example is the tall stone from Holzgerlingen in Württemberg."

To obtain a more precise picture of the extent and effects of Etruscan influence north of the Alps would require a detailed study of all the material so far discovered and now scattered in many collections and museums. At present only the vague outlines are discernible of what the civilization of central Europe owed in prehistoric times to the "forgotten people."

For the Etruscans were the teachers of the Po valley inhabitants in the arts of reading and writing, previously unknown to them. The Etruscan script gradually spread between the Apennines and the Alps, just as it had among the Umbrians, Faliscans, Latins, and Oscans, as far south as Campania. "The alphabets of the Veneti, the Raetians, the Lepontians and of the other Alpine peoples were linked to the so-called northern Etruscan alphabet adopted in the Po valley during the fifth century," says Pallottino.

> **For the Etruscans were the teachers of the Po valley inhabitants in the arts of reading and writing, previously unknown to them.**

And it seems, too, that one of the major peoples north of the Alps, the Germans, owed their earliest alphabet to the Etruscans of the Po valley, though until recently this was disputed. "It is now certain," says the Etruscologist Ambros Josef Pfiffig, "that the runic script is derived from the north Etruscan alphabet." The peoples living in the Alps transmitted it farther northward, and, if we accept Livy, Etruscans at a later date lived in the eastern Alps.

XIII

Rome's Debt
to Tarquinius Superbus

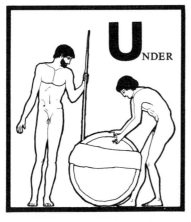

NDER

LUCIUS TARQUINIUS, CALLED SU-
perbus, the Proud, the third
Etruscan king of Rome, the reactionaries triumphed. His accession to the throne was a victory
for the old order, a return to absolute dictatorship. The constitutional reforms of Servius Tullius
were abrogated. A tyrannous rule
began, worse than anything before, and the new regime was
hated by the people.

Lucius Tarquinius, says Dionysius, "despising not only the populace, but the patricians as well, by whom he had been brought to
power . . . transformed his rule into an avowed tyranny."

A reign of terror began in Rome, according to Dionysius: "And
first he placed about his person a guard of very daring men, both
natives and foreigners, armed with swords and spears, who camped
round the palace at night and attended him in the daytime wherever he went, effectually securing him from the attempts of con-

spirators." Everywhere there were spies who "secretly inquired into everything that was said and done," and agents provocateurs who lured their neighbors into criticizing the tyrant. Trumped-up charges were brought against prominent men who were hostile to him or "those whom he thought to be aggrieved by the change and those who had great riches." Tarquinius condemned the accused to death or banishment. "There were some who were even seized in their homes or in the country and secretly murdered by him."

He began his rule by high-handed, sweeping changes. "For the laws drawn up by Tullius . . . were all abolished by Tarquinius, who did not leave even the tables on which the laws were written, but ordered these also to be removed from the Forum and destroyed," reports Dionysius. "After this he abolished the taxes based on the census and revived the original form of taxation; and whenever he required money, the poorest citizen contributed the same amount as the richest."

He selected from the plebeians "such as were loyal to himself and fit for war." "He transacted the public business at home, for the most part . . . and only occasionally in the Forum . . . His decisions in controversies relating to contracts he rendered, not with regard to justice and law, but according to his own moods."

In foreign affairs Tarquinius Superbus pursued the same line as his two predecessors. He made war on the Sabines and conquered them. On the other hand, "he made particular efforts," says Livy, "to win the friendship of the Latins . . . he went beyond mere official relations with the Latin nobility, and married his daughter to Octavius Mamilius of Tusculum, by far the most distinguished bearer of the Latin name." After a few military campaigns he scored an outstanding success for Etruscan policy when he managed to get Rome recognized as the head of the Latin league.

In home affairs, "his first concern was the temple of Jupiter on the Capitoline, which he hoped to leave as a memorial of the royal house of the Tarquins—of the father who had made the vow, and of the son who had fulfilled it." For the completion of the temple, "builders and engineers were brought in from all over Etruria." These were the specialists, the gifted artists, the modelers of terracotta, the craftsmen and building workers of whom Etruria possessed an abundance. The native population, accustomed only to farming, and inexperienced in the building trades, had to do the fetching and carrying. For after selecting the plebeians wanted for the army, Tarquinius "compelled the rest to labor on the public works in the city," says Dionysius.

The name of one of these Etruscan artists, a great master, is known, and so are some of his works. Excavations at Veii in 1916 brought to light pieces of the finest terra-cotta figures ever found in Etruria. One of these was a painted statue, over life-size, representing Apollo. The figure of the god originally stood high up on the roof-tree of what is known as the Portonaccio temple. On the same site the fragments of two other superb statues were found, one of a woman carrying a child in her arms, and the other of the god Hermes. They are all clearly by the hand of the same outstanding master and are believed to come from the workshop of the famous Etruscan sculptor, Vulca of Veii.

This was the artist who was entrusted with making the terra-cotta statue of Jupiter for the Capitoline temple. Pliny explains that the statue "was made of clay, and that hence arose the custom of painting it with minium." And he adds: "Such, in those times, were the most esteemed statues of the gods." The quadriga, the four-horse chariot, that adorned the temple pediment, was also made of terra-cotta and likewise in a Veii workshop. This is recalled in a legend told by Plutarch. According to this, the clay monument, when placed in the kiln to be baked, swelled up so much that it could only be got out by dismantling the kiln. The soothsayers, asked to interpret this unusual occurrence, declared that this meant success and power to those who possessed the quadriga. The people of Veii, when they heard this prophecy, refused to deliver the sculpture to Rome. However, another prodigy a few days later persuaded them to change their minds and hand over the quadriga.

Etrurian workshops like that of the great Vulca had long since acquired an extraordinary skill in the production of sculpture in relief and in the round. They made terra-cotta revetments used as decorative friezes on temples and the villas of the aristocracy. They were past masters in the firing of large clay statues. And these were

> *The soothsayers, asked to interpret this unusual occurrence, declared that this meant success and power to those who possessed the quadriga.*

Bronze statuette of Minerva; sixth century B.C.

a novelty to Rome. The inhabitants of Italy had previously, like the Greeks even in Homer's time, known and worshipped only aniconic gods.

A site had been prepared for the temple, as we know from Dionysius, by building high retaining walls around a hill and filling in the space with earth. When, subsequently, the foundations for the building were being dug, a strange prodigy occurred. "When the excavation had been carried down to a great depth," says Dionysius, "there was found the head of a man newly slain." Tarquinius thereupon "ordered the workmen to leave off digging and, assembling the native soothsayers, inquired of them what the prodigy meant. And when they could give no explanation but conceded to the Tyrrhenians the mastery of this science, he inquired of them who was the ablest soothsayer among the Tyrrhenians, and when he had found out, sent the most distinguished of the citizens to him as ambassadors."

The interpretation of the famous *haruspex* with which the ambassadors returned was: " 'Tell your fellow citizens it is ordained by fate that the place in which you found the head shall be the head of all Italy.' Since that time the place is called the Capitoline hill from the head that was found there; for the Romans call heads *capita.*"

This story may be no more than a pious legend later incorporated into the account of the building. But Livy knew what he was doing when he quoted it. To his readers, five centuries after the event, that "head" could only refer to the Roman empire. But Tarquinius Superbus, when he heard the interpretation, must have taken it very differently. To him it was a prophecy that the Etruscan city on the Tiber would become head of all the Leagues of Twelve. For at that time Etruscan sovereignty extended from the Alps to the Gulf of Salerno. Thus, having heard the interpretation, it was natural that Tarquinius "set the artisans to work and built the greater part of the temple."

With the new building on the Capitoline, the sacred art and architecture of the Etruscans made their appearance on the Tiber. High above the Forum, the temple was to crown their earlier pioneer civilizing work. The prototype for the new sanctuary was provided by Etruscan temples. Their sacred rules of construction, not those of the Greeks, determined the form and proportions, both external and internal, of the new building.

"It stood upon a high base and was eight hundred feet in circuit, each side measuring close to two hundred feet," says Dionysius; "indeed, one would find the excess of the length over the width to be but slight, in fact not a full fifteen feet." The temple had "three rows of columns on the front, facing the south, and a single row on each side. The temple consists of three parallel shrines." This was to provide for the triad of gods "under one pediment and one roof." The gods that Tarquinius Superbus brought to the new temple of his city on the Tiber also came from Etruria.

Which gods were they? None other than Jupiter, Juno, and Minerva. But it was only the Romans who gave them these names. North of the Tiber they were named differently. In Etruria Jupiter was Tinia, the highest of their gods and the central figure of the Etruscan pantheon. He spoke in the thunderbolt and held a symbol of it in his hand, and he was worshipped as the ruler of the gods in every Etruscan city. In a festival procession the *lucumones,* the Etruscan kings, wore the god's wreath, tunic, and toga. In the Etruscan lunar month, which the Romans also adopted for themselves, the middle of the month when the moon is at the full was sacred to Tinia, and this day of the Ides was celebrated. It gave the name *idus* to the Romans.

In the Etruscan temple, along with Tinia, the goddesses Uni and Menrva were worshipped—the Roman Juno and Minerva. Temples to the former are known in several cities of Etruria. At Veii the goddess whom the Romans called Juno had the second name Regina, that is, queen. As the symbol of her rule she carried a spear, which later in old Roman legal symbolism became the sign of the *imperium* and *municipium.* The new moon was sacred to her. Menrva is represented on many Etruscan bronze mirrors. She too was a chief goddess. Her great feast was celebrated in Etruria in March on the fifth day after the Ides. The festival was taken over by Rome and celebrated as the *quinquatrus* and—by error and for good measure—was made to last five days.

Under the skillful control of Etruscan architects and artists, a unique temple grew to completion more than fifty years earlier than the much admired Parthenon in Athens. It was built at about the time when the Greeks were dedicating on the Acropolis their *Korai,* those figures of girls with a gentle smile. And in about the same decade, a great contemporary of Tarquinius Superbus, the Persian king Cyrus, ordered the rebuilding of another temple famous in history.

In Jerusalem in 520 B.C. the Jews, who had returned from their Babylonian exile, began to rebuild the temple of Solomon which the Babylonians had destroyed in 586 B.C.

The temple high up on the Capitol did not need to fear comparisons. With its splendid, brightly colored friezes and terra-cotta reliefs and figures on roof and walls, it was one of the most beautiful in the world of its time, and one of the biggest. Jerusalem's new temple was smaller, only 102 feet 4 inches wide. And even among the most famous Greek temples which were built later, there were few that could rival the width of the new Etruscan temple on the Tiber, be it the temple of Artemis at Ephesus, the Heraion of Samos, or the Olympeion at Agrigento. The largest was the temple of Artemis at Ephesus, one of the Seven Wonders of the World, with a width of 180 feet 9 inches (55.10 m.). The temple at Rome measured 163 feet 2 inches (49.73 m.).

> This monument to Etruscan art and religion, erected at a tIme whon Etruria was at the zenith of its power, was never to serve those who inspired and built it.

And yet, there is something tragic and bitterly ironic about the building on the Capitol. This monument to Etruscan art and religion, erected at a time when Etruria was at the zenith of its power, was never to serve those who inspired and built it. It was never to celebrate their greatness, their deeds. The temple of Jupiter Capitolinus became the official sanctuary of another people, of a people who were not constructive, did not care for peaceful, civilizing undertakings as did the Etruscan pioneers. On the contrary, they were a people who conquered and destroyed, who created a military state feared all over the world. The temple the Etruscans built became the focal point of Roman religious ideology and the symbol of Roman power.

As such it was to be, for more than five centuries, the setting of the thanksgiving sacrifices at the great victory celebrations after wars and conquests. And defeated Etruscan towns were to be among the earliest to give occasion for such celebrations, the booty taken from them was to be paraded in triumphant processions which themselves were copied from the Etruscans.

Rome refused to believe, let alone officially admit, that the temple was the work of Etruscans. Everything possible was done to suppress the fact in the Roman traditions. Tarquinius Superbus, says Dionysius, in accordance with Livy's version, "built the greater part of the temple, though he was not able to complete the whole work, being driven from power too soon." The Roman historians' date for the official dedication of the temple, September 13, 509 B.C., conveniently places this event into a time when, according to their own accounts, Rome had ceased to be ruled by an Etruscan king. And posterity accepted this version.

But this is another point on which recent research has cast serious doubt. Some modern scholars now believe the Tarquin rule ended later, and Andreas Alföldi, in his *Early Rome and the Latins,* concludes that Tarquinius Superbus himself "consecrated his construction in 509 B.C." In any event, the Etruscans certainly were the actual builders of the Capitoline temple, which remained the biggest in Rome down to the end of the republic and became the model for numerous later sanctuaries in the city. These include the temples of Fortuna, and of Mater Matuta, the temple of Castor and Pollux in the Forum, that of Ceres at the foot of the Aventine, and many in the colonies. They too were made of wood and decorated with terra-cotta reliefs and statues. It was not until imperial times that the Greek taste for highly decorated buildings faced with marble became fashionable.

With the expansion of Rome the Capitoline cult spread out over the conquered lands and peoples. Tarquinius Superbus could hardly have imagined what he had started with the building he created, or what historical significance it was to acquire. For Tinia-Jupiter became a divinity acknowledged the world over.

No other building remained so closely connected with the history of Rome and for so long a time. Indeed, it outlasted the city. In 83 B.C. it burned down, but Sulla restored it, and appropriated for it Corinthian columns from the unfinished temple of Olympian Zeus in Athens. After several more fires, it was last rebuilt, even more splendidly, by the emperor Domitian in A.D. 85. When the empire collapsed under the invasion of new peoples from the north, Stilicho, the Vandal general of the western Roman empire, stripped the gold leaf off the temple doors, and Gaiseric, the king of the Vandals, seized the gilded tiles of the roof in the sack of Rome.

The ruins of the temple were still there in the fifth century A.D.

By this time, of course, a thousand years after it was built, the threefold sanctuary had ceased to have any meaning. The ancient city was now under the sway of a new religion, the Christian. Its adherents no longer honored the pagan triad; they believed instead in the Trinity.

As the temple was nearing completion, the king ordered that other works left unfinished by the first Tarquin should be completed. A large number of laborers, says Livy, "were put on to other tasks less spectacular but more laborious still, such as the construction of the tiers of seats in the Circus and the excavations of the Cloaca Maxima, or Great Sewer, designed to carry off the sewage of the entire city by an underground pipeline. The magnitude of both these projects," adds Livy, "could hardly be equaled by any work even of modern times."

> **Only one construction, seldom visited by tourists, still testifies to the ingenious architecture of the third Etruscan king and his countrymen, namely, that remarkable structure the Cloaca Maxima.**

"At these undertakings," says Dionysius, "all the poor labored, receiving from him but a moderate allowance of grain. Some of them were employed in quarrying stone, others in hewing timber, some in driving the wagons that transported these materials, and others in carrying the burdens themselves upon their shoulders, still others in digging the subterranean drains and constructing the arches over them and in erecting the porticoes . . . Thus the people, being worn out by these works, had no rest."

All that remains of the race course at the foot of the ruined imperial palaces on the Palatine, is a vast sandy, dusty field with a raised, sloping circumvallation of earth, and a few stumps of columns and fragments of masonry. There is only a plaque now to show that here was once the Circus Maximus, finally finished in imperial times, which drew spectators in tens of thousands.

Only one construction, seldom visited by tourists, still testifies to the ingenious architecture of the third Etruscan king and his countrymen, namely, that remarkable structure the Cloaca Maxima. A few yards downstream from the Tiber island, on the left bank near the Ponte Palatino, there is visible in the river wall, when the water level is not too high, an arch made of three concentric courses of stone blocks. Here is the outlet of the underground canal that runs for some six hundred yards from the Forum and keeps it dry by collecting the water that flows down from the Quirinal and Viminal. Devised and built on Etruscan initiative, this construction, which drained the swampy lowlands, became, as it were, the real "midwife" of Rome. Subsequently improved and extended, it still functions.

No one pays any attention to it now, or is at all surprised at it. And no one praises it now as Pliny the Elder did in his *Natural History* soon after the beginning of the Christian era. When he comes to speak about the "marvelous buildings at Rome," he counts among them "the enormous foundations of the Capitol" as well as "the public sewers, a work more stupendous than any; as mountains had to be pierced for their construction, and, like the hanging city . . . navigation had to be carried on beneath Rome . . . For this purpose there are seven rivers, made, by artificial channels, to flow beneath the city . . . It is said that Tarquinius made these sewers of dimensions sufficiently large to admit of a wagon laden with hay passing along them . . . Enormous as are the accumulations that are carried along above, the work of the channels never gives way. Houses falling spontaneously to ruins, or leveled with the ground by conflagrations, are continually battering against them; the ground, too, is shaken by earthquakes every now and then; and yet, built as they were in the days of Tarquinius Priscus, seven hundred years ago, these constructions have survived, all but unharmed."

Pliny did not exaggerate. The Cloaca Maxima, the beginnings of which go back to the rule of Tarquinius Priscus, is one of the oldest hydraulic constructions of this kind in Europe, probably preceded only by the drainage system to create the new *Agora* in Athens.

Tarquinius Superbus seemed determined to augment the strength, prestige, and appearance of his city. As though vast building projects were not enough, he made an interesting donation of books to the city. The books he presented, the first and for a long time the only ones in Rome, were from then on constantly consulted and studied. For at least the more eminent among the inhabitants on the Tiber had meanwhile learned to read and write from the Etruscans. It is now known for certain that the foreigners from beyond the river had successfully played the schoolmaster in this field too. Fragments of black *bucchero* vessels discovered in the deepest strata of Rome have silenced doubts, for scratched on them are inscriptions in Etruscan. Many of the shards date from 525 B.C.

The king's donation was the Sibylline Books, a work packed with oracular sayings which were believed to foretell the future. Dionysius says that securing them was "another very wonderful piece of good luck." A woman "who was not a native of the country" brought them. After "bidding him take great care of them," the woman "disappeared from among men."

"There is no possession of the Romans, sacred or profane," says Dionysius, "which they guard so carefully as they do the Sibylline oracles. They consult them, by order of the senate, when the state is in the grip of party strife or some great misfortune has happened to them in war, or some important prodigies and apparitions have been seen which are difficult of interpretation, as has often happened. These oracles till the time of the Marsian War [the "Social War," 91–88 B.C.] were kept underground in the temple of Jupiter Capitolinus in a stone chest . . . But when the temple was burned after the close of the 173rd Olympiad [83 B.C.] . . . these oracles . . . were destroyed by the fire." As is known, this did not put an end to the Sibylline oracles. There were copies of them. They continued to be consulted officially in times of national emergency until about A.D. 400. Then they were destroyed at the instigation of Christian authorities.

As for Tarquinius Superbus, he was not to remain in enjoyment of all he had created, all the great public works and buildings. Out of the blue came events that exiled him from his empire and his city.

XIV

Etruscans Establish the Republic

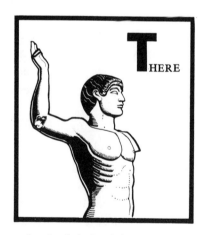

THERE HAD BEEN UNREST FOR A LONG while in Rome. The tyrannical government of Tarquinius Superbus was hated, and not only by peasants and shepherds who had been forced to labor at quite unfamiliar tasks, and complained that "like slaves purchased with money" they had "to endure shameful hardships," as Dionysius put it. The aristocrats, too, hated it because they were deprived of their rights. Tarquinius had abrogated the Servian constitution and ruled as an arbitrary despot. No one's life was safe, nor was his family or property.

Men hostile to the king and his regime began to meet secretly and concert their plans. By an irony of fate there was not a single Roman among them. The leading spirits in the revolutionary conspiracy were all Etruscans, indeed close relatives of the royal family. It was these members of the Etruscan aristocracy who were to overthrow the tyrant and introduce a new constitution and form of the state, one which the Romans were later always to speak of with pride—the republic.

Lucius Junius Brutus, son of Tarquin's sister, was the leader of the conspiracy, providing it with ideas, and urging it on. With him were Spurius Lucretius, an aristocrat of Etruscan origin, and Tarquinius Collatinus, a cousin of the king, according to tradition a son of Egerius, brother of the first Etruscan king Tarquinius Priscus.

A serious crime, committed just then, is said to have given the signal for the conspirators to put their long-plotted coup d'état into effect. One of the king's sons had raped a Roman woman. Any other event might have provided the pretext. But a crime against morality, committed by an Etruscan prince, admirably suited the purposes of later Roman historians. It offered a welcome opportunity to extol the virtue of Roman womanhood, and establish a national propaganda image of the chaste and virtuous Roman wife completely occupied with her domestic duties. It also provided an opportunity to calumniate the Etruscan ladies, whose life and respected position in society were abominations to the peasant outlook of the Romans. They were shocked that Etruscan women, elegantly dressed, jeweled, and made up, actually joined the men at banquets. What was more, they were educated, knew how to read and write, and, like Tanaquil, could interpret omens, and even took part in political discussions.

Both Livy and Dionysius make the most of the sexual crime and describe it in detail in the style of a Hellenistic novel, with lots of tears and a heroic end for the violated wife. According to Livy, when the siege of Ardea, the chief town of the Rutuli, proved a lengthy affair, "the young princes . . . spent most of their leisure enjoying themselves in entertainments on the most lavish scale. They were drinking one day in the quarters of Sextus Tarquinius —Collatinus, son of Egerius, was also present—when someone chanced to mention the subject of wives. Each of them, of course, extravagantly praised his own; and the rivalry got hotter and hotter, until Collatinus"—the only one married not to an Etruscan, but to a Roman—"suddenly cried: 'Stop! What need is there of words, when in a few hours we can prove beyond doubt the incomparable superiority of my Lucretia? . . . Why shouldn't we ride to Rome and see with our own eyes what kind of women our wives are?' "

So they galloped off to Rome, where "the wives of the royal princes were found enjoying themselves with a group of young friends at a dinner-party," and then on to Collatia, "where they found Lucretia very differently employed." She was doing her duty in the way the Roman countryfolk had always considered proper. "It was already late at night, but there, in the hall of her house, surrounded by her busy maidservants, she was still hard at work by lamplight upon her spinning."

The visit was to have an unexpected sequel. "Lucretia's beauty, and proven chastity, kindled in Sextus Tarquinius [the king's son] the flame of lust, and determined him to debauch her." A few days later, when her husband, Tarquinius Collatinus, was away, Sextus called on her again at her house, where she welcomed him hospitably. When the house was asleep and all was quiet, he "made his way to Lucretia's room determined to rape her. She was asleep. Laying his hand on her breast, 'Lucretia,' he whispered, 'not a sound! I am Sextus Tarquinius. I am armed—if you utter a word, I will kill you.' " However, the threat of death did not persuade Lucretia to yield. Whereupon Sextus used a more subtle argument. " 'If death will not move you, dishonor shall. I will kill you first, then cut the throat of a slave and lay his naked body by your side. Will they not believe that you have been caught in adultery with a servant—and paid the price?' "

Then, as Livy writes, "Even the most resolute chastity could not have stood against this dreadful threat. Lucretia yielded. Sextus enjoyed her, and rode away, proud of his success."

Lucretia sent messengers hurrying to her father and her husband. When they arrived, she told them what had happened, and killed herself, saying: " 'Never shall Lucretia provide a precedent for unchaste women to escape what they deserve.' With these words she drew a knife from under her robe, drove it into her heart, and fell forward, dead."

Nothing could have been more calculated to rouse the native population to violent indignation than this sexual crime against a virtuous Roman woman. Nothing could have better suited a plot against the hated regime. The young Etruscan aristocrats who were conspiring against Tarquinius Superbus did not miss their opportunity. Led by Brutus, an armed band hurried from Collatia to Rome. From all sides people hastened to the Forum to learn what was afoot, and Brutus spoke to the people.

He spoke, says Livy, of "the brutal and unbridled lust of Sextus Tarquinius, the hideous rape of the innocent Lucretia and her pitiful death . . . He went on to speak of the king's arrogant and tyrannical behavior; of the sufferings of the commons condemned to labor underground clearing or constructing ditches and sewers; of gallant Romans—soldiers who had beaten in battle all neighboring peoples—robbed of their swords and turned into stone-cutters and artisans. He reminded them of the foul murder of Servius Tullius . . . The effect of his words was immediate: the populace took fire, and were brought to demand the abrogation of the king's authority and the exile of himself and his family."

Upon Brutus's proposal, the constitution of Servius Tullius, which Tarquinius Superbus had flouted, was reinstated, says Dionysius. " 'Divide yourselves into your *curiae* and give your votes,' " said Brutus to the crowd in the Forum, " 'and let the enjoyment of this right be the beginning of your liberty.' " When this had been done and all the *curiae* had voted for the banishment of the tyrant, Brutus proposed another drastic innovation, something which Servius Tullius had meant to do, had it not been prevented by his violent death, as Livy confirms: "However mild and moderate his rule, he intended, according to some writers, to abdicate in favor of a republican government, simply because he disapproved in principle of monarchy."

What had not been granted to the great reformer Tullius to do was now done. Brutus, so Dionysius tells us, turned to the question of "what magistracy should be in control of affairs." He proposed "not to establish the kingship again, but to appoint two annual magistrates to hold the royal power." And "the people approved of this resolution likewise, not a single vote being given against it."

> *Thus the Roman republic was born. It was to Etruscan aristocrats and their coup d'état that Rome owed its second great reform.*

Thus the Roman republic was born. It was to Etruscan aristocrats and their coup d'état that Rome owed its second great reform. And Etruscan aristocrats held the new highest offices of state, those of the consuls. For the two men chosen "to perform the functions which had belonged to kings" were Brutus and Collatinus. "The people, being called by centuries," says Dionysius, "confirmed their appointment."

When the news of what was going on reached the king in his camp near Ardea, he was greatly perturbed and set out for Rome in haste. But it was already too late. "Tarquin found the city gates shut against him," says Livy, "and his exile decreed." The date was 509 B.C.

ROME UNDER ETRUSCAN CONSULS

ROME HAD BECOME A REPUBLIC. But how had it really happened? And what had really changed? It was not a genuine popular revolt, but a palace revolution. What had caused the overthrow of royal sovereignty was not nationalist feelings directed against foreign rule, a clash of Latins against Etruscans. It was a case of an Etruscan tyrant being expelled by his own countrymen. The great mass of Etruscans already settled in Rome, the members of the aristocracy, their clients, and many others, such as engineers, architects, priests, artists, and artisans, continued to live there.

The coup d'état did not make Rome a Latin city. As before, Etruscans still held the highest offices of state, for they provided both consuls. And the first thing they did was to again put into effect the constitution which an Etruscan ruler, Servius Tullius, had introduced. "For they restored the laws introduced by Tullius concerning contracts," says Dionysius, "which seemed to be humane and democratic, but had all been abrogated by Tarquinius . . . and they restored to the people the right of holding assemblies concerning affairs of the greatest moment, of giving their votes, and of doing all the other things they had been wont to do according to former custom."

All Etruscan ceremonies and customs likewise remained unaffected. The insignia of majesty and power were retained, the scepter and golden crown, the purple and gold-embroidered robes on festive occasions and in triumphal processions, when they were worn in honor of the gods, the ivory chair in which the consuls sat in judgment, the white robes bordered with purple and the lictors' rods borne before them in public. The Etruscan priests remained with their haruspicy and interpretation of thunderbolts and other prodigies. The spiritual and the secular powers were separated, however. A "king" of sacred rites was appointed, with no powers other than to supervise sacrifices.

So all that had happened was a change in the constitution brought about by a "putsch" in the circles that had founded Rome, had made it a large, modern city, and had ruled it for more than a century. It was no more than that. And yet this rebellion was destined to have a more far-reaching effect than anything else on the city and its inhabitants and on the whole of Etruria. For it was the republic which created the conditions for a reversal of power relationships. It made possible what could never have happened under the Etruscan kings, the seizure of power by members of the old-established indigenous Latin population. With the republic was born the future world power of the Romans. The Etruscan palace revolution was to devour its own children and the entire Etruscan nation. The coming disaster cast its shadow before it in the first serious conflict in which the city-state was involved soon after the coup d'état.

Tarquinius Superbus, in exile, began plotting revenge. Hoping for allies, he made his first approach among the Latins. "But when their cities paid no heed to him and were unwilling to make war upon the Roman state on his account," says Dionysius, "he despaired of any assistance from them and took refuge in Tarquinii, a Tyrrhenian city, from whence his family on his mother's side had originally come. And having bribed the magistrates of the Tarquinians with gifts . . . he prevailed upon the people, first of all to send ambassadors to Rome to propose terms of accommodation on his behalf, assuring them that the men in power there were working in his interest and would aid in his restoration."

> To the exiled king, "disappointed by the failure of his grand design," it was clear that the only course left to him was war.

The ambassadors first proposed that Tarquinius should be given the opportunity of appearing before the senate and the assembly of the people to give an account of his actions. This was flatly rejected, because a vote had already been taken condemning all the

Tarquins to perpetual banishment. The ambassadors then put forward another plea, that the property of Tarquinius and his family should be restored to them. The two consuls, Brutus and Collatinus, promised to consider the request. After a long debate in the senate, it was decided by one vote to restore the property. The ambassadors, who were still at Rome, had meanwhile plotted with various Etruscans still loyal to Tarquin to attempt his restoration. But the plotters were discovered and executed and the ambassadors allowed to leave. As for the Tarquins' property, the senate "let the people loose on it to take what they pleased," says Livy. Among the ex-royal property was "a tract of land between the city and the Tiber" which later became known as the Campus Martius. "It is said that there was a crop of grain, already ripe, on the land there."

To the exiled king, "disappointed by the failure of his grand

A victor's helmet with ivy wreath in gold, Vulci; fifth century B.C.

design," it was clear that the only course left to him was war. The details of the campaigns and battles in and around Rome and in Latium which resulted from the attempt to restore the Etruscan monarchy were obscured and distorted by the Romans.

Tarquinius "visited the various Etruscan towns in order to solicit their support," says Livy, "and his best hopes of success were centered in Veii and Tarquinii. 'I am of the same blood as you';—so ran his argument—'yesterday I was a king of no mean kingdom; now I am a penniless exile. Do not let me perish with my young sons before your eyes . . . It is my purpose to recover my country and my throne, to punish my ungrateful subjects. I appeal to you for aid. March with me to avenge the injuries you, too, have suffered in the past—your many defeats in battle and the loss of your lands.' " The appeal was successful; the armies of both towns joined Tarquinius.

"As the invading forces crossed the frontier," Livy continues, "the consuls marched to meet them . . . Brutus probing ahead with the mounted troops. The dispositions of the enemy were similar, the cavalry under the command of the king's son Arruns in the van . . . While the hostile forces were still some distance apart, Arruns recognized the consul by his lictors, and presently, coming near enough to distinguish his features, knew without doubt that it was Brutus. 'There is the man,' he cried in a burst of anger, 'who drove us from our country! Look how he comes swaggering on, with all the marks of a power and dignity which by right are ours! Avenge, O God of battles, this insult to a king!' Setting spurs to his horse, he made straight for the consul. . . .

"The two met with extreme violence, each without a thought for his own safety, intent only to strike his enemy down; and such weight was behind their thrust that the spear of each drove clean through his adversary's shield deep into his body, and both fell dying to the ground."

It was a fratricidal battle of Etruscan against Etruscan, king's son against the reformer of the same dynasty. The mortal duel between the two settled the issue. "Tarquin and his Etruscans seem to have been suddenly overcome by despair of success," says Livy, "and the contingents from Veii and Tarquinii both dispersed during the night and went home, as if all were lost."

On the edge of the Valle Ariccia, some sixteen miles from Rome along the Via Appia, lie the remains of an ancient tomb. At the corners of a high base of stone blocks stand four stumps of cones, likewise of hewn stone. Not many visitors make their way to this forgotten spot amid the woods. The monument is said to be the tomb of the Etruscan prince Arruns, killed in the fight with Brutus.

The ex-king's defeated attempt to return was only the overture to further conflicts in which Etruscans and Latins fought over Rome. It was not long before the Etruscans won a decisive success in a campaign originating in Clusium, one of the leading cities of Etruria, within whose walls, high above the valley of the Chiana, lived a famous king, the great Larth (or Lars) Porsena.

KING PORSENA'S FIGHT FOR ROME

"THE TARQUINS, MEANWHILE, had taken refuge at the court of Lars Porsena, the king of Clusium," says Livy. "By every means in their power they tried to win his support, now begging him not to allow fellow Etruscans, men of the same blood as himself, to continue living in penniless exile, now warning him of the dangerous consequences of letting republicanism go unavenged. The expulsion of kings, they urged, once it had begun, might become common practice."

Porsena felt that it would be to his advantage to restore the monarchy in Rome, and he quickly invaded Roman territory. "Never before had there been such consternation in the senate," says Livy, "so powerful was Clusium at that time and so great the fame of Porsena."

"On the approach of the Etruscan army," Livy relates, "the Romans abandoned their farmsteads and moved into the city. Garrisons were posted. In some sections the city walls seemed sufficient protection, in others the barrier of the Tiber. The most vulnerable point was the wooden bridge."

In the first rush, Porsena and the Etruscans captured the ridge beyond the Tiber, the Janiculum. But when his troops were about to capture the bridge, the only entrance to the city, the Romans pulled it down in time, and all the Etruscans heard was "the crash of the falling bridge and the simultaneous shout of triumph from the Roman soldiers."

"Porsena now turned to siege operations. He garrisoned the

Janiculum, took up a position on the flat ground near the river, and collected a number of vessels to prevent supplies from being brought into Rome . . . His control over the whole outlying territory was soon so complete that, in addition to other sorts of property, all cattle had to be brought within the defenses of the city."

Soon food in the city became scarce, as the siege continued. What happened then is not clear from Livy's account. In an attempt to distract attention from the facts, Livy fills in with stories about the heroic deeds of Roman men and women, until "peace was made."

Fortunately other sources have survived, and from them we know that what happened was this. Porsena's expedition was successful; he conquered Rome and occupied it. The conditions he imposed on the Romans were harsh. They were completely disarmed, and, says Pliny the Elder, "we find it expressly stipulated that iron shall be only employed for the cultivation of the fields." Furthermore the Romans had to cede all territory on the right bank of the Tiber, with the result that they no longer had exclusive control of this vital river.

Surprisingly, however, despite the victory, there is no word about the exiled Tarquinius Superbus on whose behalf the expedition had been undertaken. Porsena did nothing to alter Rome's constitution as a republic. Obviously the king of Clusium had changed his mind and now had different aims. What were the reasons for this?

> **When his army withdrew, they handed over to the famished Romans the stores collected in their camp.**

The explanation is hinted at by Dionysius. The Tarquins, who were with Porsena's army, "had during a truce been guilty of a lawless attempt upon the inviolable persons both of ambassadors and of hostages." For this reason, Porsena explained, the Etruscans now "renounced all friendly relations with the Tarquinii . . . and he ordered them to depart that very day from the camp. Thus the Tarquinii, who at first had entertained excellent hopes either of exercising their tyranny again in the city . . . or of getting their property back, were disappointed in both respects in consequence of their lawless attempt against the ambassadors and hostages, and departed from the camp with shame and the detestation of all."

204

After this, says Dionysius, the victor made a treaty of peace and friendship with Rome. When his army withdrew, they handed over to the famished Romans the stores collected in their camp. Thereupon "the Roman senate voted to send Porsena a throne of ivory, a scepter, a crown of gold, and a triumphal robe, which had been the insignia of the kings."

There was one special reason why the peaceable termination of the campaign was of the greatest importance to the economy and trade of Clusium, as of all the city-states of Etruria. It was essential not to have the Roman republic as an enemy, because otherwise the Etruscans would not have enjoyed free access to Latium, through which went the land connection with the Etruscan league in Campania.

Before long, however, the areas to the south of the Tiber were no longer to be so secure for Etruscan businessmen. For Tarquinius Superbus, faced with the failure of his plans to recover the throne with the help of Etruscan allies, endeavored to win over to his cause the Sabine and Latin towns. At first the majority hesitated, but some of them seemed disposed to join him.

Both Rome and Etruria were equally concerned to prevent the defection of Latium. To avert the threatened danger, Porsena took action first. Arruns, his son—named like Tarquin's son—"got from his father one half of the army and led an expedition against the Aricians," says Dionysius. Aricia (modern Ariccia) lies on the Via Appia, near Albano, to the south of Rome. "When he had all but taken their city, aid came to the Aricians." The aid came from the Volscians of Antium on the sea and from the Latins of Tusculum. But what was most surprising was the arrival of armed units from a people that had never previously penetrated as far as Latium, from the Greeks of Cumae, the great rival and enemy of the Etruscans in Campania. Their reasons for intervening in the war were clear. Cumae's greatest interest was to block the Etruscans' land communications with the south, in order to cut all further traffic between the Etrurian motherland and the cities in Campania.

At Aricia, however, Arruns, "arraying his small army against a superior force, put most of them to flight and drove them back to the city." When news of the defeat of the rescue operation reached Cumae, violent dissension broke out among the ruling parties. It ended with the decision to send more troops to Aricia. Command of

the new force was given to the leader of one of the factions, Aristodemus, nicknamed the Effeminate. His expedition was eventually to
make him absolute ruler of Cumae. With a fleet of ten ships and
two thousand men, Aristodemus put to sea. He landed his expedi-
tionary force in Latium and hastened to the aid of beleaguered
Aricia. Outside the city he inflicted a crushing defeat on the Etruscans.

Dionysius gives the details: Arruns Porsena "was defeated by the
Cumaeans under Aristodemus . . . and lost his life, and the Tyrrhenian army, no longer making a stand after his death, turned to
flight. Many of them were killed in the pursuit by the Cumaeans,
but many more, dispersing themselves about the country, fled into
the fields of the Romans, which were not far distant, having lost
their arms and being unable by reason of their wounds to proceed
further."

The Romans acted generously to the wounded men of the defeated Etruscan army. "These, some of them half dead, the Romans
brought from the fields into the city upon wagons and mule-carts
and upon beasts of burden also, and carrying them to their own
houses, restored them to health with food and nursing and every
other sort of kindness that great compassion can show; so that many
of them, induced by these kindly services, no longer felt any desire
to return home but wished to remain with their benefactors." This,
too, was granted. By order of the senate they were given "as a place
in the city for building houses, the valley which extends between
the Palatine and the Capitoline hills." As a result of this, adds
Dionysius, the road that leads from the Forum to the Circus Maximus was called by the Romans, even down to his own time, the
Vicus Tuscus, the Etruscan Street.

The treaty of peace and friendship between Clusium and Rome
had survived its first crucial test. In return for Roman help to the
Etruscans, King Porsena made the Romans "a gift of no slight
value, but one which gave them the greatest satisfaction. This was
the territory beyond the river which they had ceded when they put
an end to the war."

In the meantime, Aristodemus, the victor of Aricia, had returned
to Cumae where he was greeted with jubilation. He brought back
with him cargo boats full of presents he had received, and the
spoils and prisoners taken from the Etruscans. His great triumph

Gold pendant of the head of Achelous; 1⅝" long; c. 500 B.C.

The Ficeroni cista; bronze; mid-fourth century B.C.
Cylindrical container for toilet articles,
depicting scenes from the travels of the argonauts

Vase with head of a woman
showing Magna-Graecian influence

Ox-headed flask with horseman;
clay; seventh century B.C.

Head of a warrior, terra-cotta, part of facing slab from Temple of Mater Matuta, Satricum (Conca)

Gorgon's head; terra-cotta antefix from the temple of Apollo at Veii, sixth–fifth century B.C.

Head of the Apollo of Veii, terra-cotta, perhaps by the sculptor Vulca; late sixth–early fifth century B.C.

enabled him to overthrow his old opponents. Henceforth he reigned as tyrant over Cumae, having formed a bodyguard for himself from released Etruscan prisoners.

In Latium, Arruns Porsena's expedition caused bitter feelings. "The Aricians," says Dionysius, "accused the Romans of having, though kinsmen, brought upon them the Tyrrhenian war and of having caused all the Latin cities, as far as lay in their power, to be deprived of their liberty by the Tyrrhenians." In these circumstances even Tarquinius Superbus found Latins ready to listen to him and give him support. They were angry about the alliance between Rome and Porsena.

Several cities mobilized their armies. With the help of Latin forces, Tarquinius Superbus set out for the assault on Rome. But the city had been warned and reacted swiftly. "Aulus Postumius, who had been granted dictatorial power," says Livy, "proceeded with Titus Aebutius, his Master of the Horse, and a powerful army of combined cavalry and infantry to Lake Regillus near Tusculum, where they encountered the Latin forces already on the march . . . The battle which followed was . . . fought with more determination and greater savagery than usual: officers of high rank . . . joined personally in the fighting . . . and there was hardly a man amongst the nobility of either side who escaped without a wound. Postumius . . . was still making his final dispositions and urging his men to do their duty, when Tarquinius Superbus, now an old man with failing strength, came riding straight for him. The attempt failed. Tarquin was struck in the side, but his followers closed in round him and got him back to safety."

The hopes that Tarquinius Superbus had placed in this battle had come to nothing. At Lake Regillus the Romans were victorious. The defeat obliged him to leave the country, for "neither the Latins, the Tyrrhenians, the Sabines, nor any other free people nearby would longer permit him to reside in their cities," says Dionysius. He was now ninety years old, the only survivor of his family, for he had lost his children and his relations by marriage. So he retired to Cumae. Here the ex-tyrant was given right of asylum by the new tyrant Aristodemus, whom out of gratitude he made his heir.

"And after living a few days there, he died and was buried by him," says Dionysius, in the Greek city, among strangers, far from his home and his countrymen.

What remained of the two great figures, Tarquinius Superbus, the despotic, last king of Rome, and of Porsena, the heroic commander and king of Clusium, apart from the memory of their deeds, written down centuries later? The archeologists who got on their track were to make no sensational discoveries. In fact, they have so far brought to light disappointingly little. A modest remnant has been found of the great Capitoline temple which the tyrant built. At Caere (Cerveteri) traces of the royal family have been found. Soon after the coup d'état which deposed him, Tarquinius and two of his sons are said to have gone into exile at Caere. Some members of his family are believed to have remained there, and long enjoyed the respect accorded to their distinguished family. In the vast necropolis of Cerveteri, the tomb of the Tarquins was discovered in 1845. It contained an inscription in Etruscan: AVLE TARCHNAS LARTHAL CLAN—*tarchnas* being the Etruscan form of Tarquin.

As for King Porsena, his tomb seems to have been as impressive as his life. Pliny the Elder quotes a description of it by Varro: "He was buried under the city of Clusium, in a spot where he has left a monument in rectangular masonry, each side whereof is three hundred feet wide, and fifty high, and within the square of the basement is an inextricable labyrinth, out of which no one who ventures in without a clue of thread can ever find an exit. On that square basement stand five pyramids, four at the angles, and one in the center, each being seventy-five feet wide at its base, and one hundred and fifty high, and all so terminating above as to support a brazen circle and a petasus, from which are hung by chains certain bells, which, when stirred by the wind, resound afar off, as was formerly the case at Dodona. Upon this circle four other pyramids are based, each rising to the height of one hundred feet. And above these, from one floor, five more pyramids."

Varro apparently did not give the height of these last five pyramids, and Pliny adds: "According to the Etruscan fables, it was equal to that of the rest of the building. What downright madness this, to attempt to seek glory at an outlay which can never be of utility to anyone; to say nothing of exhausting the resources of the

*Bronze statuette of a dancing maenad;
late sixth century B.C.*

kingdom, and after all, that the artists may reap the greater share of the praise."

Varro, a writer and scholar of the first century B.C. in Rome, seems to have seen a part of the monument. He would hardly have included in his work such precise measurements if they were based solely on hearsay. And even the description of the upper part of the construction, with all its pyramids, cannot be merely the product of his imagination.

Who could blame scholars for wanting to hunt for a monument described in such fantastic and fabulous terms? Besides, the place where they could pick up the scent was clearly enough indicated: "under the city of Clusium," that is, at Chiusi. The little country town of Chiusi, near which the search began, lies on the road from Florence to Rome, about eight miles from the west shore of Lake Trasimene. It is situated on an eminence at the southern end of the Chiana valley. This river, a tributary of the Tiber, was navigable and provided a good connection with the south.

The prosperity of the once prominent city declined. But the fertility of the soil in the neighboring countryside, which the Etruscans had cultivated twenty-five centuries earlier, remained. Silvery olive groves and vineyards cover the green slope, only interrupted by cemeteries again and again rifled since the days of antiquity, whose dark chambers have long been empty, robbed of their precious votive gifts of gold jewelry and magnificent bronzes. "Here, traveller, if curious and enterprising, you may thrust your arms up to the elbows in adventures," wrote George Dennis in the last century.

Some three miles to the north of Chiusi is a hill called Poggio Gaiella, with a conical crest some nine hundred feet in circumference. It was here that excavations were begun in the winter of 1839–40. What they revealed was remarkable enough. Within the hill was, in fact, a kind of labyrinth of narrow passages, with tombs arranged in several tiers or terraces, one above the other. However, the excitement of the discoverers soon subsided. There was no sign of the monumental stone tomb of Porsena.

And yet the ground underneath Chiusi is perforated like an antheap by innumerable mysterious tunnels, some of them reaching as far as the outermost points of the town. Many of these passages are used by the inhabitants as cellars.

Some years ago, a large underground chamber, possibly a cistern, was discovered some thirty feet below the cathedral square. Vaulted with carefully dressed blocks of travertine, it is a remarkable structure. This too might be part of a labyrinth, but again there was no sign of King Porsena's legendary mausoleum, which seems to have vanished completely.

XV

Rome Comes of Age

By THE YEAR 500 B.C. THE DICE HAD been cast and the road ahead was settled. Tarquinius Superbus had been expelled by nobles of his own people. The rule of Etruscan kings on the Tiber had come to a sudden end. These were the hard facts as the sixth century B.C. drew to a close, the century in which the proudest and most glorious chapter of Etruscan history had been written.

When Tarquinius Superbus began to reign, Etruria was at the peak of its power and glory. Etruria's name carried weight and commanded respect throughout the Mediterranean from Miletus and Athens as far as Carthage, from the Bosporus to the Pillars of Hercules. In alliance with the strongest sea power, Carthage, its ships held undisputed sway over the Tyrrhenian Sea. Its trading empire was worldwide. The products of its art, industry, and handicrafts were highly prized by Greeks and Carthaginians, and in great demand among the peoples beyond the Alps.

On land too, its empire was powerful, stretching from the Po valley to Campania, from the Celtic tribes in the north to the cities of Greek colonists in the south. Large areas of Italy with their old-established, still half-barbarous population had been lifted permanently out of their prehistoric primitive existence, and throve and prospered.

Whatever the Etruscans put their hand to succeeded. It seemed as though undiminished fortune and success were theirs, as though the gods never ceased to smile on this extraordinary people, so gay and yet so dreamy, like the smile of their princes and princesses that still greets us in the dark chambers of their tombs, from their frescoes and terra-cottas, and from the sarcophagi and vases in the museums. *"In Tuscorum iure pene omnis Italia fuerat,"* said Cato; nearly all Italy had been under Etruscan domination. And Virgil tells us that Etruria grew great, *"sic fortis Etruria crevit."*

What an opportunity there had been in the days when Porsena occupied Rome, for Etruria to rule all Italy. "It seemed," wrote Mommsen, "as though the unification of Italy under Etruscan supremacy were not far distant." But the Etruscans did not seize that great, unique opportunity. They frittered it away, because the city-states were incapable of joint political action for common political aims. The individualism of each of the separate members of the League of Twelve was too strongly developed, for all that they met annually for the great ritual festival at the Voltumna sanctuary. They had archaic governmental structures, each had its own clearly defined culture, and in thought and action they moved on separate ways. They loved to conquer, if conquest meant acquiring and opening up new markets and outlets for trade. But the idea of subjugating foreign peoples by force was alien to them. They took to the sword only when they were themselves threatened, when they had to defend their own interests.

They had built up their great empire by peaceful methods. It was their trail-blazing work that created their flourishing cities in Tuscany, the Po valley, and Campania. Tradition is silent about the Etruscans ever waging a war of conquest for such purposes. All their efforts were directed toward production and commerce, toward bountiful harvests from soil which their technicians were the first to make fertile, toward the establishment of industries and workshops for the manufacture of articles of daily use and the production of choice luxury items and works of art.

The opportunity they missed decided their fate. For another people was to rise and to conquer by the sword what lay almost within reach of the Etruscans thanks to their peaceful work of development.

> **Even when Rome had become a republic, it continued to enjoy the collaboration of the Etruscans.**

Even when Rome had become a republic, it continued to enjoy the collaboration of the Etruscans. After the coup d'état, as before, Etruscan nobles played an important part in affairs that were no longer their own. They had sponsored the young republic and they lent it their aid in the first difficult, crucial years.

Roman historians subsequently tried to conceal this fact, but it is evident from the long series of Etruscan names in the *fasti consulares,* the list of annually appointed chief government officials. The two Etruscans, Lucius Junius Brutus and Tarquinius Collatinus, were the first two consuls. Three years later, in 506 B.C., there were again Etruscans in this office, Titus Herminius and Spurius Larcius. In about 501 and 498 the latter's brother, Titus Larcius, was twice consul. In the following year he is recorded as having held the extraordinary office of dictator, with supreme powers. In about 490 Spurius Larcius was again consul. Down to about 448 B.C. the names of Etruscan aristocrats appear in the *fasti consulares* in high civil and military offices. Spurius Cassius, who was consul three times, in 502, 493, and 486, succeeded in concluding the *foedus Cassianum,* a treaty of perpetual peace and mutual aid with all the Latin cities. The parties to this treaty undertook not to make war upon one another as long as heaven and earth remained in their places, and in addition not to allow safe passage to any enemy attacking either of them, but, if that happened, to mobilize all their armed forces to repel the invaders.

But Etruria, too, had no objection to assisting the new state in an emergency. During the rebellion and general strike of the plebeians, says Livy, "work on the land had been suspended, and the result was a steep rise in the price of grain; famine followed so severe that Rome might have been a beleaguered city." In this crisis the consuls "sent agents over a wide area to arrange for the purchase of grain." They had to go a long way, "to travel northwest along the Etrurian coast and southeast along the Volscian coast to Cumae, and even as far as Sicily."

"Aristodemus, the reigning prince of Cumae, was the heir of the Tarquins, and after supplies had been bought there he retained the Roman grain-ships in lieu of the property he ought to have inherited. From the Volscians and the people of the Pontine marshes nothing could be obtained; indeed, the agents were actually in danger of violence."

Who actually supplied Rome with the food without which "the slaves and the poorer members of the community would undoubtedly have starved to death"? "From Etruria," says Livy, "supplies reached Rome by way of the Tiber, and this was enough to keep the people alive." The agents, Dionysius records, "who had been sent to the cities of Tyrrhenia bought there a quantity of millet and spelt and brought it down to Rome in river-boats."

Yet all this did not help the Etruscans any more. In Rome they were more and more excluded and pushed aside. The descendants of the people who, a century earlier, lived in straw huts had come of age. From now on, they took charge.

The character of the city was by now fixed. A modern, impressive, thriving town had been made out of a colony of shepherds amid marshy fields and ponds. The great Etruscan buildings, and the Forum, the temple of Jupiter, and the Circus Maximus stood like a huge, brightly colored stage-set amid rural surroundings. The streets were lined with houses of brick and tufa, and the city had its sewage system. All this development aid had been worthwhile —for those at the receiving end.

But one element had remained unaffected by foreign rule, and that was the inhabitants themselves. In life and character, in thought and action, they remained uninfluenced, unchanged. North of the Tiber as far as the Arno, among the Umbrians and Faliscans, the native population had become "Etruscanized." But in Rome the Etruscans failed in this. The time had been too short. A mere century was not enough to arouse among the backward, illiterate inhabitants sufficient enthusiasm for a sophisticated civilization. Like other peoples, the Romans had admittedly learned how to read and write from the Etruscans. But they wrote Latin, not Etruscan, and Latin remained their language. They did not succumb to the charms of the foreigners.

Now, free of their foreign masters, they pulled the tiller hard over and set their own course. They did not follow the example of their Etruscan teachers. Nothing that they introduced into the country was developed further. Rome pursued different aims. Gradually, through overlapping military involvements, it became conscious of a destiny to rule the world, and everything was subordinated to that. It became a military state, a community of armed farmers, a dreary, drilled garrison. There was no room for Mercury, for the Muses. The future was with Mars. Almost uninterruptedly for five hundred years the doors of the temple of Janus were to remain wide open as a sign that Rome was at war.

> **From the rich legacy of the Etruscans, the Romans adopted only what served their political organization and military needs.**

From the rich legacy of the Etruscans, the Romans adopted only what served their political organization and military needs, such practical things as roads, bridges, fortifications, aqueducts, public baths and hygienic installations. Everything else, trades, industry, commerce, the arts and crafts, all these were pushed aside. Apart from agriculture and arms manufacture, there was no production. "A workshop is no place for a gentleman!" sneered Cicero centuries later. Life became plain and bare, without gaiety and beauty. A workaday drabness settled on the Tiber, the dreary civilization of a barbarous peasantry, the atmosphere of an everlasting barracks yard.

Every kind of luxury was frowned on, the ownership of gold and silver forbidden and punishable. In the streets the shops in which Etruscan goldsmiths displayed their beautiful jewelry closed down, as did the workshops with their stocks of bronze articles. Pottery was no longer imported. In the rubble strata of early republican days only isolated shards of Attic vases have been found. Nowhere else, said Livy, "have thrift and plain living been for so long held in such esteem."

Whereas mass production in factories had long been normal practice in Etruria, with a resulting superabundance of goods, Rome returned to the primitive level of production at home for domestic use. Shut up in her house, the Roman woman sat with her distaff and loom and made her plain clothes herself. Everything the family needed was made at home. Even when he was emperor,

Augustus wore homemade clothes. The only artisans who worked for general consumption were the smiths. Homes became plain and bare, food basic and unattractive. The pleasures of the table, of a varied cuisine, such as the Etruscans had appreciated, were forgotten. An insipid gruel or porridge called *puls,* cooked with water, was the national dish.

The enchanting music, the fascinating sound of the Tuscan flute and the twanging of the cithara, was heard no more. All that remained was the trumpet calling to arms, to battle and the victor's triumph. And the one big sports ground, used not for gymnastic games or Olympic competitions, but only for pre-military training and drill, became the Campus Martius, the prototype of all the later drill grounds of Europe, of the Märzfeld of the Merovingian kings, the Champ de Mars of the French, and the Tempelhofer Feld in Berlin.

On Rome's Campus Martius the young men were trained for military service. They practiced javelin throwing, running with weapons, thrusting the spear, and riding; they were toughened up to endure heat and cold. Young and old flocked voluntarily and enthusiastically to the field for their favorite recreation—practice in the handling of weapons. And after practice on the Tiber came use; came, in short, battles.

It was not by work and industry that Rome was to become great and one day to acquire immense wealth. Its road to world domination led over the ruins of conquered and plundered foreign lands and peoples. And among the first to be crushed by the Roman steamroller where the disseminators of the oldest advanced civilization in Italy, Rome's first teachers and the founders of its capital city, the Etruscans.

SHADOWS OVER THE ETRUSCAN EMPIRE

THE GOLDEN AGE OF ETRURIA was coming to a close. The gods suddenly seemed angry with those whom they had so long favored. The tale of Etruscan reverses and losses by land and sea began. In this century, the fifth, they were to lose one of the most important buttresses of their empire—their command of the sea, and with it a most valuable colonial area, that of the League of Twelve in Campania. Two great battles in 480 B.C. ushered in the coming historical change. The Greeks won both—at Himera against Carthage and at Salamis against the Persians.

The aims of the Carthaginians' sea power were far-ranging, their secret contacts worldwide. They had attentively watched the devel-

**Bronze mirror showing Hercules seizing a maiden;
c.480 B.C. Found at Atri in the Abruzzi**

opments in the Near East that followed the rise of the Achaemenid dynasty of Persia under Cyrus, especially those on the coasts of Asia Minor and the Levant. The whole of Ionia had fallen under Persian rule. The mighty maritime fortresses of ancient Phoenicia, with the exception of Tyre, had soon afterward shared the same fate under Cambyses.

For a little while it seemed as though the Persians could not maintain their grip. In Ionia there was discontent in the Persian-occupied cities, and in 499 B.C. it flared up in revolt. Aristagoras, the tyrant of the powerful trading city Miletus, became the leader of the revolt.

Supported by the motherland, with help from Athens and Eretria, the Greeks advanced on Sardis and captured it. The residence of the Persian governor went up in flames. But the power of the new ruler of Asia was too great to be defied. The rebels were driven back, their army was destroyed. One single city still resisted— Miletus. But though it held out longest, it too was crushed in 494 B.C. The Persians took it by storm, and the great, splendid city that controlled dozens of trading stations and settlements throughout the Mediterranean was razed to the ground.

What was not forgotten was the memory among the Persians of those who had helped the Ionians in their revolt, who had aided them in battle. Thus the idea was born at the court of Persepolis of one day sailing for the Greek mother country and taking revenge on Athens. When Darius heard that Sardis had been captured by the Athenians and Ionians and set on fire, "he did not give a thought to the Ionians," says Herodotus, "knowing perfectly well that the punishment for their revolt would come; instead, the first thing he did was to ask who the Athenians were, and then, on being told . . . commanded one of his servants to repeat to him the words, 'Master, remember the Athenians,' three times, whenever he sat down to dinner."

As the Persians brooded on retaliation against Greece, so the Carthaginians and their Etruscan allies looked on the Greek colonies and Greek trade as an opponent that was growing continually stronger, and an increasingly active competitor. That the Greeks did not shrink from occasional acts of war had recently been made plain. After the Persian defeat of the Ionian fleet, in connection with the attack on Miletus, says Herodotus, the Phocaean commander

Dionysius, who had fought with the Ionians, "sailed for Sicily, which he made his base for piratical raids against Carthaginian and Tyrrhenian shipping."

Carthage and Persia had a common interest, different though the reasons for it might be. The Carthaginians prudently put out feelers. In their Phoenician mother country they had good friends, also threatened by Greek trade, who were quite ready to stir up the Persians against Greece. Phoenician anti-Greek feelings were well known in Carthage. Herodotus, in narrating the preparations for the attack on Miletus, mentions that: "Amongst those who sailed with the fleet, it was the Phoenicians whose heart was most in the business."

Accordingly the Phoenicians were to be told, and to pass it on, that the Carthaginians would be only too happy to associate themselves with Persian plans. As a mark of confidence they would even allow Persian representatives to visit their trading stations at the Pillars of Hercules from which all foreigners were normally banned.

A delegation from Carthage, which was making the usual annual visit to Tyre to pay tribute to the god Melkart, made the first contacts. Confidential discussions took place on the subject dearest to both Carthage and Phoenicia, namely, war against the hated Greeks. The Phoenicians were in a good position to make an important contribution to such a war.

> The defeat of Greece would be the signal for Carthage and her Etruscan friends to take action.

It was not for nothing that the Persians, natives of a mountainous land as they were, and ignorant of everything to do with the sea, treated the skilled Phoenician mariners of the coast more as friendly advisers and experts than as subjects. Tyre, however, no longer occupied the leading position, which it had been obliged to yield to its old rival Sidon. The ruler of this city became chief admiral to the Persian king.

Darius, advised by his Phoenician supreme naval commander, began to prepare his grand design—and it became known in Carthage—which was to transport a huge army across the Hellespont and the Aegean Sea to Greece. The defeat of Greece would be the signal for Carthage and her Etruscan friends to take action. That would be the moment for their united forces to conquer the

Greek colonies in Sicily and southern Italy. With the help of the Phoenicians, they would then make their economic and maritime predominance in the eastern and western Mediterranean the biggest and strongest ever.

A worldwide alliance thus took shape. "A common interest," says the French archeologist Gilbert Charles Picard, "bound the representatives of the old Oriental powers, Persians and Carthaginians alike, as well as the Etruscans, the last representatives on European soil of the old Mediterranean world. The Etruscan-Punic alliance extended to the west the block of eastern nations constituted by the Persian conquest."

The plan was put into effect. The armies moved into position simultaneously in two theaters of war, in the west and in the east. Xerxes, son and successor of Darius who had died during the preparations, invaded Greece with the help of a vast fleet. In Sicily a Carthaginian army led by Hamilcar landed at Panormos, the modern Palermo, and moved along the coast to the town of Himera, the most westerly outpost of the Greeks on the north coast of the island.

"It was a superb piece of political scheming," commented Mommsen, "to throw the Asiatic hordes upon Greece and the Phoenician upon Sicily at the same moment."

But in those September days of 480 B.C. fate decided upon a quite different outcome, one that went against the Persians, Carthaginians, and Etruscans. Events took an unexpected course, for both attempts, both attacks failed.

The jubilant shouts of the victorious Greeks at Salamis in 480 B.C. echoed over the water. They had routed and destroyed the numerically far larger Persian fleet, few ships of which managed to escape. And on the very same day, according to the Sicilians, says Herodotus, outside the walls of Himera, Theron of Akragas and his son-in-law Gelon, tyrant of Syracuse, who had been summoned to his assistance, inflicted a crushing defeat on the enormous Carthaginian army, said to have numbered three hundred thousand. Its general, Hamilcar, vanished; the Carthaginians who survived were taken into slavery.

The triumphant Greeks of Sicily declared that they had killed thirty-five to forty thousand of the enemy, had destroyed several hundred ships, had taken over six thousand pounds weight of gold on the battlefield. In addition Carthage had to pay a war indemnity of two thousand talents of silver. These were losses serious enough to endanger the Carthaginian economy.

Thus, fifty-five years after the great victory of Alalia over the Greeks, the high hopes of the Carthaginian and Etruscan allies had come to nothing. The Etruscans were soon to feel the effects of the terrible defeat and humiliation of Carthage.

The Etruscan merchant ships had already received a serious blow a couple of years earlier when Anaxilas, the tyrant of Rhegium (modern Reggio di Calabria) and Zancle (modern Messina), built a naval station at the rock of Scylla to close the Strait of Messina. Etruscan shipping thus lost access to the Ionian Sea.

Six years after the battle of Himera another disaster befell the Etruscans with the defeat of their battle fleet by the Greeks of Cumae, which resulted in the isolation of the Etruscan colonies in Campania. The Etruscans had already suffered severely by the defection of Latium and the hostility of its peoples. For this deprived them of their land connection with the most southerly part of their empire. Quite apart from the economic results, this meant a great loss of prestige to the Etruscan leagues. Their dominant position in Italy was threatened for the first time.

Naturally the sea communications with Campania became more important than ever. If the Campanian cities were not to become completely isolated it was essential to keep the sea lanes open and defend them with all possible means. The only way to guarantee that was to have undisputed mastery of the southern Tyrrhenian Sea. Thus everything impelled the Etruscans toward a showdown with the Greeks, above all with Cumae which, with its important harbors in Campania, was becoming more troublesome than ever.

Once before, in about 524 B.C., the Etruscans, as Dionysius reports, "undertook to overthrow Cumae . . . though they could allege no other just ground for their animosity than the prosperity of the city. For Cumae was at that time celebrated throughout all Italy for its riches, power, and all the other advantages, as it possessed the most fertile part of the Campanian plain and was mistress of the most convenient havens around about Misenum."

But it was an ill-fated expedition. Sudden storms and floods turned the land around the city into a swamp, and the attack, with a huge force of cavalry and infantry, petered out.

Now once more the leaders of the Campanian league turned their sights on the powerful Greek city and began to lay plans. Aristodemus, the tyrant of Cumae, who had intervened so decisively in the Etruscan-Latin battle for Aricia, was suddenly overthrown, and this seemed a favorable moment for attacking the city and finishing it off for good. The attack was to be made simultaneously by land and sea. Pompeii provided an ideal base for the operations. Messengers were sent to the mother country to ask for naval support, and meanwhile preparations went forward in Campania.

When Cumae learned from spies what the Etruscans were planning, the Greeks appealed to Syracuse in Sicily for help. Since the victory of Himera, this Greek city had much increased its prestige and power in the western Mediterranean, and its tyrant, Hieron, eagerly seized any opportunity for still further extending his dominance. He acted without delay, and dispatched to the aid of Cumae "a considerable number of triremes," as Diodorus reports.

In the meantime the troops from Campanian cities had concentrated in a wide ring around Cumae, ready to attack as soon as the Etruscan warships from the mother country had blockaded the city and begun to land troops. The Etruscan warships and transports had begun their operation when the fleet from Syracuse appeared on the scene and threw the Etruscan vessels into confusion.

This victory over the reputedly unbeatable Etruscan naval might was proudly recorded by Greek historians.

The Etruscans were forced to turn about and make for nearby Cape Misenum. There, at the foot of the five-hundred-foot-high cliff that projects into the Gulf of Naples, a furious battle took place. The surprise of the Etruscans at being suddenly faced by the combined Greek fleet seems to have paralyzed them. The Greek commander forced his opponents to fight hand to hand, from ship to ship, and thus prevented the Etruscans from adopting their ramming technique.

The Syracusans captured or sank many of the enemy's ships. The remainder fled. The Campanian land forces, dismayed and discouraged by the defeat of the Etruscan fleet, abandoned the siege of Cumae and departed.

This victory over the reputedly unbeatable Etruscan naval might was proudly recorded by Greek historians, and Pindar, in the first Pythian Ode, written for Hieron of Syracuse, commemorates the triumph of his Greek countrymen at Cumae:

[*Zeus*], *I beseech you, bend your head in assent*
that the Phoenician and the war-crying Tyrsenian keep
  quietly at home, beholding the shame of their wreck by
  sea at Kyme,
the things they endured, beaten at the hands of Syracuse's lord,
how he hurled their young men out of their fleet-running
  ships on the sea,
gathering back Hellas from the weight of slavery.

The poet's coupling of Phoenicians with Tyrsenians means, according to A. J. Pfiffig, that Carthaginian ships also took part in the battle. In the poem, Pindar puts the Syracusans' victory on a level with the great victories of mainland Greece over the Persians at Plataea and Salamis. The triumph of Salamis has remained common knowledge down to the present day. But no one knows of the successes and failures of the Etruscan fleets, of the battles of Alalia and Cumae.

Two souvenirs of the naval battle of Cumae have survived to the present day. One of them is in the British Museum, London. It is the plain, hemispherical bronze helmet of an Etruscan warrior. The inscription on it shows that it was captured in battle. In Greek letters, it says: "Hieron, son of Deinomenes, and the Syracusans (dedicated) to Zeus the Etruscan spoils won at Cumae."

The helmet was found at Olympia in 1817. Hieron dedicated it at the great sanctuary there, where he himself, it is said, had been celebrated for his two victories in horse races and one in the four-horse chariot race. In 1959 a second helmet with an almost identical inscription was found at Olympia.

In return for his help to Cumae, Hieron was richly rewarded by being given the island of Pithecusae (modern Ischia), on which he rapidly planted a settlement with a garrison. For the Etruscans this was the worst blow of all. It meant that the Campanian harbors of Pompeii, Herculaneum, and Sorrento were permanently under the surveillance and domination of the neighboring Syracusan base and its reconnaissance ships. The harbors would no longer fulfill their purpose, in fact could not be held.

Etruscan Campania, its land and sea connections with the northern city-states interrupted, was thus finally isolated, and Etruscan rule over the southern waters was at an end. This was a serious blow also to the mother country. The chief sufferers from the terrible defeat of 474 B.C. were the two old, great coastal cities Caere and Tarquinii. From now on, their maritime trade contracted, their wealth declined, and with it their political and military power.

The Greeks' tremendous success at Cumae had at a stroke

Etruscan helmet, with dedication by Hieron of Syracuse celebrating a naval victory over the Etruscans near Cumae in 474 B.C. Found at Olympia

changed the situation in the western Mediterranean. Syracuse was now the first of all the Greek cities in Sicily. Its navy would now rule the waters north of the island, replacing that of the Etruscans who had given their name to the Tyrrhenian Sea. They were soon to feel their powerlessness.

Twenty years after the victory of Cumae, Syracuse launched another expedition, this time against Etruria itself. In 454 B.C. a strong fleet under Admiral Phayllos appeared suddenly off the coasts of Elba and Corsica. It had been sent to put a stop to what the Greeks called Etruscan piracy. But it never got to the point of any act of war. Prosperous Etruscan merchants found a way to bribe the Syracusan admiral, and heavily laden with gold, he and his warships quitted central Italian waters. His Etruscan gifts were to cost him dear when he got home. "The Syracusans found him guilty of treachery and exiled him," reports Diodorus Siculus.

A year later, in 453 B.C., another commander, Apelles, was sent north with sixty triremes and very firm instructions. This time the expedition did what was expected of it. Apelles, says Diodorus, overran the coast of Tyrrhenia, then passed over to Corsica where he sacked many places, and finally "subdued" Elba. Having accomplished all this, "he returned to Syracuse accompanied by a multitude of captives and not a little other spoil."

From these bare bones of the story, it is easy to reconstruct what must have happened. On the mainland coast, the Greeks must have wrecked the ports of Vetulonia, Populonia, and Tarquinii, and plundered their warehouses and stores, and no doubt sacked a number of smaller places too. They raided the coasts of Corsica, and, as regards Elba, they actually seem to have gained control of it for a time, or at least must have established settlements there. The fact that the Etruscans were unable to repulse these attacks on their own coasts and offshore islands shows how their power had declined.

In Syracuse the Greek fleet was welcomed with great rejoicing. There the meaning of this successful raid was well understood. It meant that henceforth the Etruscans and the Carthaginians would no longer control Italian waters. It was the victorious, powerful fleet of Syracuse that now ruled the Tyrrhenian Sea.

In the south, not long after this, came the end of Etruscan Campania. As a result of being cut off from the mother country and any reinforcements from it, the southern League of Twelve had been obliged to form units of mercenary troops for the defense of its cities. These mercenaries were recruited among the native population, and consisted largely of the wild mountaineers belonging to the Sabellic peoples who inhabited the high, pathless hinterland.

It was not long before these mountain tribes, driven by population pressure and hunger, began to descend like an avalanche from their inhospitable mountain valleys into the fertile plain of Campania. They swept far and wide over the country, reached the coast, and demanded land for settlement. There was nothing the Etruscans and the Greeks in the Cumae region could do but allow them to settle. Nor could they prevent the newcomers from penetrating even into the towns and establishing themselves there. The streets of Capua, Pompeii, and Naples were soon swarming with the uninvited guests.

The Etruscan rulers took defensive action. They began to fortify the cities. Pompeii was walled round; Capua, the capital, was protected by huge earthworks. It was all to no avail. The flood of Samnites had brought destruction into the land; nothing could now avert disaster.

The Campanian capital was the first victim. A Samnite conspiracy ended Etruscan rule in Capua forever. Samnite settlers in the surrounding countryside got together with their fellow countrymen serving in the garrison of Capua and worked out a plan to take the city by surprise. The foreign mercenaries had no scruples about betraying their Etruscan commanders and the inhabitants of the city which had taken them into its service. They waited for a public holiday, when everyone had enjoyed the local fiery wine in good measure and was sleeping off the effects. Then, at night, the Samnite mercenaries opened the gates and let in the armed hordes of their fellow countrymen. The slaughter went on all night, and by dawn few Etruscans were left alive.

> *That was the end of Etruscan Capua, the capital of the League of Twelve and the heart of Campania.*

That was the end of Etruscan Capua, the capital of the League of Twelve and the heart of Campania. It came in about 425 B.C., and its fate decided that of the rest of the country. It quickly fell under the control of the Italic peoples. Of all the Etruscan cities in Campania only one, Pompeii, was able to hold out for some time against the Samnite attacks.

Even mighty Cumae suffered the same fate. Strongly fortified though it was, this Greek city, which for decades had successfully defied the Etruscans, fell before the savage hordes of barbarians. Only Naples, the offspring of Cumae, and the islands of Ischia and Capri, guarded by Syracusan troops, put up a successful defense.

Toward the end of the century it seemed for a moment as though a more hopeful turn of events for Etruria was coming. It was during the Peloponnesian War, when Athens, on the advice of Alcibiades, in 415 B.C. decided on a naval expedition to Sicily, to wage war against Syracuse, the friend and ally of hated Sparta. The Athenians, says Thucydides, "also sent to Etruria, where some of the cities had offered of their own accord to join them in the war."

The Etruscans, old trading partners and friends of Athens, sent three fifty-oared ships, and also "there were some Etruscans fighting because of their hatred for Syracuse," says Thucydides. They fought heroically with the Athenians at the great battle of Syracuse. But the Athenians proved inferior at sea. "When Gylippus [a Spartan general helping the Syracusans] saw that the enemy fleet was defeated and then driven ashore beyond the shelter of their stockade and camp, he took part of his army and came along by the breakwater to give support, with the intention of destroying the crews as they landed and of making it easier for the Syracusans to tow off the ships, this part of the shore being in their hands. On the Athenian side the Etruscans were watching this point, and when they saw Gylippus's men advancing in disorder, they went out against them, charged and routed their vanguard, and drove it into the marsh of Lysimeleia . . . The Athenians put up a trophy for the fighting where the Etruscans had driven the enemy infantry into the marsh and where they themselves had won the victory with the rest of their army."

But the luck of war changed—against Athens and its Etruscan allies. Reinforcements that arrived from Athens under Demosthenes did put fresh heart into the Athenians, but all the same they were defeated. The Greek invaders lost the remainder of their fleet in Syracuse harbor, and their land forces were driven down to the river Assinarus and slaughtered there. It was a complete disaster.

The generals of the Athenian expedition were executed by the victors in Syracuse, and seven thousand prisoners were shut up in the city's stone quarries, the famous *latomie,* as they are still called. Here many died, others were sold as slaves, and others after long delay sent for hard labor in the public prison.

The Sicilian campaign was to be the last one of any size in the south in which Etruscan naval and land forces took part. With the defeat of the Athenian expedition, which was tragic for Etruria too, Syracuse became the leading Greek sea power. Its rulers could now think of extending their dominion over the whole of Sicily and southern Italy, and even over Italy's second sea, the Adriatic.

The Etruscans in northern Italy, the cities of the League of Twelve in the Po valley, were soon to feel upon their coast the power of victorious Syracuse.

XVI

The End
of the Golden Age

THE ETRUSCAN CUP OF BEATEN GOLD is king, and any bronze whatever that adorns the house for any purpose." This was not said by an Etruscan merchant advertising his wares. Far from it. The words, quoted by Athenaeus in his famous encylopedic symposium, occur in a poem by Critias, one of the thirty tyrants of Athens. And this was not the only tribute to Etruscan craftsmanship. There must have been many Greeks who admired Etruscan bronzes as did Pherecrates, the comic playwright. A character in one of his comedies is quoted by Athenaeus as saying: "The lamp stand was Tyrrhenian . . . for manifold were the crafts among the Etruscans, since they were skilled and loving workmen."

Depressing though the prospect was in the Tyrrhenian Sea after the Syracusans' naval victory, and the grievous loss of Campania, Etruria rapidly adjusted to the new situation. It was still extremely wealthy. The mother country and the league in the north were still unaffected; the productive capacity of the country's many industries, of its mines, foundries, and workshops, was still intact, as was the diligence of its people and the enterprise of its businessmen.

The unsafe waters along Etruria's coast were replaced by other routes and means of communication. Exports and imports were carried over the Apennines. In the Po valley the flow of goods continued unhindered, from ports on the Adriatic, to Athens and other friendly Greek cities, and across the Alps to the Celtic peoples. Both were markets of expanding consumption, and demand was especially keen for bronze articles, in the production of which the Etruscans were past masters.

What Etruria offered in the way of bronzes was as unique in quality as its variety was astonishing. The range included everything from superb works of art by gifted sculptors to mass-produced household goods. A work by one of the great Etruscan bronze sculptors survives in the Capitoline Museum in Rome. This is the famous *lupa,* the she-wolf that is still Rome's symbol. The name of the artist who made it around the middle of the fifth century B.C.

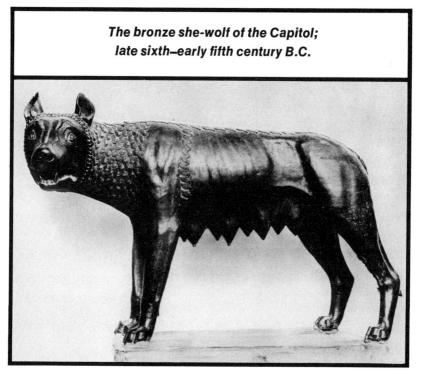

The bronze she-wolf of the Capitol; late sixth–early fifth century B.C.

is unknown. It was forgotten, like those of all the other great masters among his compatriots, with the sole exception of Vulca of Veii. What they created was lost too. The Romans carted their works away by the thousands during the conquest and destruction of Etrurian cities. From Volsinii alone they took some two thousand statues. These works of art went to Rome and then disappeared forever.

Vitruvius, the famous architect and engineer who dedicated his work on architecture to the emperor Augustus, refers to the magnificent gilded bronze statues of the Etruscans. And Pliny the Elder several times mentions such works of art: "There are also Etruscan statues dispersed in various parts of the world, which beyond a doubt were originally made in Etruria." And, "The ancients were in the habit of making the door-sills and even the doors of the temples of brass." He says too: "We see the Tuscan Apollo, in the library of the temple of Augustus, fifty feet in height from the toe; and it is a question whether it is more remarkable for the quality of the metal, or for the beauty of the workmanship."

> **Such fine old bronze statues as existed in Rome were by Etruscan masters.**

Such fine old bronze statues as existed in Rome were by Etruscan masters. The few surviving references, both Greek and Roman, are unanimous in their testimony that Etruria was famous for its bronze casting, and was in its own way as productive and creative as Athens in this branch of art. The works of the Etruscan masters were great art, even if they did not, as has so often been urged against them, conform to the rules of proportion for the human body exemplified in Polykleitos's "Canon" statue and widely followed in Hellas.

It was not the Etruscan way to concentrate on externals, to aim at an unreal, idealized perfection of form. Their dynamic, vital works pulsed with life. Whether figures of animals or of human beings, they were not regular, balanced, or ideal. Proportions, correct anatomy, were often disregarded. Etruscan artists aimed above all at bringing out the quintessence of their subject, its individual characteristics. They strove to express the inner driving force, the unconscious depths.

This purpose is quite plain in very early times, around 700 B.C.

The Chiusi cremation urns of that date, or canopic urns, as they are called, are the beginnings of a great art of portraiture of a kind which Hellas neither knew nor appreciated. Whereas Greek statues and portraits always appear idealized, Etruscan artists sought to grasp the personality of a man, its tough, basic core, and to convey this realistically, regardless of aesthetics. It was their works that inspired the sober realistic art of the Roman portrait, as it flourished in the Augustan Age.

The standards established in the much-praised Athens of the Periclean Age by the works of Phidias, Myron, and Polykleitos, provided a stereotype of beauty. These sculptures afterward came to be considered in Europe as the highest summit of all Western art. They eclipsed the masterpieces of anonymous Etruscan artists. And it was no different when some of these sculptures again saw the light of day after many centuries, works such as those magnificent bronzes, the *Chimera,* the *Minerva,* and the *Arringatore* (Orator), which are now the pride of the Archeological Museum at Florence. They were judged according to the standards of the Greeks. It was

Bronze chimera; second half of fifth century B.C.
Restored in the Renaissance

not understood that the canon of form is not the only one, that art can pursue other ideals, those governed by the canon of expression and content.

Thus Etruscan works of art were never awarded top marks. Their intrinsic value and significance, their quite different aims, were not recognized. Mommsen, the great admirer of the Roman military state, was not the only one to pass a harsh judgment: "There is no getting away from it . . . ," he wrote, "in the history of Italic art, the Etruscans will have to be shifted from first place to last." And one of the last supporters of this out-of-date view was the American art expert, the late Bernard Berenson, who declared that "only through the originality of incompetence can [Etruscan art] be distinguished from the art of the Greeks."

It is only recently, as shown by the success of exhibitions of Etruscan art, that this art has experienced a resurrection, has been accepted and appreciated. The diffusion of Freud's ideas about the human unconscious has contributed not a little to this change. It helped to open people's eyes to the completely non-Greek expressionism of Etruscan art.

The glass cases in the Etruscan sections of Italian museums are packed to bursting. Stacks of boxes, of bronze finds alone, repose unsorted and uncatalogued in the storerooms. All these objects attest the range of an extraordinarily productive industry turning out works of art and articles of utility. There are the accessories of luxurious villas, engraved caskets for the ladies, for their perfumes and makeup and jewels, for their combs, earrings, bracelets, and necklaces. The lid handles often consist of two standing figures carrying a third, horizontal one. There are the bronze mirrors, with portraits and scenes engraved on the back, the front being brilliantly polished; the richly ornamented lamp holders and incense burners, the tripods and bedsteads; the ornamented helmets and armor, the shields and greaves, the lamps of all kinds.

A unique great bronze lamp was found in 1840 at Cortona and is now the pride of the local museum. Cast in one piece, the lamp is twenty-three inches in diameter and weighs over a hundred pounds. The lower surface contains in the center a huge Gorgon's face, "the visage of a fiend," says Dennis, "with eyes starting from their sockets in the fury of rage—a mouth stretched to its utmost, with gnashing tusks and lolling tongue—and the whole rendered more terrible by a wreath of serpents bristling around it . . . In a band encircling it, are lions, leopards, wolves and griffons, in pairs, devouring a bull, a horse, a boar, and a stag."

A circle of wave ornament follows, with eight dolphins leaping the crests. Above them squat eight naked Sileni, or satyrs, with hooves and animals' ears, each playing either a double flute or Pan pipes. Between each pair of Sileni is a Siren, half woman, half bird, with wings and tail spread out. Above these figures and symbols of a magical, all-encompassing world, is the rim of the lamp containing sixteen spouts of classic form in which was placed the oil.

"A comparison with the huge coronas of our Ottonian and early Romanesque churches is inevitable," writes Otto-Wilhelm von Vacano. "But it is just this comparison with medieval coronas which brings out clearly the peculiarity and profound heterogeneity of the Cortona lamp. Whereas the former are heavenly bodies, as it were, orbiting around the golden celestial sphere that is the sun and God himself, the latter is turned to the night and the unconscious . . . it is an image of a mighty subterranean world."

> **"But it is just this comparison with medieval coronas which brings out clearly the peculiarity and profound heterogeneity of the Cortona lamp. Whereas the former are heavenly bodies, as it were, orbiting around the golden celestial sphere that is the sun and God himself, the latter is turned to the night and the unconscious . . . it is an image of a mighty subterranean world."**

We do not know all the places where the factories and foundries, studios and workshops were located. It was not yet customary to affix a "made in so-and-so" label on everything to indicate the place of origin. But they were in the interior of Etruria, in towns which experienced a boom after the decline of the previously important seaports. The names of some—only of the most important bronze-making centers—are known. Chiusi was one of them; its specialty was splendid cauldrons and candlesticks. From the north, possibly from Bologna, came branched candlesticks ornamented with mythological figures and groups. From Vulci came a variety of highly esteemed drinking vessels and vase handles, tripods with feet shaped like lion's paws, and incense burners with dancers and Sileni.

Among the principal customers were the Greeks. Etruscan bronzes have come to light in various parts of Hellas and in Magna Graecia. They have been found in excavations at Locri in southern Italy, at Lindos on the island of Rhodes, and at Olympia and Dodona in Greece. Tripods from Vulci were buried in the graves of Spina on the Adriatic, and when, in Athens, the rubble from the time of the Persian wars was cleared away, the excavators found on the Acropolis a fragment from one of the finest of Etruscan bronze tripods.

On the middle Rhine and in Burgundy the first indigenous artistic style appeared in response to the stimulus and inspiration brought by the foreign articles that came over the Alps from the south. Specimens of the La Tène culture, named after the place where they were first found, appear around 450 B.C. It is precisely to the same period that we can date Etruscan deliveries of a special type of war material that was much appreciated by the indigenous Celtic tribes and played an important part in their later far-ranging military expeditions. Burials of Celtic chieftains near Coblenz, and on the river Marne at La Gorge Meillet, were found to contain two-wheeled war chariots of Etruscan provenance.

In the course of their assistance to the development of the city on the Tiber, the Etruscans had already supplied modern arms and military training to their future greatest and deadliest enemy, the Romans, and now they aided their second most dangerous coming foe with the latest military techniques. Their deliveries of arms helped the barbarous tribes of the north to come of age, just as it had earlier done for the Latins. Half a century later the leaders of the Celtic hordes bursting into the plains south of the Alps came in war chariots modeled on those exported by Etruscan merchants.

No ancient writer has left the slightest reference to Etruria's flourishing economy and industry of those days, nor to its foreign trade. Even Herodotus has nothing to say about it, or about life in Etruria. And for him it would have been easy to obtain accurate information. He lived for years in southern Italy, at Thurii, not far from Croton, whose inhabitants in the previous century had destroyed Sybaris, Etruria's most important trading partner in Magna Graecia. He was well placed for gathering most interesting historical details.

236

Only one of his great Greek contemporaries once briefly mentions the Etruscans. This is Aeschylus, who several times stayed with the tyrant of Syracuse to organize stage festivals for him at the local theater, during which his famous work *The Persians* was given its first performance. In a surviving fragment we find the remark that the Etruscans are "a people good at preparing medicines." That is all.

Posterity first gained some notion of the extent of the trade in bronzes and vases between Etruria and Athens from the activities of treasure seekers who in the last century began to dig about in the soil of Tuscany, especially in the necropolis near Vulci, which was one of the most important centers of the bronze industry. "Every one who had land in the neighbourhood tilled it for this novel harvest," says Dennis, "and all with abundant success; the Feoli, Candelori, Campanari, Fossati—all enriched themselves and the museums of Europe with treasures from this sepulchral mine."

Dennis himself witnessed the methods used by the excavators employed by Lucien Bonaparte's widow in a necropolis situated on her property. "And a pretty property it is," he says, "rendering an excellent return to its possessor; for while her neighbours are contenting themselves with well-stocked granaries, or overflowing winepresses, the Princess to her earlier is adding a latter harvest—the one of metaphorical, the other of literal gold, or of articles convertible into that metal. Yet, in gathering in the latter harvest, the other is not forgotten, for, to lose no surface that can be sown with grain, the graves, when rifled, are refilled with earth. . . .

"At the mouth of the pit in which they were at work, sat the *capo*, or overseer—his gun by his side, as an *in terrorem* hint to his men to keep their hands from picking and stealing. We found them on the point of opening a tomb. The roof . . . had fallen in, and the tomb was filled with earth, out of which the articles it contained had to be dug in detail. This is generally a process requiring great care and tenderness, little of which, however, was here used, for it was seen by the first objects brought to light that nothing of value was to be expected . . . Coarse pottery of unfigured, unvarnished ware, and a variety of small vases in black clay, were its only produce; and as they drew them forth, the labourers crushed them beneath their feet as things 'cheaper than seaweed.' In vain we pleaded to save some from destruction; they were *roba di sciocchezza*—'foolish stuff'—the *capo* was inexorable; his orders were to destroy immediately whatever was of no pecuniary value, and he could not allow us to carry away one of these relics which he so despised. It is lamentable that excavations should be carried on in such a spirit; with the sole view of gain, and with no regard to the advancement of science. Such is too frequently the case."

In the third (1883) edition of his book, Dennis noted that the control of excavations had been much improved since the time of the Princess of Canino, when "facts, often, it may be, of great importance, were unnoticed and unrecorded. We saw, in the Museums of Europe, from Paris to St. Petersburg, the produce of these Vulcian tombs, we admired the surpassing elegance of the vases and the beauty of their designs, and marvelled at the extinct civilization they indicate; but they afforded us no conception of the places in which they had been preserved for so many centuries, or of their relations thereto."

By 1856, Dennis said, more than fifteen thousand tombs had been opened in the Vulci necropolis. This figure is all the more astonishing when it is remembered that the burials at Vulci, like those of all the other great Etruscan cemeteries, had already been rifled for some two thousand years, during which time tens of thousands of graves had been long filled in and had vanished from the earth.

"All the tombs are empty," wrote D. H. Lawrence, who visited Etruria in the 1920s, in his description of the great necropolis at Cerveteri. *"All have been rifled."*

"All the tombs are empty," wrote D. H. Lawrence, who visited Etruria in the 1920s, in his description of the great necropolis at Cerveteri. "All have been rifled. The Romans may have respected the dead, for a certain time, while their religion was sufficiently Etruscan to exert a power over them. But later, when the Romans started collecting Etruscan antiques—as we collect antiques today—there must have been a great sacking of the tombs. Even when all the gold and silver and jewels had been pilfered from the urns—which no doubt happened very soon after the Roman dominion—still the vases and the bronze must have remained in their places. Then the rich Romans began to collect vases, 'Greek' vases with the painted scenes. So these were stolen from the tombs. Then the

238

little bronze figures, statuettes, animals, bronze ships, of which the Etruscans put thousands in their tombs, became the rage with the Roman collectors. Some smart Roman gentry would have a thousand or two choice little Etruscan bronzes to boast of. Then Rome fell, and the barbarians pilfered whatever was left. So it went on."

"What sacred trophy marks the hallow'd ground?" asked Byron in another context, and answered, "The rifled urn, the violated mound."

The rediscovered vases of Vulci, which were expensive imports from Athens, speak volumes for the immense wealth of Etruria, testify to a luxurious way of life that could be enjoyed only thanks to the efficiency and output of Etrurian industry and handicrafts, and to the country's worldwide foreign trade.

The main cities of Etruria such as Caere, Tarquinii, Vetulonia, and Vulci were really large towns by the standards of the time, with populations exceeded only by the major Greek cities, chiefly by Athens, which expanded rapidly after the victory over the Persians, when it enjoyed an exceptional boom, and became the largest Greek city. Only Syracuse and Corinth came anywhere near it in population. And the Etruscan cities at their peak of prosperity may well have excelled even Athens in their standard of living.

A faint reflection of the brilliance and splendor of that period has survived in the unique wall paintings of Etruscan chamber tombs. In the necropolis at Tarquinia there are many of the finest, which have become world-famous. And they are only a mere fraction of the multitude that once existed. Two of them take us back into the life of great Etruscan families in the fifth century B.C., as it were, make us eyewitnesses to their banquets and festivals in a long-buried past. They revive a long-forgotten era of the Etruscans, a people to whom the West, and indeed the whole of Europe, owes more than is yet realized.

While Rome, within a few decades of becoming a republic, had relapsed into Spartan simplicity and a drab, utilitarian atmosphere, a mere sixty miles or so to the north stood Tarquinii, in spirit a whole world away, as were its sister cities. A few narrow stairs take us down into the Tomb of the Leopards in the great cemetery outside the city, and we enter a world that was rich, highly civilized, and familiar with every refinement.

The tomb, hewn out of the rock, is bathed in color. The frescoes on the creamy white walls shine with red ocher, blue, olive green, all as fresh as though the artist had brushed them in yesterday instead of twenty-four centuries ago. A checkerboard pattern in red, black, yellow, and blue decorates the ceiling, and dark red, yellow, and blue circles the stone beam. In the pediment facing the entrance two leopards confront each other across a tree.

A sumptuous banquet is in full swing. On the right and left walls the broad, brightly colored frieze shows a servant and musicians advancing amid shrubs, olives perhaps, or laurels, toward the banqueting room depicted on the end wall. The figures on the left wall are stepping calmly, while those on the right look as though they had difficulty in controlling their excitement. At the end of this wall, nearest the diners, is a servant holding a large, shallow goblet, and looking back over his shoulder to the musicians, to whom he beckons. First is a curly-headed young man who is playing the double flute; after him hurries another holding a cithara, a lutelike instrument, by its strings. The musicians wear loosely hanging knee-length mantles; the cup-bearer nothing but a broad sash, the Etruscan *tebenna,* draped over the shoulders. These figures seem to move like dancers, pulsing with life, instinctively rhythmic to their fingertips. There is an extraordinary zest in their gestures, their precise steps, in the posture of each one of them.

There are six banqueters on three couches, a man and woman on

Banquet, detail of fresco
from the Tomb of the Leopards, Tarquinia; c.470 B.C.

the center one, the same on the right, and two men on the left. More shrubs are placed behind and in front of their couches. The men are dark-haired, the women are blondes. All wear wreaths, possibly of myrtle, in their hair, as do the attendants and musicians. The men's shoulders and chests are bare above a white, blue-edged wrap; the women wear a diaphanous robe, the *chiton,* and over it a colored mantle. They wear three bracelets on each arm. Slaves pass between the upholstered couches, which are covered with colored rugs, to serve the banqueters.

A naked slave holds a wine jug horizontally, to show that it is already empty. To the right, one of the reclining men holds up to his companion the symbol of fertile immortality, an egg, for which she reaches out her hand. Their neighbors to the left have turned round, wave their hands and look interested in what is going on. The whole mood is one of gaiety and festivity. And yet at the same time there is something indescribably mysterious about the figures and the scene.

To the same period, about 470 B.C., belongs another tomb of the same necropolis, the Tomb of the Triclinium. In this case the frescoes were carefully removed from the walls and are now preserved in the museum at Tarquinia. They were included in the first big international exhibition of Etruscan art, which was seen in a number of European capitals from 1956 on, and which everywhere excited admiration.

They also depict a festive meal with music and dancing. Part of the fresco showing the banqueters is damaged and barely recognizable. When Dennis saw it in the last century it was in better condition. "There still remain, little impaired," he wrote, "two figures of opposite sexes, reclining on a couch, attended by a female servant with an *alabastos,* or pot of ointment, and a boy with a wine-jug, while a *subulo* stands in one corner playing the double-pipes . . . In front of each couch is an elegant *trapeza* or four-legged table, bearing dishes full of refreshments . . . Depending from the ceiling above the banquet are chaplets of different colours."

Before the imperial era the Romans were scandalized by sumptuous banquets such as those which were quite common among the Etruscans, and by other customs of theirs. Indeed, the frescoes might well have served as a shocking example of what was not proper. The Roman code of propriety was strict, tailored for a masculine society of peasant soldiers. Pliny the Elder proudly describes what was considered right in ancient Rome and what was held in contempt and was punishable: "The worst crime against mankind was committed by him who was the first to put a ring upon his fingers . . . It was the hand, and a sinister hand, too, in every sense, that first brought gold into such high repute: not a Roman hand, however, for upon that it was the practice to wear a ring of iron only, and solely as an indication of warlike prowess . . . For a great length of time . . . not even the Roman senators wore rings of gold: for rings were given, and at the public expense, to those only who were about to proceed on an embassy to foreign nations, the reason being, I suppose, because men of highest rank among foreign nations were perceived to be thus distinguished.

"Nor was it the practice for any person to wear these rings, except those who for this reason had received them at the public expense; and in most instances, it was without this distinction that the Roman generals celebrated their public triumphs. For whereas an Etruscan crown of gold was supported from behind over the head of the victor, he himself . . . had nothing but a ring of iron upon his finger . . . Those, too, who had received golden rings on the occasion of an embassy, only wore them in public, resuming the ring of iron when in their houses. It is in pursuance of this custom that even at the present day, an iron ring is sent by way of a present to a woman who is betrothed, and that, too, without any stone in it."

This custom, praised as a virtue in Rome, arose from necessity. Livy himself let slip the admission that for a long time there was very little gold in Rome. It was so scarce that the Law of the Twelve Tables, promulgated about 450 B.C., not only imposed severe penalties on the possession of gold, but even prohibited the burying of gold with the dead. Only one exception was permitted, gold dental fixtures, an invention of Etruscan goldsmiths.

Myrtle-wreathed men, let alone women, on festive occasions, as in Etruria, were something unthinkable to the Romans, for as Pliny states, they were acquainted only with wreaths given as the reward of military prowess. Of those, however, the Roman people had "more varieties . . . than those of all nations put together." The highest honor was the civic crown made of oak leaves. Its award was subject to strict conditions, "to the effect that the life of a fellow citizen"—and a Roman citizen at that—"must be preserved, and an enemy slain."

Festivities were not for women in the Rome of early times. They were not only barred from participating in banquets; total prohibition of alcohol was their lot. And woe to them if they were caught defying the ban. "At Rome it was not lawful for women to drink wine," says Pliny, and he cheerfully records some instances of what happened to transgressors. "We find that the wife of Egnetius Mecenius was slain by her husband with a stick, because she had drunk some wine from the vat, and that he was absolved from the murder by Romulus. Fabius Pictor, in his Book of Annals, has stated that a certain lady, for having opened a purse in which the keys of the wine-cellar were kept, was starved to death by her family." He further quotes Cato for the method of keeping a check on women with a taste for wine: "It was the usage for the male relatives to give the females a kiss, in order to ascertain whether they smelt of 'temetum,' for it was by that name that wine was then known."

It is obvious that uncouth peasant soldiers would not understand the customs of an old, highly civilized people and would accuse them of immorality. But for the Greeks to take a high moral line, especially in regard to Etruscan women, was more impertinent. The Greek writers Timaeus of Taormina, and Theopompus, depicted Etruscan women as given over to a lack of sexual restraint and to depravity which, says Mommsen, "in no way fell short of the worst immorality of Byzantium and France."

They were fine ones to complain. For when it comes to morality, the ancient Greeks far outdid the sex mania of the present day. Herodotus did not mince his words when he told his countrymen in Athens the truth about their morals. The Persians, he says, imported their vices and lust from foreign countries—"a notable instance is pederasty, which they learned from the Greeks."

The Greeks judged the Etruscans by themselves. Women at a banquet, with men on a couch—in the horizontal position too—

that could mean only one thing. By ancient custom throughout Hellas the women who did that must be venal, must be *hetaerae*. Demosthenes, the great orator and statesman, said flatly: "We have courtesans for our pleasures, concubines for the requirements of the body, and wives for the procreation of lawful issue."

Among the Greeks the women's quarters in the house were separate from those of the men. Women lived apart and ate by themselves. They were strictly forbidden to participate in the men's meals and banquets in the main hall. Nor were they allowed to discuss politics or attend gymnastic displays, as was taken for granted in Etruria. Herodotus states that in Miletus in the fifth century B.C. a wife never ate together with her husband, and was, in fact, not even allowed to address him by name.

Homer still allowed a privileged place to women. The Achaeans were monogamous. It was only Priam, the king of Troy, who maintained a harem. But about 700 B.C. the old ways changed. The idea that woman was inferior gained ground. Hesiod, the pious poet and rough farmer whose family came from Asia Minor, preached misogyny. For him, woman was a calamitous gift of the gods. She was Pandora, the giver of all evil, from whom was descended the race of women, who bring misfortune to mortal men. From his time, women in Hellas were banned from public life. They began to live in a harem.

The future housewife got no schooling as a girl. She was simply left uneducated. Greek men found their amusement and stimulation in the company of "companions," *hetaerae*. Some of them were, in fact, highly cultivated, with a knowledge of music, literature, art, and philosophy. It was they, and not the married women, who were admired and highly respected. Greek history is full of them, and the names of many have survived, such as Glycera, "Sweetie," loved by the poet Menander, Aspasia, the mistress of Pericles, Lais, who gave herself for nothing to the penniless Diogenes and made up for it by exacting yet bigger presents for her services from the rich philosopher Aristippus, down to Phryne, whom Praxiteles immortalized in marble and whose breasts the lawyer Hypereides uncovered to win over the judge of the case in which he was defending her.

The Greek woman had only one respectable public employment open to her—that of priestess. It was the same among the Romans.

Apart from that, the man, as pater familias, was absolute master, and woman had no say outside the household.

The position of women marked the division between two opposed worlds, that of the Greeks and Romans and that of the Etruscans. In Etruria, women were highly regarded and enjoyed social equality. Tanaquil, the wife of the first Tarquin king of Rome, was not only involved in politics; she was also an adept of the arcane science of the priests.

But the example of Etruria was not to prevail. Victory lay with the ideas of Hellas and Rome. Thus the path was laid down which the women of Europe had to follow until recent times, a path over-shadowed by the world of men.

Nothing changed in woman's social position and in the prejudices to which she was subject. Christianity, which chose Rome for its highest see, left things as they were, indeed, even made them worse. *Mulier taceat in ecclesia,* "Let your women keep silence in the churches." Women could not be priests nor preachers. No matter how much the Holy Virgin might be revered, this did not improve women's position.

Maybe the *Minnesänger,* who sang the praises of the loveliest of the lovely, might have brought about a change. But the service of love died out with medieval chivalry. It was not until the English suffragettes that the struggle began for the rights which Etruria had conceded to women twenty-five centuries earlier, for Europe re-mained obsessed by the ideas which prevailed among the Greeks in the seventh and sixth centuries B.C.

There was still a chance in the fifth century B.C. that the Etruscan attitude would become the model for the West. At that time, even after the loss of Rome and Campania, the rich, industrialized city-states still had the means and the power to make themselves masters of the whole of Italy, if only they had been united and determined to do it. Rome would not have been an obstacle. Militarily it was still in kindergarten, being insignificant and small in comparison with Etruria. Its entire territory could be viewed from any one of the seven hills. But the struggle for political power was something alien to the Etruscans. Their energies were directed to other ends. What those were can be seen from their painted tombs.

The image of the Etruscans that has survived is of a people won-derfully relaxed and gay, devoted to the pleasures of life. They are figures from a different, strange, and happy world. Yet the skirmishes and clashes of those days were already part of the Etruscans' great conflict with Rome which was to destroy them and their grandchildren, their whole people and civilization.

PART FOUR

Decline of the Etruscan Empire

Because the Roman took the life out of the Etruscan,
was he therefore greater than the Etruscan?

D. H. Lawrence, 1932

XVII

The Rediscovery of Veii

AT NO GREAT DISTANCE FROM ROME, to the north of the Tiber, the Campagna spreads out in a more or less level plain cut into by ravines. In the midst of this region once lay mighty Veii. Its territory extended northward to Lake Vico and the Ciminian Mountains, was bounded in the west by the city-state of Caere (Cerveteri) and in the east and south stretched from the middle Tiber to its mouth, the present Ostia, where the *salinae,* the salt works, were. The right bank of the Tiber, opposite Rome, with the Janiculum and Monte Mario and what is now the Vatican City, was at that time known as the "Etruscan bank."

The remains of Veii lie deserted. Among all the many thousands of annual visitors to Rome hardly anyone goes out there and climbs the steep tufa plateau, desolate in its solitude. It does not look very different now from what it must have been a few years before the Christian era when the Roman poet Propertius stayed there, and, moved by the melancholy fate that had befallen the once famous city, wrote:

Veii of old had monarchs of her own,
And in her forum stood a golden throne:
Now in her walls the plodding shepherd's horn
Sings, and amid her bones men reap the corn.

Veii at the height of its prosperity is said to have had about a hundred thousand inhabitants. Dionysius says that it was as big as Athens, which had a circumference of six to seven miles. At a time when Rome was still a modest settlement, Veii had long crowned its tableland with temples and other splendid buildings. For two centuries it eclipsed Rome, until at last, having become great and strong, the latter was able to deliver an annihilating blow to its proud Etruscan neighbor. Veii was never to recover, and after the decline of the Roman empire, complete oblivion descended on the Etruscan city.

In the Middle Ages no one knew where the once great rival of Rome had stood. Civita Castellana was at one time thought to be the site, but, as is now known, it was built over the ancient Falerii Veteres. It was not until the last century, with its general rediscovery of the Etruscans, that Veii was located. It lies on the right of the Via Cassia, some twelve miles from Rome, near the hamlet of Isola Farnese.

But at first, few remains were found. "It is to be regretted that so little is to be seen of the long-forgotten dead of Veii," says Dennis. "It was the largest, and, in Romulus's time, the most mighty of Etruscan cities, and yet in scarcely another cemetery are there so few tombs to be seen . . . Yet excavations are frequently, almost yearly, carried forward, mostly by dealers in antiquities at Rome; but as lucre is their sole object they are content to rifle the tombs of everything convertible into cash, and cover them in immediately with earth."

At the time of Dennis's visit, only one tomb was open, that dis-covered in 1842–3 by the Marchese Campana and named after him. It is described by Dennis in some detail: "Half way up the slope of a mound, the Poggio Michele, is a long passage, about six feet wide, cut through the rock towards the centre of the hill. At the entrance

250

on each side crouches a stone lion, of that quaint, singular style of sculpture, that ludicrously clumsy form, which the antiquary recognises as the conventional mode among Etruscan sculptors of representing the king of beasts. At the further end of the passage crouch two similar lions, one on each side of the door of the tomb—all intended as figurative guardians of the sepulchre."

In a footnote Dennis adds: "Figures of lions, as images of power, and to inspire dread, are of very ancient use, and quite oriental. Thus Solomon set lions around his throne . . . and the Egyptians and Hindoos placed them at the entrance of their temples . . . The monuments of Lycia, now in the British Museum, and the tombs of Phrygia . . . show this animal in a similar relation to sepulchres; and moreover establish a strong point of analogy between Etruria and the East."

Dennis describes what he saw on entering the tomb: "It is a moment of excitement, this—the first peep within an Etruscan painted tomb; and if this be the first the visitor has beheld, he will find food enough for wonderment. He enters a low, dark chamber, hewn out of the rock, whose dull greyish hue adds to the gloom. He catches an imperfect glance of several jars of great size, and smaller pieces of crockery and bronze, lying on benches or standing on the floor, but he heeds them not, for his eye is at once riveted on the extraordinary paintings on the inner wall of the tomb, facing the entrance. Were there ever more strangely devised, more grotesquely designed figures?—was there ever such a harlequin scene as this. Here is a horse with legs of most undesirable length and tenuity, chest and quarters far from meagre, but barrel pinched in like a lady's waist . . . His neck and fore-hand are red, with yellow spots—his head black—mane and tail yellow—hind-quarters and near leg black—near fore-leg corresponding with his body, but off-legs yellow, spotted with red. His groom is naked, and his skin is of a deep-red hue. A boy of similar complexion bestrides the horse; and another man precedes him, bearing a hammer, or, it may be, a *bipennis,* or double-headed axe, upon his shoulder; while on the croup crouches a tailless cat or dog, parti-coloured like the steed, with one paw familiarly resting on the boy's shoulder. Another beast, similar in character, but with the head of a dog, stands beneath the horse. . . .

"In the band below is a sphinx, standing, not crouching, as is usual on ancient Egyptian monuments, with a red face and bosom, spotted with white—straight black hair, depending behind—wings short, with curling tips, and striped black, red, and yellow . . . A panther, or large animal of the feline species, sits behind, rampant, with one paw on the haunch, the other on the tail of the sphinx; and beneath the latter is an ass, or it may be a deer, of smaller size than the panther. Both are painted in the same curious parti-colours as those already described. . . .

"On the opposite side of the doorway (for there is a door in this wall, opening into an inner chamber), in the upper band, is a horse, with a boy on his back, and a 'spotted pard' behind him sitting on the ground. In the lower band is another similar beast of great size, with his tongue lolling out and a couple of dogs beneath him. All these quadrupeds are of the same curious patchwork of red, yellow, and black . . . The land of the Nile however may be seen in the ornamental border of lotus-flowers, emblematical of immortality, which surmounts the figures. . . .

". . . The most untutored eye can perceive at a glance that the paintings belong to a very early age of the world. After having carefully studied every other painted tomb now open in Etruria, I have not a moment's hesitation in asserting that this is in point of antiquity pre-eminent; and, I believe, that few other tombs in Italy, though unpainted, have any claim to be considered anterior to it."

Dennis was right. The Campana tomb dates from the end of the seventh century B.C.

In January, 1958, another, even older painted tomb was discovered at Veii, the Tomba delle Anatre, the Tomb of the Ducks. In this too the artist used only black, red, and yellow. Above a bright red band is a frieze of five ducks profiled against a yellow background, head and neck stretching up, and moving toward the tufa pedestal of the dead. Believed to have been painted between 675 and 650 B.C., they are, according to the Italian scholar Alfredo d'Agostino, "the oldest wall painting so far found

> *Despite the discoveries, the desolate tableland of Veii, covered only with sparse grass and scrub, is still solitary and silent but for the sound of rushing waters falling into the depths of the earth.*

The "Aurora" vase from Eaterli; fourth century B.C.

in Etruria." Mario Torelli calls the painting "a document of extraordinary importance, both historically and artistically," which attests the existence in Etruria of monumental forms of art even at that early date.

Despite the discoveries, the desolate tableland of Veii, covered only with sparse grass and scrub, is still solitary and silent but for the sound of rushing waters falling into the depths of the earth. Springs still flow into the ancient tunnels which the Etruscans once cut into the brown tufa.

In the sacred temple area springs bubble up, and after heavy rainfall the Cremera, or Valchetta, as it is now called, rushes in a wild torrent through the Ponte Sodo, the so-called solid bridge which is really a tunnel, at places some twenty-five feet high and twelve feet wide, dug through the cliff. Etruscan engineers made it to cut off a spur of the hill, and it still carries the stream for more than seventy yards in a straight line through the solid rock.

Up above on the bare plateau, where the cliff drops perpendicularly some 180 feet, a fragment of wall remains, part of the fortifications that guarded the Arx (now called Piazza d'Armi), the citadel of Veii.

On a rocky platform somewhat below the crest, excavators shortly before the First World War made the first significant discoveries. At the edge of the cliff, widely visible from afar, once stood a great temple, bright and colorful with its painted terra-cottas and statues aloft on the roof. It was badly damaged, and only a stone base, with traces of the sanctuary building, remained.

An elaborate system of water conduits, runnels, and tanks surrounds the altar, which must mean, as John Ward-Perkins states, that "water evidently played an important part in the ritual associated with the cult." It is possible that sulfurous springs were channeled into a wide stone basin, in which those seeking a cure for their ailments may have bathed. Many ex-voto objects of terra-cotta have been found nearby, from which it has been concluded that the temple had a reputation for its medical cures.

Within this temple area the Italian archeologist G. Q. Giglioli had the good fortune to make the finest discovery yet in the soil of Etruria. On May 19, 1916, in an exploratory trench along a wall, he came upon a statue, life-size, of terra-cotta, buried upright among layers of rubble. It was the head that first became visible. Once it had been carefully disengaged from the surrounding soil and rubbish, there appeared intact a face with an enigmatic smile and slanting eyes seemingly gazing into the far distance. It was the face of a god, of Apollo, the son of Zeus.

The excavators were struck dumb at the unexpected sight of the divine head thus suddenly brought to light after millenniums. Overcome by the excitement of the moment, Giglioli fell upon the head and covered it with kisses. With immense care the excavators went on digging. The statue was found to be nearly six feet high and painted, the flesh reddish brown, and the hair, shoulder-length, black. The figure is dressed in a soft, pleated, knee-length tunic.

Thus wrested from his ancient sacred precinct, the god found a new home in the Villa Giulia Museum in Rome. In a strange setting surrounded by admirers, Apollo seems to want to hasten away, back to that world and time which have long passed irrevocably away with the god himself.

What can the statue mean to us now, what can it tell us? It has become a precious relic of a distant past; the sight of it moves us strangely and yet it seems to have become devoid of meaning. It has become alien and incomprehensible by the mere passage of so many centuries which have changed and destroyed so much.

The statue is attributed to Vulca by Pallottino. Its creator, whoever he was, had a profound understanding of this god. The Apollo belonged to a group representing Hercules's theft of the sacred hind from the temple of Apollo at Delphi. Pieces of the other figures were found nearby, as well as the head of a Hermes, discovered later. Finally, in 1939, the statue of a woman holding a child in her arms was excavated.

But what do the Greek legends and myths signify in this context? In these works the Etruscan artists exploded Hellenic models, broke formal laws that had become rigid. At the same time they demonstrated a realism uncommon for that early period, and unknown to the Greeks, a realism which nonetheless expresses the incomprehensible powers of creation, the blind cruelty of the cosmos. The enigmatic smile of this Apollo seems to reflect the knowledge of a long-lost image of the universe. Another such figure is a Gorgon head of diabolical hideousness, encircled by its brightly painted snakes, with tongue hanging out, an expression and symbol of those same primeval forces of nature. It decorated the roof-tree of the sanctuary near which it was only recently found, along with other fragments of Sileni and maenads.

There is an extraordinary desolation about the site of ancient Veii, now stripped of its most precious treasures and relics. At sunset the dark russet tufa glows in the dying light, until dusk blurs the colors and night covers the rocky summit, and its black silhouette stands out against the distant, twinkling lights of modern Rome, successor to that imperial Rome whose rise began 2,600 years ago with the destruction of Veii.

No one knows about it now. Nor about the long-drawn struggle that raged around this mighty Etruscan city. No less than fourteen wars are recorded, the first six being as early as the period of the kings in Rome. But those were mere family quarrels, fought out between Etruscans, for even on the Tiber Etruscan kings reigned.

But once Rome had become a republic, the situation changed completely. Veii, the rich, foreign state at its gates, was to be Rome's first victim. Not to have recognized this in good time, not to have taken the necessary measures when at the height of her power, was what decided the fate of Veii.

THE HUNDRED YEARS' WAR

FROM THE BEGINNING OF THE fifth century B.C. Veii was never left in peace. In almost uninterrupted feuding and fighting, Rome suffered its occasional defeats, but stubbornly kept up its aggression until, shortly after 400 B.C., it finally subdued its neighbor.

In 485 B.C. Roman troops made their first raid over the border. Two years later, in 483 B.C., began the first long war, which lasted almost ten years, and, in the annals of Rome, became the glorious tale of the fame and destruction of the Fabii. Livy has given us a full account of it all.

At a time when hostilities with Veii prevented Rome from turning her attention elsewhere, "trouble was imminent from other quarters as well." There was a threat from the Volscians and the Aequians, "and it was clear that the Sabines, Rome's inveterate enemies, and all Etruria would before long be on the march." In this situation, Caeso Fabius, head of the Fabian family and at that time one of Rome's two consuls, put a proposal before the senate. "As you know," Livy reports him as saying, "in our dealings with Veii what we need is a regular permanent force, not necessarily a large one. Our suggestion therefore is that you put the task of controlling Veii into our hands, while you attend to other wars elsewhere."

On the following day all the Fabian clan, equipped for service, assembled at the appointed place. "The consul, in the crimson cloak of a commander . . . took his place among them and gave the word to march. Never before had an army so small and so glorious marched through the streets of Rome."

There were 306 men, and not one of them came back alive save one boy, we are told. They erected a stronghold on the Cremera River and from there raided the enemy's land. But one day, in a pitched battle, "they were all killed and their fort taken." Rome had its first heroes, the first shining example for its warriors.

Thereafter the Veiians went over to the offensive. Some of their troops occupied the Janiculum hill, others crossed the Tiber and threatened the city itself. Having broken the Romans' resistance in a first bout of fighting at the Temple of Hope, the Veiians subsequently suffered heavy losses in a battle at the Colline Gate, when the Romans, reinforced by Latins from Tusculum, expelled the invaders.

The war came to an end a couple of years later, when two Roman armies, under the command of the consuls, managed to encircle the Etruscans, who "thus found themselves caught between two fires; in trying to escape first one contingent and then the other, they were severely mangled." A forty-year truce was concluded in 474 B.C.

Veii lost its hold on the Etruscan town of Fidenae on the left bank of the Tiber, and the position of the regal period was fully restored. But well before the truce had run out, hostilities again broke out in 445 B.C. At first, they amounted to nothing more than border incursions and raids. But then, in 438 B.C. Fidenae suddenly defected. Rome's garrison was driven out, four of its envoys were murdered, and the town went over to Lars Tolumnius, king of Veii. War ensued. Again we have Livy's account of what happened.

Before the walls of Fidenae, Lars Tolumnius was killed by Aulus Cornelius Cossus, who "stripped the lifeless body of its armor, cut off its head and, sticking it on the point of a lance, returned to the fight with his spoils. At the sight of their dead king, the enemy broke and fled."

The "linen corselet" of the slain king was hung, as *spolia opima*, spoils of honor, in the temple of Jupiter Ferentius, where it remained for the emperor Augustus still to see and read the inscription.

The following year, under the consulship of Marcus Cornelius Maluginensis and Lucius Papirius Crassus, renewed Roman raids into the territory of Veii and Falerii brought home a number of prisoners and some captured cattle. When the Romans besieged and took Fidenae, both Veii and Falerii in 435 B.C. sent envoys to all Etruscan cities, asking for an immediate meeting of the heads of the League of Twelve at the shrine of Voltumna. This was agreed to, and when Rome got the news through its spies and realized how big a danger threatened it from "a united Etruria," it did at once what was customary in times of great danger: it appointed a dictator as sole supreme commander.

However, "Veii failed to secure support: having started the war on her own initiative she must carry it on with her own resources, and not expect friends to share her troubles when they had not been offered a share in the prospect of success." As far as Rome was concerned, therefore, "the whole affair ended more peacefully than anyone expected."

> *No one recognized Rome's threat to all of them. Only this can explain the hesitation, the indecision, the postponement of action.*

Nor was Veii more successful with its pleading at the next annual meeting of the Etruscan cities, where, although war plans were discussed, "a decision was postponed for a year and a decree issued forbidding any further meeting until the year was over, in spite of the urgent and bitter representations of Veii that she was threatened with the same disaster as that which had brought destruction to Fidenae."

No one recognized Rome's threat to all of them. Only this can explain the hesitation, the indecision, the postponement of action. Each city seemed to be concerned only with its own affairs and interests. It may be, of course, that the Etruscans' attitude owed something also to another worry. Disturbing news had come from the Po valley in the north; messengers told of a Celtic march upon the Apennines. The city-states began to strengthen their fortifications. Powerful cyclopean walls, fortified with towers, were built of huge hewn blocks of stone, rectangular and polygonal. Tarquinii surrounded itself with a wall seven and a half miles in circumference; Volterra built a similar wall of over four miles, and Volsinii one of some three miles. In many places remnants are still visible of these impressive structures, which became the model for Rome's own fortifications.

In despair, Veii once more seized the initiative. Success seemed to be with its armies at first. In a single battle, three Roman commanders were beaten, and this news attracted to Veii's cause a good many volunteers hoping for loot. But the only town to pledge support was Fidenae, which thereupon was made the combined military base. It was against Fidenae, therefore, that the dictator Mamercus Aemilius marched with a Roman army. Not far from the town, a fierce battle took place and the Romans were winning, when an astonishing thing happened, as Livy records.

"The Etruscans were already reeling under the weight of the Roman attack, when suddenly through the open gates of Fidenae came pouring a stream of men armed with fire. It was like an army from another world—something never seen or imagined before that moment. There were thousands of them, all lit by the glare of their blazing torches, and like madmen, or devils, they came rushing into the fray."

In the first moment of terror and confusion the front ranks of the Roman troops gave way. But then the cavalry galloped into the thick of the flame and the troops took new heart. The Fidenaetes' unusual stratagem availed them nothing. The Etruscans were beaten, Fidenae was taken and sacked, and all able-bodied survivors sold as slaves. Veii obtained from victorious Rome a truce of twenty years.

But Rome from that day on secretly armed for the final struggle with Veii, now deprived of its only ally, Fidenae. When the truce ended in 408 B.C., Rome was ready with a huge army. The senate issued a proclamation "that anyone who pleased might go to Camillus and the army at Veii to claim his share in the plunder. Thousands took advantage of it, and swarmed into the camp."

Livy gives this account of what followed: "Camillus . . . ordered all troops to stand to. 'Pythian Apollo,' he prayed, 'led by you and inspired by your holy breath, I go forward to the destruction of Veii, and I vow to you a tenth part of the spoils. Queen Juno, to you too I pray, that you may leave this town where now you dwell and follow our victorious arms into our City of Rome, your future home, which will receive you in a temple worthy of your greatness.' From every direction and with overwhelming numbers Roman troops moved forward to the assault."

The events that followed, with the siege of this fortified town which, like Troy, is supposed to have held out for ten years, became the subjects of Roman legend and Roman poets. And rightly so, for it was a great fight for a great prize. For the first time in their history the Romans undertook to subdue a nation not of their blood, and to gain a permanent foothold beyond the old northern frontier of the Latin country, beyond the Tiber.

For the first time, too, a Roman army remained in the field year in year out, summer and winter, and the soldiers were paid out of public funds. For once begun, the siege of Veii could not be broken off.

While the Romans had the military support of the Latins and the Hernici, to whom the fall of the dreaded Etruscan neighbor promised as much satisfaction and gain as to Rome itself, Veii stood alone, abandoned by its kin, helped only by a few neighboring cities, including Capena, Falerii, and Tarquinii. A last appeal for solidarity went unheard. "The Etruscan communities at a full council at the shrine of Voltumna failed to agree upon whether or not the whole nation should unite in defense of Veii."

This was tantamount to a death sentence, and it was the council's last word. In the following year at the Voltumna shrine the question of aid to Veii was again discussed, and again the majority of city-states was against it.

There must have been deep-seated resentments behind this stubborn refusal. Like all the other city-states, Veii had been ruled by annually elected officials since its last king, Lars Tolumnius, had been killed in battle. But then, Livy explains, the Veiians, "in disgust at the annually recurring scramble for office which had not seldom given rise to bitter quarrels," appointed another king. And it was he, says Livy, who was the cause of the Etruscan communities refusing Veii their help, for he had once deeply offended them. Every year when they met at their national shrine, the spokesmen of the Etruscan communities elected a priest. Once, this king of Veii had stood for this coveted office of *"sacerdos Etruriae,"* but he was not elected and in a rage withdrew all his actors, dancers, and musicians from the sacred games "without warning, and while the show was still in progress." This greatly angered and upset the Etruscans, a people more than most deeply concerned with religious matters and averse to departing in even the slightest way from the prescribed sacred rites.

It will never be known whether this incident really was the only reason why the league refused to come to the aid of Veii. Be that as it may, what Rome feared did not happen—the Etruscans as a whole nation failed to enter the war on Veii's side.

Yet the Romans could not be certain of their good luck. Spies reported that at Voltumna there had been a strong anti-Roman faction, even though Veii's request was rejected. So, on the principle that it is better to be safe than sorry, the Roman besiegers of Veii "took the precaution of constructing their field-works both for offense and defense—facing the town to prevent sorties, and also confronting the open country to block any assistance which might come from elsewhere in Etruria."

Once only, after six long years of siege, Veii had a brief hour of triumph. The Faliscans and Capenates, upstream on the Tiber, had long realized that if Veii fell, the whole country would be open to invasion, and they, being nearest, would be the next to suffer. After long hesitation, they suddenly made up their minds, equipped an army, and sent secret messengers to beleaguered Veii.

And so it happened that when the Faliscans and Capenates suddenly appeared in the Romans' rear, the Veiians made a strong sally from the town, and the panic-stricken Romans had to fight on two fronts at once. They suffered heavy losses, had to abandon their forward positions and strong points, and such survivors as were not taken prisoner took to flight. For the first time in many years, Veii was not surrounded by enemies. But the respite was not to last.

Rome, after this setback, immediately raised new troops and returned with reinforcements. This time the Faliscans and Capenates were beaten and driven out of the country, and the Veiians were forced back into the town.

Veii, after years of effort, was nearing exhaustion. The people were short of food, which could be brought in only by night. They were short, above all, of weapons, and their position was becoming desperate. At yet another meeting at the shrine of Voltumna, envoys from Capena and Falerii pressed for a common effort to raise

261

the siege of Veii, but all they obtained was a promise that no objection would be raised if Etruscan fighting men volunteered for that service.

It was too little and too late. Things had gone too far; the Romans were too determined now to finish off their cornered quarry. For, so Livy boasts, "the terror of the Roman name will be such that the world shall know that, once a Roman army has laid siege to a city, nothing will move it—not the rigors of winter nor the weariness of months and years—that it knows no end but victory and is ready, if a swift and sudden stroke will not serve, to persevere till that victory is achieved. Perseverance is necessary in all kinds of warfare, but most of all in sieges."

> *It was too little and too late. Things had gone too far; the Romans were too determined now to finish off their cornered quarry.*

That particular siege had been going on for eight years, when stories started coming in "of a number of inexplicable and ominous occurrences." Rome did not pay much attention at first—perhaps, as Livy suggests, because "Rome always employed Etruscan soothsayers, and because of the war with Etruria there were none, at the time, in the city." "One occurrence, however," he adds, "caused universal anxiety: the lake in the Alban Wood, without any unusual rainfall or other natural cause, rose much above its normal height."

This happened in 398 B.C. Plutarch, in *Camillus,* gives this account of the prodigy: "It was the beginning of autumn, and the summer now ending had, to all observation, been neither rainy nor much troubled with southern winds; and many of the lakes, brooks, and springs of all sorts with which Italy abounds, some were wholly dried up, others drew very little water with them; all the rivers, as is usual in summer, ran in a very low and hollow channel. But the Alban lake, that is fed by no other waters but its own, and is on all sides encircled with fruitful mountains, without any cause, unless it were divine, began visibly to rise and swell, increasing to the feet of the mountains." Eventually, "when the earth, which, like a great dam, held up the lake from falling into the lower grounds, through the quantity and weight of water was broken down, and in a violent stream it ran through the ploughed fields and plantations to discharge itself in the sea, it not only struck terror into the Romans, but was thought by all the inhabitants of Italy to portend some extraordinary event."

There was a danger that the whole rim of the crater might give way, and the waters flood all the agricultural land of the Campagna. Sacrifices were of no avail, the gods seemed unwilling to be propitiated, and the waters of the Alban lake went on rising. The nonplussed Romans at last decided to send a mission to the Delphic oracle to find out the meaning of the prodigy. But another interpreter of the fates was much nearer at hand, for before the envoys returned from Delphi, the Romans happened to get hold of an Etruscan soothsayer at Veii. This is how Livy describes the episode:

"An old man of Veii . . . while Roman and Etruscan soldiers were exchanging chaff as they faced each other on their respective guard-posts, suddenly burst into prophecy and declared that Rome would never take Veii until the water in the Alban lake was drained off. The soldiers at first merely laughed, taking what the old fellow said as a meaningless gibe; but after a minute or two they began to talk it over, and finally one of them asked a man belonging to the town who the old fellow was . . . The answer was that he was a soothsayer.

"Now the Roman sentry who had asked the question was of a superstitious turn of mind, so pretending a wish to consult the soothsayer . . . about some private puzzle of his own, got him to come out and talk to him. Neither was armed and they walked off together some distance in apparently perfect mutual confidence, when the sentry, who was young and strong, suddenly seized his aged companion and carried him bodily to the Roman lines. The Etruscans who saw the act . . . raised a tremendous outcry but could do nothing to stop it.

"The soothsayer was taken to headquarters and then sent on to the senate in Rome, where he was asked to explain what he had meant. In reply he said that the gods must indeed have been angry with Veii on the day when they put it into his mind to reveal the doom which was destined to fall upon his country, and for that reason what he had then been inspired to speak he could not now recall as if it had never been spoken; for it might well be that it was as great a sin to conceal what the gods wished to be known as to speak what should remain concealed.

"He went on to say that it was known to Etruscan lore and written in the books of fate that if the Romans drained the water from the Alban lake after it had risen high, then they would be granted victory over Veii; till then, the gods of Veii would never desert her city walls. He then began to explain in detail the proper method of drawing off the water.

"The senate felt that the old man's authority was hardly adequate in a matter of such importance, so they decided to await the return of their mission to Delphi with the answer of the Pythian oracle."

The answer they brought home confirmed the old soothsayer's prophecy, but, as Zonaras tells us, Apollo, while requiring certain rituals, did not reveal just what they were and how they were to be performed. But the soothsayer knew. Under his instructions, sacrifices were offered and the water of the lake was let into a hidden passage and discharged into the plain, where it trickled into the fields instead of rushing down to the sea.

This legendary episode is most instructive. It shows, for one thing, that there was a prescribed ritual not only for the founding of cities, but even for hydraulic engineering. And it also makes it clear that at the time of the siege of Veii, a good deal more than a hundred years after the draining of the Roman Forum and the construction of the Cloaca Maxima, the Romans still had not mastered the technical knowledge and skill of their Etruscan teachers. They did not even know the precise position of the Etruscans' subterranean drainage and irrigation canals, some of them more than forty-five feet deep, which formed a dense network throughout Latium. The Etruscan experts, on the other hand, knew all about them, and also about the big emissary from the Alban lake.

The soothsayer of Veii must have had very accurate information about the "hidden passage," which had obviously been long neglected and was blocked up with rubble and mud. "Under his instructions" the tunnel was cleared and restored to working order. The emissary is still intact today, twenty-five hundred years later. It has often been repaired since, of course, but it still functions, just like the Cloaca Maxima in Rome. Even now, said George Dennis in 1883, "the Emissary of Albano calls forth the admiration of the traveller"—and if the traveler have a mind for the technical achievement of ancient peoples, in particular the Etruscans, this statement surely holds true in the 1970s as well.

On the edge of Lake Albano lies Castel Gandolfo, the papal summer residence, built on the site of ancient Alba Longa, the capital of the Latin league. From the Galleria di Sopra, a road along the edge of the crater lake shaded by evergreen oaks, a stairway leads down, in a few minutes' walk, to the famous emissary. It can also easily be reached from the railway station.

The tunnel was driven through the layers of lava that form the crater wall. It leads in a southwesterly direction and ends in the Campagna, near Le Mole. The tunnel is about two thousand yards long, four feet wide, and from six to nine feet high. A modern installation regulates the flow of the lake water through the entrance of the tunnel, by reducing excessive pressure, while filters and a screen prevent rubble and silt from choking up the tunnel. At the exit the water flows off into a number of channels that distribute it among fields and vineyards. The emissary is much bigger than the famous Siloam tunnel cut through the hill under Jerusalem by King Hezekiah in about 700 B.C. to bring water into the town. It measured about 550 yards in length.

No inscription, such as that at the Jerusalem tunnel, has ever been found recording the date or other historical details of the Alban emissary, and it is doubtful if there ever was one. The Romans were not interested in informing posterity about the achievements of Etruscan engineering.

While the tunnel was being cleared under the supervision of the soothsayer, fierce fighting broke out anew at Veii, to the great surprise of the Romans. Volunteers from Etruria, including some from Tarquinii, had arrived, and, together with the troops from Capena and Falerii already in the field, they succeeded in trapping two bodies of Roman forces. One of their commanders was killed and the other escaped only with difficulty. "The incident was only a minor defeat," says Livy, "but . . . the moral effect of it was tremendous; in Rome . . . there was something like panic."

To meet the threat of an Etruscan offensive, Marcus Furius Camillus, who had again been appointed dictator, recruited new forces from Rome and Latium, and marched north. Near the Faliscan town of Nepi he encountered the enemy, the forces of Falerii and Capena. He at once gave battle, and thanks to his superior tactics, defeated the Etruscans, captured their camp and a mass of booty. Camillus then turned around and proceeded back to Veii.

He knew that an attempt to storm the walls would be a hopeless undertaking. The Romans had not yet learned the well-tried technique of cracking a fortified city which the peoples of the ancient Orient, the Assyrians and Babylonians, had found indispensable in their campaigns, namely, the use of the battering-ram and the wheeled siege tower. It was only centuries later that the Romans learned it from the Greeks who had copied it during Alexander the Great's expedition in Asia.

> The Romans had not yet learned the well-tried technique of cracking a fortified city which the peoples of the ancient Orient, the Assyrians and Babylonians, had found indispensable in their campaigns, namely, the use of the battering-ram and the wheeled siege tower.

A city as strongly defended as Veii could only be captured by a stratagem. Camillus found a way similar to that of David attacking the Jebusites in Jerusalem, when he is reported to have said, "Whoever would smite the Jebusites, let him get up the water shaft." The Roman general had learned from patrols that the rocks were in many places pierced by narrow passages which the inhabitants had dug, probably either as secret ways of escape or in order to draw water from the Cremera, which flowed alongside the walls, without being seen. Closer examination revealed a tunnel leading upward. It was blocked with rubble; so men were set to work to dig this out and were kept at it day and night. They had come upon a passage that led up into the citadel and ended under the temple of Juno.

As soon as the tunnel was cleared, Roman assault troops took up their position in it. What happened then is described by Livy thus: "There is an old story that while the king of Veii was offering sacrifice, the priest declared that he who carved up the victim's entrails would be victorious in the war; the priest's words were overheard by some of the Roman soldiers in the tunnel, who thereupon opened it, snatched the entrails and took them to Camillus . . . The enemy, who were manning the walls against the threat from outside, were attacked from behind; bolts were wrenched off the gates; buildings were set on fire as women and slaves on the roofs flung stones and tiles at the assailants.

"A fearful din arose: yells of triumph, shrieks of terror, wailing of women, and the pitiful crying of children; in an instant of time the defenders were flung from the walls and the town gates opened: Roman troops came pouring through, or climbed the now defense-less walls; everything was overrun, in every street the battle raged. After terrible slaughter, resistance began to slacken, and Camillus gave the order to spare all who were not carrying arms. No more blood was shed, the unarmed began to give themselves up and the Roman troops with Camillus's leave, dispersed to sack the town . . . So ended that famous day, of which every hour was spent in the killing of Rome's enemies and the sacking of a wealthy city.

"Next day, all the free-born townsfolk were sold, by Camillus's orders, into slavery."

Finally, when all private property had been removed from the houses and palaces and public buildings, Camillus ordered the re-moval of the temple treasures and images of the gods. The heavy, magnificently worked bronze doors were taken away; these the dic-tator did not intend to hand over, but to keep for himself. The first great victory of a Roman general was marked by the beginning of Roman corruption.

The temple statue of Uni, Queen Juno as the Romans called the goddess, was removed for transport to Rome. It was done with the deepest reverence, says Livy: "young soldiers were specially chosen for the task . . . having washed their bodies and dressed them-selves in white, they entered her temple in awe, and shrank at first from what seemed the sacrilege of laying hands upon an image, which the Etruscan religion forbade anyone except the holder of a certain hereditary priesthood to touch.

"Suddenly one of them said: 'Juno, do you want to go to Rome?' Whether the question was divinely inspired or merely a young man's joke, who knows? But his companions all declared that the statue nodded its head in reply. We are told, too, that words were uttered, signifying assent. In any case—fables apart—she was moved from her place with only the slightest application of mechanical power, and was light and easy to transport—almost as if she came of her own free will—and was taken undamaged to her eternal dwelling-place on the Aventine, whither the dictator had called her in his prayer. And there Camillus afterwards dedicated to her the temple he had vowed."

Even Livy could not forbear to pay a tribute to the defeated enemy. "Such was the fall of Veii," he says, "the wealthiest city of Etruria. Even her final destruction witnessed to her greatness, for after a siege of ten summers and ten winters, during which she inflicted worse losses than she suffered, even when her destined hour had come she fell by a stratagem and not by direct assault."

In Rome the news of the fall of Veii was received with indescribable jubilation. "The return of Camillus drew greater crowds than had ever been seen on such an occasion in the past," says Livy, "people of all ranks in society pouring through the city gates to meet him; and the official celebration of his triumph left in its splendor all previous ones in the shade. Riding into Rome in a chariot drawn by white horses he was the cynosure of every eye . . .

"The ceremony over, Camillus contracted for the building of Juno's temple on the Aventine, consecrated a shrine to Mater Matuta, and resigned his office—his duties to religion and to the state being all accomplished."

Out of the proceeds of the booty the Romans, according to tradition, made a gift to Apollo in Delphi of a golden mixing bowl as a

Apulian flask in the shape of a duck; fourth–third century B.C.

thank-offering; it was preserved there in the treasury of the Massaliotes. The plunder from Veii, in particular the gold, was to come to the rescue of the Romans only a few years later when at a moment of dire need it enabled them to ransom the freedom of the city and themselves.

The Romans' enormous success in the war for Veii was one of the most crucial events in their history. Indeed, it became a milestone even for the historical records. Shortly before 400 B.C. there appeared, along with the list of the consuls in Rome, the tablets set up by the Pontifex Maximus, which formed the basis for the city chronicles. From then on, the principal events of each year were recorded on the white tablets under the name of the magistrate of the year. These *tabulae pontificum* provided the material for later Roman historiography and were the main source of the great chronicle in eighty books, the *Annales Maximi,* which were published by the Pontifex Maximus P. Mucius Scaevola when the priests' tablets ceased to be displayed.

> **Rome's war against Veii ended in 396 B.C., and with this campaign, the first of any length which Rome had fought, the rise of the city really began.**

Rome's war against Veii ended in 396 B.C., and with this campaign, the first of any length which Rome had fought, the rise of the city really began. A century earlier, Lars Porsena had been close to destroying Rome. Things were very different now. By the victory over the strong city of Veii, Rome had thrown off the shadow of mighty Etruria. Now the Tiber belonged to Rome alone. For the first time Rome had taken a firm hold on ancient Etruscan soil. Marcus Furius Camillus had opened the way to the future conquest of foreign peoples and states, and secured a base for all later campaigns against the Etruscans. With the capture of Nepi and neighboring Sutri, the Faliscan towns allied with Veii, the victors gained the most important key positions on the road to central Etruria.

"The fact . . . that it was possible for the remaining cities, despite all Veii's efforts to drag the Confederation as a whole into the war, to intervene so little in these events while there was still time to do so and Rome might still have been contained," says Otto-Wilhelm von Vacano, "demonstrates that the other Etruscans did not foresee how the Romans would act and did not recognize in time Rome's significance for their own existence. This underlines once again what other reports also make known, namely that the Confederation was not a body consisting of powers with a policy aimed at certain goals and developing dynamically, but a union of an old-fashioned kind based on religion and worship and deeply rooted in magical conceptions."

Rome's territorial gain was important. The victorious battles against Fidenae and Veii, which ended with the incorporation of their lands, nearly doubled the area of the Roman state from 316 to some 580 square miles. Some of this land was subsequently assigned to Roman colonists, who acted as a sort of frontier guard.

The conquest of Veii was long remembered in Rome. An echo of the rejoicing persisted through the centuries in the custom of the "sale of the Veiians." This was a mock auction sale of booty which culminated in the offer of the "King of the Veiians," a cripple draped with a purple mantle and hung with gold trinkets.

But Camillus, whose efficiency and skill had made the great success possible, got no thanks. He was involved in a dispute about the distribution of the plunder taken at Veii, and was indicted before the commons. He did not wait for the judgment and voluntarily went into exile at Ardea. But not for good. A mere decade later an event occurred which threatened to overwhelm Rome in disaster and brought Camillus back to new successes and honors.

Rome made good use of its victory. A year later, Veii's "accomplices," the people of Falerii and Capena, were punished for having given military assistance to Veii. Rome demonstrated how it would in future treat those who dared to oppose her plans of conquest. The order was given to strip "every acre of land bare of its produce, fruit or grain."

The thriving vineyards, orchards, and olive groves, the fields of grain, were cut down and set on fire. Flourishing plantations and gardens where generations of work had made the land productive were turned into wasteland by the barbarous depredations of the Roman soldiery.

The people of Capena were appalled and begged for peace. The people of Falerii, however, prepared for battle, and after their troops had been defeated by Camillus outside the city, they settled down to a siege. It was not until 394 B.C. that they surrendered.

"Where once fierce hatred and savage rage had made even the destruction of Veii seem a better fate than the tame capitulation of Capena," says Livy, "there was now a unanimous demand for peace . . . Falerii was laid under tribute for a sum to cover the cost of the army's pay for the year, thus relieving the Roman people of the war-tax. The war was over, and the Roman troops returned to the city."

Two years after the conclusion of these punitive expeditions, the Romans were suddenly attacked from another direction. The people of Volsinii, the big city-state on Lake Bolsena, together with those of Sappinum, invaded Roman territory with large forces. Volsinii, which possessed the famous Voltumna sanctuary of the League of Twelve, had made no move to assist Veii in its hour of need, but now decided, after that disaster, to face up to Rome. What the motives for this were is a mystery. Did Volsinii want to avenge Veii, which she had, like the other Etruscan cities, left in the lurch? Or did she cherish the forlorn hope of wiping out the disgrace, of undoing what was done? Tradition is silent on the reasons.

What is clear, however, is that the Roman army soon got the better of the Etruscans. At the first engagement, eight thousand of them, cut off by the Roman cavalry, laid down their arms, and the rest fled. The aggressors got off lightly. They were granted peace in return for restoring all the Roman property they had seized and defraying the Roman army's pay for the year.

This epilogue brought to an end Rome's hundred years' war against Veii.

XVIII

The Celtic Invasion of Etruria

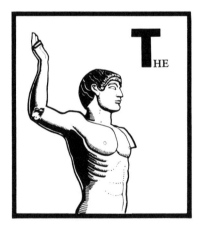

PEOPLE OF ROME WERE NOT TO enjoy their success for long. The city's rise to power and victory was soon followed by a great setback. The disaster was set off by a tremendous movement of peoples into Italy from the north.

In a vast migratory tide the restless Celtic peoples had already spread out from their original homeland over a large part of western Europe. From the Rhine and upper Seine they had thrust northward across the Channel into Britain and southward over the Pyrenees into the Iberian peninsula. There they occupied the north of Spain. In about 400 B.C. these peoples were again on the march. This time they turned south for their conquests. From their settlements in south Germany and north Switzerland they moved over the Alps and descended into the Po valley. The invasion was begun by the Insubres, after whom the region of the north Italian lakes was named Insubria

Livy gives the reason for this invasion of the sunny south by the warlike inhabitants of the northern Alps. "There is a tradition that it was the lure of Italian fruits and especially of wine," he says, "a pleasure then new to them, that drew the Gauls to cross the Alps."

In this connection both Livy and Dionysius recount a legend that came from Etruria. In Livy's version it goes thus: "Arruns of Clusium . . . had sent wine into their country deliberately to entice them over, as he wanted his revenge for the seduction of his wife by his ward Lucumo, a man in too powerful a position to be punished except by the help of foreigners called in for the purpose. It was he who guided the Gallic hordes over the Alps and suggested the attack on Clusium."

So it was an Etruscan triangle drama that led to an act of vengeance which was to have catastrophic consequences. For the Celtic invasion threatened the whole of Etruria, and Rome came within an ace of being wiped out forever. But there may be a grain of truth in this Arruns story. It is a fact that the region around ancient Clusium, modern Chiusi, produces an exceptionally satisfying wine, much praised by the knowledgeable. It is named after the dreamy little medieval town of Montepulciano in the neighborhood. That the people of Clusium enjoyed their wine is shown by the scene depicted in relief on a vessel of *bucchero pesante,* the heavy black ware typical of the city, dating from the sixth century B.C. Two men are seated at a table on which they are playing a game with stones or counters. Above the table, between them, is depicted a large kantharos, a typical two-handled drinking vessel.

The Etruscans of the Po valley, inadequately armed to meet the surprise attack, could not repulse the invaders. The Celts, as Livy records, settled in regions previously cultivated by the Etruscans.

It may have been only a coincidence, or just a legend, but on the very day when Veii was taken by the Romans, Melpum, the wealthy Etruscan city in the Po valley, possibly near the site of modern Milan, is said also to have been captured and destroyed by hordes of Insubres, Boii, and Senones. This double onslaught in the north and south, ending with the fall of two frontier cities, seems to have heralded the coming decline of the great Etruscan nation.

The Celtic flood meant the doom of the Etruscan League of Twelve in the Po valley. But other parts of Italy, especially central Etruria, were likewise in serious trouble, and Rome was in mortal danger. The hordes of Celts swept on over northern Italy and toward the Adriatic. "When the Celts divided up the territory by tribes," says Diodorus Siculus, ". . . those known as the Senones received the area which lay farthest from the mountains and along the sea. But since this region was scorching hot, they were distressed and eager to move; hence they armed their younger men and sent them out to seek territory where they might settle."

When this advance party returned with a favorable report, the the tribes got on the move again toward the south. They poured down to the Apennines and then over the mountain passes. Central Etruria, the mother country that had not seen a foreign conqueror for centuries, nor known war, that had prospered by peaceful development of the soil, did not expect this overwhelming invasion of savage armed hordes.

> *Plundering and devastating the fields, the Celts poured down the valley of the Chiana, past Lake Trasimene, and appeared before Clusium, whose king had once been Lars Porsena.*

"Now they invaded Tyrrhenia," continues Diodorus, "and being in number some thirty thousand they sacked the territory of the Clusini." The inhabitants were quite unprepared for such an attack, and panic gripped the country from the Apennines to the Tyrrhenian Sea. No Etruscan army opposed the foreign warriors. The terrified countryfolk took flight and hid in the forests. The cities bolted their gates and posted sentries.

Plundering and devastating the fields, the Celts poured down the valley of the Chiana, past Lake Trasimene, and appeared before Clusium, whose king had once been Lars Porsena. They surrounded the city, but were unable to make any impression on it. It was strongly fortified and the Celts were only accustomed to battle in open country.

"The plight of Clusium was a most alarming one," records Livy; "strange men in thousands were at the gates, men the like of whom the townsfolk had never seen, outlandish warriors armed with strange weapons, who were rumored already to have scattered the Etruscan legions on both sides of the Po." In this grim situation the city sent a mission to Rome to ask for help, although they "had no official ties with Rome or reason to expect her friendship, except perhaps that they had refused assistance to their kinsmen of Veii."

However, no help came. Instead of troops, Rome sent a three-man delegation authorized to investigate and conciliate. They were to "remonstrate with the Gauls in the senate's name and to ask them not to molest a people who had done them no wrong." They explained that Rome would protect the people of Clusium by force if necessary, "although it would be better, if possible, to avoid recourse to arms and to become acquainted with the new immigrants in a peaceful manner."

But the delegation failed in its aim, indeed, brought down disaster upon the Romans. When the envoys had explained their object to the Gauls, the latter, says Livy, replied: " 'You say you prefer to help your friends by negotiation rather than by force, and you offer us peace. We, for our part, need land, but we are prepared to accept your offer on condition that the people of Clusium cede to us a portion of their territory—for they have more than they can manage. You can have peace on no other terms.' . . .

"When the three envoys asked by what sort of justice they demanded land, under threat of violence, from its rightful owners, and what business Gauls had to be in Etruria anyway, they received the haughty reply that all things belonged to the brave who carried justice on the point of their swords.

"Passions were aroused and a fight began . . . the envoys . . . took up arms . . . laying about them in the Etruscan van. Quintus Fabius, riding ahead of the line straight for the Gallic chieftain as he was making for the Etruscan standards, killed him with a spear-thrust through the side and began to strip him of his armor. It was then that the Gauls realized who he was . . . that he was the envoy from Rome. At once the trumpets sounded the retreat; the quarrel with Clusium was forgotten and the anger of the barbarian army was turned upon Rome."

The Gauls sent envoys to the senate to complain about the breach of international law committed by the Roman representatives and to demand their surrender. The request was rejected, and the three members of the Roman delegation were promoted. When the Gauls heard of this insult to their embassy, "they flamed into the uncontrollable anger which is characteristic of their race, and set forward, with terrible speed, on the path to Rome."

Southern Etruria lived through frightening days as the swarms of Celts swept across the land. "Terrified townships rushed to arms as the avengers went roaring by," says Livy; "men fled from the fields for their lives; and from all the immense host, covering miles of ground with its straggling masses of horse and foot, the cry went up 'To Rome!' "

A Roman army, hurriedly mustered, crossed the Tiber and advanced to meet the enemy. They had barely gone eleven miles when they clashed with the advance guard of the Celtic force. The Romans were terrified at the mere appearance of these outlandish savages, with their streaming hair stiffened by a wash of lime, their long, drooping, shaggy moustaches, their naked, or half-naked bodies, with a broad gold ring around their necks. The effect of their appearance was intensified by the deafening noise they produced, by what Livy calls "the dreadful din of the fierce war songs and discordant shouts of a people whose very life is wild adventure."

All this created confusion, and in no time the Romans were being encircled. Before they knew where they were, "the ground in front and on both sides was already swarming with enemy soldiers." The opposing armies were at the point where a little tributary of the Tiber, the Allia (modern Rio de Rosso on the Via Salaria) joins the river. Here, on July 18, 390 B.C., the battle was fought. It proved an appalling disaster for the Romans, a black day, if ever there was one, and the most catastrophic defeat in the annals of Rome until then.

The Gauls, yelling their war cries, fell upon the Romans with their long swords, and routed them. The main body of the beaten army turned and fled. Most of them made for Veii, where the strong walls of the conquered city still stood intact, but many were drowned as they tried to cross the Tiber. The others fled back to Rome with their tidings of disaster.

Rome was now at the mercy of the Celts. The few troops still available were not enough to man and defend the walls. The population was given over to panic, and did not even have the presence of mind to close the gates. Thousands streamed out of the city to the Janiculum and the surrounding countryside. The priests of Quirinus and the Vestal Virgins took what sacred objects they could carry and hurried to Caere. They found asylum in the ancient Etruscan city. In Rome the citadel on the Capitoline hill, high above the Forum, was garrisoned and stores were laid in. Three tense and anxious days passed, and then the Celts walked into the open city. They came, they killed, they plundered. Then, before the horrified eyes of the Romans on the Capitol, they set fire to the entire city. While destruction spread through street after street, only the citadel held out.

For seven months the Gauls remained, besieging the Capitoline hill. All their attempts to storm it failed.

So the Capitol and the temple of Jupiter on it remained intact. The brilliantly colored terra-cotta figures, made by Vulca and his pupils in Veii for the roof of the sanctuary built for Etruscan kings, looked down on the grim desolation below. There the besiegers now had to fight disease which attacked them from the ruined houses and drainage installations. The sickening smell of burned and burning corpses blew over the devastated city. But the Gauls did not yield. They demanded a ransom so high that the Romans could not meet it. The republic had been fighting for years, had scarcely been able to till the land properly or do any trade, much less accumulate quantities of treasure.

"At Rome," says Pliny, "for a long period of time, the quantity of gold was but very small. At all events, after the capture of the city by the Gauls, when peace was about to be purchased, not more than one thousand pounds' weight of gold could be collected." That was all, and even that, it may be assumed, had not come to the public purse by hard work and diligence, but from the booty taken in Veii when it was captured not many years earlier.

The Gauls, who did not know the history of the city, refused to believe that the Romans were so poor, and stuck to their demands. But when the news came through to Brennus, the Gallic chieftain, that the recently acquired territory of the Senones in the Po valley had been invaded by the Venetii, he decided to accept the offered ransom. Then, unharmed and laden with rich booty, Brennus and his hordes departed, back through Etruria to the north.

Rome had come through. And from far and near the fugitives began streaming back. From Veii, to which the men of the army beaten on the Allia River had retreated, came soldiers. And from Ardea came Camillus, who had been sent for while the Gauls were burning Rome, and had been appointed dictator.

All that mattered now was to rebuild the shattered city. Nothing else was more urgent. Nevertheless, a large part of the population showed no inclination to set about it. Nothing appeared as distasteful to them as hard physical work. Two centuries earlier their forefathers had been driven by the Etruscan kings to build the city. Now that it was to be done again, this time voluntarily, they refused.

> **It took all Camillus's persuasive oratory to bring home to his fellow countrymen how great a sin it would be to abandon Rome because it was rubble and ashes.**

They wanted to find an easier way. Was there not, they argued, an empty, still almost undamaged Etruscan city near at hand? And a large one at that, strongly fortified, where most of the houses and public buildings were still standing, and all that was needed was to go and occupy them?

"The tribunes," says Livy, "were . . . still holding continual mass meetings at which they urged the abandonment of the ruins of Rome and the migration to Veii . . . The people themselves were increasingly inclined to favor it." It took all Camillus's persuasive oratory to bring home to his fellow countrymen how great a sin it would be to abandon Rome because it was rubble and ashes. "I cannot believe," he declared scornfully, "that you would commit so shameful a crime simply because you shrink from the labor of restoring these ruins."

The emigration to Veii was prevented, and the rebuilding of Rome began. "Tiles were supplied at the state's expense; permission to cut timber and quarry stone was granted without any restrictions except a guarantee that the particular structure should be completed within the year."

But the shepherds and farmers of yesterday who, apart from the plow, knew only the sword, had learned nothing. What their Etruscan teachers had once shown them was now long forgotten. They had no architects and engineers of their own to direct the rebuilding. It was not surprising that "the work of reconstruction was ill-planned." The ruined houses were rebuilt entirely without system. "All work was hurried and nobody bothered to see that the streets were straight," records Livy; "individual property rights were ignored, and buildings went up wherever there was room for them." The narrow, crooked streets, which lasted down into imperial times, date from this rebuilding.

Even the layout of the Cloaca Maxima and other underground drainage channels, built by the Etruscans, seems to have been no longer known. In ignorance, new buildings were in part put up right above them. "This explains why the ancient sewers," says Livy, "which originally followed the line of the streets, now run in many places under private houses, and why the general layout of Rome is more like a squatters' settlement than a properly planned city." However, the Servian walls, built by the second Etruscan king, were restored and improved. For this purpose, great blocks of tufa were brought from the quarries near Veii. The fortifications thus strengthened proved equal to all demands through more than six centuries.

The priests and Vestal Virgins brought the sacred objects back from Caere. This Etruscan city earned Rome's gratitude, expressed in a treaty of friendship and hospitality, because it "had given asylum to Roman priests and the sacred objects of Roman religion, thereby ensuring the continuity of religious observance and worship," says Livy. No other Etruscan city was granted so high an honor.

Gradually life began again in Rome. There was no threat from outside; even the Etruscans left it in peace. In the neighborhood of Veii there had been some skirmishes while the Gauls were besieging Rome, but they were of merely local significance. A couple of

Tomb of the stucco reliefs, Cerveteri; third century B.C.

Etruscan columns, chiefly exiles from Veii, had seized the favorable opportunity to raid Roman territory. Roman soldiers who had taken refuge in Veii "had noticed a certain amount of activity in the neighborhood; then they had seen Etruscan columns driving off the cattle they had stolen—and the Etruscan camp, too, was in sight, not far from the town." Other Etruscans were camped near the salt works. Livy's account makes it clear that no major forces were involved. The Veii garrison had no difficulty in dealing with the Etruscan units in a couple of night raids.

But the remainder of Etruria, or at least the strongly fortified cities which the Gauls left alone, made no move when Rome lay helpless and undefended, its army defeated and scattered, while the Gauls occupied and burned the city. The Etruscan rulers had taken no military action while the Roman legions tightened the ring around mighty Veii, nor did they make any attempt to recover their fellow countrymen's lost territory when they had a good opportunity after Rome's defeat on the Allia.

It was a once-only opportunity for the Etruscan league. And it was missed. The Etruscans could not change their spots; they could not overcome the separatism which blocked any union and alliance of all the city-states.

How differently the Greeks had acted a century earlier, in rallying their forces and giving the world an example of what could be done in a desperate, seemingly hopeless situation. The army of a handful of city-states had defeated the great power Persia. By a supreme effort they had beaten back the eastern offensive and preserved their independence.

So too the twelve tribes of Israel had reacted six centuries earlier. Like the twelve Etruscan city-states they also, in the beginning, were united only in a religious league centered on a sanctuary, in their case that of Shiloh, and on their faith in Jehovah, whose presence was symbolized and embodied in the Ark of the Covenant kept there. But the threat from the Philistines, who were beginning to occupy the land, made them realize the need for a stronger political union. So the twelve tribes gave up their freedom and independence, if hesitantly and unwillingly, and, at the moment of supreme danger, chose a king and submitted to him. By which means they preserved their country and their greatest possession, their faith.

But Etruria never emulated either example. The road it was henceforth to follow seemed thereby predestined.

XIX

Rome Takes Etruria's Frontier Fortresses

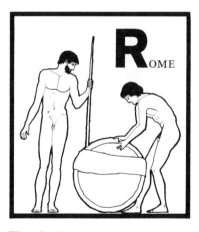

ROME RECOVERED QUICKER THAN WAS to be expected. She resumed her old policies with unabated energy and was not disposed to renounce a tittle of her old power or lose a single one of her former alliances or conquests.

The disaster after the battle on the Allia did not merely interrupt the foreign developments which had just begun. It shook the very foundations of Roman power. The Latin peoples did not feel under any obligation to a Rome that had been weakened and shamefully beaten in battle. They broke off the old relationship. At the same time, other neighboring peoples revolted. "A serious foreign war broke out," says Livy, "set on foot by the Volsci, in conjunction with a revolt on the part of the Latins and Hernici."

The fact that Rome's forces were tied down in the south gave Etruria an opportunity to smash the wedge which the Romans had driven into some of the oldest Etruscan territory after the fall of

Veii. The Romans had astutely moved to secure their newly conquered bastion against the north by making an alliance with the Faliscan towns Sutrium (Sutri) and Nepete (Nepi). They could not have made a better choice, for with these two strong positions Rome gained "the barriers, so to speak, and gateways" to Etruria, as Livy puts it.

Now as then, the road from Rome to the heart of Etruria passes through the Sutri gap. Less than thirty miles as the plane flies separate the two places, and yet the journey is like a trip into another world. The Via Cassia that goes northwest from Rome past the ruins of Veii lies at first in level, pleasant, but monotonous country. Then the scene changes. Narrow, deep gorges, at the bottom of which rushes a stream, lie among steep, reddish brown pinnacles of tufa; separated by deep valleys, the rocky plateaux are crowned by picturesque little villages. Here the volcanic landscape of southern Etruria begins. It is wild country that has been gashed, torn, and piled up by geological upheavals in a remote past, and then reshaped over millenniums by torrents and rivers into the present bizarre scenery.

To the left lies Lake Bracciano, like a tarnished metal mirror among its surrounding hills. It occupies the crater of a former mighty volcano. Another twelve miles or so to the north, at the foot of Monte Venere in the Ciminian Mountains, lies Lake Vico, also in an extinct volcano. Halfway between the two lakes is Sutri, and some seven miles to the east of it, Nepi.

Sutri, like a citadel, grips a rocky plateau among the deep ravines that furrow the plain all around. Steep cliffs, prolonged and strengthened by walls, make it a stout stronghold. Nepi, among deep gorges, is also by its position a fortress difficult of access. Both places seem predestined by nature to act as frontier fortifications, as gates to control exits and entrances in any direction. Whoever held these two cities had a clear road to the west through the valley of the Mignone, to powerful Tarquinii and the sea, as well as to the east to Falerii, the modern Civita Castellana. The latter controlled communication with the upper reaches of the Tiber, and northward to the very heart of Etruria.

Marcus Furius Camillus had set out with a new army against the Volscians, leaving only a part of his total forces to defend the Tiber crossing. The Etruscans, profiting from his preoccupation with the Volscians, had mobilized and were besieging Sutrium, an ally of Rome, says Livy. The city appealed to the Roman senate for help and was told that Camillus would march to their aid as soon as possible.

However, the population could not hold out, owing to hunger and exhaustion, and they surrendered the city. Forced to leave their homes, they were making their way in a long procession toward Rome when Camillus appeared with his army, and, at the last minute, when all seemed lost, brought rescue. Camillus marched on to Sutri, captured it and slaughtered the Etruscans or led them away captive, and restored the inhabitants to their homes.

> **Forced to leave their homes, they were making their way in a long procession toward Rome when Camillus appeared with his army, and, at the last minute, when all seemed lost, brought rescue.**

In the same year, 387 B.C., a Roman army invaded the district of Tarquinii. The expedition, Livy records, was directed at two frontier fortresses which defended the entrances to this Etruscan territory. The first, Cortuosa, situated at the source of the Mignone, was taken by surprise and captured at the first assault. Then it was sacked and burned. At Contenebra, the other fortress, the approach of the legions was discovered, the alarm was sounded, and defense organized.

As the Romans needed their troops urgently elsewhere, they did not wish to start on a possibly lengthy siege which would tie them down for some time, and they decided on another tactic. The army was divided into six corps, each of which went into action for six hours, and was then relieved by the next. Unceasing attack was maintained at the only accessible point of the fortifications. The defenders, few in number, were thus forced to remain on the walls, day and night, to throw back the attackers. This continuous fighting wore down the defense. After a few days the townsmen were exhausted, and the Romans captured the place and plundered it.

The swift fall of these two fortresses was a serious blow to the Tarquinians. Their defense line, which stretched in a wide arc along the Tolfa and Sabatini mountains to the Ciminian forest, was broken, and a practically unobstructed route into Tarquinian territory now lay open to the Romans. Only one fortress, Luni, on the main westward road, still offered some protection. But it was scarcely in a position to withstand a long siege. Luni lay on a plateau surrounded by ravines, and was an Etruscan settlement which had been given walls after the fall of Veii. But the fortifications were constructed hastily, as is clear from the remains of a wall put together carelessly from large and small blocks of tufa, which is still to be seen near the little railway station of Monte Romano.

The Etruscans seem to have planned a counteroffensive by secret negotiations with anti-Roman factions in Sutri and Nepi, as well as with the Volscians, whose capital was Antium (modern Anzio). The latter were to strike simultaneously with the Etruscans and thus force the Romans to fight on two fronts.

In Nepi everything went according to plan. The anti-Roman faction surrendered the city to the Etruscans, who mounted guard on the walls and gates, says Livy. But in Sutri the Etruscan plot was only a half success. They gained part of the town, but in the remainder "the townspeople had barricaded the streets and were defending themselves with great difficulty . . . The arrival of succor from Rome, and particularly the great reputation which Camillus enjoyed . . . checked for the moment the disastrous course of events and afforded time to render assistance," says Livy. The Romans then attacked from two sides; the Etruscans in panic abandoned the city and fled into the open country where they were pursued and massacred "until night made it impossible to see."

It was then the turn of Nepi, where the Etruscans were in complete possession and refused to surrender. The Romans first laid waste all the surrounding fields to intimidate the town's inhabitants. Then they filled up the moat and erected scaling ladders against the walls, and, says Livy, "carried the town at the first shout and charge." To set an example, the Nepesini who had been responsible for the surrender of the city to the Etruscans were promptly executed. As a result of these battles, all the southern tip of Etruria from the Tiber to the Ciminian forest was again in Roman hands.

Soon after the departure of the Gauls, Rome had annexed the territory of Veii and formed it into four new rustic tribes, and now, in about 385-3 B.C., veterans from the Latin wars were settled in colonies at Sutri and Nepi. The fortifications of these two frontier towns were put in order, and the Romanization of this fruitful region went steadily ahead.

The picturesque landscape around Nepi is well described by Dennis: "The dark ravine, deepening as it recedes, leading the eye to the many-peaked mass of Soracte in the distance, by the towers and battlements of the town on one hand, and by a stately stone-pine raising its spreading crest into the blue sky on the other, is set off like a picture in its frame. It is one of those scenes in which you could scarcely suggest an improvement—in which Nature rivals the perfection of Art."

Today it is a quiet little country town whose inhabitants put their maize to dry in the sun on the roofs of their houses and in the streets. Remains of the walls that Camillus's soldiers once stormed are still there. Few visitors come to this weathered ancient scene of bitter struggles; the foreign tourists roar by on the Autostrada del Sole far away from here. Occasionally, a visitor coming up the Via Cassia from Rome stops at nearby Sutri, maybe to see the birthplace of a certain Pilate, a Roman official of some notoriety. A medieval township occupies the site of the former Faliscan town. Remains of the ancient walls still exist, and the gate called the Porta Furia recalls the invincible opponent of the Etruscans, Furius Camillus.

THE DIONYSIUS RAID

MISFORTUNES SELDOM COME singly. The Etruscans had not yet got over the failure at Sutri and Nepi when they suffered another severe blow, this time not from Rome. The defeat in the interior of the country was followed by a loss on the coast which had no less painful consequences. Tarquinii's great neighbor Caere, together with the wealthy port of Pyrgi, was the victim of a raid by the Greeks who came with a large naval force.

In Syracuse the help that Etruria gave to Athens during the Sicilian war of 414–3 B.C. had not been forgotten. It was not forgotten, nor forgiven, that several Etruscan cities had offered their support to Alcibiades, and that Etruscan units and fifty-oared warships had fought on the side of the enemy.

Thirty years later, Syracuse, after its long, victorious struggle against the attempt of Carthage to subjugate the Greeks of Sicily, stood at the zenith of its power and was reaching out to southern Italy. This was the work of one man, the ambitious tyrant Dionysius I. But war, armaments, and a prodigal building program had ruined the city's finances. Enormous sums had been swallowed up by the army of eighty thousand men, the huge fleet of three hundred large warships, the famous high wall of rectangular hewn stones that fortified the city, and by the pomp and display of the court, with its great theatrical festivals and such eminent guests as Aeschylus and Plato.

Such an institution as a world bank, which might have provided credit, did not yet exist. There remained self-help, by, to put it simply, robbery. The choice of a suitable victim was not difficult. They would make Etruria pay, somewhat belatedly, perhaps, for having fought alongside Athens. In Syracuse, they recalled too, how profitable the raids a century earlier had been on Corsica, Elba, and the Etruscan coast. The unscrupulous tyrant had no difficulty in finding an excuse. The Etruscans, he asserted, were still indulging in piracy at sea and were a menace to peaceful shipping.

And so Dionysius, says Diodorus Siculus, "set out to make war against Tyrrhenia with sixty triremes." Like a flock of ravenous birds of prey the ships passed the coast of Latium and the mouth of the Tiber, and then turned toward land at the sight of the first Etruscan town. They dropped anchor and set their swarms of heavily armed fighting men ashore.

The first violent shock of the Greek attack fell upon the city-state of Caere, where enormous damage was done. All three harbors and bases, Alsium (Palo), Punicum (Santa Marinella), and Pyrgi (Santa Severa) were destroyed, their warehouses and stores, packed with valuable goods, were plundered. Even the famous temple of Leucothea, the goddess of childbirth and of sailors, was not spared by the Syracusans. They seized every gold, silver, or other valuable object, and loaded everything into their warships. The temple treasury was full of precious votive gifts; the spoils from it alone are said by Dio-

> **The formerly wealthy city of Caere never recovered from the damage done to its economy by the Greek expedition.**

286

dorus to have been worth one thousand talents, and another five hundred talents were obtained from the sale of prisoners and the rest of the booty.

The scene of this Syracusan raid of 384 B.C. has recently been rediscovered. Some thirty-two miles north of Rome, the Via Aurelia passes the little bathing resort of Santa Severa. In a straight line it is about eight miles from Caere. At the edge of the waves stands the massive round tower of a medieval castle. By rowing out from the beach it is possible to see, through the translucent water, the squared stone blocks on the sea bottom which were once the quay wall of Pyrgi, the main harbor of Caere. The castle stands squarely on the site of the ancient harbor. In the course of the centuries the sea has gradually gnawed away at the beach and reached farther inland. The coast was once much farther out than now.

During the 1950s, in the course of the land reform, much of the land around Santa Severa was deep-plowed with motorized implements for the first time, and as a result large quantities of pottery shards were turned up. But what in particular alerted the Etruscologists was the bearded head of a man modeled in painted terracotta in the late archaic style. It did not appear to come from a necropolis. It seemed clearly to be part of a temple decoration. This assumption was correct, and was confirmed by careful search. The foundations of a large temple were discovered, measuring 78 feet 9 inches by 112 feet 10 inches, and made of regularly dressed stone blocks. The temple had contained three cellae, in front of which was a colonnaded porch, with three rows of columns like the Jupiter temple on the Capitol.

Close by, the excavators found the shattered remains of a group of terra-cotta figures. The subject is the battle of the gods and giants represented by four figures—Athena, Zeus, and an unknown bearded god wrestling with a giant. Investigations showed that the statues must have been made about 460 B.C. They had decorated the temple pediment for some eighty years when the Syracusan raiders set fire to the building.

It was in this area, between the temple described above and the foundations of another, that in 1964 the important find was made of three gold sheets, two inscribed in Etruscan and one in Punic, which have thrown new light on the Etruscan language.

From the port of Caere the Greek fleet went on to Corsica, according to Strabo. All the Etruscans were expelled, and Dionysius caused a harbor to be constructed there. The Porto Vecchio of today appears to have been built on a former Etruscan settlement. This Greek invasion put an end to Etruscan rule on the island.

The formerly wealthy city of Caere never recovered from the damage done to its economy by the Greek expedition. Its harbors, even if they were repaired, no longer enjoyed the busy traffic of foreign and native ships which had once anchored here. And they got no protection from Etruscan warships. The fact that the Syracusans did not encounter the slighest opposition shows clearly that the former thalassocracy, the once admired and dreaded Etruscan mastery of the sea, was a thing of the past.

It was not only Caere and the neighboring towns and harbors which suffered. The complete blockade by sea affected also the industry, crafts, and trade of inland cities. An important gate to the outside world that had been open for centuries was suddenly and violently closed. Trade across the Tyrrhenian Sea was paralyzed, and the large income it had formerly yielded was lost.

XX

Etruscan Dancers Against the Pestilence

TWENTY-THREE YEARS AFTER THE GAULS' SACK of Rome, the Romans were thrown into "great terror," says Livy, by the news that the Gauls were on the march again. The "sudden rumor of a Gallic war drove the state to appoint Marcus Furius Camillus to his fifth dictatorship." This time the clash came in the Alban hills. "Many thousands of barbarians fell in battle, and many after the camp was taken. The others roamed about, making mostly toward Apulia, and owed their escape from the Romans to their distant flight and the dispersion which resulted from their panic and their straggling."

This Celtic invasion too must have come through Etruscan territory. For the second time, Etruria's cities and lands must have experienced the passage of the savage hordes, with all it meant in attacks, robbery of cattle and grain, looting and burning. But there is no record of what happened between the Arno and the Tiber. Rome recorded only what concerned herself.

In 365 B.C., two years after the victory over the Gauls, Rome was struck by a grave calamity in the shape of an outbreak of pestilence which lasted throughout the following year, killing thousands. In desperation the Romans resorted to an unusual measure. "With the object of appeasing the divine displeasure," says Livy, "they made a . . . banquet to the gods, being the third in the history of the city." It proved an ineffective treatment. "When neither human wisdom nor the help of Heaven was found to mitigate the scourge, men gave way to superstitious fears." Someone recalled that the Etruscans knew special plays, or mimic dances, for disarming the wrath of the gods. These were performed "without any singing, without imitating the action of singers." So the Etruscan mimes were summoned to Rome. "This was a new departure for a warlike people," Livy rightly observes, "whose only exhibitions had been those of the circus." Music and singing were never seriously practiced by the Romans, and dancing was something alien to Roman *gravitas*. Such music as they did have was limited to that of a few wind instruments, the horns adopted from the Etruscans, and, above all, the trumpet used in military parades and war.

The Roman public at the first performance watched with surprise as "players who had been brought in from Etruria danced to the strains of the flautist and performed not ungraceful evolutions in the Tuscan fashion," as Livy puts it.

What the Etruscan art of mime was like we can to some extent imagine from the figures of dancers preserved in wall paintings, on bronze mirrors, and on vases. Students of Etruscan dances as represented in art say that they are unlike those of other peoples.

Once again, Etruria became Rome's teacher. "Next the young Romans began to imitate them," says Livy, ". . . and so the amusement was adopted, and frequent use kept it alive." Livy further informs us that the word for the Roman professional actors, *histriones,* was derived from *ister,* the Etruscan word for player.

The Roman view of dancing was summarized at a later date by Cicero, who declared, *"Nemo fere saltat sobrius, nisi forte insanit"* —"Almost no one dances when he is sober—except perhaps a lunatic." It is hardly surprising that this people of peasants and soldiers produced something quite different in imitating what they had

290

gaped at when the Etruscan dancers performed. The Romans, their taste being what it was, made a crude, popular farce out of the ancient, magical, cultic dance. The young men who imitated the Etruscans, says Livy, at the same time exchanged jests in uncouth verses. It was not till a few centuries later, in imperial times, that the Romans acquired a real taste for mimetic dancing, but it was hardly for aesthetic reasons, or those of a magic ritual. What then became fashionable, and was to be seen in the palaces of the rich, was nude dancing for purposes of erotic stimulation.

However, the new importation from Etruria did nothing to stop the pestilence of 364 B.C. It "neither freed men's minds of religious fears nor their bodies of disease," notes Livy.

Nevertheless the Romans were not discouraged from having recourse to another ancient Etruscan usage when a new calamity occurred. "The games were in full swing when an inundation of the Tiber flooded the circus and put a stop to them," reports Livy, "an accident which—as though the gods had already turned away, rejecting the proffered appeasement of their anger—filled the people with fear."

This time it was a custom once before adopted from Etruria, but meanwhile long forgotten, which was recalled. This was the custom of driving a nail into the wall of the Jupiter temple on the Capitol. "The elders recollected that a pestilence had once been allayed by the dictator's driving a nail."

> But to the Etruscans
> this metal calendar
> of the past acquired
> a profoundly fateful
> significance.
> For each nail marked
> more than just the end
> of yet another brief
> space of time in the life
> of their people.

During the annual Etruscan festival a solemn ceremony was held at the Voltumna sanctuary, in the course of which the highest office-holder drove a nail into the wall of the temple of the goddess Nortia. Cincius, in Livy's words "a careful student of such memorials," stated that the nails were driven in to record the years. So nail after nail accumulated on the walls of the temple. But to the Etruscans this metal calendar of the past acquired a profoundly fateful significance. For each nail marked more than just the end of yet another brief space of time in the life of their people. It symbolized the irrevocability and limitation of all earthly events and existence. The annual nails brought home to them the irresistible passage of time which, for nation and individual alike, was bringing their certain, predestined decline.

Year by year, those who came to Voltumna saw the diminution of the area of temple wall that was still uncovered by nails. They knew that when it was completely covered, the last hour of the "Etruscan name" would also have come.

This idea was carried into everyday life. Etruscan ladies were reminded of the transience of all things even when they were dressing for dinner in their handsome villas. This is demonstrated by a bronze mirror, dated about 320 B.C., which was found at Perugia in 1797. The back of the brilliantly polished metal disk is engraved with a scene from Greek legend. Knowledge of such stories was a recognized part of the Etruscans' culture. And they transmitted them to the Romans—it was the latter's first lesson in the humanities—long before Rome conquered Greece. The legend narrates how during a hunt in Aetolia the young Meleager killed a gigantic boar which had devastated the country around Calydon. He succeeded in this because Atalanta, a huntress, had already severely wounded the furious monster in a thicket with her spear. Meleager, head over heels in love with Atalanta, presented the animal's hide to her. In a quarrel over this trophy, Meleager killed two uncles, his mother's brothers, who grudged the presentation to Atalanta and took the boar's hide away from her. His action was to cost Meleager his life, at his own mother's decision. When he was newly born, the goddess of Fate had told his mother that he would live as long as a brand from the fire was unburned. She had kept it all this time, but now, angry at his killing of her brothers, his mother threw the log into the fire, and as it burned to ashes, Meleager breathed his last.

The mirror is one of the largest and finest of any that have been found. The artist who made it used the foreign legend as the basis for a different message, one that was important to him. Beside Meleager sits the brave young huntress with whom he was in love. The scene illustrates the moment immediately after the killing of the boar. Yet the faces of the two do not express joy. Their eyes are fixed in a rigid stare. For now the inevitable must take its course. Next to the couple stands the goddess of Fate, with widespread wings as though she had just alighted. Her name is Athrpa, the Etruscan form of the Greek Atropos. She gazes piercingly at the young man. With her left hand she holds to the wall the nail, which she is about to drive in with the hammer in her right. Nothing can now hold back the predestined event. Athrpa is also Nortia, who presides symbolically over the inescapable course of years and events.

The ritual observed every year at the Fanum Voltumnae was transplanted to Rome. In their anxiety not to do anything wrong, the Romans adopted it in all its detail. As in the Etruscan ceremony, the vital action could only be performed by the highest office-holder: "the senate ordered the appointment of a dictator to drive the nail." In the Jupiter temple on the Capitol an inscription still recalled in imperial times the importation from Etruria. On the right partition wall of the cella of Jupiter, separating it from that of Minerva, there was a tablet which, says Livy, "recorded in archaic words and letters, that the chief magistrate shall on the thirteenth of September drive a nail."

However, on the Capitol, the ceremony never became a regular, annual one—no doubt because the Romans, not understanding the inner meaning of the ritual, slavishly followed the letter of the Etruscan prescription that only the holder of the highest office must drive in the nail. But Rome only appointed a dictator in times of great emergency.

TARQUINII DEFIES ROME

IT WAS CLOSE TO A GENERATION after the defeat on the river Allia before Rome had restored her badly shaken position vis-à-vis the Latins and the other peoples south of the Tiber who had meanwhile become restless. After prolonged, testing struggles, Rome achieved her aim. In 358 B.C. the Hernici were readmitted to alliance with Rome and the treaty with the Latins was renewed; Rome's hegemony was thus reestablished. Four years later an alliance was made with the turbulent and warlike Samnites. In all those years there is not a word in the Roman annals about the Etruscans, which seems to indicate that there was peace in their country.

Then, just at a time when Rome had her hands free, the northern frontier regions flared into revolt, and the Etruscans, in particular the people of Tarquinii, made a new attempt to recover the territory lost to the Romans.

"The Tarquinians," records Livy, "bent on plundering, ranged over the Roman territory, particularly that part which adjoins Etruria." When Rome, angry at the unexpected incursion which was "terrifying to the countryside," demanded reparation and failed to get it, she declared war. But the consul Gaius Fabius, who was sent to crush the revolt, proved incompetent. So great was the accumulated bitterness of the Etruscans against the Romans, that when they defeated Fabius in battle the Tarquinians indulged

Terra-cotta winged horses, from the pediment of a temple at Tarquinia; third century B.C.

themselves in an act of savage cruelty by slaughtering 307 Roman prisoners in the marketplace of Tarquinii as a sacrifice.

What had begun with the attack of a single city-state now expanded to an ever-growing revolt. The Faliscans also took up arms against Rome and joined with the people of Tarquinii. Together they opposed the Roman consul Marcus Fabius Ambustus, who, in the following year, was given command of the army sent to deal with them.

The Etruscans, fighting with wild fury, put the Romans to flight. The consul, says Livy, "was routed by the Faliscans and Tarquinians in his first engagement." The reason, as Livy explains, was a repetition of what had happened before in the battle for Fidenae. "The panic was chiefly due to this, that their priests, bearing serpents and blazing torches before them, came rushing on like Furies, and utterly dismayed the Roman soldiers with the extraordinary sight. At first they were like men frantic and distraught, and flung themselves in a disordered mob into their own camp."

Pictures in many tombs and the reliefs on sarcophagi give an idea of their terrifying appearance. It was thus that the Etruscans imagined the demons of the underworld. They were eerie figures, swinging hammers and holding snakes in their hands. However, the panic which the unexpected, uncanny figures of the priests aroused in the Roman soldiers was quickly overcome. "When the consul, the lieutenants and the tribunes laughed at them and upbraided them for being scared like children at idle tricks," says Livy, "shame caused a sudden revulsion in their feelings, and they rushed, as if blinded, on the very objects from which they had fled. In this spirit they brushed aside the enemy's vain paraphernalia, and hurling themselves on his real fighting men, they routed the whole army, and even captured the camp that day. As they returned victorious with the rich plunder they had won, they jested in soldier-fashion and scoffed not only at the enemy's devices, but at their own fright as well."

The news of the defeat sounded the alarm to the whole of Etruria. "All who bore the Etruscan name then rose in arms," reports Livy.

Now a new strategy was worked out. The idea was abandoned of trying to break through between Lake Vico and Lake Bracciano, a district which was firmly held by the strong Roman forces at Sutri and Nepi. Instead, it was decided to surprise the enemy in his own territory by a skillful outflanking movement along the coast.

Messengers hastened to Caere, through whose land the Etruscan troops would have to move, and informed those of the city fathers who were anti-Roman of what was planned. The messengers returned with the information that while Caere could not officially side with their kinsmen of Tarquinii, the city would not oppose the expedition, in fact would secretly give it all possible support.

> **This time the fortunes of war seemed to be with the Etruscans.**

This time the fortunes of war seemed to be with the Etruscans. The surprise succeeded. The Etruscans, "led by the men of Tarquinii and Falerii, advanced as far as Salinae" (the salt works), says Livy.

The appearance of hostile forces at the almost undefended mouth of the Tiber near Ostia caused great alarm in Rome. It was reported that "the countryside lying near the Roman salt works had been pillaged, and a part of the booty carried into the borders of the Caerites, whose soldiers had, without question, been among the depredators." Rome, as usual in an emergency, appointed a dictator. "Marching out from the city and setting his army across the Tiber by means of rafts," says Livy, "wherever a rumor of the enemy called him, he surprised many straggling pillagers as they roamed about the fields, on both sides of the river; he also captured their camp in a surprise attack, and with it eight thousand soldiers; and having slain the rest, or driven them out of Roman territory, was granted a triumph by the people."

The Romans followed up this victory by ruthless action against the three city-states involved. In 354 B.C. and the following year they ravaged the lands of Tarquinii, killed large numbers of the city's soldiers in battle, and took a vast number of prisoners. Then they took their revenge for the 307 legionaries who had been massacred at Tarquinii. Of the prisoners, says Livy, "three hundred and fifty-eight were selected—the noblest of them all—to be sent to Rome, and the rest of the populace were put to the sword. Neither were the people less stern toward those who had been sent to Rome, but scourged them all with rods in the middle of the Forum and struck off their heads. Such was the vengeance they exacted of their enemies for the Romans sacrificed in the marketplace of Tarquinii."

For years the Romans showed no mercy. In 351 B.C. while one consul, Gaius Sulpicius Peticus, was devastating the territory of Tarquinii, the other, Titus Quinctius Poenus, marched against the Faliscans. Then, says Livy, "nowhere encountering their enemies in battle, they warred rather with the land, which they burnt and pillaged, than with men; until the obstinacy of both peoples was overcome, as by the wasting of a lingering illness." Thus beaten down, the two peoples asked the senate for a truce. "They were granted one for forty years," reports Livy.

The Etruscans paid a terrible price for their desperate, unsuccessful struggle to regain their independence. Thousands of their young men were killed or carried away into slavery. Their lands, after years of devastation by the legionaries, were a pitiful sight. The olive groves and vineyards were burned or felled. Far and wide, the once fertile fields were overgrown with weeds because for years they had not been tilled, for fear of the marauding Roman armies. Many of the irrigation installations had been destroyed, silted up, or fallen into ruin. Many a workshop and manufactory was burned down, many a hamlet pillaged and afterward abandoned by its inhabitants.

There was not enough labor to make good all the damage. The once-thriving farmland lay devastated; the work of generations was undone. Here too Etruria's fertile soil began to go to waste as it had in the rich lands of conquered Veii. In the meantime Rome had also punished and humiliated Caere. This city, in view of its old treaty of friendship with the Romans, had not dared to take part openly in the war, but it had allowed the forces of Tarquinii and the Faliscans to march through its territory, and volunteers to join the two allies. So Caere sent envoys to Rome "to beg forgiveness for their error."

The envoys approached the senate, but were referred by this body to the people. They pleaded that the Romans should "not give the name of 'purpose' to what should properly be called 'force' and 'necessity.' The Tarquinians, marching in hostile array through their territories, had sought nothing of them save permission to pass, but had drawn certain rustics after them in their train, who had borne a part in the pillaging with which the people of Caere were now taxed. If it pleased the Romans that these men should be surrendered, they would surrender them; if they would have them punished, they should be made to suffer."

Caere's representatives recalled what they had done for Rome in her hour of need, when the city had received the sacred emblems of the Roman gods and protected them during Rome's war with the Gauls. "They invoked the flamens and Vestals whom they had entertained with a pure and scrupulous hospitality." The upshot of Caere's appeal, says Livy, was that "the people were moved, not so much by their present claims as by their ancient merits . . . So peace was granted to the people of Caere, and it was resolved that a truce of a hundred years be made."

However, despite this peace, Caere seems to have ceased to be an independent state, which represented an irreparable loss to the Etruscan league. For it meant that after the fall of Veii and the Roman advance to the slopes of the Ciminian forest, the last defense in the south against further conquests by Rome was gone. The coast road to the north now lay open to the Roman armies.

DISASTER IN THE NORTH

THE WHOLE WORLD SEEMED ALL at once to be conspiring against Etruria. It seemed as though it were not enough for Tarquinii and the Faliscans to have been defeated by Rome, for the Greeks to have raided and pillaged Caere's harbors and seized Corsica. There came as well the culminating misfortune of grave news from the north, from the country beyond the Apennines.

In about 350 B.C., Felsina, the principal city of the League of Twelve in the Po valley, of Etruria Padana, fell to Celtic attacks after years of resistance. The invaders also surprised and destroyed the wealthy city of Misa (near the modern village of Marzabotto) in the valley of the Reno. Thus the two bastions that defended the route to the Apennine passes had fallen. The entry to the heart of Etruria stood open to the Gallic hordes.

The fall of the two cities marked the end of Etruscan rule in the Po valley, barely half a century after the first onslaught of the Celts, when Melpum (modern Milan) is said to have fallen to them on the same day in 396 that Veii fell to the Romans. Etruria's loss of Campania in the south was now followed by that of its second and last great dominion. The consequences, especially in the economic field, were immeasurable, not to speak of the loss of prestige and political power. Etruria, with its highly developed industry and handicrafts, depended upon a brisk foreign trade. The occupation of the Po valley by hostile Celtic tribes meant an end to the movement of goods over the Apennines to the Adriatic Sea, meant that the last remaining trade route to Greece and other countries was cut. Etruria was isolated from the rest of the world. The Celts had

Bronze head of a youth; third century B.C.

burst violently into the largest and most fertile plain of Europe and had seized it piecemeal. Nothing could withstand their advance, for they came in overwhelming numbers. Like swarms of locusts they invaded from the north and the northwest in endless straggling droves of thousands and thousands, with women, children, carts, and cattle.

They began by settling in the southern valleys of the Alps and in the neighboring plains. The Insubres took Melpum; the Cenomani settled around Brescia and Verona. They were followed by other tribes pressing from the north, by the Boii who gave their name to Bononia (Bologna), and by the Senones. They crossed the Po on rafts and pushed on, fighting and plundering, to the Adriatic.

The cities of Etruria Padana could not deal with this mass migration. Their armies were beaten; city after city surrendered, village after village. The population sought safety in flight. Streams of Etruscan refugees poured over the Apennines to their kinsmen in ancient Etruria. Others found refuge in the eastern Alpine valleys where they intermarried with the Raetians, and, says Livy, became "so barbarized by their wild surroundings that they have retained nothing of their original character except their speech, and even that has become debased."

This would suggest that Raetic, which in the form of Romansch, is still spoken in the Grisons and the Engadine, may contain in corrupted form traces of Etruscan. Inscriptions in an Etruscoid alphabet have in fact been found on the southern fringes of the Alps. They come from Tresivio in the Valtellina, from Voltina on Lake Garda, and from Rotzo in the Val d'Assa, near Asiago. Inscriptions in what is known as the Bolzano alphabet have been found in the valley of the Adige above Verona, and even at Matrei near Innsbruck. There is a trace of an Etruscan past in certain place names ending in "-enna," such as the Raetian town Chiavenna, north of Lake Como.

The countryside which had previously teemed with agricultural produce, which had been transformed into one vast, thriving oasis, began to deteriorate, to go to waste.

The Celtic invaders persisted in their barbarous way of life. The countryside which had previously teemed with agricultural produce, which had been transformed into one vast, thriving oasis, began to deteriorate, to go to waste. The land that the Etruscans had cultivated, the irrigation and drainage systems they had installed, the tunnels and channels they had built, were not looked after and began to go to wrack and ruin. Archeological discoveries have confirmed the rapid decay. In Celtic graves only primitive wares and household goods have been found.

A few places in the east escaped the invasion and kept their predominantly Etruscan population. Among them was the city of Mantua. Situated on an island in the river Mincio it could be reached only over long wooden bridges. Thanks to this defensible site it was able to resist the Gallic attacks. It survived longest and preserved its character down to the Imperial Age. Pliny describes Mantua as "the only remaining Tuscan town across the Po." The famous *periplus* (sailing directions) compiled under the name of the Greek Scylax in about 325 B.C. also describes the area of Adria and Spina as still Etruscan.

Spina with its harbor was protected by its position between the sea and the lagoon; it remained undamaged and for some time continued to function as a port of transshipment. Nonetheless its great days as an important trading center on the Adriatic were past. It lacked a rich hinterland to provide a market. The Celtic masses who now dwelt between the Alps and the Apennines were poor and had few needs. The only thing they could supply was grain. They exploited the Etruscan farmland. Eventually Spina's trading activity was limited to shipping grain. Its chief customer was Athens which, with its growing population, had urgent need of foodstuffs.

By an irony of fate it was precisely Athens' friends of many years who tried to stop the export of grain from the Po valley. Privateers, fitted out by Etruscan refugees who had settled at various remote spots on the Adriatic coast, seized whatever they could get hold of. Their aim was revenge on the Celts. But it was Athens that suffered most.

The Etruscan privateers soon became such a menace that Athens had to do something about them. Two famous Attic orators, Hyperides and Dinarchus, warned the Greek public of the danger threatening the state. In 325 B.C. a decree was issued which speaks of the urgently needed defensive measures to be taken against

Etruscan ships in the Adriatic in order to safeguard Athenian trade and food imports.

"Though something of Etruria might here still endure," wrote Mommsen, "it was but fragments of its former power. The Etruscan nation got no profit from what individuals might still achieve in the way of peaceful traffic or maritime acts of war."

It was a gloomy epilogue, that in any case soon came to an end, and with it a great chapter of Etruscan history.

XXI

Roman Legions in Tuscany

INFORMATION FROM ROMAN SOURCES ONCE more dries up after the events of 351 B.C., the defeats and heavy losses of the Tarquinians and Faliscans and the humiliation of Caere. For forty years we hear nothing about the Etruscans.

Seemingly nothing happened in Etruria during an age when in other parts of the world great events took place that played an important part in determining the future of Italy. It was the age when Alexander the Great made his victorious progress through the East and established one of the greatest of world empires.

However, the Etruscans seem to have been not inactive in foreign affairs. Some fragmentary information indicates that they made contact with the Greek conqueror. Did they perhaps secretly cherish hopes of his becoming their liberator? Arrian, the military man and historian, who in the second century A.D. wrote an account of Alexander's campaign based on the official journal of the expedition, says that Etruscans sent an embassy to Alexander as he was returning to Babylon in 323 B.C. Another notice says he received them and recommended them to give up piracy at sea. He was evidently referring to the Etruscan privateers in the Adriatic. "It seems incidentally," says Lopes Pegna, "that with this embassy went the famous soothsayer or seer Peithagoras of Amphipolis who, when he saw that the sacrificial victim had a 'liver with no lobe,' predicted a mortal peril facing Alexander."

Meanwhile the Etruscans remained quiet in Italy. At the same time that a Greek empire was being created in the east, Rome, undistracted by unrest or hostilities in Etruria, was free to extend her rule by conquests in the south. In southern Italy a power of some significance had grown up. This was the Samnite league. Tribes belonging to this strong, extraordinarily brave and warlike people had once before played a decisive part in history. A century earlier the Samnite invasion, together with the Greek attack, had put an end to the Etruscan League of Twelve in Campania. The descendants of that first wave of mountain peasants and shepherds had long since become settled and urbanized. Now the population of the old tribal centers had again increased to the point when the Samnites once more had to look for land.

Samnite tribes, united in a rather loose association or league, had established a foothold in Apulia and in eastern Italy that reached as far as the Adriatic. In the west they advanced to the Gulf of Salerno. For the second time the Campanian plain was threatened with a Samnite invasion. But the inhabitants, especially of the wealthy city of Capua, had no mind to lose their independence, and appealed to Rome for help against the Samnites. This was agreed, and thus Rome, without lifting a sword, extended her sphere of influence into Campania.

But Rome's promise of protection amounted to a challenge, and shortly afterward led to war. When the Samnites in 343 B.C. devastated the country around Capua, the First Samnite War broke out. In the first year the legions gained three victories. Nevertheless two years later, Rome, with a semblance of generosity, made peace with the Samnites on easy terms for the latter. There was good reason for this.

A grave crisis was threatening the very foundations of Roman

304

power. Rome's allies of the Latin league were in revolt; they demanded independence or equality and in 340 B.C. took to arms. But Rome overcame this threat, too. The Latins were defeated in a great battle, and the legions subsequently marched through the Latin territory, conquering town after town. After two years the revolt was at an end. In 338 B.C. the Latin league was dissolved, the Latins lost their independence and joined a confederacy with Rome which absorbed their territories. Thus Rome, stronger than ever, once again extended to the frontiers of Samnium.

Through all this, Etruria had looked on passively. And it continued thus when, in 326 B.C., war broke out again between Rome and the Samnites. The Etruscans made no move in 321 B.C. when Rome suffered one of the most shameful defeats in its history in the valley of the Caudine Forks. Nor did they stir when, in 315 B.C., the Romans were defeated by the Samnites at Lautulae near Terracina, the natural frontier between central and southern Italy.

It was not until 311 B.C., when "the war with the Samnites was practically ended," that "the rumor of an Etruscan war sprang up," says Livy. For forty years Etruria had kept quiet, years during which Rome had more than once faced serious threats to its existence. Now, when Rome once more gained the upper hand, the Etruscans became active. Had it taken the Samnite War to make them realize the true character of Roman aims? Had they only now grasped that Rome's whole policy was directed to one single end, the subjugation of all other peoples, the conquest of all Italy?

Ancient authors provide no answers to these questions. According to tradition, the rumor of war with the Etruscans caused great alarm in Rome. A rebellious Etruria was still a tremendous threat. Livy openly admits that "in those days there was no other race—setting apart the risings of the Gauls—whose arms were more dreaded, not only because their territory lay so near, but also because of their numbers."

The senate reacted as was to be expected. Gaius Sulpicius Longus was appointed dictator and he, "as the gravity of the circumstances required, administered the oath to all those of military age, and made ready arms and whatever else the situation called for, with the utmost assiduity." Nevertheless he was not so presumptuous as to think of an offensive war. He well knew that that would create for Rome the most dangerous situation imaginable—a war on two fronts. So the dictator decided "to remain inactive unless the Etruscans should first take the field." However, "the Etruscans followed the same policy, preparing for war but preventing it from breaking out. Neither side went beyond their own frontiers."

But in 310 B.C. what Rome feared came about. The Etruscans opened hostilities. A large army was gathered together in central Etruria and suddenly marched south where it laid siege to Sutrium (Sutri), an ally of Rome. Once again a struggle began for the possession of this stronghold, whose walls had often seen fighting between Etruscan and Roman. Livy describes in detail what happened when the consul Quintus Aemilius Barbula brought up his army to the relief of the city.

"As the Romans came up, the Sutrini obligingly brought provisions to their camp, which was formed before the city. The Etruscans spent the first day in deliberating whether to accelerate the war or to draw it out. On the following day, their generals having decided on the swifter plan in preference to the safer, the signal for battle was displayed at sunrise and their men in fighting array marched out upon the field.

"When this was reported to the consul, he at once commanded the word to be passed round that the men should breakfast, and having recruited their strength with food, should then arm. The order was obeyed; and the consul, seeing them equipped and ready, bade advance the standards beyond the rampart, and drew up his troops a little way off from the enemy. For some time both sides stood fast, observing one another closely, each waiting for the other to give a cheer and begin to fight, and the sun had begun his downward course in the heavens ere a missile was hurled on either side.

"Then the Etruscans, that they might not withdraw without accomplishing their purpose, set up a shout, and with sound of trumpets advanced their ensigns. The Romans were equally prompt to begin the battle. The two armies rushed together with great fury, the enemy having a superiority in numbers, the Romans in bravery. Victory hung in the balance and many perished on both sides, in-

306

cluding all the bravest, and the event was not decided until the Roman second line came up with undiminished vigor to relieve their exhausted comrades in the first; and the Etruscans, whose fighting line was supported by no fresh reserves, all fell in front of their standards and around them.

"There would never in any battle have been more bloodshed or less running away, but when the Etruscans were resolved to die, the darkness shielded them, so that the victors gave over fighting before the vanquished. The sun had set when the recall was sounded, and in the night both armies returned to their camps."

Both sides sustained heavy losses in this undecided battle. "The enemy," says Livy, "had lost their whole first line in a single engagement, and had only their reserves remaining, who barely sufficed to garrison their camp; whilst the Romans had so many wounded that more died of their hurts after the battle than had fallen on the field." Instead of raising the siege of Sutrium, as they had hoped, the Romans found themselves involved in a war of attrition. Livy concludes with the bare statement: "Thereafter there was nothing done that year at Sutrium worth recording."

Rome had to resign itself to being unable, with the armed forces at its disposal, to wage war successfully in two widely separated theaters at once, in the north and in the south. The decision was taken to remain on the defensive on the Samnian front, and to concentrate the main force in Etruria, now the chief danger.

In the following spring, both consuls, Quintus Fabius Rullianus and Gaius Marcius Rutulus, marched against Etruria. The former took over the campaign at Sutrium, with reinforcements from Rome; but, Livy tells us, from Etruria, too, a new army came to strengthen the enemy. Again Livy gives a detailed account of the ensuing engagement and the subsequent course of the campaign.

"The consul Fabius, leading his army along the foot of the mountains to relieve the allies, and, if in any way practicable, to attack the works of the besiegers, encountered the enemy drawn up in line of battle. The plain spreading out below him revealed to the consul their exceeding strength; and in order to make up for his own deficiency in numbers by the advantage of position, he altered slightly his line of march, so as to mount the hills—which were rough and covered with stones—and there turned to face the enemy."

By this tactical maneuver Fabius forced the Etruscans to fight on an upward slope. "The Etruscans, forgetting everything but their numbers, in which alone they trusted, entered the combat with such haste and eagerness that they cast away their missiles in order to come the sooner to close quarters, and drawing their swords rushed at the enemy. The Romans, on the contrary, fell to pelting them, now with javelins and now with stones, of which latter the ground itself provided a good supply; and even such of the Etruscans as were not wounded were confused by the blows that rattled down on their helms and shields."

The Etruscan attack lost its impetus, and this gave the Romans their chance. "The Roman first and second lines, giving a fresh cheer, charged them, sword in hand. Their onset was too much for the Etruscans, who faced about and fled headlong toward their camp. But the Roman cavalry, riding obliquely across the plain, presented themselves in front of the fugitives, who then abandoned the attempt to reach their camp and sought the mountains; from which they made their way in a body, unarmed and suffering from their wounds, to the Ciminian forest. The Romans, having slain many thousand Etruscans and captured eight-and-thirty standards, took possession also of the enemy's camp, with a very large booty."

The Romans had sustained only slight casualties, and their troops were by no means exhausted. Nevertheless they did not at once follow the beaten Etruscans, but stopped to "consider the feasibility of a pursuit." They did so for the very good reason that the legionaries, still under the shock of their defeat at the Caudine Forks, had no heart for entering the gloomy mountain forests into which the Etruscans had fled. Centuries later, Livy's account still reflected the awe with which the army must have viewed this inhospitable stretch of land: "In those days the Ciminian forest was more impassable and appalling than were lately the wooded defiles of Germany, and no one—not even a trader—had up to that time visited it. To enter it was a thing that hardly anyone but the general himself was bold enough to do."

Eventually, Marcus Fabius, the consul's brother, "offered to explore and return in a short time with definite information about everything." He was well suited for such a mission, for "he had been educated at Caere in the house of family friends, and from this circumstance was learned in Etruscan writings and knew the Etruscan language well . . . In that age, Roman boys were regularly wont to be schooled in Etruscan literature, as nowadays they are trained in Greek."

Livy, we may note in passing, here makes the remarkable admission that Roman schools and the whole Roman educational system must still have been very backward at that time. Two centuries after the fall of the Etruscan kings, Rome was still unable to provide adequate education at home for the sons of the most eminent Roman families.

> Two centuries after the fall of the Etruscan kings, Rome was still unable to provide adequate education at home for the sons of the most eminent Roman families.

Marcus Fabius set out, accompanied only by one slave, who likewise knew Etruscan. Their mission was more than a mere incursion across the frontier; it was a reconnaissance patrol into an unknown world. No Roman had ever set foot on the Ciminian forest, no one knew what lay behind. Before setting out, the two men gathered what scanty information they could about "the nature of the region they must enter and the names of the chief men in those tribes," so as to avoid giving themselves away in conversation by revealing their ignorance of the most commonly known facts. They disguised themselves as shepherds, each armed with "billhooks and a brace of javelins" like the Etruscan countryfolk, and set out. None of the people they met and with whom they exchanged a few words thought them at all suspect, for quite apart from their shepherds' clothes and their knowledge of the language, it simply did not enter any Etruscan's mind that Romans might set foot in the Ciminian forest.

It was a highly successful mission. The two men returned with detailed information about the lay of the land, its roads and towns and fortifications, as well as about the strength and equipment of Etruscan units and the names of their leaders. On hearing the patrol's report, the consul decided to take a chance on leading his army into the forest. But, convinced that success depended on his movements remaining undetected by the Etruscans, he waited for the cover of night.

"He sent the baggage ahead, in the first watch," says Livy, "and directed the legions to follow the baggage. He himself stopped behind with the cavalry, and at dawn of the following day made a demonstration against the enemy's outposts, which had been stationed at the entrance to the pass." Having thus deceived the enemy and, above all, made sure that they had not noticed the nocturnal march of his own infantry, "he retired within his camp, and emerging from it by the opposite gate overtook the column before night."

The feint succeeded. "Next day, with the first rays of light, he was on the crest of the Ciminian mountain and, looking thence over the rich plowlands of Etruria, sent his soldiers to plunder." They took the peaceful peasants completely by surprise. The men were tending their fields and vineyards and olive groves, and looking after their herds and flocks as usual. Instead of the military encounter which the Romans had expected, they were free to ravage the country as they pleased.

"The Romans had already brought away enormous booty when certain improvised bands of Etruscan peasants, called together in hot haste by the chief men of that country, encountered them, but with so little discipline that in seeking to regain the spoils they had nearly been made a spoil themselves. Having slain or driven off these men and wasted the country far and wide, the Romans returned to their camp, victorious and enriched with all manner of supplies." There, at Sutri, "they found five legates, with two tribunes of the plebs, who had come to order Fabius in the name of the senate not to cross the Ciminian forest. Rejoicing that they had come too late to be able to hinder the campaign, they returned to Rome with tidings of victory."

Rome's misgivings about the affair turned out to have been only too justified. For "this expedition of the consul's, instead of putting an end to the war, only gave it a wider range." The news of the Romans' military incursion into the peaceful hinterland and the devastation wrought by the legions "aroused not only Etruria to resentment but the neighboring parts of Umbria also." A general revolt broke out, and the whole of Etruria took to arms. "An army came to Sutrium that was larger than any they had raised before."

On arrival, the Etruscans were so anxious to engage the Romans at once, that, says Livy, "not only did they move forward their camp, out of the woods, but even, in their eagerness for combat, came down into the plain at the earliest opportunity in battle formation At first, after forming up, they stood still in their positions, having left their enemies room to draw up opposite. Then, finding the Romans in no haste to engage them, they advanced up to the rampart. When they saw that even the outguards had retired within the works, they began shouting to their generals to have their rations for the day sent out to them from the camp; they would wait under arms, they said, and either at night, or at daybreak at the latest, attack the enemy's stockade."

This was a fatal decision. The Roman general, meanwhile, calmly took his dispositions. His troops were restless at the enormous numbers of the enemy, but he encouraged them by a brief address, and for the rest ordered them to eat and sleep, but to be armed and ready for his signal at any time.

In the dead of night, the soldiers "at about the fourth watch were awakened without noise." "Then, on the signal being given a little before dawn, which on summer nights is the time of deepest sleep, the rampart was thrown down, and the Romans, rushing out in battle formation, fell upon their enemies, who were lying about the field. Some were slain without even stirring in their sleep, some were but half awake, the greatest number were reaching in terror for their weapons. Only a few were given time to arm themselves; and even these, with no definite standard to follow and no leader, the Romans routed and chased from the field. Some made for the camp and others for the mountains, as they fled this way and that. The forests afforded the surer refuge; for the camp, being situated in the plain, was captured the same day. Orders were issued that all gold and silver be brought to the consul; the rest of the booty went to the soldiers."

A Roman general's experience and superior tactical skill, together with the discipline of legions tried in numberless combats, inflicted a crushing defeat on a numerically far superior but inexperienced Etruscan popular army. The Etruscans' losses were appalling. "On that day the enemy lost sixty thousand slain or captured." As a result of this heavy blow the Etruscans did what they had so often failed to do since Rome's war against Veii. They united. Invoking the *lex sacrata,* by which each man recruited a comrade, they raised a huge army. All over Etruria volunteers flocked to the standards. Forgotten, at long last, was the separate city-states' customary concern with only their own affairs, which in the past had always obstructed any common action and had so fragmented the Etruscan forces as to aid and abet the Roman conquest of Etruscan lands for more than a century. A joint policy was adopted.

This Etruscan army met the Roman legions at Lake Vadimo. On the banks of this small, sulfurous crater lake west of the Tiber, not far from today's little railway station of Orte on the Rome–Florence line, a battle took place so fierce and so violent as to overshadow anything Etruria had ever known in the past.

> *"That day," so Livy concludes his account, "for the first time broke the might of the Etruscans, which had long flourished in prosperity. Their strength was cut off in the battle, and their camp was taken and plundered in the same attack."*

"The field was contested with such rivalry of rage," says Livy, "that neither side discharged a missile. The battle began with swords, and, furious at the outset, waxed hotter as the struggle continued, for the victory was long undecided. It seemed as though the Romans were contending, not with the so oft defeated Etruscans, but with some new race. No sign of flight was visible in any quarter."

To the Roman general's concern, the lines of the legionaries were thinning. "As the front-rankers fell, the second line moved up to replace the first, that the standards might not want defenders." Even the last reserves were soon decimated. In this "extremity of distress and danger" the Roman cavalry were ordered to dismount, and "made their way over arms and over bodies to the front ranks of the infantry."

This sudden intervention of fresh forces saved the hopeless situation. "Like a fresh line springing up amongst the exhausted combatants, they wrought havoc in the companies of the Etruscans. Then the rest of the soldiers, following up their charge, despite of weariness, at last broke through the enemy's ranks. At this, their stubbornness began to be overcome, and certain companies to face about; and when these had once turned tail, the rest likewise took to flight."

"That day," so Livy concludes his account, "for the first time broke the might of the Etruscans, which had long flourished in

312

prosperity. Their strength was cut off in the battle, and their camp was taken and plundered in the same attack."

The Romans lost no time in pressing home their advantage. Soon the army of the consul Quintus Fabius Rullianus appeared near Perugia (Perusia), some sixty miles to the north, and "fought a battle with the remnants of the Etruscan forces." He did not need to trouble to take the town itself, for it surrendered at once after his victory. "Having placed a garrison in Perusia and having sent on before him to the senate in Rome the Etruscan deputations which had come to him seeking friendship, the consul was borne in triumph into the city," where, "in recognition of his remarkable conquest of Etruria, Fabius was continued in the consulship."

One last attempt at resistance was crushed during the following year. The consul Publius Decius, who was entrusted with the war in Etruria, marched with a well-equipped army to Tarquinii. He ordered the city to surrender and the inhabitants were evidently convinced of the impossibility of resistance, for Livy reports that he "frightened the Tarquinians into furnishing corn for the army and seeking a truce for forty years." This was granted. In addition Tarquinii had to give up a stretch of its coast, near the present-day Porto Clementino. Here, more than a century later, in 181 B.C., the Latin colony of Graviscae was established.

From Tarquinii, Decius marched to Volsinii. But the order to surrender and accept Roman suzerainty was answered with armed revolt. There was, of course, no question of engaging the far superior Roman army in open battle, but the people took to their strongholds in a last desperate attempt to defy destiny. It was of no avail. Before long Decius broke the resistance of Volsinii, and in addition forced other neighboring Etruscan cities to submit to Rome.

Decius, says Livy, "captured by storm a number of strongholds belonging to the people of Volsinii. Some of these he dismantled, lest they should serve as a refuge for the enemy, and by devastating far and wide he made himself so feared that all who bore the Etruscan name begged the consul to grant them a treaty. This privilege they were denied, but a truce for a year was granted them. They were required to furnish the Roman army with a year's pay and two tunics for each soldier; such was the price they paid for a truce."

Before 308 B.C. had drawn to a close, there was once more complete peace in Etruria. The war of independence had failed. Economically exhausted by the widespread destruction and pillaging of its land, drained of its manpower by the heavy losses in battle, Etruria could do nothing but submit to the superior military power of Rome. In a couple of years the Romans had overcome the threat presented by the coalition of all the Etruscans.

THE DEMONS IN THE TOMBS

THERE SEEMED NO WAY OF ARresting the decline of Etruscan power. The nation which two centuries earlier had held sway over the most important lands of Italy was now reduced to a narrow space between the Apennines and the Ciminian forest. Gone forever, it seemed, was the age of far-reaching power and worldwide respect. Even by the middle of the fourth century B.C. only a memory of that still remained.

For a long time no Etruscan ship had dared to venture into the open sea. Even the limited coastal traffic that still remained was threatened. And Etruria's oppressor and enemy, Rome, was offering friendship to Carthage, the great maritime power that had once been allied with the Etruscans. The two powers made treaties of trade and friendship in 348 and 306 B.C.

There seemed little hope for the future of the Etruscans. The defeats and losses which their armies and fleets had suffered at the hands of the Romans, Celts, and Greeks had far-reaching consequences. Those reverses made a deep impression upon the Etruscan soul and paralyzed the nation's willpower. A somber mood, a kind of gloomy foreboding of the coming decline, became widespread. What no chronicler relates is expressed unmistakably in the excavated cemeteries. On the walls of the tomb chambers figures and scenes full of terror and dread begin to appear. The banquets in honor of the dead are no longer characterized by gaiety and carefree happiness. The erstwhile smiling dead disappear for ever. Their faces are set and rigid with lamentation. Joy and exuberant acceptance of life give way to melancholy seriousness and finally to somber fatalism.

314

The idea of a frightening other world, inhabited by terrifying demons and uncanny figures gradually cast its spell over everything. The buoyant steps of dancers and musicians gave way to a mournful procession of souls in a subterranean realm of shades where grim monsters dwelt. The long funeral processions move like ghosts to the gate of the underworld. They are accompanied by demons with snakes in their hair, swinging hammers and clubs, brandishing tongs and ropes. The face of death, once so calm and peaceful, is now savage and horrifying.

The soil of ancient Tarquinii has preserved a moving testimony to that period. This is in the Tomba dell'Orco, the tomb of Orcus, which was discovered in 1868. It is really two tombs, connected by a passage, the earlier of which belongs to those very decades when Tarquinii was engaged in its desperate struggle with the Roman legions.

The entrance to this tomb of the underworld is in the midst of a field of grain. A short, steep stairway leads down to the older of the two tomb chambers and into the world of Etruria in the fourth century B.C. Members of the aristocracy of Tarquinii had the sepulcher hewn out of the rock for the burial of their family. It is a quadrangular room, with a low bench around the walls, on which stood the sarcophagi. Only a part of the wall decoration still exists; it evidently represented a banqueting scene.

On the right of the entrance, the profile of a young woman looks out from the damp rock wall of the chamber. She is wearing her prettiest jewelry, grape-cluster earrings and two necklaces, and a light-colored dress. On her head is a chaplet of laurel, and her hair is gathered in a snood at the nape of the neck. Lower down the wall are traces of a couch with colored covers and cushions. The young woman's family name was Velcha, as appears from an inscription. The face is pale, melancholy, with an expression of sadness about the full, sensuous lips, as though she were vainly recalling the joys of life from which she was suddenly taken away.

Right next to her, on the wall at right angles, stands Charun, the Etruscan messenger and herald of death, who guides souls on their last, gloomy journey, a frightening figure, like a shade, a creature of darkness, with vast wings outspread. Pointed animal ears stand up from his red, snakelike locks; he has an eagle's beak of a nose and his flesh is grayish green, as though moldering in decay. A

315

snake springs up beside him, and he grasps the shaft of what must be a hammer, the symbol of his power, with which he gives the blow that ends life. This monster, this demon, has nothing in common with the Greek Charon, the peaceable ferryman of Hades.

At the entrance to the second chamber two figures are carved in relief, one on each side of the door; though now rather damaged, they seem to represent dancers, between whose legs a serpent is entwined. Within the second chamber the wall paintings, which are several decades later than those of the first room, depict mainly scenes from Greek myths mingled with demons and spirits from the Etruscan underworld. The funeral banquet is transported to the underworld of Hades and Persephone.

> *On another wall appears a demonic figure, more terrible of aspect than Charun.*
> *The ferocious head, with donkey's ears and snakes growing from it, has the beak of a vulture or eagle.*

Persephone, with little snakes sprouting from her hair, stands next to Hades (or Pluto or Orcus), who has the skin of a wolf's head pulled over his own. He is seated on his throne, as judge and lord of the shades, his right arm outstretched, with a snake twined around it, and his left uplifted grasping another snake. "His gesture," writes Pietro Romanelli, "is one of power rather than of menace, and seems to anticipate Michelangelo's figure of Christ in judgment in the Sistine Chapel."

On another wall appears a demonic figure, more terrible of aspect than Charun. The ferocious head, with donkey's ears and snakes growing from it, has the beak of a vulture or eagle. This is Tuchulcha. Winged, brandishing a huge snake, he stands menacingly between Theseus and Pirithous, the figure of the latter being barely recognizable. Theseus is seated, his expression sad, as though he were overwhelmed by the vicious, piercing look of the demon. On the first wall to the left of the entrance are shown the preparations for the banquet of the dead. Beside a table stand two naked youths, one with wings, presumably a demon, and one without. On the table are goblets and bowls. Much of the tomb decoration was destroyed soon after its discovery, but enough remains to indicate the terrors of an underworld that is rather like the later Christian vision of Hell.

From the fourth century B.C. we continually meet the demon of death with the bird-of-prey beak who carries a hammer. This image and its name appears in the wall paintings of tombs, on vases, mirrors, and sarcophagi, like a symbol of fear and dread that has welled up from the unconscious. Increasingly, Etruscan artists

Vase in the form of the head of Tuchulcha

chose from the subject matter of Greek gods and heroes episodes of blood and tragedy. Human sacrifice, the murder of Clytemnestra, the killing of the Trojan prisoners, the duel of Eteocles and Polynices ending in the death of both—these are the typical themes.

On an Etruscan sarcophagus of the fourth century found at Torre S. Severo, near Orvieto, are reliefs showing the sacrifice of Polyxena at Achilles's tomb and the slaughter of the Trojan prisoners by Achilles at the tomb of his friend Patroclus. In the same scene appear two Furies with huge wings, holding snakes in their hands. The dead hero's shade leans against the stele of his grave.

Charun is always present when death approaches, at the moment when life is about to be extinguished, whether peacefully at home or in battle. Either singly or in couples his powerful figure with a ferocious countenance appears in battle scenes, at the removal of the dead or as doorkeeper to the grave. His weapon is always the mighty hammer. At the gladiatorial contests of imperial Rome the man who dragged the dead bodies from the arena, dressed as Dis Pater, the underworld god, wore this same mask of Charun and carried his hammer.

Charun and Tuchulcha seldom appear alone. They are accompanied and assisted by a whole throng of male and female death demons, including the spirit Vanth, representing implacable fate. She is winged, half-clad, with crossed baldrics over a bare bosom, short skirts, and hunting boots. She brandishes snakes or burning torches. These demons or spirits are sometimes armed with clubs, pincers, a rope or mallet; they hover over scenes of battle or the killing of prisoners, or they stand at one side, expectantly. They take charge of the dying, drag them from their relatives, and take them away. They lead the funeral horse, accompany the bier, or themselves pull it. They sometimes precede or follow the funeral procession, or wait at the gate of the underworld.

Other symbols of death that populate the beyond are wild, ravenous beasts and monsters, such as chimeras, sphinxes, lions, panthers, and griffins. They lurk in the gables of tombs, crouch in the friezes that run around the walls. They attack animals as well as men, pursue, rend, and devour their victims. The rule of the everlasting cosmic powers was as merciless and ineluctable as the decline of the Etruscan nation.

XXII

Revolt in Arezzo

ETRURIA LAY PROSTRATE. ROME, FREED of that nightmare, could now direct all her energies to ending the Samnite War. The Samnites had found new allies in the Umbrians in northern Italy and the Marsi and Paeligni of the center. Some volunteers from the Hernici also joined them. But the Etruscans, who might have tipped the balance against Rome, were missing.

It is true that when the Umbrians got together a large new army, with the intention of marching to assault Rome, a "great part of the Etruscans" were also induced to rebel. But the Romans took such swift action against the Umbrian forces that there was no occasion for Etruscan intervention.

Quintus Fabius Rullianus, the consul, says Livy, "advanced by long marches to Mevania [near Perugia and Assisi], where the forces of the Umbrians at that time lay.

"The sudden arrival of the consul, whom they had believed to have his hands full with another war in Samnium, a long way from

Umbria, so dismayed the Umbrians that some were for falling back on their fortified cities, and others for giving up the war." Only the forces of one canton attacked Fabius as he "was entrenching his camp." They were defeated, however, and "on the next and on succeeding days the other peoples of Umbria also capitulated."

The campaign against the rebellious minor tribes continued until they were subdued. Three years later, in 305 B.C., the Samnites submitted after their lands had been devastated. Their commander, Statius Gellius, was taken prisoner and the city of Bovianum captured. The fall of this main center was followed by a treaty between Rome and Samnium, and thus the Second Samnite War came to an end after twenty years of fighting.

This was another important step forward in Rome's progress toward control of Italy, but all the same her hegemony was not yet assured. The Romans well knew that the Samnite mountain folk remained strong and that there was still the possibility of war breaking out again. They knew too the danger of an alliance between Samnites and Etruscans and took the necessary measures to ward it off. To put a barrier between these peoples, two military roads were built into the mountainous country northeast and east of Rome, and these were defended by fortresses and bases. On the northern edge of the Fucine lake (now drained and reclaimed land), a Latin colony of six thousand settlers was established at Alba Fucens, some fifty-five miles east of Rome. South of this and about sixty miles southeast of Rome, four thousand men were settled at Sora in the bend of the river Liris.

While Rome was taking all possible steps in order to be armed and prepared for new conflicts, her opponents hesitated and allowed precious time to pass without action or planning. It was, in fact, simply a local rising in Etruria, in which Rome intervened, that led to new hostilities.

In 302 B.C. strife between different factions broke out in Arretium (modern Arezzo). This city in the Chiana valley southeast of Florence was at that time one of the chief cities of northeast Etruria, along with Perugia and Cortona. "It was reported that Etruria was up in arms," says Livy, "in consequence of an outbreak that had its origin in dissensions at Arretium, where a movement was begun to drive out the Cilnii—a very powerful family—because of the envy occasioned by their wealth."

The Austrian Etruscologist Ambros Josef Pfiffig notes that, "After the abolition of the monarchy toward the end of the sixth century, first the Etruscan aristocracy everywhere seized power, and then the upper bourgeoisie, in imitation of the aristocrats. The twelve cities were at this time republics controlled by a plutocratic nobility. The lower classes, who were mostly of Italic origin, increasingly felt themselves to be bondsmen of the rich merchants and landowners. Real slavery like that of Greece and Rome probably did not exist in free Etruria. It was more a sort of vassalage of the older Italic population.

"It is understandable that the condition of the peasant vassals became more onerous as the sources of Etruscan wealth in overseas trade dried up. For then the upper class had to fall back on the profits from their own land."

On hearing about the party strife in Arretium the Romans promptly intervened. In itself this domestic conflict might have been a matter of indifference to the Romans, or even desirable, as tending to weaken Etruria. But Rome was a power of law and order and could not tolerate violent upheavals. The senate decided to send military forces to help the exiles. The Cilnii were an ancient noble family, from whom in later times Maecenas, the friend of the emperor Augustus, was descended, and they may have been guarantors to the Romans of the thirty-year truce which Arezzo, Perugia, and Cortona had signed eight years earlier, a truce which clearly was not at all popular.

At an early stage of the campaign against the Etruscans, the Romans suffered a reverse. Marcus Aemilius Paulus, the master of the horse, "went out to forage," says Livy, "and being ambushed, lost a number of standards and was driven back into his camp, with a shameful rout and slaughter of his soldiers.

"The news of this reverse gave rise in Rome to a greater alarm than the situation warranted. For, as though the army had been destroyed, a cessation of legal business was proclaimed, guards were called into service at the gates, and night-watches in the several streets, arms and missiles being heaped upon the walls."

The dictator Marcus Valerius Maximus, who had been in Rome consulting the auspices, then returned to Etruria with new forces to restore the position. "He advanced without delay into the district of Rusellae" says Livy.

Less than ten miles southeast of Vetulonia, Rusellae (modern Roselle) was one of the most important and oldest of Etruscan

cities. It lay on a hill between the Ombrone and the Bruna rivers and was about fifteen miles in a straight line from the coast. It was strongly defended by a wall of limestone blocks some two miles long, parts of which survive. From the Lacus Prillius, a brackish lake that is now reclaimed land, its ships had access to the Tyrrhenian Sea. It was to this place that the Etruscans followed the Roman troops. Though they had confidence in their ability to cope with the Romans in the open field, they decided to try an ambush like that in which they had previously succeeded.

> **It was to this place that the Etruscans followed the Roman troops. Though they had confidence in their ability to cope with the Romans in the open field, they decided to try an ambush like that in which they had previously succeeded.**

"Not far from the Roman camp," says Livy, "stood the half-ruined buildings of a village which had been burned when the country was laid waste. Concealing armed men in these ruins, they drove out some cattle in full sight of a Roman outpost, which was under the command of the lieutenant Gnaeus Fulvius. But when this tempting bait failed to lure any of the Romans from their post, one of the shepherds came up under the very works and called out to the others, who were hesitating to drive out their flock from amongst the tumble-down buildings, asking why they were so slow, for they could safely drive them through the midst of the Roman camp."

When some men from Caere had interpreted this to Fulvius, he ordered them to listen to the shepherds' talk and note whether it was that of rustics or city folk. His men reported that the supposed shepherds' accent, carriage, and appearance were too refined for countrymen. Fulvius then ordered his men to tell the "shepherds" that their trick had been discovered. At which the Etruscans lying in ambush "all rose up from their hiding-places and advanced in martial array into the plain which was spread open to the view on every side. Their army seemed to the lieutenant to be greater than his own detachment could withstand, and he therefore sent in all haste to the dictator to summon help."

After the fighting had gone on for some time, and all the Etruscan troops were engaged, the dictator brought up the cavalry. Then, says Livy, "the legionaries gave a cheer, and simultaneously the horsemen were let loose and with a free course galloped straight upon the enemy, who were not prepared to resist a shock of cavalry and were overwhelmed with a sudden panic."

The battle did not last much longer. "The routed enemy fled back to their camp, and when the Roman standard-bearers pressed in after them, they gave way and huddled up together in the farthest part of the enclosure. The narrow gates became choked with fugitives and a great part of them climbed upon the mound and palisade, in hopes that from that elevation they might be able either to defend themselves, or to climb over somewhere and escape. It chanced that in a certain place the mound had not been solidly rammed down, and this, overburdened with the weight of those who stood upon it, slid over into the trench. By that opening . . . they saved themselves, but more got away without their arms than with them.

"In this battle the might of the Etruscans was broken for the second time."

The Etruscans were allowed to send envoys to Rome to ask for peace. This the senate refused, but they were granted a truce for two years. In return for it they had to provide a year's pay for the soldiers and two months' grain.

By this victory Rome had made another deep penetration of Etruscan territory. The important mining areas of the north, the hinterland of the rich city-states of Vetulonia, Populonia, and Volterra, were at the mercy of Roman armies. The last great strongholds were now in the front line.

WITH THE SAMNITE ARMIES AGAINST ROME

THE NEW, PAINFUL REVERSE gave Etruria no chance of peace. The defeat at Rusellae had shown how powerless it was if left to itself. Only in a great coalition was there a possibility of recovering the lands lost to the insatiable Romans. The Etruscan city-states now put all their hopes in such a coalition. Moves to organize it were made even before the truce expired. Etruscan envoys were sent secretly to negotiate an alliance of Umbrians, Sabines, and Samnites.

Ill luck would have it that just at this time a huge army of Gauls invaded Etruria, "and diverted them for a little while from their purpose," says Livy. Then the Etruscans tried to buy the Gauls' help against Rome. The Gauls seemingly had no objection to an alliance, and negotiations were needed only to fix the price.

But the Etruscans soon found that they had been swindled. "When this had been agreed upon and received, and the Etruscans, having completed the rest of their preparations for the war, bade their new allies follow them, the Gauls demurred. They had made no bargain, they said, for a war with Rome; whatever they had received had been in consideration of their not devastating the Etruscan territory and molesting its inhabitants; nevertheless they would take the field, if the Etruscans were bent on having them, but on one condition only—that the Etruscans admit them to a share in their land, where they might settle at last in a permanent home."

The Etruscans discussed this proposal at great length. "Many councils were held," says Livy. But in the end it was turned down "not so much from a reluctance to see their territory lessened as because everyone shrank from having men of so savage a race for neighbors." As they could not get what they wanted, the Gauls then "departed with a vast sum of money, acquired without any toil or risk."

Through this unfortunate incident the Etruscans lost valuable time, and the Romans, having learned about the war preparations and the negotiations with the Gauls, took the initiative. The Roman legions marched through the countryside "wasting their lands and firing their buildings," says Livy, till "the smoke was rising on every side from the conflagration not only of farmhouses but of many villages as well." But despite this devastation the Etruscans did not move out of their fortified cities.

In 298 B.C., in the midst of this campaign, the Romans received news that the Samnites had risen again.

In 298 B.C., in the midst of this campaign, the Romans received news that the Samnites had risen again. This meant war on two fronts. The Romans seem not to have realized what a dangerous conspiracy and coalition lay behind the rising. The consuls divided the commands between them. Lucius Cornelius Scipio got Etruria and Gnaeus Fulvius the Samnites, and they set out for their respective theaters of war. "Scipio looked forward to a slow campaign like that of the previous year," says Livy. But he got a surprise.

In the north of Etruria, near the city of Volterra in the valley of the Cecina, he was met "by the enemy drawn up in a column," and all ready for battle. "The fighting, which lasted for the best part of a day, was attended with heavy losses on both sides; and night came on while it was yet uncertain to which nation victory had been vouchsafed." The darkness separated the combatants, but "morning showed who was victor and who vanquished, for in the silence of the night the Etruscans had decamped."

The Romans marched on and occupied the Etruscan camp. It was deserted but contained much booty. Laden with their spoils the army marched southward again into Faliscan territory where they deposited their baggage at Falerii. The consul Scipio then ordered punitive measures, the sort of scorched earth policy that Rome's peasant soldiery were so good at executing. "The whole country was laid waste with fire and sword, and booty was brought in from all directions," is how Livy describes it. "Not only was the soil left bare for the enemy, but even strongholds and villages were burned." In the south the Samnites too had achieved nothing, and in fact had lost a battle and two cities to the Romans.

The consular elections were now approaching, and in Rome it was rumored, reports Livy, "that the Etruscans and Samnites were levying huge forces; it was said that in all their councils the leaders of the Etruscans were openly censured for not having brought the Gauls into the war, on whatever terms; and the Samnite magistrates were attacked for having confronted the Romans with an army raised to oppose a Lucanian foe." Thus it seemed to Rome that "their enemies were girding themselves for war, in their own might and the might of their allies, and they would have to contend with them on far from even terms."

Two consular armies were called up, one to take the field in Etruria, the other in Samnium. But shortly before they set out, reports were received from the north which upset all the plans. Messengers came from Sutrium, Nepete, and Falerii "with the news that the nations of Etruria were counseling together how they might sue for peace."

326

This story may have been deliberately planted in order to lull the Romans into a sense of false security and to conceal the preparations for the great coalition that were then going ahead. Anyway, it "diverted upon Samnium the whole burden of war." The two consular armies spread out over a wide front and "laid all waste within five months' time."

The following year, after the election of new consuls, the old consuls were ordered to carry on the war in Samnium and their commands were extended for six months as proconsuls. They continued to lay waste the farms, and captured and sacked three cities. The Samnite army, however, would not risk battle, but retreated into Etruria.

"Whilst these operations were being carried out in Samnium," says Livy, ". . . a mighty war was preparing against the Romans in Etruria, on the part of many nations, at the instigation of a Samnite named Gellius Egnatius." The Samnite forces had broken through the Roman barrier of fortifications in central Italy, and reached the frontiers of Etruria and Umbria. The Etruscans had almost all agreed to war, records Livy. The nearest Umbrian tribes had joined in, and efforts were being made to recruit Gallic mercenaries. "All this multitude was assembling at the camp of the Samnites." Thus four of the peoples of Italy had mobilized their armies against the hated enemy.

The Etruscan city-states had spared no expense to get the help of the Gallic warriors. As they would fight only for hard cash, large sums were collected. In Tarentum, friendly to Etruria, the gold and silver coins that the Gauls demanded were minted from the metal obtained from temple treasures.

The news from Etruria caused the greatest alarm in Rome. The senate ordered the suspension of the courts and a levy of all men. "Not only was the oath administered to free citizens of military age, but cohorts were also formed out of older men, and freedmen were mustered into centuries." Command of the army in Etruria was entrusted to two of the most experienced generals, Quintus Fabius Rullianus and Publius Decius. It numbered some sixty thousand men. Two further armies were held in reserve, one near Falerii under Gnaeus Fulvius and the other just outside the Servian wall, where the Vatican now is, under Lucius Postumius Megellus.

In the meantime the four allied armies, Etruscan, Samnite, Umbrian, and Gallic, had met in Umbria and were completing their preparations. They divided their camp into two, says Livy, because one place was not big enough to hold so great a multitude. "Consultations were then held amongst the enemy and they decided not to . . . give battle all together; to the Samnites were joined the Gauls and to the Etruscans the men of Umbria. A day was designated for the battle, and the Samnites and Gauls were appointed to make the attack; in the midst of the engagement the Etruscans and the Umbrians were to assault the Roman camp."

The consuls then marched their armies along both banks of the Tiber northward to Umbria. Even before they had made contact with the enemy, the latter's plans were betrayed to them by "three Clusinian deserters who came over secretly in the night to Fabius, and having informed him of the enemy's designs were rewarded and sent back again, so that from time to time, as each new step should be decided on, they might find it out and report upon it."

The consuls immediately issued new orders to counter the threatening pincer movement—the advance of the Etruscans and Umbrians on the Roman camp. Gnaeus Fulvius and Lucius Postumius were ordered "to march from their respective posts in the Faliscan and Vatican districts to Clusium, and lay waste the territories of the enemy with the utmost rigor." The object of this maneuver was to draw Etruscan troops away from the area where the decisive battle would have to be fought.

The Romans did in fact succeed in this. "The reports of this devastation drew off the Etruscans . . . to the defense of their own frontiers." They were followed by the Umbrians who were also afraid of their territory being plundered. As a result the ranks of the coalition army were considerably reduced. Nevertheless the Romans had a hard day's fighting ahead of them.

When they learned of the departure of the Etruscans, the consuls hastened to bring about an engagement. They came up with the enemy at Sentinum, on the eastern slopes of the Apennines, near where the little town of Sassoferrato stands on a height. For two days they harassed the enemy. On the third came the battle. "At the first shock," says Livy, "the strength put forth on both sides was so equal that if the Etruscans and the Umbrians had been present either in the battle or at the camp, in whichever quarter they had thrown their weight the Romans must have suffered a disaster."

On the right wing, where Quintus Fabius Rullianus with his two legions faced the Samnites under their general, Egnatius, the fighting was long indecisive. "The Romans were rather defending themselves than attacking." On the left wing, where Publius Decius was in command, the Romans had some initial success against the Gauls, but things began to go wrong "when they were subjected to a new and terrifying kind of assault; for, standing erect in chariots and wagons, armed enemies came rushing upon them with a mighty clattering of hoofs and wheels, frightening the horses of the Romans with the unfamiliar din. Thus the victorious cavalry were scattered, as if by a panic fit of madness, and, suddenly fleeing, were overthrown, both horse and rider." The infantry, too, began to weaken.

At this point, Publius Decius "spurred his charger against the Gallic lines, where he saw that they were thickest, and hurling himself against the weapons of the enemy met his death." The general's heroic death steadied the ranks. At the same time, Fabius gathered up all the troops he had held in reserve and ordered the cavalry to charge. Their unexpected attack on the flank and rear of the enemy threw the Gauls into confusion and drove them to flight. At the same time a furious attack upon the Samnites forced them to give way. They fled in panic back to their camp, where their commander Egnatius was killed.

This was the end of the battle. It was a great victory for Rome. The losses on both sides were enormous. On the Roman side 8,700 were killed; the coalition armies lost 25,000 dead and 8,000 prisoners. It was the end, too, of the coalition. The army dispersed, the Gauls drifted away, such of the Samnites as survived went back to their homes in the Abruzzi Mountains. Umbria remained in Roman hands.

> It was the end, too,
> of the coalition.
> The army dispersed,
> the Gauls drifted away,
> such of the Samnites
> as survived went back
> to their homes
> in the Abruzzi Mountains.

In Etruria itself the Romans were also successful. "Gnaeus Fulvius . . . besides the enormous damage which his forays inflicted on the enemy, fought also a victorious battle with them. The Perusini and Clusini lost upward of three thousand men, and some twenty military standards were captured from them."

Quintus Fabius ordered the army of Decius to remain on guard over Etruria and "led down his own legions to Rome and triumphed over the Gauls, the Etruscans, and the Samnites." But despite the victory, the year 295 B.C. brought no peace to Rome. Neither of the two strongest peoples, the Etruscans and the Samnites, had been subjugated in their own countries. The war went on.

Perugia, after the Roman army was withdrawn, had formed a new army and sent out envoys to other cities urging a resumption of the war. Volsinii was the only one to join in. "Fabius dealt with the new outbreak in Etruria, where he slew four thousand five hundred of the Perusini and took one thousand seven hundred and forty prisoners." The Etruscans had to pay 310 *asses* ransom for each prisoner. The booty was distributed among the Roman soldiers.

The following year Rome sent out two armies, which marched first against Samnium. As there was not enough to do there for both, that of the consul Lucius Postumius Megellus marched north to Etruria, where he devastated the lands of Volsinii. When the city's troops came out to put a stop to this barbarous destruction they were defeated "at no great distance from their own walls," and 2,800 of them were killed.

The consul then led his men to Rusellae (modern Roselle) not far from the Tyrrhenian coast. Here too the Romans laid waste the fields and proved to the Etruscans that resistance was useless. The town was captured, nearly two thousand were killed in fighting about the walls, and over two thousand taken prisoner.

Rusellae remained silent and forgotten until the present day. It lies only some six miles northeast of Grosseto, on the landward side of the Via Aurelia; a signpost by a footpath points to the "rovine di Roselle," the ruins of Rusellae. A winding path leads past the rust-red boles of barked cork oak up to the site of the ancient city. Some eight centuries ago the last inhabitants left with the bishop whose see this was and moved to Grosseto. "Since that time Rusellae has remained as it is now seen—a wilderness of rocks and thickets—the haunt of the fox and wild boar, of the serpent and lizard—visited by none but the herdsman or shepherd, who lies the live-long day stretched in vacancy on the sward, or turning a wondering gaze on the stupendous ruins around him, of whose origins and history he cannot form a conception."

What Dennis wrote over a century ago is just as true today. Long stretches of the vast fortifications still stand, in places made of huge stone blocks, some of which are four cubic yards in size. A swine-herd lives on the lonely hill from which the view extends to the sea. There is a unique opportunity here in this remote spot to bring to light the whole of one of the most important Etruscan cities, right down to the foundations. But so far it has not been used.

Diggings have been made at a few points only. In 1960, to the southeast of the hill, traces were found of streets, canals, and reservoirs. Below them ruins from the sixth century B.C., the Etruscan golden age, lie undisturbed and with them the secrets of once mighty Rusellae. So far no permission has been given for even one systematic excavation.

After the conquest of Rusellae, the Etruscans at last gave in. "Three very powerful cities, the chief places in that country, namely Volsinii, Perusia, and Arretium, made overtures of peace, and arranged with the consul, in return for clothing and corn for his troops, to be permitted to send ambassadors to Rome, who obtained a truce for forty years." The three cities had to pay 500,000 *asses* each, and at once, by way of reparations. Etruria seemed to have bowed to its fate.

Four years later, in 290 B.C., the campaigns against the Etruscans' allies came to an end by the conclusion of peace with the Samnites.

CELTS IN ETRUSCAN PAY

BARELY A DECADE AFTER THE great international battle at Sentinum, all the enemies of Rome in both the north and the south were to come together again in alliance. In southern Italy, the Lucanians and the Bruttians, who lived south of Samnium, revolted and started parleys with their neighbors to form another coalition of Italic peoples. When Rome sent envoys to warn them, they imprisoned them and started hostilities. At the same time they summoned the Samnites, Tarentines, Etruscans, Umbrians, and Gauls to join the common struggle for independence.

When agents from the south appeared in Etruria, opinion proved to be divided. The northern cities were firmly opposed to participating in any anti-Roman alliance. Some other city-states, however, among them Volsinii and Vulci, and possibly also Clusium, agreed, and at once began to make plans. The agents also succeeded in finding supporters among the Gauls who had long been itching to avenge the defeat at Sentinum. Many Gallic warriors were engaged as mercenaries.

In 284 B.C. an impressive body of warriors of the Senones tribe, with Etruscan volunteers, suddenly appeared before the walls of Arretium (Arezzo), which was allied with Rome. They laid siege to the city in order to bring pressure on it to join the alliance. The Romans hastened to relieve the besieged city, but their army was defeated and its commander, Lucius Caecilius Metellus, was killed along with thirteen thousand of his men. Not since the Allia battle had Rome met with such misfortune. The news of the Roman defeat was a signal to Etruria and all northern Italy to take up arms.

The Romans sent two new legions to Arezzo and at the same time envoys to the Senones to ask for the release of the prisoners. But during the negotiations, in which the Gauls openly sided with the Etruscans, there was a violent clash and the Roman envoys were killed.

Rome replied with a punitive expedition. The consul Publius Cornelius Dolabella with a strong army advanced into the territory of the Senones and pushed as far as the Adriatic. Ruthlessly the legions made a clean sweep. Those who were not put to the sword were driven out of the country, the whole of which was occupied by the Romans. "This was the first part of Gaul in which they planted a colony," says Polybius, "calling it Sena after the name of the tribe who formerly inhabited it." This colony in an Adriatic port (the modern Senigallia) gave Rome a dominating maritime base.

The merciless extermination of the Senones caused the greatest alarm among their Gallic neighbors and kinsmen, the Boii. They streamed over the Apennines in full force, thirsting for revenge, and joined up with Etruscans who, together with the survivors of the Senones, were continuing the war.

An armed host of Gauls and Etruscans set out along the Tiber for Rome. After crossing the river near Lake Vadimo, only fifty miles from Rome, they encountered the Roman army under the consul Publius Cornelius Dolabella. "In this battle" says Polybius, "most of the Etruscans were cut to pieces while only a few of the Boii escaped." It was said that the defeat was so disastrous that the Tiber ran red with the blood of the Etruscans and Gauls, and that thus the inhabitants of Rome knew of the battle even before the consul's messengers arrived with the news of victory.

> **For the second time Lake Vadimo had been the scene of a crushing Etruscan defeat.**

For the second time Lake Vadimo had been the scene of a crushing Etruscan defeat. Near its banks, in 309 B.C., the Romans "for the first time broke the might of the Etruscans." Barely a generation later, in 283 B.C., it happened a second time. The lake is now a small pond; overgrown with rank grasses and reeds that float in small islets on its milky, shimmering surface and drift here and there in the wind, it seems as though haunted.

Now known as Lago di Bassano, it lies but a few minutes' walk from the railway station Bassano in Teverina, near where the great viaducts of the Rome–Florence motorway cross the Tiber three times in close succession. In Etruscan times the lake must have been larger, and even in the first century A.D. Pliny the Younger described it as "of no great size, but large enough for the wind to raise waves on its surface." It was perfectly round, and there were no boats on it, because it was sacred.

Today there is little enough to recall the events which were so decisive in Etruscan history. Now and then the plow turns up in the dark soil of the banks a fragment of armor, of a sword or a helmet, the only things that still speak of the terrible battles that raged here.

The alliance between Etruscans and Boii came to an end in 282 B.C. when their forces were again defeated. The Gauls made peace with Rome and turned their energies to plans of conquest elsewhere. They left Italy for the Balkans. Spreading terror and collecting plunder, they outflanked Thermopylae and appeared at Delphi, where they were defeated, and moved over into Asia Minor. The region of Anatolia where they settled was named Galatia after them. It was to their descendants that St. Paul in a later age addressed his famous Epistle to the Galatians.

The Roman victories over the Gauls settled matters in the north. Etruria became a secondary front, and Rome no longer faced any serious threat from that direction.

XXIII

A Pyrrhic Victory

R_{OME} WAS NOW FREE TO ATTEND TO its wars elsewhere. And the Romans lost no time. They took up vigorously the campaign in southern Italy which they had so long conducted with delaying tactics and limited means. At first, all went well. A consular army defeated the Lucanians. The Greek cities which had been hard-pressed by the latter welcomed the Romans, whom they considered as saviors, with open arms. Thurii, Locri, Croton, and Rhegium accepted Roman garrisons within their walls. But this led to trouble.

Rome's success provoked resistance from Tarentum, the strongest city in Magna Graecia, which saw a threat to its maritime activity and its predominant position. There was a serious incident in the harbor of Tarentum, where the population attacked a Roman fleet that had dropped anchor there while on the way from the Tyrrhenian Sea to the Adriatic. The incident led to a breach with Rome and war. Tarentum, which was, of course, no match for Roman arms, turned to a foreign power. The city appealed for help to one of the leading soldiers of his time, King Pyrrhus of Epirus, and was given it.

In the autumn of 281 B.C. an advance party of three thousand Epirots arrived and occupied the citadel. Early in the following year Pyrrhus himself came with a powerful army consisting of twenty thousand infantrymen, two thousand archers, five hundred slingers, and three thousand cavalry—not much less than the force with which Alexander had crossed the Hellespont fifty years before. And he had a secret weapon which was tactically effective, to wit, twenty elephants. It was their first appearance in Italy, says Pliny, where they "were called 'Lucanian oxen,' because they were first seen in Lucania."

The news of the arrival of Pyrrhus spread like wildfire throughout Italy. Rome's enemies saw their chance. The Samnites, Lucanians, and Bruttians lost no time in allying themselves with the Greeks. Even from the north, from Etruria, came an offer of assistance. Suddenly it seemed as though Rome's predominance was in danger.

The Romans hastened to take countermeasures. One army was left to defend the capital; another, under the consul Tiberius Coruncanius, moved to Etruria, where bands of volunteers were assembling around Vulci and Volsinii. The main army, consisting of four legions plus the troops of the allies, and totaling about fifty thousand men, was led by the consul Publius Laevinus against Pyrrhus. The opposing armies met near Heraclea, a Tarentine colony on the river Siris. Despite their numbers the Romans were not really a match for the highly skilled Hellenistic army of Pyrrhus, whose elephants, moreover, terrified the horses of the Roman cavalry. Pyrrhus won the battle, with heavy losses. The Romans were now in a difficult situation, the more so in that in the meantime soldiers from the Lucanians, Samnites, and Bruttians were flocking to Pyrrhus. Except for Rhegium, all the cities of southern Italy went over to him, and he marched into Campania without encountering any resistance. There the king ordered an advance on Rome. His plan seems to have been to join up with the Etruscans, to overawe Rome's allies and threaten the city itself.

Pyrrhus succeeded in reaching Anagnia (modern Agnani), less than forty miles from Rome, without any army opposing him. Publius Laevinus, it is true, followed him like a shadow—at a respectful distance—but took care to avoid any engagement. But what the Greek leader was hoping for did not happen. None of Rome's allies broke away. Everywhere in Latium the cities closed their gates to him. Even the Sabines and Umbrians made no move.

Pyrrhus would perhaps have continued his expedition but for the fact that at this time Vulci and Volsinii, the only Etruscan city-states that had revolted, capitulated to the Romans. Vulci lost its independence and its territory along the coast and inland.

The possibility of a general rising against Rome, which had seemed so close after the Greek victory at Heraclea, faded away. Pyrrhus was now faced in addition by the northern Roman army which had finished its work in Etruria and by the reserve stationed in Rome. There seemed no option for him but to turn about. For a while he hesitated in Campania, and with the approach of winter moved back to Tarentum.

THE END OF THE LAST FREE CITY

AFTER VULCI'S LOSS OF ITS INDEpendence in the last Roman offensive, the only free Etruscan city-state that survived was rich and powerful Volsinii. But its days too were numbered, and the history of the Etruscans as a free people was nearing its end. The final act of the centuries-old struggle between Etruria and Rome remains obscure. Livy's book on the decline and fall of Volsinii is lost. Fragments of other chronicles yield only a vague picture of what happened. The endless wars with their heavy losses in men compelled the aristocracy increasingly to arm their bondsmen and freedmen and lead them into battle. In return for this military service they had been obliged to make concessions and step by step to grant them important civil rights.

According to Valerius Maximus, Volsinii fell upon evil days. It had been a wealthy, well-organized city, with excellent laws and customs, and was considered the capital of Etruria. But gradually it slid into the depths of dishonor as it surrendered to a tyranny of the former slaves. First these managed to infiltrate the senate. Eventually they seized the government. They issued arbitrary decrees on inheritance, prohibited the banquets and assemblies of freeborn citizens, and even married the daughters of their former masters. The so-called slaves, says A. J. Pfiffig, "were really the plebs, the mass of vassals, peasants, tradesmen, and laborers."

During the decade after the defeat of 280 B.C., the internal strife in Volsinii seems to have grown to such a pitch that the aristocrats could no longer feel sure of their lives and property. In desperation they decided to apply to Rome for help. Envoys arrived for secret discussions. As they did not want anyone to learn about the move, the senate agreed to their request that the discussions should take place at a private house. As bad luck would have it, a Samnite who was a guest in the house overheard the conversations and betrayed everything.

When the unsuspecting envoys got back to Volsinii they were seized by an excited crowd, tortured, and executed. A revolt broke out, and the insurgents seized power in the city. There began a reign of terror such as Etruscan history had never known. The nobles were driven out or slain. Their wives and daughters were seized, their possessions pillaged, and their lands divided up among the people. This revolt provided Rome with a welcome pretext for military action against the last great city-state. With the excuse of helping the exiled nobility to recover their rights, Rome sent out its legions.

The inhabitants of Volsinii realized too late what they had provoked by their revolt. The desperate spirit of resistance that filled the city on the approach of the hated Romans could not save it. The consul Quintus Fabius Gurges defeated the forces hurriedly sent out to oppose him, but was himself mortally wounded. The following year, 264 B.C., the new consul, M. Fulvius Flaccus, took over the command, and when Volsinii refused to surrender, threw up earthworks around the walls, and invested the town. Worn out by hunger and fighting, the city surrendered after a long siege.

Those ringleaders who were captured were executed. And then the plundering of the city began. Even the nearby venerable sanctuary of the Etruscan league, the Fanum Voltumnae, did not escape the legionaries' attentions. They despoiled it of all its precious treasures, its votive offerings and other gifts. A long line of wagons, packed with objects of incalculable value, set off for Rome. According to tradition the plunder included no less than two thousand bronze statues. They vanished completely. It was an immeasurable loss when one thinks of the few uniquely beautiful Etruscan bronzes that have by chance survived.

Metrodorus of Scepsis, the Greek writer of the first century B.C., is reported by Pliny the Elder as having reproached the Romans for conquering Volsinii just for the sake of the two thousand statues. These precious bronzes were stolen, not from enthusiasm for Etruscan art, or in order to decorate Rome. They were, it is said, simply all melted down. And the reason for that was the senate's urgent need of cash to pay for new campaigns of conquest. The preparations and armaments for the intended war against Carthage were swallowing up vast sums. They were found, since there was a shortage of silver, by minting *aes grave* of bronze. Thus the art treasures of Volsinii ended up as bronze coins used for purchasing arms with which to fight Etruria's former friend and ally in Africa.

In her mania for destruction, Rome went so far as to order the eradication of Volsinii from the face of the earth. Nothing was to remind posterity of the proud city that for centuries had embodied the power and greatness of the Etruscans. All the buildings were destroyed, the walls and fortifications laid level with the ground. Such inhabitants as survived and were not sold into slavery were rounded up and driven away to compulsory settlement elsewhere.

> **The fall and destruction of Volsinii represented the final capitulation of the Etruscans and was the end of their history as an independent nation.**

On November 1, 264 B.C. the consul M. Fulvius Flaccus celebrated his triumph in Rome. For the last time the tablets recording the *fasti triumphales* included the name of an Etruscan city—*de Vulsiniensibus*. The fall and destruction of Volsinii represented the final capitulation of the Etruscans and was the end of their history as an independent nation. It came 132 years after Rome had made its first great inroad into Etruria by the conquest of Veii, and nearly 250 years after the expulsion of the Tarquins from Rome.

Etruria was now under the thumb of a foreign power. Rome granted only a semblance of autonomy to the subjugated city-states. The military colonies at Sutri and Nepi, the garrison at Arezzo, police, and a network of informers kept watch on everything.

The cities were still allowed to trade and their pottery manufacture and crafts continued, but the whole of the metal industry, which was important for armaments, was subject to strict control and directives from Rome. All the iron ore that was mined was now sent to the victor's smelting furnaces at Puteoli (modern Pozzuoli), while the bronze was dispatched to Brindisi. The once flourishing heavy

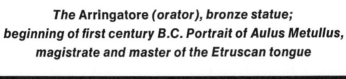

The Arringatore (orator), bronze statue; beginning of first century B.C. Portrait of Aulus Metullus, magistrate and master of the Etruscan tongue

industry gradually declined. The ironworks were replaced by work-shops and factories turning out painted pottery. And they began the mass production of cheap goods. Buyers with taste were no more.

The history and the fate of Volsinii fell into oblivion. Even knowledge of the site it had once occupied was lost. Scholars have looked for it in various places. Some thought it might have been at Orvieto, the Etruscan name of which is still unknown. Was this perhaps the site of Velzna, as Volsinii was called on Etruscan coins? Many finds have shown that the city on the Paglia, so strikingly situated on an isolated cone of brownish red tufa surrounded with vineyards, must have been an important place even in Etruscan times. Among these finds are fragments of terra-cotta temple decorations, frescoed tomb chambers, and a large painted sarcophagus. This came to light when lightning struck and uprooted a huge old tree. At the foot of the plateau the necropolis known as the Crocifisso del Tufo has been excavated. Here the tombs, built of massive masonry, are arranged side by side in streets crossing at right angles. The names of the dead are inscribed by the doorways in large Etruscan characters.

But what could be more reasonable than to look for the ancient city-state where a place name, and the name of a lake, have preserved its memory down to the present day? Lake Bolsena lies amid the piled-up lava of what was once a mighty crater from which a volcano of prodigious size flung its fire and smoke into the sky. On the north bank, some twelve miles southwest of Orvieto, lies a little town with the same name, Bolsena.

One looks in vain for boat or sail on the dull silver mirror of this vast piece of water. The monotony of its surface is broken only by two tiny islands, Bisentina and Martana. Like serrated reefs, they rise from unplumbed depths. The steep sides of the crater, like a gloomy amphitheater formed by the primeval forces of nature, are covered from top to bottom by forest and pathless scrub. It is an eerie place, full of mysterious melancholy even when the sun shines from a cloudless sky.

It was on the banks of this lake that the hitherto fruitless search for vanished Volsinii came to an end.

This lake and its surroundings have witnessed much in the course of the millenniums, even in historical times. On Martana island, in

340

A.D. 535, Queen Amalasuntha, daughter of the Ostrogothic ruler Theoderic the Great, was taken prisoner by order of her husband Theodahad, and strangled in her bath. This murder provided the emperor Justinian with a pretext for his attack on the Ostrogothic kingdom and led to its fall.

At the church of Santa Cristina at Bolsena, in the crypt, one of the sights is the altar of the saint on which is a tenth-century ciborium. It was here that the famous Miracle of Bolsena took place. A priest from Prague, tormented by doubts about transsubstantiation, was on a pilgrimage to Rome and, when he stopped at Bolsena, took the opportunity to celebrate mass in Santa Cristina. To his amazement he suddenly saw blood on the consecrated Host. It was in memory of this miracle that Pope Urban IV in 1264 instituted the festival of Corpus Christi.

Southeast of Bolsena at the little town of Montefiascone a stone commemorates the death of a high ecclesiastic who clearly had no pangs of conscience on his journey to Rome. The curious inscription begins: *Est! Est! Est!* It recalls a somewhat uncommon episode. Bishop Johannes von Fugger, of Augsburg, a great wine lover, had the habit, when traveling, of sending his servant ahead of him to sample the wine at the inns, and to write on the door where it was best, the word *Est,* meaning, "It's here." At Montefiascone the wine was so good that he marked it up three times. The bishop never reached his journey's end. He drank himself to death on the spot. The local wine growers still use the *Est! Est! Est!* of the clerical wine-bibber as the brand name for their product.

It was on the banks of this lake that the hitherto fruitless search for vanished Volsinii came to an end. One day excavations near some ancient ruins on the periphery of Bolsena brought to light streets of dressed stone blocks, an amphitheater, a forum, and the foundations of a villa. But on closer examination it became clear that they were of a later, Roman period. They were the remains of the place where the exiles had, by Roman order, been obliged to settle, in short, the new Volsinii. Its continued existence until imperial times is attested. Tacitus names it as the birhplace of Sejanus, the favorite of Tiberius, who for a long time pulled the strings in Rome, until the emperor had him executed. Strabo, living into the first century A.D., lists Volsinii as one of the principal cities of Etruria in his time.

But precisely where was the original city, the once celebrated *urbs vetus,* the old city? The answer came from excavations conducted by the Ecole française de Rome that began in 1946 on the bank of the lake.

A little over a mile east of Bolsena, a hill, known as Mozzetta, rises from the lakeside. It is over two thousand feet high and on its slopes the excavators' picks and spades struck upon strong fortifications. Amid the vineyards and scrub they unearthed the remains of a wall some five feet thick made of large tufa blocks. On some of these are inscribed Etruscan letters or signs which are taken to be masons' marks. The circuit of the walls is about three miles and includes several minor heights. The construction is dated to the fifth or fourth century B.C. The position and careful masonry of the impressive fortification indicate the importance of the city it defended. Steep ravines protected it on the north and west. Within the walls huge cisterns ensured a supply of drinking water. One such artificial reservoir discovered by the French excavators measures more than 120 feet in length. "Girdled by walls" was the expression ancient writers used to describe Velzna.

These excavations, in the opinion of M. Pallottino, "have definitely proved that Volsinii corresponds to modern Bolsena, as the latter name implies (an earlier hypothesis connected it with Orvieto). A powerful girdle of city-walls crowned the acropolis dominating the lake."

However, these discoveries have not answered the other great question, which has long preoccupied scholars, as to the whereabouts of the often mentioned Fanum Voltumnae. According to tradition, this famous central sanctuary at which all the Etruscans assembled for their great religious festival was located in the territory of Volsinii. Two deities were worshipped there. One was Nortia, into the walls of whose temple the nails were driven. The Roman annalist Cincius claimed to have seen them with his own eyes around 200 B.C. The other god was Veltune (otherwise Velta, Voltumna, or Vertumnus), whom the antiquarian Varro called *deus Etruriae princeps,* the chief god of Etruria. For this reason some have supposed that he was identical with the Tuscan god Tinia. Varro specifies that the companions of Caelius Vibenna brought this god to Rome, where he was worshipped by the Etruscan colony. As late as the Imperial Age, a statue of Vertumnus still stood at the spot where the Vicus Tuscus, the Etruscan Street, joined the Forum.

Once every year great religious celebrations were held at the Fanum Voltumnae. Representatives of the twelve states discussed the political and economic affairs of the league, and elected a president, known as the *sacerdos Etruriae*. After the leaders had concluded their discussions, priests performed the sacred ritual outside the temples and invoked the good deities and spirits in the east and the evil ones in the west. The sacrifices and prayers were followed by athletic contests and poetic and musical entertainments. People came from far and near to this festival and to the annual fair connected with it, at which wares from the whole country were displayed. Merchants from Rome and abroad regularly visited the festival.

So far, all attempts to find the scene of these pan-Etruscan celebrations have proved fruitless.

UNDER ROMAN OCCUPATION

ALMOST IMMEDIATELY AFTER the campaign against Volsinii the victor was involved in a life-or-death struggle. In 264 B.C. the war against Carthage broke out. This tremendous conflict was to last nearly 120 years until Rome achieved its ambitious aims by the destruction of the Punic capital in Africa. The war began over the control and possession of Sicily, in the west of which Carthage had long had important bases, as it had in Sardinia.

For the first time in its history Rome reached out beyond the Italic lands and fought a war at sea. Meanwhile Etruria, remote from the scene of events, was granted years of peace. Its people had time to recover from the grave social and economic upheavals which had resulted from war and the loss of its independence. Gradually there came a certain relaxation of tension in relations with Rome.

The Romans, indeed, just at this time adopted one of the Etruscans' ancient funeral customs. At the games in honor of his late father, in 264 B.C., Decimus Brutus arranged for a display of fighting between three pairs of men. This was the beginning of the gladiatorial combats in Rome. Such bloodthirsty fights were known in Etruria from early days, but only at funeral celebrations, where they replaced the former human sacrifices.

The tomb paintings of Tarquinia depict some sinister-looking masked games. The Tomba degli Auguri preserves frescoes of the sixth century B.C. depicting somber scenes from a burial ritual which are barely comprehensible to modern man. They make us eyewitnesses of a cult belonging to an alien, mysterious, long-vanished world. In the gable of the end wall two beasts of prey, a leopard and a lion, are tearing at a wild goat. Below this, on either side of a massive painted door, stands a bearded man with one hand on his head and the other extended, in gestures of lament and farewell. On the right wall two wrestlers are locked in combat. They are completely naked. A priestly umpire, carrying his mark of office, the *lituus,* or crook, watches the wrestlers.

Alongside this group a macabre game is being played out to its fatal end. A masked man with a pointed cap and a beard—named *phersu* in an inscription—is setting a dog, which he holds on a long cord, against a half-naked man. The dog is biting the man's left leg. The man is desperately trying to defend himself with a club. But he does so blindly, without being able to direct his blows, for his head is covered in a sack or cloth. His frantic efforts at hitting the dog are made all the more difficult by the fact that the leash is twined around his legs. He is already bleeding from deep wounds.

This cruel game offers no hope to the victim. It has only one end —his sacrifice for the deceased. Presented as a spectacle at the funeral ceremonies, it reminds the living of the ineluctability of death, and in ritual and its mysteries embodies the limitations and finitude of all existence, whether of the individual or the nation. The Etruscan name of the masked man, *phersu,* corresponds to the Latin word *persona.* And to the Romans this signified first a theatrical mask, or actor, before it came to include the sense of personality.

Among the Romans too, the combat displays which were introduced from Etruria were at first given only on the occasion of burials. It was not long, however, before they were to be emptied of their meaning in their new, alien surroundings and, as presented to a different, more matter-of-fact people, to lose for all time their original, more profound significance. From being a sacred, ritual act, reflecting the incomprehensible, cruel power of the cosmos, they became, toward the end of the Roman republic, a purely secular spectacle.

344

It was not until the First Punic War was approaching its end that Etruria felt its effects. The country was even more firmly incorporated in the Roman military system. Experience of war with Carthage, whose warships penetrated into Campanian waters, drove the Romans to send colonies to the Tyrrhenian coast for defense purposes. In territory taken from Caere three such colonies were established, those of Pyrgi (modern Santa Severa), Alsium (modern Palo) in 247 B.C., and Fregenae in about 245 B.C., near the present-day Maccarese. Four years later the construction of the great coast road, the famous Via Aurelia from Rome to Cosa, was begun and later extended to Pisa. It owes its name to C. Aurelius Cotta, to whose censorship it is traditionally attributed. As with some other great highways the Romans made use to a large extent of an existing Etruscan route.

> *It was not until the First Punic War was approaching its end that Etruria felt its effects.*

In 241 B.C. the first phase of the long, bitter struggle with Carthage ended in victory for Rome, its first outside Italy. The peace terms required Carthage to surrender all its possessions in Sicily, and thus, with the exception of Syracuse, the island became Roman, as did also the little Lipari Islands to its north.

Rome had already seized Corsica, once Etruscan, from the Carthaginians in 259 B.C., and had established its own naval base at Aleria. The only major Carthaginian possession off the coast of Italy was Sardinia, and that remained in their hands for only another three years. For in 238 B.C., after an insurrection of mercenaries against Carthage, the Romans intervened against the Carthaginians, and only made peace when the island was surrendered to them. After that, it was the Roman fleet which ruled the Tyrrhenian Sea.

By its victory in the First Punic War, Rome became a great power. The long-drawn-out war that lasted nearly a quarter of a century tested Rome's strength to the utmost. It may be presumed that it was not entirely without repercussions in Etruria. Did some city-states perhaps try to renew friendly relations with Carthage and secretly conspire with their former great ally? Were there acts of passive disobedience, or even of sabotage in Etruria?

One case of open resistance to Rome is on record. The summary of the lost Book XX of Livy states: "The Faliscans, having revolted,

345

were on the sixth day subdued and permitted to surrender." And Polybius adds: "At Rome there followed a civil war against the Falisci, but this was brought to a speedy and favorable conclusion, taking Falerii in a few days."

In 241 B.C. four legions under the command of the consuls Q. Lutatius and A. Manlius carried out the campaign against the rebellious city. Falerii, on its 450-foot-high hill, was quickly stormed. Its strong fortifications were razed, and it suffered the same fate as Volsinii. Its inhabitants had to evacuate the site, which was hard to attack, and were compelled by the Romans to resettle three miles away in a strategically indefensible position in the plain, at Falerii Novi.

The site of the ancient Faliscan city lies beneath Civita Castellana, a little town close to the Via Flaminia, some thirty-four miles to the north of Rome. For a thousand years after its destruction by the Romans, the place remained deserted. Then, in the eighth or ninth century A.D., its defensive position attracted a fresh settlement; it was rebuilt, refortified, and began a new life. Only the soil preserved the memories of its great past.

Many relics of Etruscan time have come to light, fragments of terra-cotta statues, tiles, and other temple decorations. West of Civita Castellana, in a dusky ravine spanned by the double tier of a partly medieval bridge, the Ponte Terrano, lies an extensive cemetery. It is an eerie place, silent, mysteriously fascinating, and the same today as it was more than a century ago when Dennis visited it and described it: "Where could be found a more impressive, a more appropriate cemetery than a ravine like this—a vast grave in itself, sunk two hundred and fifty feet below the surface—full of grandeur and gloom? Here, far below the noise and tumult of the city, they might sit by the tombs of their departed relatives, listening to the incessant murmurs of the stream, which to their imaginations, so prone to symbolize, might seem an emblem of eternity. The lofty perpendicular cliffs shutting them out from the world, the narrow strip of sky overhead, the subdued light, the damp chill, would combine with the sacredness of the spot to impress solemn feelings upon their minds. The wild pigeons nestling in the crannies of the precipices, and wheeling above their heads, to their rapt fancies might seem the souls of the departed, haunting the neighbourhood of their earthly abode."

346

Only a few weeks were required to suppress the Faliscans' revolt and destroy their capital. Nothing could more forcefully have impressed upon defeated Etruria its powerlessness and the end of its independence. Before the century came to an end its cities again went through bad times as they were dragged into Rome's wars of conquest. Twice the Etruscan lands became the theater of war. Each time the attack came from the north. The Gallic threat, as enormous as on the first occasion, loomed once more.

Rome, having once set out on the road to the conquest of other nations, never called a halt. After the success against the Carthaginians in the south, the Roman drive for expansion turned to the north. The objective was all the land as far as the Alps.

In the west, says the summary of Livy's lost Book XX, "for the first time an army marched against the Ligurians." In 238 B.C. the Romans began to develop a supply and naval base at the mouth of the Arno near Pisa. And on the east coast of Italy, on the Adriatic, they decided to found colonies in the territory already conquered. But in 232 B.C. when they began dividing up and distributing the land among their settlers in the region south of Ariminium (modern Rimini), the Gauls were roused to revolt and took the offensive.

The Boii of Bologna and the Insubres of Milan began to arm and demanded help from kindred tribes beyond the Alps. "They urged and incited their kings Concolitanus and Aneroestus to make war on Rome," says Polybius, "offering them . . . a large sum in gold." From their homes in the mountains on the upper reaches of the Rhone a large army of *Gaesatae,* which in Celtic means spearmen, hastened to the spot, and other Cisalpine tribes, such as the Taurini from farther west, also joined in.

> **Devastating the country as they went, the great horde swept through the Arno valley, bypassed fortified Arezzo that was occupied by Roman troops, and reached Chiusi, only three days' march from Rome.**

Altogether forces of fifty thousand infantry and twenty thousand on horseback or in chariots assembled in the Po valley. In 225 B.C. they began to march over the Apennines to the south. "The Celts," says Polybius, "descending on Etruria, overran the country without let or hindrance, and, as nobody appeared to oppose them, they marched on Rome itself." Devastating the country as they went, the great horde swept through the Arno valley, bypassed fortified Arezzo that was occupied by Roman troops, and reached Chiusi, only three days' march from Rome.

In the meantime couriers had been sent by the senate to Sardinia to recall the consul Gaius Atilius Regulus with his two legions. The troops of the other consul, Lucius Aemilius Papus, stationed at Rimini on the Adriatic, were ordered to cross the Apennines and march into Etruria. In Rome itself a reserve of some fifty thousand men was mustered. An advanced force was posted in Etruria to protect the western Apennine passes. Everywhere, including Etruria, men fit for service were called up, and weapons and supplies were collected.

The army from Rimini, hastening by forced marches toward Chiusi, intended to join up with the advance guard in Etruria, which was following the Gauls. Thus threatened from the rear, the latter decided to abandon the march toward Rome and to lead the Romans into an ambush. The Gauls, says Polybius, lit their campfires and then retreated secretly to a town called Faesulae (modern Fiesole), leaving their cavalry behind to follow after. The Romans hastened in pursuit of the cavalry; at Montepulciano, northwest of Chiusi, the Gauls turned and fought. "The numbers and courage of the Celts prevailed," says Polybius, "not fewer than six thousand Romans falling and the rest taking to flight."

But now Aemilius arrived from the Adriatic coast; his appearance decided the Gauls to avoid any further combat, and to return home with their abundant booty. To mislead the consul as to their plans, the Gauls made a big detour around Mount Amiata, then turned northward up the coast road. They were not to know that this very turn-about was to lead them straight to disaster.

The legions from Sardinia under the consul Atilius Regulus had by now landed at Pisa and at once set off for Rome, on the very coast road along which the Gallic army was marching on its way home. The Romans had covered about half the distance to Rome when the two armies met near Telamon (modern Talamone), and a tremendous battle was fought. At first the Gauls were winning. But then the army of Aemilius Papus, from Rimini, caught up with them from behind and attacked furiously. In the melee the consul

Atilius Regulus was killed and "his head was brought to the Celtic kings."

With great courage the Celts formed a double line, back to back, to face the onslaught from two sides. Polybius gives a vivid account of the savage fighting: "The Romans . . . were terrified by the fine order of the Celtic host and the dreadful din, for there were innumerable trumpeters and horn-blowers, and, as the whole army were shouting their war cries at the same time, there was such a tumult of sound that it seemed not only the trumpets and the soldiers but all the country round had got a voice and caught up the cry."

In the Gallic ranks the *Gaesatae,* the spear-men from beyond the Alps, fought naked, with nothing but their weapons. Against the hail of javelins from the Romans they had no real defense and suffered heavy losses. Their comrades, the Insubres, Boii, and Taurisci, fought furiously, but were gradually beaten down. "Finally," says Polybius, "attacked from higher ground and on their flank by the Roman cavalry . . . the Celtic infantry were cut to pieces."

Their defeat was overwhelming. Forty thousand Gauls were killed and ten thousand were taken prisoner, among them King Concolitanus. The other king, Aneroestus, escaped with a few followers, but they then killed themselves. The battle of Telamon at one stroke put an end to the war. The Gallic peril was exorcised like an evil spirit.

The Romans had to pay dearly for their victory, for the losses among the legionaries were high. But the Etruscans suffered even more. The tempest of foreign warriors had roared through their country. Their fields were laid waste, their harvests and cattle commandeered, their cities plundered. All this caused incalculable damage to their whole economy and trade. And nothing of what the Gauls had pillaged in the way of gold, silver, and other precious articles was ever seen again in Etruria. For the tremendous booty which fell to the Romans after the fighting all made its way to the treasuries on the Tiber.

There is nothing visible now at the scene to recall the great decisive battle of 225 B.C. Talamone, the Roman Telamon, a sleepy village with a little harbor, sheltered from the north by the Monti dell'Uccellina, still preserves its name of Etruscan origin, Tlamne.

It must have been a town of some importance, for it minted its own coins, marked with TLA. Across the quiet blue bay, directly on the Via Aurelia which closely follows the curve of the coast, rises the hill Talamonaccio, crested by an old fort. At its foot, on the coastal plain, the Romans and Gauls clashed in battle.

In the last century the local peasants turned up with the plow memorials of the battle against the Gauls: a hoard of bronze votive tools, probably dedicated to celebrate the Roman victory, and arms. They are now in the Museo Archeologico at Florence, along with architectural terra-cotta fragments that once decorated a temple at Talamone. The clay plaques show two figures of warriors, perhaps illustrating the battle of the Seven against Thebes, or perhaps the Gallic kings Aneroestus and Concolitanus.

> *It was the last great Celtic invasion to threaten Rome and lay waste Etruria.*

It was the last great Celtic invasion to threaten Rome and lay waste Etruria. After their victory the Romans set to work with determination to subjugate Gaul between the Apennines and the Alps. With the capture of Mediolanum (modern Milan) after the overthrow of the Insubres in 222 B.C., Gallic rule in the Po valley came to an end.

To safeguard the Po crossing, the fortified colony of Placentia (modern Piacenza) was founded on the right bank of the river, replacing an Etruscan settlement, and not far away on the left bank, Cremona. In the territory taken from the Boii another fortified outpost was built at Mutina (Modena), once also an Etruscan town.

Among the Etruscans the news of the conquest of Milan could awaken only sad memories. One hundred and seventy-five years earlier, on the same day when Veii fell, the Etruscan league in the Po valley lost Melpum, the city's earlier foundation. Now Rome, their conqueror, had itself reached that most northerly point to which their own empire had once extended. But Rome was not to develop and encourage the economy of the Po valley, its agriculture and trade, as they did; and when Romans crossed the Alpine passes to the north, it would not be as peaceful traders, laden with wares.

XXIV

Hannibal Woos Etruria

LESS THAN FIVE YEARS HAD PASSED when Etruria, now indissolubly tied to the fate of Rome, found itself once more involved in a military conflict. In 218 B.C. the Second Punic War broke out.

Carthage, still smarting under its defeat, hit back. The attack was launched from Spain, the new Carthaginian dominion conquered after the loss of Sicily and the imporant islands in the Tyrrhenian Sea. With elite shock troops, ninety thousand infantry, twelve thousand cavalry, and thirty-seven elephants, Hannibal set out in the spring on his campaign against Italy. He took the land route, crossed the Pyrenees and southern France, and in late September or early October crossed the Alps with infinite labor.

Five months after leaving New Carthage the Punic general surveyed the plains of northern Italy and received reinforcements from a new source. Swarms of Gauls, fresh from their defeats by the

351

Romans, flocked to his standards, buoyed up with ever-new hope of booty. Before the onset of winter, the invaders clashed with the Roman legions. In a cavalry engagement to the west of the Ticino River, the Numidian horsemen carried the day and forced the consul Publius Cornelius Scipio to retreat. The Romans had to evacuate the country north of the Po. Hannibal pursued them and crossed the river on a bridge of rafts. In the meantime the other consul, Sempronius Longus, had hastened up. Hannibal inflicted a severe defeat on both the Roman armies which attacked on the Trebia, a right-hand tributary of the Po. The whole of northern Italy was lost to Rome. Now it was Etruria's turn.

Hannibal settled down in his winter camp, preparatory to a further advance southward as soon as the season should permit. His aim was to humiliate Rome. Hordes of Gallic warriors, infantry and cavalry, joined his army. But Hannibal was putting his hopes less in them than in bringing about the defection of Rome's allies. "Freedom for the peoples of Italy" might have been his watchword. As a demonstration, he had all the Romans among his prisoners put in slaves' fetters, and let all the other Italic prisoners go free. They were to convey the message to their countrymen at home that Hannibal was not waging war against Italy, but only against Rome. The liberator would follow those he had liberated. No sooner was the winter over than Hannibal set out once more.

Two consular armies had meanwhile advanced to resist the Carthaginian invasion of central Italy. The consul Gnaeus Servilius Geminus was ready with his legions on the Adriatic. Near Arezzo lay the camp of the other consul, Gaius Flaminius.

Nevertheless Hannibal crossed the Apennines without hindrance. He boldly outflanked Flaminius, marched for four days through the swamps caused by an exceptionally heavy flooding of the Arno— a disaster such as that which struck Florence a few years ago—and burst into Etruria.

"The region (the Etruscan plains between Faesulae and Arretium) was amongst the most productive in Italy," says Livy, "rich in cattle, grain and everything else." Hannibal, "leaving the Roman camp on his left, made for Faesulae, harrying and devastating Etruscan territory with the intention of forcing upon Flaminius the spectacle of as much damage as fire and sword could produce." Hannibal's deliberate intent was to provoke the consul, "to bait and prick him into action." The Carthaginians marched on through the rich valley of the Chiana in the direction of Perugia. "Hannibal, determined to inflame his antagonist and drive him to avenge the sufferings of his allies, left nothing undone to reduce to a desert the whole stretch of country between Cortona and Lake Trasimene."

The Punic leader's tactics hardly seemed designed to attract volunteers, let alone to inspire the Etruscan people as a whole to revolt against Rome. The hopes Etruria had placed in his invasion of the Po valley must have been sadly disappointed.

All the same, Hannibal had made the right move. He achieved his purpose. Flaminius, when he saw "that everything his friends possessed was being ruined or carried off almost before his eyes," felt that it was "the gravest reflection upon himself that a Carthaginian army should be roaming at large through central Italy, marching without any attempt at resistance to attack the very walls of Rome."

A meeting of his staff was called, and "all his officers urged a policy of caution; . . . he should wait for the other consul, so that the two of them might join forces and cooperate in the coming campaign." Furiously he brushed all such advice aside and gave the order to march and prepare for action. Flaminius led his men at top speed toward the enemy, and to their own destruction.

On the north the mountains come down close to Lake Trasimeno, and the only road is squeezed in between the two. In this terrain as though made by nature for an ambush, Hannibal awaited his opponent. "Here, at the eastern exit, Hannibal took up a position, in full view, with his African and Spanish veterans; his light troops . . . he concealed amongst the mountains north of the lake, and stationed his cavalry, also hidden by hills, close to the narrow western entrance, so that they could block it the instant the Romans had passed within."

Flaminius, who had reached the lake the previous evening, and suspected nothing, fell into the trap. "No sort of reconnaissance had been made. When his column began to open out on reaching the wider area of level ground north of the lake, he was aware only of those enemy units which were in the direct line of his advance; of the units concealed in his rear and in the hills above him he had no inkling whatever. Hannibal had achieved his purpose: as soon as he had his antagonist penned in by the lake and the mountains and surrounded, front, rear and flank, by his own men, he gave the order for a simultaneous attack by all units."

The end came in a few hours. There was neither time nor space for the Romans to take up their usual battle order. The consul was killed, and with him many of his men. "All was nearly over when at last the heat of the sun dispersed the mist, and in the clear morning light hills and plain revealed to their eyes the terrible truth that the Roman army was almost totally destroyed." It was June 21, 217 B.C.

The Roman dead numbered fifteen thousand, as many were taken prisoner. Some ten thousand scattered in flight. It was "one of the few memorable disasters to Roman arms," says Livy.

Once again Hannibal put the Roman prisoners in chains, and liberated all the others. "This time," says Pfiffig, "the gesture worked. On the news of Rome's defeat at Lake Trasimeno, the Gauls, the Ligurians and the Etruscans in the Apennines and north Etruria rose and openly declared their support for Hannibal. They attacked the Romans in their districts and killed them or handed them over to the Carthaginians. Neither Livy nor Polybius, for understandable reasons, says anything about this. A large part of northern Etruria was now loyal to the victor of Lake Trasimeno."

But Hannibal did not exploit his opportunity. Was he so certain of ultimate success? He pushed on. Bypassing Rome, he marched into southern Italy. In the following year, 216 B.C., at the battle of Cannae, he inflicted on the Romans the greatest defeat in their history. The site of the battlefield lies on the river Ofanto some five miles inland from the coastal town of Barletta in Apulia; the settlement that once stood there was destroyed by the Normans in 1083 and now all that remains is one vast archeological dig important enough to warrant a railway station of its own. It is called Canne della Battaglia.

After this victory a large part of Apulia and Bruttium went over to Hannibal. In Campania Capua welcomed him and in Sicily so did Syracuse. In the winter of 213–212 B.C., when Hannibal got control of Tarentum, disturbances broke out in Etruria as well. This obliged Rome to station two legions permanently there. But the unrest went on.

Even among the Latins, public feeling changed. There were open complaints at meetings about the mobilization of troops and taxes. And in 209 B.C., when thirty Latin colonies sent delegations to Rome, twelve of them told the consuls "that they had not the resources to supply either men or money."

Among the objectors were the representatives of Ardea, Nepi, and Sutri. In vain the consuls pleaded with them, told them that their reckless decision "would mean the betrayal of the Roman empire and the yielding of victory to Hannibal." The envoys were unmoved and replied simply that they had "nothing new to lay before their governments, for they had not a single soldier to conscript or any money to pay him with."

It was not surprising that in these conditions resistance in Etruria was even more considerable. For there, too, only a year earlier, in 210 B.C., two Roman commissioners had been buying up supplies for the army, backed by a thousand troops sent there on garrison duty. A conspiracy in Hannibal's interest was discovered.

In 209 B.C. the senate received disturbing news from Arezzo. Gaius Calpurnius, who was in command of the troops camped outside the city, had discovered preparations for a revolt. M. Claudius Marcellus, the consul, was sent there at once to look into the matter, and he swiftly put an end to the disorder.

But a year later there were again signs of conspiratorial unrest in Arezzo, and the pro-praetor Gaius Hostilius Tubulus, now in command in Etruria, was sent written instructions from the senate to take deterrent action. "Tubulus promptly ordered the one legion which was encamped in front of the town to march in," says Livy, "and posted his guards wherever he thought fit; then he summoned the town's senators to the forum and demanded hostages. The senate asked for two days to consider their answer, but were told by Tubulus that they must themselves provide the hostages immediately, or, if they refused, that he would take all the children of the senators on the following day." However, before guards could be posted at the gates, "seven leading senators got away with their children during daylight."

The next day, when their flight was discovered, Tubulus took harsh measures. The property of those who had fled was seized and sold. From the senators who remained, 120 of their children were taken as hostages. They were put in charge of the pro-praetor Gaius Terentius Varro, who took them to Rome. In the meantime Tubulus, with his two legions, was scouring the whole area so as "to nip in the bud any movement toward a revolutionary outbreak."

Thus order was restored. Rome's energetic intervention had forestalled open revolt. But the underground opposition remained. When Varro came back from Rome and demanded the keys to the town gates, so that they could be locked at night, the magistrates bluntly told him that they could not be found. Accordingly he had new locks and keys made and charged them up to the town.

More than once at this time the anti-Roman feelings of the Etruscans came to the surface. We hear of secret conspiracies with the Carthaginians, sabotage of the Roman military machinery, or of acts of resistance, local noncooperation, and mutiny. This situation went on for years until finally an ingeniously contrived deception that caused serious harm to the Roman state came to light. It was a widely ramified, gigantic fraud. And, as Roman police investigations revealed, two distinguished Etruscans were the promoters of the affair.

In 215 B.C., a year after the disaster at Cannae, the senate had been constrained, for lack of funds, to commission private contractors to ship supplies overseas. The armies in Spain, Sardinia, Sicily, and Corsica had to be furnished with what they needed, and the contracts provided for regular shipments of food and clothing, arms and war material of all kinds. These were to be carried in cargo boats sailing at regular intervals. As the Roman navy was occupied with urgent tasks elsewhere, convoy protection by warships could be given only exceptionally. In short, it was a contract essential to the prosecution of the war, and one that demanded unconditional confidence on both sides. Much depended on its prompt execution.

But it was to cost the state dear. For only after a long time was it discovered what the contractors and shipowners had been doing with the supplies entrusted to them. When the truth became known to the public, the indignation was so great that not only was the enlistment of two legions postponed, but Rome was on the brink of serious disturbance. There was an angry demand for the punishment of the guilty men. They were a certain Marcus Postumius, a tax-farmer from the port of Pyrgi, and his colleague, Titus Pomponius, from Veii. Both were Etruscans.

What were they accused of?

"Their method," reports Livy, "was to load small and more or less worthless cargoes into old, rotten vessels, sink them at sea after taking off the crews in boats standing by for the purpose, and then, in reporting the loss, enormously to exaggerate the value of the cargoes." The inflated statement of loss incurred they then presented to the authorities and cashed vast sums in compensation, thanks to "the assumption by the state of all risks from tempest in the case of goods carried by sea to armies in the field."

As nobody became suspicious, Postumius and Pomponius unscrupulously carried things a stage further. They invented completely fictitious shipwrecks. They reported the sinking of heavily laden cargo vessels which had never set out, or did not exist, and did even better business with this shadow fleet. A whole chain of bribed accomplices, suppliers and storekeepers, ships' captains and seamen, contributed to their fake reports and falsified evidence. As a result the public treasury incurred heavy losses, and what was worse, the legions overseas were reduced to a wretched plight by shortages. The network of accomplices before and after the fact, of those who connived or cooperated, and of those who were bribed, must have been very thoroughly organized, for the swindle went on undisturbed for years. Even when suspicion was aroused and reported to official quarters in Rome, nothing happened. The matter was brought to the attention of the senate, but received no official condemnation because the senate in view of the circumstances at the time did not wish to make enemies of the tax-farmers.

However, the scandal could not be hushed up. Too much had leaked out. There was great indignation in Rome, and the people were sterner judges than the senate. "Two people's tribunes, Spurius and Lucius Carvilius, recognizing that the scandal was a serious one, were at length aroused to action and proposed to fine Postumius 200,000 *asses*." As a result of this there was a riot.

"When the day came for his appeal, the people attended the assembly in such numbers that the open space on the Capitol was packed to capacity." Postumius made his speech, defending himself, and witnesses were heard. And then something unbelievable happened. The tax-farmers, doubtless associates of the accused and also involved in the affair, violently disrupted the proceedings. "Shoulder to shoulder," says Livy, "like troops breaking through the enemy's line, they thrust their way into the space left by the crowd when it was ordered to stand back, hurling insults as they went at people and tribunes alike." It nearly came to blows. In order to forestall an insurrection, the tribunes had no alternative but to stop the hearing. "The assembly was dismissed."

This was going too far. A meeting of the senate was called, and "the consuls brought forward the matter of the lawless violence of the tax-farmers which had led to the break-up of the assembly." Expressing the general indignation, they pointed out that "Postumius of Pyrgi . . . had robbed the people of their right to vote, wrecked the assembly, degraded the tribunes, threatened his countrymen with battle, forced himself and his friends in between the tribunes and the crowd deliberately to prevent the tribes being called on to vote. Nothing, they went on, had stopped a bloody struggle from developing but the forbearance of the magistrates who had temporarily yielded to the outrageous self-assertion of a small group, allowed themselves and the populace to be worsted, and, to deprive those who wanted it of an excuse for bloodshed, had of their own free will broken up an assembly which Postumius and his gang were prepared to wreck by armed force."

The senate agreed on the "atrocious nature of Postumius's behavior, which was formally declared to be an act of violence against the state and a most dangerous precedent." There was now no longer any question of his getting away with a fine. The tribunes "brought a capital charge instead, adding an order that if Postumius failed to furnish sureties he was to be arrested and taken to prison." He did produce sureties but failed to appear himself on the appointed day. The matter was put to the people who, Livy reports, decided: " 'If Postumius fails to appear before the first of May, and, being summoned on that day, does not reply and is not excused, then it shall be understood that he is an exile; his property shall be sold and he shall be refused water and fire.' "

The tribunes then brought capital charges against all who had

358

made a violent disturbance in the assembly and caused the proceedings to be interrupted. They ordered them to produce sureties. "Those who failed to do so were imprisoned at once; then others who were in a position to do so were imprisoned too; the majority avoided the risk by going into exile." The other principal accused, Titus Pomponius, appears to have got away unpunished. In Lucania he "passed himself off as a recognized military commander . . . scraped together some sort of an army," and engaged the Carthaginian commander, who captured him.

The fact that Etruscans were the leading spirits in this massive fraud suggests that what was behind it was not mere profiteering but a plot to sabotage Rome's prodigious war effort. Such an interpretation is supported by another circumstance. Livy mentions that as the Punic War dragged on, a wave of superstition swept over the country, and prophets and priests of foreign cults were introducing "unaccustomed rites."

These were prohibited by the senate, which also ordered the surrender of books of prophecies or prayers. Lopes Pegna ventures an explanation of this curious episode: "Clearly these mystical trappings were part of a deliberate defeatist propaganda campaign launched by the Etruscans, who without doubt secretly and anonymously spread depressing and dire predictions. It can be taken for granted that these had to do with the current war, and warned that its outcome would be ruinous for trade and industry, and indeed the whole economy of all the Italic peoples who were Rome's willing or unwilling allies."

The Carthaginians had been in Italy for more than a decade when events suddenly and dramatically came to a head. In this period of unrest and conflict news arrived that brought alarm and despondency to Rome, but joy and hope to Etruria. Hannibal's brother Hasdrubal had suddenly left Spain and had crossed the Alps. In 207 B.C. he arrived with his army in north Italy.

> **The Carthaginians had been in Italy for more than a decade when events suddenly and dramatically came to a head.**

For Rome it seemed that once again everything was in the balance. The war in Italy had at last begun to go against Hannibal, but a junction of his army and that of his brother could give it an unexpected new turn, dangerous to

Rome. Soon reports were received that Hasdrubal was on the Po and attacking Piacenza. The Gauls flocked to his banner, as they had done to his brother's. Etruscan and Umbrian volunteers also added to his numbers. Soon the people of Tuscany were awaiting the "liberator." But Hasdrubal picked another route to the south, that along the Adriatic coast, through Gallic territory. Fate caught up with him on the way and put an end to all his ambitious plans. South of Rimini, on the river Metaurus, he was defeated by two consular armies. He himself was killed in the battle. Like a torch plunged into water, Etruria's hopes went out.

When the Romans had recovered from their alarm, their next move was to bring to account and to punish all who had stabbed them in the back. By order of the senate the proconsul Marcus Livius Salinator, one of the victors on the Metaurus, set out for Etruria to "hold an inquiry and find out which of the Etruscan or Umbrian communities had planned to go over to Hasdrubal on his arrival in their territories and which had sent him aid in the form of men, supplies, or anything else."

Judicial inquiries were instituted, and in order to strengthen his authority in searching out the cases of treason Marcus Livius was given two legions of slave volunteers. Roman annalists do not say what those inquiries revealed, how many people were tried, or how many death sentences were passed. But what is recorded is eloquent enough. Marcus Livius had to remain in Etruria until 205 B.C. to complete his assignment. And in that same year Etruria suffered yet another penalty, this time an economic one.

In 205 B.C. Publius Cornelius Scipio brought the war in Spain against the Carthaginians to a victorious conclusion and was elected consul. He planned to take the war to Africa. The senate agreed, but did not provide sufficient means for the job. Nevertheless Scipio obtained what was needed for his overseas expedition. "The considerable costs of building the necessary fleet," wrote Mommsen, "were covered by so-called voluntary contributions from Etruscan cities, that is to say a war levy imposed as a penalty on Arretium and other pro-Carthaginian cities."

Livy records in detail what Scipio got from Etruria: "Caere offered grain for the crews and supplies of all sorts; Populonium promised iron"—which was mined in the island of Elba and smelted in furnaces on the mainland—"Tarquinii sailcloth; Vol-terrae grain and timber for keels and garboards . . . Perusia, Clusium, and Rusellae offered fir for building and a large amount of grain."

But one city, Arretium, outdid all the others. It supplied "3,000 shields, 3,000 helmets, and a total of 50,000 pikes, javelins, and spears, an equal number of each, together with enough axes, shovels, sickles, basins and handmills to equip forty warships; also 120,000 measures of wheat and a contribution toward traveling allowances of petty officers and oarsmen."

"All this," comments Pfiffig, "represents Rome's bill for their support of Hannibal and Hasdrubal. The 'voluntary donors' were those convicted of war crimes."

How little Etruria was trusted is shown by the fact that according to Livy's account there is no word of its providing troops. There was not a single Etruscan among the seven thousand volunteers whom Scipio recruited. Thus the Etruscan towns were compelled to furnish their hated enemy with huge quantities of armaments and other supplies. Moreover, these were for use against Etruria's friend Carthage. It is doubtful whether Scipio could have equipped an expedition so rapidly without these forced contributions. His fleet was ready to sail forty-five days after felling the timber. The weapons that Arezzo alone furnished were enough to arm far more soldiers than Scipio engaged.

Livy's account throws a lot of light on the economic situation of Etruria. The cities were evidently still productive. And yet the picture is very different from what it had once been. "What strikes us at once in this list is that the centers of Etruscan prosperity had moved inland," comments Jacques Heurgon, "and that to judge by the importance of both its metallurgical and agricultural contributions Arezzo really appears to have become the economic capital of Etruria. But if one considers the contribution from the towns in the coastal area, we notice, chiefly in between Tarquinii and Rusellae, which, upstream from modern Grosseto, had formerly taken the place of Vetulonia, a wide gap of about a hun-

> **Two hundred years of Roman conquests, reprisals, and punitive measures, not to speak of the loss of important territory, had left a deep mark.**

dred kilometers. In this cradle of Etruscan grandeur, where so many sites had brought themselves honor by signal gifts to civilization, Telamon, Ansedonia-Cosa, Sovana, Saturnia, Vulci, not one quintal of wheat could be collected. Vulci particularly, Vulci on the Fiora, is conspicuous here by its absence, not that life had altogether left it: it still had, at that period, its *zilath* [chief magistrates] who were preceded by lictors in solemn processions. Later, it would recapture its old enchantment in the glorious memory of Aulus and Caelius Vibenna in the François tomb. But the fact that it could not be taxed proved that it was ruined. And even Tarquinii, that boasted having seen the divine dwarf Tages spring out of one of its field-furrows, had been able to produce only a bundle of cloth from its depleted stores."

Two hundred years of Roman conquests, reprisals, and punitive measures, not to speak of the loss of important territory, had left a deep mark. The splendor and wealth of Etruscan cities which had flourished in the south and along the shores of the Tyrrhenian Sea were a thing of the past; the great centers radiating a pioneering spirit of enterprise had fallen into insignificance. Where the heart of the motherland once beat there was now only decay. Those regions never recovered from their enormous losses and damage. They sank into provincial unimportance, became mere hinterland, intersected by the conqueror's military roads, guarded by strongly fortified bases, occupied by colonies of foreign veterans.

Etruria had long ceased to be a granary on which Rome could draw in time of famine. Where once arable farming and fruit growing had extracted bountiful harvests from the soil were now vast livestock ranges. It was useless now for mariners approaching the coast to look out for the smoke of the former many smelting furnaces. The great iron-smelting works at Populonia were no longer active. And farther inland the metal works of Vulci and Visentium (modern Bisenzio) on Lake Bolsena had closed down, those of Volsinii were in ruins. For reasons of strategy or armaments supply the conqueror had moved the heavy industry elsewhere, or, as at Arezzo, kept it under the strict supervision of a garrison.

The factories of Perugia were dilapidated and the crafts of Vetulonia had died out. Caere, once one of the most splendid cities in the world of its time, now devoted itself, like Tarquinii, solely to agriculture and the manufacture of ropes and cloth. Everywhere small industries had replaced big ones. Etruria had become a country of innumerable artisans. They produced articles of everyday use, especially tools and implements for agriculture—plows, sickles, shovels, knives, axes.

In the summer of the year when Scipio set out for Africa, the anti-Roman feeling in Etruria received fresh stimulus. To the general surprise yet another Carthaginian commander appeared in Italy. In 205 B.C. Mago, another brother of Hannibal's, landed at Genoa, captured it, and occupied part of the coast. As he did not have enough troops for an offensive he set to work recruiting the tribes of Liguria and the Gauls. Gold and the prospect of booty attracted many.

Mago also sent messengers, recruiting agents, and detachments of troops into Etruria. They met with considerable success. Volunteers joined up, arms were distributed, and there were outbreaks of armed resistance in several places. The two Roman legions of slave volunteers under the proconsul Marcus Livius were moved away from Etruria to Ariminium (Rimini), says Livy, and were replaced by two city legions from Rome under Marcus Valerius Laevinus. But force failed to quell Etruscan resistance. The following year the Romans were obliged to start a new round of judicial inquiries under the consul Marcus Cornelius Cethegus, "engaged in holding Etruria, almost the whole of which was beginning to look to Mago, and through him, to the hope of throwing off its dependence upon Rome."

So the terror of Roman tribunals began again. A wave of arrests spread over the country as all who were suspected of disloyalty or fomenting unrest were rounded up for questioning. The consul had been ordered by the senate to conduct the inquiries without any respect to persons. "Many noble Etruscans," says Livy, "who had either gone themselves to Mago to tell him of the readiness of their communities to revolt from Rome, or had sent others to do so, had appeared in court and been condemned, and later others whom a guilty conscience had driven into exile were sentenced in absence, thus avoiding the death penalty and leaving for the satisfaction of the law only such property as was liable to confiscation." Innumerable death sentences were pronounced, and the confiscations were so extensive that they made a considerable contribution to Rome's exhausted treasury.

The Etruscans, who had once again set their hopes on liberation, were mercilessly punished. But the unrest and conspiracies continued, for in the following year, 203 B.C., the consul Gaius Servilius Geminus, says Livy, "was detained in Etruria by the inquiries he was conducting, on the senate's instructions, into conspiracy amongst the leading citizens." It looks as though the Etruscans were still desperately counting on a victory for their former great ally.

At this time Hannibal, summoned home by Carthage, was already preparing to leave Italy to make his last stand on the soil of his African homeland.

A year later, in 202 B.C., at Zama, five days' march southwest of Carthage, came the decisive battle which put an end to the mighty struggle and to the last hopes of all opponents of Rome. Hannibal, never before defeated in the field, was beaten by Scipio.

The peace which Carthage was forced to accept ended her rule over the western Mediterranean. She ceased to count as a great power. But Rome had by this victory become the leading power in the Mediterranean world. The entire West was now under her influence. None of Rome's near or distant neighbors could measure up to the military resources at her command.

THE DECLINE OF CARTHAGE AND HELLAS

AFTER THE EXTRAORDINARY EXertions and strains of the Punic War the victor barely took a pause for breath. A mere year after the peace with Carthage Rome set about a campaign in the East. By the declaration of war on King Philip of Macedon in 200 B.C., Rome began a struggle which was to establish her superiority in the eastern Mediterranean as that against the Carthaginians had established it in the West.

Three years after a Roman army landed at Apollonia in Illyria, in the autumn of 200 B.C., the first decisive engagement took place. Heavily defeated in Thessaly, Philip was obliged to make peace on terms which reduced him to virtual powerlessness. At about this time new disturbances broke out in Tuscany.

"A slave insurrection rendered Etruria almost a battlefield," says

Livy. Strong action was immediately taken by a high judicial official to suppress the rebellion. "Manius Acilius Glabrio, the praetor exercising jurisdiction in cases between citizens and aliens, was sent with one of the two city legions to investigate and suppress it." He succeeded in his mission, thanks to somewhat drastic measures. In a clash with the rebels "many of them were killed and many captured." Against the others Roman justice made use of a cruel form of capital punishment which came from Asia, and was previously common only among the Scythians, Assyrians, Persians, and Phoenicians. Those who had been the instigators of the revolt, says Livy, the praetor "scourged and crucified."

Was it really only an uprising of slaves in Etruria? There is reason to think that what happened was a revolt of the oppressed Etruscans, indeed "enslaved" by the Romans. With reference to the crucifixions, Lopes Pegna argues that: "the punishment was reserved for slaves, but also—as we know from an outstanding historical case—for those who tried to usurp the powers of the state. According to the annalist tradition Rome intervened three times in Etruria, and always as a result of mutiny by slaves or plebs. This version is a misrepresentation; in this case, as in the others before it, it is a historical calumny intended to conceal the facts of the most glorious and heroic attempt by the Etruscans to recover their lost freedom."

All efforts at resistance by the Etruscans were doomed to failure. Rome's power had become too great, and Etruria had become too important as a transit land for the legions on their way north and northwest. Its inhabitants could do nothing but look on impotently as the net of Roman military bases was pulled yet tighter. By the third century B.C. Etruria already had Roman colonies in territory taken from Caere, one at Pyrgi (S. Severa) and one at Castrum Novum (S. Marinella). In 183 B.C. in the territory of Vulci, "a colony of Roman citizens was established at Saturnia . . . Ten *iugera* were given to each colonist." Two years later a colony was settled at Graviscae on land taken from the people of Tarquinii. Each settler received five acres. Traces of this colony are still to be seen in the Roman remains at Porto Clementino, about three miles from the mouth of the Mignone. With the foundation of these fortified places Rome completed the defensive line along the Tyrrhenian coast.

Meanwhile a new military highway from Arezzo to Bologna

linked northern Etruria with the Po valley, where the Celts had been finally defeated in 191 B.C., and safeguarded communications over the Apennines with the Roman colonies in Cisalpine Gaul. The consul Gaius Flaminius had it built by his legionaries in 187 B.C. "Because he had brought it to pass that the province was free from war," reports Livy, "that he might not leave his army idle, he built a road from Bologna to Arezzo."

This road, like the earlier Via Aurelia, also for the most part followed an old Etruscan trading route. "I have been able to make out the traces of this road, now largely obliterated," writes Lopes Pegna. "Two fine funeral steles have been found at Londa and S. Agata." Many other places along this road have yielded archeological material of Etruscan and Roman times.

Etruria's name crops up again only once in these years, though in a context anything but political or military. A cult with orgiastic ceremonies had spread far and wide. Men and women, it was said, participated in "secret rites performed by night." Very belatedly the senate discovered that these rites, the Bacchanalia, had "long been celebrated all over Italy and now even within the city in many places." The consuls were directed by the senate to investigate the Bacchanals and their nocturnal orgies. They discovered that "a nameless Greek came first to Etruria . . . a dabbler in sacrifices and a fortune-teller," and that it was he who performed the initiatory rites of the cult. Then "the destructive power of this evil spread from Etruria to Rome like the contagion of a pestilence."

> A cult with orgiastic ceremonies had spread far and wide.

After lengthy deliberations and investigations, the senate decreed in 186 B.C. that for the future there should be no Bacchanalia in Rome or Italy. The cult was treated as a conspiracy and there was a general round-up of persons who had participated in the rites and orgies. Innumerable arrests were made, and some people were executed. Indeed Livy says that "More were killed than were thrown into prison." Thus an end was put to the exotic scandal.

The Bacchanalia were not an Etruscan invention, for they came from the East, from Greece. Nor were they more widespread in Etruria than in Rome and elsewhere. But the mud stuck; Etruria was given a reputation for religious aberrations.

366

The people of that occupied country learned only by hearsay about the great conflicts that were going on far away from Italy. By unceasing wars Rome was subduing country after country in the East and the West, reducing them to the status of provinces, and extending her empire. In 168 B.C. King Perseus was defeated by the Romans at Pydna, and the following year Macedon was divided into four. Rhodes was humiliated and lost its possessions. A tremendous amount of booty came to Rome.

The treasures and property stolen from the conquered peoples suddenly made the have-nots on the Tiber extraordinarily rich. Corruption and embezzlement increased. As early as 190 B.C. an action was brought against the Scipios, who were accused of enriching themselves from the booty taken in the campaign against Antiochus.

Rome's military strength had grown to a point at which no one else could rival her, and she acted everywhere with complete ruthlessness. After Greece her next victim was Carthage.

Since the Second Punic War the city had been politically quite defenseless, but it had enjoyed an economic revival and great prosperity. Cato, one of the most influential men in the senate, visited Carthage in 153 B.C. and came back full of envy for its wealth. Henceforth he never ceased to agitate for war against Carthage; every public speech of his ended with the words: "For the rest, I am of the opinion that Carthage should cease to exist."

In 149 B.C. war was declared on Carthage, and the consuls sailed to deliver Rome's outrageous demands. These were that the inhabitants must evacuate Carthage, which would be destroyed; they could settle where they liked as long as it was ten miles from the sea. Carthage refused to accept the terms, but lost the ensuing war. In 146 B.C. the city was captured and destroyed. For seventeen days fires raged in the streets; large numbers of the inhabitants died and thousands were led away into slavery. The ruins were razed. The ill tidings spread through Etruria that Carthage, the mighty ally and friend of the country in its great age, was no more.

XXV

The Death of the Republic

THE YEAR THAT CARTHAGE WAS left a burned-out ruin, once proud Macedonia came under direct Roman rule as a province and shortly afterwards the independence of Greece was brought to an end. In 146 B.C., following a revolt, four legions arrived in Corinth. The city was destroyed, its inhabitants sold into slavery, and Greece put under the governor of Macedonia. Rather more than a decade later, in 133 B.C., Rome finally subdued Spain by the successful siege of the key fortress of Numantia —which was also burned to the ground. And in that same year Rome got a first foothold in Anatolia and constituted its province of Asia: Attalos III, king of Pergamon, bequeathed his kingdom to the senate and people of Rome.

It was all a colossal success, a fantastic expansion of power. In addition to the whole of Italy, the empire now included Sicily, Sardinia and Corsica, Spain and Africa, Macedonia, Greece and

368

Asia Minor. But these far-flung victories brought the victor anything but peace and happiness. For the vast conquests all over the world had grave consequences at home. Italy itself was racked by economic and political crises. A period of party conflict, dangerous unrest, revolts, and terrible civil war began. And the last flickers of Etruscan life began to dwindle amid the bloodthirsty clashes in which the republic foundered.

Rome, the one-time cluster of villages, had become a city rolling in money. During the wars it had raked in unimaginable riches. Along with the booty in kind came the property of the treasuries and temples of conquered and plundered lands and peoples, as well as the taxes and tithes from the newly constituted provinces. And the quantity of human booty, the slaves brought into the country, seemed beyond counting.

An age of general prosperity might well have begun. Once the devastating wars had been banished from its own soil, once Rome had become ruler of the known world, there should have come a time for reward and thanks to all those who had made sacrifice after sacrifice through long years. But Rome's ruling clique let no one share in the fruits of victory. Selfishly set upon its own profits, it denied the population not only a share in the enormous booty, not only any benefit from the new wealth, but even the right to any improvement of the economic position.

The vast harvest was enjoyed by a small circle alone. It was the *optimates,* the aristocratic upper crust of senators and knights, who profited. Under their control a capitalist economy developed which was to have its most disastrous effects on farming. Huge estates came into being which were worked, not by an independent rural population, but by armies of cheap slave labor. Vast ranches with herds of livestock more and more replaced arable farming, as grain was imported dirt-cheap from Sicily. Irresistibly the latifundia spread and threatened the free peasants. The small and medium-sized farms which could not cope with the competition were increasingly driven out of business. Their owners, forced to sell or lease their land, became impoverished and joined the proletariat of the towns. This development did not spare Etruria, where the number of giant farm enterprises grew alarmingly.

There was a crying need for land reform. But the senate did nothing. Against its wishes, nevertheless, a bitter struggle broke out for an equitable distribution of land. In the brothers Tiberius

369

and Gaius Gracchus the impoverished peasants found the men to espouse their cause. The desolate appearance of the Etruscan latifundia is said to have inspired the elder of the two with the determination to do something about the growing evil. "His brother Gaius has left it us in writing," says Plutarch, "that when Tiberius went through Tuscany to Numantia, and found the country almost depopulated, there being hardly any free husbandmen or shepherds, but for the most part only barbarian, imported slaves, he then first conceived the course of policy which in the sequel proved so fatal to his family."

Neither of the brothers succeeded in his aim of rescuing the Italian peasantry. The resistance of the *optimates* was too much for them, the power of the senate party's adherents too great. The people's cause was defeated.

Tiberius Gracchus was elected tribune in 133 B.C., and pushed through a revision of an existing law limiting the amount of public land an individual could use and providing land for those who had little or none. A commission was set up to supervise the operation of the new law.

But the nobles had no intention of accepting the land reform, and they plotted revenge. They were powerful enough to carry through their purpose, and they had many on their side outside Rome. In Etruria and Umbria, as Appian says, the owners of latifundia were afraid that they might not only lose the public land they were cultivating, by force or clandestinely, but their own private holdings as well. So they too sided with the senate party.

> On the day Tiberius Gracchus stood for reelection a riot was started, and a mob of nobles armed with cudgels and chair legs burst in and murdered him and three hundred of his supporters.

A year after the passing of the land reform, the nobles made short shrift of the reformers. On the day Tiberius Gracchus stood for reelection a riot was started, and a mob of nobles armed with cudgels and chair legs burst in and murdered him and three hundred of his supporters. His brother Gaius continued to work for Tiberius's policies, and ten years later when he was elected tribune, he attempted to go further. He was well aware that only a thoroughgoing reform of the state could put an end to abuses. So he took up the challenge of limiting the power of the ruling clique, and into the bargain the attempt to grant Roman citizenship to the Latin people. Fearlessly he launched a campaign against the senate. Like his brother, he failed and came to a violent end.

The death of Gaius Gracchus in 121 B.C. spelled the triumph of the reactionaries. The land reform petered out. The vast latifundia remained and with them the depopulation of wide areas. Their primitive pastoral economy completed the devastation of land once made fertile by the Etruscans, which had begun when the legions laid waste so many fields and plantations. The extensive network of drainage and irrigation channels constructed by the Etruscans decayed and silted up. River valleys became marshy and swamps formed, especially in the lowlands along the coast. They became the breeding ground of mosquitoes that carried malaria. This was the origin of the dreaded lethal regions, the notorious Maremma.

The dire consequences were not long in appearing. At Graviscae, the coastal garrison town founded in 181 B.C. in former Tarquinian territory, fever killed off the inhabitants. Cato attributed the deaths to the "unhealthy air," and Virgil called Graviscae a place of "bad weather." Sidonius Apollinaris, in the fifth century, wrote that "pestilence rules in Tuscany," and Pliny the Younger in a letter notes that "the Tuscan strip of seacoast is relaxing and dangerous to the health."

For close on two thousand years the land suffered from this scourge. The Maremma persisted all through the Middle Ages and down to modern times. In 1848, and still in 1883, Dennis described the wide, disease-ridden region: "Etruria was of old densely populated, not only in those parts which are still inhabited, but also, as is proved by remains of cities and cemeteries, in tracts now desolated by malaria, and relapsed into the desert; and what is now the fen or the jungle, the haunt of the wild-boar, the buffalo, the fox, and the noxious reptile, where man often dreads to stay his steps, and hurries away as from a plague-stricken land, of old yielded rich harvests of corn, wine and oil, and contained numerous cities, mighty and opulent, into whose laps commerce poured the treasures of the East, and the more precious produce of Hellenic genius. Most of these ancient sites are now without a habitant, fur-

rowed yearly by the plough, or forsaken as unprofitable wilder-
nesses."

It was not till the last century that efforts were once more made
to improve the land. In 1828 the Grand Duke Leopold II of Tuscany signed a decree providing for the reclamation of the Maremma. But it was only in recent years that this tremendous undertaking was completed with the help of comprehensive measures by
the Italian government. Today there is, at long last, fertile farmland again in the places where more than twenty-five hundred years
ago the Etruscans, with their techniques learned from the ancient
Orient, had first wrested it from nature.

THE ITALIAN WAR

ITALY KNEW NO PEACE. THE OP-
position to the old order stirred up
by the Gracchi could not be suppressed. Even if they failed of their
aims, the revolution they started
went on. The *populares,* representing the people, gained more and
more supporters and fought for their just cause against the *optimates,*
against senate rule and the aristocracy.

Dissatisfaction and anger mounted when the government opposed another, even more insistently voiced demand. The Italian
allies, who, along with Rome, had borne the heavy burden of the
wars, demanded Roman citizenship. It was over this question that
the storm broke in 91 B.C. The tribune M. Livius Drusus proposed a law to grant citizenship to the Italians. But before it came
to a vote, he was murdered. His assassination showed the Italians
what they could expect from Rome. Central and southern Italy rose
in arms. The old hatred for Rome flared up once more. The fiercest
agitators among the rebellious peoples were the Samnites, who re-
named one of their cities and made it their capital under the sym-
bolic name of Italia. They even minted their own coins; these
depicted the Italian bull goring the Roman wolf.

Thus began a conflict that shook the very foundations of Roman
power—the Italian or Social War.

The rebels took the offensive. Samnite troops advanced into
Campania and won over many towns. For Rome the situation was

serious. There was no telling what might happen if the revolt spread to yet other peoples. But in the early stages, at least, this fear proved groundless. Nothing stirred in Etruria, and Umbria remained quiet.

The Romans were driven to extreme measures. Owing to the scarcity of soldiers, says Appian, freedmen were for the first time enrolled in the army. But the outlook for Rome was grave when at the end of 90 B.C. the army of the consul Publius Rutilius Lupus was defeated and he himself was killed.

At the news of this and other successes by the Italian rebels, their cause threatened to gain new allies in the north. "The inhabitants of Etruria and Umbria and other neighboring peoples . . . were excited to revolt," says Appian. The danger to Rome seemed as great as in 310 B.C. But whereas the alliance of Etruscans and Samnites at that time had goaded the Romans to the utmost exertion of their strength, this time they reacted differently. They took alarm and declared themselves ready to make concessions. What they had stubbornly resisted for years, now under the pressure of events they conceded. Toward the end of 90 B.C. the consul L. Julius Caesar carried a law granting Roman citizenship to Latin and Italian allies who had remained loyal to Rome. The next year a supplementary measure granted citizenship to all who laid down their arms.

Rome's astute political moves did not fail of their effect. They took the wind out of the sails of all further attempts at rebellion. Etruria's revolt, which had barely begun, collapsed. Only in the south of Italy did the war go on, until even the Samnites, who stubbornly continued the fight, were beaten down.

> **Three centuries
> after the fall of Veii,
> which opened the Roman
> career of conquest,
> Etruria's history
> as an independent nation
> had run its course.**

Three centuries after the fall of Veii, which opened the Roman career of conquest, Etruria's history as an independent nation had run its course. The inhabitants of the once powerful country had become nationals of the victor state, were now Roman citizens. Many may have welcomed the new dispensation when the senate's laws were proclaimed in Etruscan towns and villages.

A memorial to that time survives in a famous tomb, some three miles outside Perugia. Discovered in 1840, it is known as the Ipogeo dei Volumni, the mausoleum founded by Arnth and Larth Velimna, as an inscription states, for four generations of the family. It was dug out of the tufa rock and is in the form of a house, with *atrium, tablinum,* and other rooms. The large, rectangular urns have handsomely carved upper parts representing sumptuous, draped couches on which the figures of the dead recline. The base of the urn that contained the ashes of the head of the family, Arnth Velimna, is embellished with two winged, female figures guarding the gate to the underworld. These figures have been compared with the work of Michelangelo or Jacopo della Quercia.

Terra-cotta cinerary urn, Vignagrande near Chiusi; mid-second century B.C.

It was this tomb which inspired Dennis, who visited it soon after its discovery, to undertake his study of Etruria. "Never shall I forget," he wrote, ". . . with what strange awe I entered the dark cavern—gazed on the inexplicable characters in the doorway—descried the urns dimly through the gloom—beheld the family-party at their sepulchral revels—the solemn dreariness of the surrounding cells. The figures on the walls and ceilings strangely stirred my fancy. The Furies, with their glaring eyes, gnashing teeth, and ghastly grins—the snakes, with which the walls seemed alive, hissing and darting their tongues at me—and above all the solitary wing, chilled me with an indefinable awe, with a sense of something mysterious and terrible. The sepulchre itself, so neatly hewn and decorated, yet so gloomy; fashioned like a house, yet with no mortal inhabitant—all was so strange, so novel. It was like enchantment, not reality, or rather it was the realisation of the pictures of subterranean palaces and spell-bound men, which youthful fancy had drawn from the Arabian Nights, but which had long been cast aside into the lumber-room of the memory, now to be suddenly restored."

At Tarquinia, in the Tomba del Tifone, are the last Etruscan paintings known to us, dating from the second or beginning of the first century B.C. The low roof of the tomb is supported by a thick, squat pillar cut out of the rock, and around the sides is a ledge consisting of three steps, also cut in the rock, on which the sarcophagi originally stood, some of them having lids carved with recumbent figures of the deceased. Among the faded and much damaged frescoes is a group of white-robed figures, advancing, it would seem, into the world of the shades. They are accompanied by demons with snaky hair and greenish flesh. On the central rectangular pillar are painted three fantastic beings. Two of them are the winged giants, or typhons, who give the tomb its name. Their legs terminate in snakes, and they are depicted as holding up the roof. The third figure is a winged *Lasa,* a female being who accompanies the dead. The inscriptions are not in Etruscan but in Latin, and the style of the paintings is Roman. A decorative band with a motif of leaping dolphins is the only thing that recalls the bygone, joyful archaic period. Deep mourning and grave solemnity permeate this tomb, this monument at the boundary between two worlds. The great age of the ancient Etruscan people has passed away.

After their long tribulations a new period seemed to have begun. But those who cherished such expectations were sadly disappointed.

> "The sound of a trumpet rang out from a perfectly clear and cloudless sky with a shrill, prolonged and dismal note." The haruspices announced that the eighth saeculum in the life of the Etruscan nation had come to an end, and, ominously, the ninth had begun.

The senate party had no desire to give up the reins of power and in practice refused to implement the new law to the full extent. They arranged the franchise in such a way that the new citizens were disadvantaged in respect to the old. This let loose a storm of indignation. There were violent clashes between *optimates* and *populares*. Barely was the Social War over when civil war broke out.

Rome, already threatened with war in Asia Minor, became the scene of bloodthirsty conflict. The struggle for power lay between Sulla, who blindly upheld the cause of the senate with its opposition to change, and Gaius Marius, the defender of the people's rights.

L. Cornelius Sulla, who had finished off Samnite resistance, was rewarded by election to the consulship in 88 B.C. and then appointed to the command against Mithridates in Asia. But the tribunes of the people's party secured the transfer of this command to Marius. Sulla refused to accept the change and, at the head of six legions, marched on Rome, captured it, and made short work of his opponents. He induced the senate to outlaw Marius and his associates. One tribune was hunted down and killed, but Marius, after many adventures, escaped to Africa.

Sulla did not remain long in Rome, but long enough to put the reactionaries back in command again. Then he left Rome and Italy for his war in Asia. But the great conflict was far from decided. The *populares* were defeated but not destroyed. They still had a large number of supporters throughout the country. The power basis of the victors in Rome was too weak, and the strength of their opponents was too great.

The prospects for the future were gloomy. In that year, 88 B.C., an extraordinary prodigy occurred. According to Plutarch in the *Life of Sulla,* "the sound of a trumpet rang out from a perfectly clear and cloudless sky with a shrill, prolonged and dismal note." The *haruspices* announced that the eighth *saeculum* in the life of the Etruscan nation had come to an end, and, ominously, the ninth had begun.

<table>
<tr><td>

**SULLA'S
BLOODBATH
IN TUSCANY**

</td><td>

THE SOOTHSAYERS WERE SOON proved right in their interpretation of the strange portent. Civil war was once more to inflict on Etruria loss of life and destruction. While Sulla was busy in

</td></tr>
</table>

the East fighting Mithridates, the storm broke at home against the forcibly restored rules of the *optimates*. Before 87 B.C. came to an end, the regime that Sulla had installed was overthrown, and the new masters in Rome were precisely those leaders of the popular party who had been banished and outlawed.

In response to his supporters' pleas, Marius returned from Africa. He landed at Telamon on the Etruscan coast, with a small force. This he rapidly increased by promising to fight for the freedom and independence of all the Italian peoples subjugated by Rome. Volunteers came flocking to him, and soon he had six thousand men and forty ships. With these he blockaded the mouth of the Tiber and intercepted grain on its way up the river to Rome.

Meanwhile the consul L. Cornelius Cinna, whom the senate had declared a public enemy, had won over troops which Sulla had left in Campania. Marius and Cinna then made a concerted attack on Rome. A new reign of terror began, and the leading men of the *optimates* party were murdered. For four years the supporters of Marius remained in power. Then their rule ended as violently as it had begun. Neither Marius, who died in 86, nor Cinna, who was killed by mutinous troops in 84, lived to see it.

In 83 B.C. Sulla, who had defeated Mithridates and concluded peace with him, was back in Italy. At the head of forty thousand troops he landed at Brindisi and marched for a second time on Rome. He was joined by M. Licinius Crassus, whose father had died in Marius's reign of terror, and by Gnaeus Pompeius, later named the Great.

The Marius party knew that Sulla was their greatest enemy, was the champion of reaction. In Rome and all over Italy they prepared for war, mobilized all their forces. Two of their most determined leaders, Gnaeus Papirius Carbo and Gaius Marius, the son, took over the consulship. Their forces, says Appian, "were constantly increasing from the major part of Italy, which still adhered to them, and also from the neighboring Gauls on the Po." Some cavalry were even recruited in Spain. In Etruria large numbers of the late elder Marius's veterans flocked to support the son. The Etruscans did not foresee what a terrible price they would have to pay for their enthusiastic support of the revolution.

But many may have seen a bad omen, a warning from the gods, in what happened in Rome at this time. On the night of July 6, 83 B.C., the temple of Jupiter on the Capitoline hill went up in flames, and was destroyed down to its foundations. For nearly five hundred years the splendid building had proclaimed the greatness of Rome's Etruscan kings. When the sculptor Vulca was summoned from Veii to make the figures of the gods that adorned the roof, Etruria with its league of cities was at the zenith of its power. It was almost as though the sudden collapse of the sanctuary in rubble and smoking ashes announced the misfortune which was facing the Etruscans. A year later it began.

In 82 B.C. Sulla, who had spent the winter building up his army in Campania, advanced to Rome. Gaius Marius, who tried to stop him, was defeated and driven to take refuge in Praeneste, where he was besieged. Sulla then occupied Rome, remaining there only long enough to take the most urgent measures before hurrying on northward, to Chiusi in Etruria.

There was some small-scale fighting on the banks of the river Glanis (modern Chiana) and at Saturnia. And a great battle was fought near Chiusi between Sulla and Carbo; it lasted a whole day but was indecisive. Carbo then sent two legions to Praeneste in an attempt to relieve Marius, who was still besieged, but they were driven back by Sulla's forces. Meanwhile the Gauls living between Ravenna and the Alps went over to Sulla's officer Metellus Pius, and the latter won a battle over Carbo's lieutenant, Norbanus, at Faventia (modern Faenza), reportedly killing some ten thousand of his men, while another six thousand deserted. When Carbo learned how things were going against him, he lost heart and fled to Africa, leaving behind some thirty thousand troops at Chiusi, in the Chiana valley. The young Pompeius inflicted a disastrous defeat on this army, which lost twenty thousand men, among them many Etruscans. The army broke up, and many men went back to their homes. Some reached Arezzo and began to recruit new volunteers to continue the revolt. The legions and a body of Samnites in the neighborhood of Praeneste marched to Rome and camped outside the walls. Here, on November 1, 82 B.C., at the Colline Gate, Sulla engaged them, late in the afternoon. The fighting continued through the night, and fifty thousand were estimated to have been killed on the two sides before Sulla gained the victory. Shortly afterward Praeneste surrendered and Marius committed suicide.

This was the end of Carbo's army. Sulla was now master of Italy. Only in one part of the peninsula did resistance continue—in Etruria. Populonia held out, and Volterra, strongly defended on its high cliffs, defied Sulla.

Four legions encamped below the town and laid siege to it. But Sulla, who could boast of never having lost a battle in his life, found himself at a loss. His attempts to capture the fortress failed, despite his personal command of the operations. Finally he handed over to Gaius Papirius Carbo, brother of the consul who had fled to Africa, the continuation of the siege in the hope that starvation would accomplish what force of arms had not.

But the bloodshed did not end with the military operations. The victor was not satisfied with defeating, crushing, and humiliating his opponents. He wanted to be sure that they were destroyed forever. Having got himself made dictator in November 82 B.C., Sulla then went ruthlessly to work. After the victory at the Colline gate he had more than eight thousand prisoners massacred, says Appian, "because they were mostly Samnites," and this treatment he continued with mass exterminations such as had never before been known in the history of Roman conquests.

> **Sulla's vengeance fell most heavily on Samnium and on Etruria, the land that had defied him longest. Mercilessly he rooted out the Etruscan families.**

He introduced proscription lists of his victims. They were outlawed and their property was confiscated. Anyone who killed them was paid the previously announced reward. The victims' sons and grandsons were barred from public office. There were no trials and no pardons. And naturally there was a wild rush to buy up the confiscated properties. The cities which had opposed Sulla were also punished; their land was seized wholesale and they were deprived of their Roman citizenship.

Sulla's vengeance fell most heavily on Samnium and on Etruria, the land that had defied him longest. Mercilessly he rooted out the Etruscan families. Special squads of officers traveled from place to place, carried out executions and drove the inhabitants from house and home. Influential Romans and friends of the dictator enriched themselves out of the movable property and the real estate of the murdered wealthy families. Domitius Ahenobarbus acquired great estates near Cosa. The famous and profitable pottery factories at Arezzo came into the hands of Roman speculators. Communal as well as private owners lost large tracts of their land; Arezzo, Chiusi, and Fiesole were among the cities thus despoiled.

The Sullan terror lay like a nightmare over the country, and it seemed as though it would never end. On the upper Cecina the dictator's troops were still camped outside Volterra. It was not till 80 B.C., two years after the last great battle outside Rome, that the defenders of this last center of Etruscan resistance capitulated. In the following year Sulla resigned his dictatorship. In 78 B.C. he died of a hemorrhage.

Etruria never recovered from the treatment it received. The losses and damage which the civil war and then Sulla's punitive measures inflicted on land and people alike were too great. It had received a mortal wound, and the nation's will to live succumbed under the iron hand of Sulla's officers. Roman veterans were settled in colonies on the land of the conquered and plundered cities. The old, established families at Fiesole, Arezzo, Cortona, at Populonia, Volterra, and many other places were obliged to receive new, foreign citizens within their walls, while in the country the farms passed to foreign owners. From that time Romanization made rapid strides. Within a few decades assimilation was to extinguish the last independent expressions of Etruscan culture and way of life.

The rural districts were depopulated more than ever before. The inhabitants, dispossessed of their farms, and unemployed, drifted to the towns where the mingling of Etruscan and other Italian peoples went on rapidly. Many of the indigenous inhabitants intermarried with the new colonists; aristocratic families turned their backs on their homeland. They handed over to managers the administration of their properties and settled in Rome. Life in that city, which was fast becoming a metropolis, seemed more attractive and interesting, and its thriving international trade offered new opportunities. They soon became Romanized, adopted the customs and habits and language of their new environment, and forgot their origin.

Only in a few places the old crafts still flourished, especially pottery making. Arezzo even enjoyed a new period of prosperity. Its main product, the famous Arretine ware of *terra sigillata,* was in very wide demand. It was manufactured in large potteries, the biggest of which belonged to an Etruscan family, the Perennii.

The inhabitants of Arezzo owed it chiefly to Cicero that they got back lands confiscated after the civil war, and once again enjoyed full rights of Roman citizenship. Cicero also took up the cause of Volterra and secured the remission of the severe penalties imposed upon the town by Sulla. The inhabitants of both cities had become, as Cicero emphasized, loyal subjects and good Romans.

While the old traditions survived, they were, like everything else, gradually altered and pushed aside by the new way of life. As in the past the dead were still buried according to traditional rites in the family vaults, but more and more Latin inscriptions appear alongside Etruscan ones.

It was at about this time that the Etruscan priests ordered the codification of the ancient sacred doctrine of their people. Tarquitius Priscus later translated part of these sacred books into Latin, but both translation and original have been lost.

Rome itself was most anxious that the ancient *disciplina Etrusca* should be preserved in its original purity. The Romans did not want to be without the arts of the *haruspices,* especially in what concerned the interpretation of unusual events and phenomena. Cicero, in his *De divinatione,* refers to a senate edict of the second century B.C. on the subject. It laid down that "of the sons of the chief men, six should be handed over to each of the Etruscan tribes for the study of divination, in order that so important a profession should not, on account of the poverty of its members, be withdrawn from the influence of religion, and converted into a means of mercenary gain." Cicero himself proposed in one of the religious laws of his ideal state that "prodigies and portents shall be referred to the Etruscan soothsayers, if the senate so decree; Etruria shall instruct her leading men in this art."

Nothing of great moment happened in Etruria during its waning years. Even so, there was little peace in the land between the Tiber and the Arno. Several times it was the scene of rebellious, politically significant events, and military clashes. First the soldiers who had been compulsorily settled in Tuscany revolted. Sulla's attempt to make diligent tillers of the soil out of veterans habituated to war and adventure misfired. It was hardly to be wondered at. These colonies, said Cicero in his second oration against Catiline in Rome on November 9, 63 B.C., "are all composed of very fine citizens and very brave men." But, he went on, so many of them were so heavily in debt that the only way out of their plight was through insurrection. They were not accustomed to honest hard work, and had so little taste for it that they began to be rebellious.

The discontented soldiers found a leader in L. Sergius Catilina, who demanded the cancellation of their debts. The revolt was joined by Etruscans from Fiesole and Arezzo who had been dispossessed of their lands. Troops sent from Rome soon disposed of the bands of veterans and restored order. Catilina himself was killed in 62 B.C. near Pistoia.

In 59 B.C. Julius Caesar, in his first consulship, set about dealing with the disorders in Etruria. He wanted to bring peace to this troubled land, and his first measure was a bill to provide farms for the veterans and some of the impoverished city folk. He hoped by this means to improve the lamentable state of agriculture and to promote peaceful relations with Rome. The bill was opposed by the senate and the big landowners, but Caesar pushed it through. During the next few years a number of colonies were established; Cicero mentions the settlement of veterans at Veii and Capena, both in southern Etruria, in 46 B.C. Farther north, new settlements were made, one near Arezzo and the other in the plain not far from Fiesole. Etruscan peasants who had earlier been driven off their land got holdings along with numbers of veterans.

It was on the northern border of Etruria that the three masters of the Roman world, Caesar, Pompey and Crassus, met in confer ence in 56 B.C. At Lucca they renewed their pledge to continue to work together and do nothing which would displease any one of them. But within a few years the triumvirate began to break up. After the death of Crassus in 53, followed by a period of jockeying for position by Caesar and Pompey, the decisive steps were taken in 49. Caesar sent Mark Antony with five cohorts of troops to Arezzo, to guard his flank, while he himself advanced southward from Ravenna. Then, on January 10, 49, by crossing the Rubicon, a little river between Ravenna and Rimini which marked the boundary of Cisalpine Gaul and Italy, he stepped outside his own province and thus began the civil war.

Caesar, it would seem, was well disposed toward the Etruscans, and had among his advisers the *haruspex* Spurinna. It was he who warned Caesar, in vain, of the Ides of March. And in 44 B.C. when the news came that Caesar had been murdered during a session of the senate, he was mourned throughout Etruria. At that time there was widespread alarm and fear at the sight of a great comet in the night sky. With dismay the Etruscans learned that the *haruspex* Vulcatius had announced to the Roman assembly during Caesar's funeral that the end of the ninth *saeculum* had come. He is said to have declared that he announced this in full knowledge that he was acting against the will of the gods and that he would have to pay for so doing with his life. And thereupon he is said to have died on the spot, without any apparent cause.

> **With dismay the Etruscans learned that the haruspex Vulcatius had announced to the Roman assembly during Caesar's funeral that the end of the ninth saeculum had come.**

THE END OF ETRURIA

CAESAR'S TESTAMENT LED TO the last great conflict, which was to put an end to the republic. This was the quarrel between C. Octavius (Octavian), Caesar's grand-nephew, his adopted son and heir designate, and Marcus Antonius (Mark Antony). The conflict did not end till the battle of Actium in northwest Greece in 31 B.C. Amid the rivalries and clashes which shook the Roman world from end to end, the name of an Etruscan city—Perugia—crops up for the last time.

In the autumn of 42 B.C. the battle of Philippi, in eastern Macedonia, ended in the defeat of Caesar's murderers and the suicide of Cassius and Brutus. In the following year while Mark Antony was enjoying himself with Cleopatra in Alexandria, Octavian began the settlement of veterans in Italian cities which he had promised after Philippi. But when the first confiscations and expulsions resulted in a serious clash between soldiers and farmers and an outbreak of disorders, the consul Lucius Antonius, Mark Antony's brother, backed the dissidents. And this led to fighting between the eight legions L. Antonius managed to raise and Octavian's forces; it led to the war of Perugia.

For a short while, L. Antonius even occupied Rome. Then he was driven out and forced into Etruria, where he took refuge in the city of Perugia. Octavian blockaded the city and cut it off completely from the outside world. In March, 40 B.C., after a winter's siege and starvation, L. Antonius had to surrender. Nothing happened to him, other than being made governor of Spain, but the reprisals inflicted on the unfortunate town were all the more frightful.

Octavian, the much-eulogized future emperor Augustus, treated the conquered city with unbounded ferocity. All the town councilors and Octavian's Roman political opponents were put to death. Three hundred of the leading citizens were rounded up as scapegoats, and, it is said by Suetonius, Octavian "offered them on the Ides of March at the altar of the god Julius, as human sacrifices." It was one of the worst atrocities of the whole revolutionary age, and eclipsed even Sulla's proscriptions. Only once in the past had Rome been guilty of anything approaching it in horror, when in 353 B.C. the 358 prisoners from Tarquinii were butchered in the Forum.

After the human sacrifice, tremendous clouds of smoke were visible from afar. One of Perugia's citizens, a certain Cestius Macedonicus, overcome by despair, "set fire to his house," says Appian, "and plunged into the flames, and a strong wind fanned the conflagration and drove it over the whole of Perusia, which was entirely consumed, except the temple of Vulcan." Perugia, the once splendid Etruscan city, was nothing but a heap of rubble and ash within its high stone walls. A wave of fear spread through Etruria at the news of Perugia's fate. Many Etruscans, afraid of further reprisals, buried their valuables in the country and took refuge in the forests. During the last century several finds were made which recall the terror of those times. In 1851 near the Coniaia spring at Arezzo a buried hoard of five hundred silver coins of the Roman republic was discovered; in the neighborhood of Lucca another cache came to light that consisted of more than three thousand silver coins of that time. In 1871 more coins were dug up at Montefalco near Perugia. As early as the fourteenth century, large quantities of coins from the republican period are reported to have been found in "ancient Casentino," that is, the area in which Arezzo lies.

Octavian, who became sole ruler after his victory at Actium over Antony and Cleopatra, subsequently tried to make good what he had done to Perugia. As emperor he ordered that the town was to be rebuilt in all its splendor. In memory of him it was henceforth known as Augusta Perusia. That name, chiseled into the stone of the city gate known as the Arco di Augusto, has survived down to the present day.

Was it repentance for his monstrous fury that made Augustus decide on the rebuilding? We can but speculate. It certainly seems likely that the influence of his friend and adviser Gaius Cilnius Maecenas played a part in his decision. Maecenas came from Arezzo, of a royal Etruscan family.

It is recorded that Augustus in his travels through the provinces several times stopped at Florence and other neighboring places. Before his great administrative reforms he founded a number of new colonies in Tuscany. They were intended to bring abandoned farms back into cultivation and to instill new life into agriculture. Saena Julia, modern Siena, built on an old Etruscan site, was one of them.

Perugia "seems to have flourished under the empire and was raised to the rank of a colony by the emperor Trebonianus Gallus," says Emeline Richardson, who adds: "Another Etruscan city to get a new lease of life under Augustus was Arretium, which became rich and famous again from the manufacture of a particularly handsome and delicate pottery, the coral-colored Arretine ware, whose walls are decorated with scenes of hunting, banqueting, and lovemaking, or with masks and garlands and all the pretty, Hellenizing paraphernalia of the new imperial style."

Roman merchants exported this pottery all over the world, even as far as India. Fragments of it have been found in England as well as in the Sahara. The first potteries in Gaul, including those at Lezoux in the Auvergne and at Graufesenque near Clermont (Puy de Dôme), were imitated from those of Arezzo and produced the similar, so-called Samian ware; others were set up later in Roman Germany.

Rome, now an imperial residence, was given a new look—a newly rich look of overdone ornament. Augustus made a pretentious metropolis out of the city with its ugly, centuries-old brick buildings. Whole districts of winding, narrow alleys were demolished to make room for the new, marble splendors, such as those exemplified by the Forum of Caesar, the temple of Venus Genetrix, and the Forum of Augustus containing the temple of Mars Ultor.

Seven centuries earlier the Etruscans had been the first great legislators of Italy and teachers of Rome in all forms of architecture. The Romans, spartan and uncreative, had not developed any architectural ideas of their own during this long period. Now Greece became their paragon and Hellenistic art appeared in Rome, in the city which previously had had no thought but of war and conquest.

Now at last, under Augustus, the Romans produced their own poetry. In this too a descendant of the ancient Etruscan people played an outstanding part of leadership. It was Maecenas who awoke Rome's enjoyment of art and became the great patron and stimulator of poetry. He had an acute eye for young talent and formed a circle of brilliant writers and intellectuals. Besides Virgil, Propertius, and other poets, it was above all Horace whom he counted among his closest friends. He gave him a farm in the Sabine hills, and thus made it possible for him to devote himself to his writing, free from financial worries.

> *Maecenas's name became proverbial and has remained so. But his Etruscan origins are seldom remembered.*

It was Horace too who wrote enthusiastically about the royal origins of his great patron after visiting him at his villa on the Esquiline in Rome. There the walls of the atrium were decorated with the painted garlands of a genealogical tree bearing the names of Maecenas's ancestors. The family tree reached back to

386

the fourth century B.C., when the Cilnii ruled in Arezzo. "Of all the Lydians that are settled in Tuscan lands," writes Horace, "none is of nobler birth than you, and . . . grandsires of yours, on your mother's and your father's side alike, commanded mighty legions in days of old." Maecenas's name became proverbial and has remained so. But his Etruscan origins are seldom remembered.

The new and pompous style of architecture spread from the capital to Etruria. Private and public buildings sprang up, copied from those on the Tiber, with colonnades, wide terraces and gardens with fountains and artificial lakes. Public baths, theaters, and amphitheaters were built. But even the look of lonely, country places was changed. Rich Romans began to appreciate the pleasures of rural life, and built splendid country houses where they spent their vacations surrounded by crowds of servants, and went hunting and fishing. The famous Roman villas spread over the landscape from the Apennines to the coast.

And a new kind of tourism appeared at this time. Thousands of visitors, seeking recreation or recuperation from their ailments, came to the famous healing springs which Etruria owed to its volcanic soil. No other part of Italy could offer, so close to the capital, such an abundance of curative waters. A regular spa industry grew up. Many of these watering places have remained in use to the present day. *Chianciano—fegato sano* (Chianciano for a healthy liver) announce the billboards along the Autostrada del Sole to Rome. Ultra-modern sanatoria for the treatment of liver and gallbladder complaints now stand where the inhabitants of Etruscan Clusium once treated their liver troubles.

Under Augustus's great administrative reform of all Italy Etruria was redefined within new frontiers which differed from those at the time of the League of Twelve. The name by which the Romans had called it, Tuscia, was abolished and it became the Seventh Region, "in which is Etruria," as Pliny the Elder wrote; but it was not the same in area as before. In the north, toward the Ligurians, it was extended to the river Magra, near the town of Spezia. In the south it reached only to the Tiber. The old Etruscan-speaking region beyond the river was attached to Umbria. It was not until Charlemagne that the old name Tuscia (Tuscany) was restored to the region north of Viterbo and Bolsena. The southern region, formerly Etruscan, with Tarquinii, Veii, and Caere, became part of

Latium. A thousand years later, the original name of the country reappeared in modern history when in the Treaty of Lunéville of 1801, Tuscany was made into the kingdom of Etruria under Louis, Duke of Parma.

In his *Odes,* Horace celebrates the happy state of Italy under Augustus's rule—the end of the civil war, the peace and security from foreign foes, the undisturbed labor of farmers and merchants. But no poet raised his voice in lament at the hour of death which came for Etruria when the "golden age" began for Rome.

The Seventh Region did not remain a purely formal administrative arrangement. The assimilation process was quickly completed. Augustus's rule covered nearly half a century. During the Classical Age that began with him, the last traces of the distinctive way of life of the ancient Etruscan people disappeared.

A visit to any museum with a collection of Etruscan art and antiquities soon shows how quickly the Etruscans, in the words of Diodorus Siculus, "adapted themselves to the new masters." They offered no resistance to the new art which swept all before it. Their spirit was broken; they had lost their soul. They were content to swim with the stream, and Augustan classicism characterized everything that was still made in Etruria, from public monuments and private villas to articles of everyday use.

In the crafts they began the mass production of copies of the fashionable new style. Even the graves contain fewer and fewer memories of the ancient people, and then they cease altogether. After the middle of the first century A.D. there are no more tomb inscriptions in Etruscan. And even the living, as Seneca suggests, had ceased to understand Etruscan. In Romanized Etruria, Latin was the language.

Latin too was the language used in the great commemorative tablets to Etruscan notable men which were erected in the Forum of Tarquinii around A.D. 40. Only small fragments remain of these *Elogia,* discovered in 1948 by Pietro Romanelli. They celebrate heroes of Etruscan tradition who are otherwise unknown to us. It is presumed that they are based on the Etruscan authors mentioned by the emperor Claudius.

On one of the fragments appears the name Tarchon, the legendary founder of the city named after him, together with the names Etruria and Tarquinii. In another fragment eight lines record the

388

deeds of a ruler (whose name is missing) who was the first Etruscan general to lead an army to Sicily, and was rewarded for his success with the insignia of a triumph: a scepter with an eagle and a golden wreath. Nothing has survived to indicate the period of this expedition.

A third fragment commemorates the deeds of an Etruscan who came from Norchia. His name too is lost. All that remains is the statement that he defeated a king of Caere, triumphed over Arezzo in war, and conquered nine fortified places.

The great past survived still in superb works of art and painted terra-cottas, though their real significance had gone and they were little heeded. They recalled the great age of Etruscan art when the finest statues of the gods were made of clay.

Outside the ruins of former Etruscan cities there still lay the vast cemeteries, with their huge tumuli within whose depths the frescoed vaults enclosed great treasures. But few knew now about the dead whose last resting place they were, nor about the times when they lived, about the wealthy and famous families who had given the land its rulers for centuries.

The deeds of the great, ancient people had begun to fade from memory, when unexpectedly the ranks of its enemy and conqueror produced a man who put together everything important that could still be discovered about the Etruscans' past. He was none other than the later ruler of the Roman empire, Claudius. The story of how he came to do this begins in the lifetime of Augustus.

> *The deeds of the great, ancient people had begun to fade from memory, when unexpectedly the ranks of its enemy and conqueror produced a man who put together everything important that could still be discovered about the Etruscans' past.*

One of the ladies often seen at the imperial court was Urgulania. She was, as is clearly proved by the recent discovery of her name in an inscription at Tarquinia, a member of an Etruscan noble family. She was a close friend of Livia, the emperor's wife, and as such enjoyed so privileged a position that, as Tacitus puts it, she was placed "above the law." Tacitus paints an impressive picture of the personality of this influential Etruscan lady. One day, he tells us, "when she was summoned to the senate as witness in a case, she refused to attend. A praetor was dispatched to interrogate her at her home." On another occasion she defied a summons to appear in court in connection with a debt. Instead she hurried off to the imperial palace to complain about the summons. In the end, to smooth things over, Livia gave instructions that the sum demanded should be paid.

Urgulania made good use of her position and connections to push the advantage of her own family. She even managed to meddle in the imperial family's private affairs, especially as regards young Claudius, her friend Livia's grandson. Claudius was regarded as the family idiot and despised by all; he was also a sickly boy, and the emperor was at a loss what to do with him, as witness a letter of his to Livia reproduced by Suetonius.

What especially worried Augustus, it is clear from the letters given by Suetonius, was how to prevent Claudius from making a fool of himself in public on state occasions. He suggested to Livia that "his cousin, young Silvanus" should accompany him at one such function to see that he did not do anything silly. This Silvanus was the eldest grandson of the formidable Urgulania, his father being her son M. Plautinus Silvanus, who had made a brilliant official career, and was also married to an Etruscan. Finally Urgulania brought off her masterstroke in gaining influence with the imperial family—she found Claudius his first wife, who was none other than her granddaughter Plautia Urgulanilla.

Claudius was thus closely connected with some of the last members of the Etruscan aristocracy, and it was not surprising that he became deeply interested in their history. He set to work to study it thoroughly. "It is clear," says Jacques Heurgon, "that the son-in-law and brother-in-law of the authentic representatives of the principal Etruscan *gentes* of the time, having access to family archives jealously guarded within the severe walls of Tuscan palaces at Tarquinii, Volterra, Chiusi, and Perugia had found there his vocation as Etruscologist." He devoted years of work to the composition of his *Tyrrhenica,* a history of the Etruscans in twenty books.

Claudius did not forget the Etruscans even when fortune had taken an unexpected turn for him and he had become emperor, and married other wives. He made special efforts to ensure that the ancient priestly lore of Etruria was kept in being. In this he was advised by Tarquitius Priscus, a member of the famous family of

Etruscan *haruspices,* an earlier member of which had translated into Latin a number of books on the art of divination, supernatural events, and the legendary doctrine. In A.D. 47 Claudius made a speech to the senate about the sacred college of *haruspices.* "This oldest Italian art," he said, according to Tacitus, "ought not to die out through neglect." He recalled that "leading Etruscans, on their own initiative—or the Roman senate's—have kept up the art and handed it down from father to son. Now, however, public indifference to praiseworthy accomplishments has caused its neglect; and the advance of foreign superstitions has contributed to this."

The senate ordered that the priests should consider what institutions of the soothsayers needed support. And it seems that the necessary action was taken, for during Claudius's reign we hear of an order of the sixty *haruspices,* organized as a college. Its center was first at Tarquinii and then in Rome. "It played the role of authorized guardian of the Etruscan discipline," says Heurgon, "and assured its long survival, right to the end of antiquity and even into the Byzantine epoch."

However, the *Tyrrhenica,* the priceless fruit of Claudius's labors, and thus the history of the Etruscans, never became known to posterity. It disappeared completely. No copy has survived, nor any extracts. There are only a few fragments cited by other writers. The Romans were not interested, not even the learned men. The *Tyrrhenica* dealt with a past of which Rome did not wish to be reminded now that she had become the capital of the world and was at the zenith of her power.

People made fun of Claudius's studies. This comes out in a satire, possibly by Seneca, published very soon after his death. The satire is entitled the *Apocolocyntosis,* literally the "Pumpkinification." The pumpkin was reckoned a symbol of stupidity. The satire describes with venomous spite the death, ascent into Heaven, and descent into Hell of the murdered emperor. In that year, A.D. 54, reports Tacitus, in the consulate of Marcus Asinius Marcellus and Manius Acilius Aviola, "a series of prodigies indicated changes for the worse." And the emperor's death, like that of Caesar, was marked by a flaming comet in the night sky.

PART FIVE

The Great Legacy

*The Etruscans were undoubtedly
one of the most remarkable nations of antiquity—
the great civilizers of Italy.*

George Dennis, 1848

*Their position as cultural mediators
is what gives the Etruscans
far-reaching importance.*

Franz Altheim, 1956

*In respect to the oldest period
of Italian history the Etruscan world
was a revelation as unexpected
as was Cretan civilization
in respect to Greek history.
In neither case have
the full consequences yet been drawn.*

Pierre Grimal, 1961

XXVI

The Forgotten Heritage

REMEMBER THAT YOU HAVE BEEN SENT TO the province of Achaea, to the pure and genuine Greece, where civilization and literature, and agriculture, too, are believed to have originated . . . Respect the gods their founders and the names they bear, respect their ancient glory and their very age . . . Do not detract from anyone's dignity, independence or even pride, but always bear in mind that this is the land which provided us with justice and gave us laws . . . that it is Athens you go to and Sparta you rule, and to rob them of the name and shadow of freedom, which is all that now remains to them, would be an act of cruelty, ignorance, and barbarism."

These words of adjuration were written by Pliny the Younger in about A.D. 108 to Valerius Maximus, the imperial legate in Greece. After subjugating Hellas, seizing its treasures, and removing to Rome thousands of columns, statues, friezes, and books, the Romans succumbed to the fascination of Greece. Things Greek became fashionable. Rome decked itself with borrowed Greek plumes just as it had done centuries earlier with Etruscan ones.

Not a line has survived expressing similar sentiments in respect to Etruria. The memory of nations is short and they have no room for gratitude. They hate being indebted to others. When Pliny wrote, the rich legacy that Etruria had handed on to Rome was long forgotten, and legends had obscured the fact that it was Etruscans who founded the city and the state, who taught the Romans to read and write, and first made them acquainted with Greek art. For five centuries before the Romans came in direct contact with Greece during their campaigns in southern Italy, the Etruscans had brought them marvelous vases from Hellas, and with them a knowledge of Greek myths and legends.

The imperial descendants of the shepherds on the Tiber hills did not want to know about that past, and did everything possible to eradicate all memory of it. Just as newly rich upstarts like to acquire the titles and ancestors of famous families, so Rome had meanwhile embellished its origins with a distinguished family tree. They claimed Aeneas of Troy for themselves.

Conquered, with their country occupied by foreign soldiers and settlers, the Etruscans no longer existed as a nation. And yet they survived and their influence persisted. The works they created and the examples they set were still strong and vital. The roots they had put down, especially in Tuscany, were deep and widespread, and they were to send up new shoots for a long time to come.

What they bequeathed was still to provide many a stimulus in various fields, both material and spiritual, from their architecture and art to their religion. They were the first people in Italy to build, or strive to build, vaults and arches. Their city gates, of which parts survive to the present day at Perugia and Volterra, provided a model for the Romans which the latter developed magnificently, as for example in the great triumphal arches built in the Imperial Age. The Etruscan liking for round buildings and vaults—the earliest examples of which are the Cerveteri tombs dating from the seventh century B.C.—was shared by the Romans who enlarged Etruscan architecture to gigantic proportions.

The monumental family tombs of the Roman emperors were imitations of the huge, stone-girdled tumuli of earth in the depths of which Etruscan princes were buried. Examples are the famous, much admired mausoleums of Augustus and Hadrian (the Castel Sant' Angelo). Architecturally they closely followed the model of the vast hemisphere on a circular base. Only the proportions changed. The low drum of hewn stone which girdled the Etruscan tumuli became the high, circular, marbled-faced wall. On the other hand the hill, planted with cypresses, which crowned the structure, became shallower.

The ideas of Etruscan tomb architecture were later applied by Roman builders to secular constructions. The enormous public baths, the *thermae,* were often built with cupola vaults. And from Rome, mausoleums and *thermae* spread all over the empire. Copies appeared in all the major cities and garrison towns.

The Etruscan religion and religious observances still occupied an important place in imperial Rome. The emperor Caligula, according to Suetonius, carried his daughter Julia Drusilla "around the temples of all the goddesses in turn before finally entrusting her to the lap of Minerva, whom he called upon to supervise his daughter's growth and education."

The ancient *disciplina etrusca* continued to be fostered by Etruscan priests. But despite all efforts to preserve the purity of the teaching, it did not escape contamination from foreign sources. A variety of philosophical and mystical doctrines reached Rome from the eastern provinces of the empire and the Orient generally, among them the Egyptian worship of Isis, the cult of Mithras from Persia, and Christianity. It

> **Even the emperors turned to Etruscan priests when there was some question of interpreting omens and divining the future.**

is not known whether and to what extent Etruscan survived as a language of worship, or at least in ritual formulas and phrases. But it does seem that even after it had long ceased to be a current, everyday language, it still persisted for some time, rather as Sanskrit does now. Lucretius, in the first century B.C., speaks of the "Tyrrhenian songs" which are read backwards, i.e., from right to left. The order of the sixty *haruspices* known to have existed at Tarquinii in the reign of the emperor Claudius survived even into the Byzantine epoch.

Even the emperors turned to Etruscan priests when there was some question of interpreting omens and divining the future. There are many examples of this, and even the names of some *haruspices* have been preserved. A change began to appear under Constantine the Great after his Edict of Milan in A.D. 313, which made Christianity a tolerated religion. Constantine at first forbade the practices of the *haruspices* and then later modified his ban, specifically allowing the official, public activities of the priests in connection with the state religion. As an example of what was permitted, the emperor decreed that if lightning struck the imperial palace or any other public buildings, the *haruspices* should investigate the event and announce their interpretation of what it portended. The festival of the Etruscans at the sanctuary of the Fanum Voltumnae near Volsinii was still being celebrated in the fourth century A.D., according to ancient custom. Constantine took no action against it; if anything he strengthened its Etruscan character by authorizing the neighboring Umbrians to have a festival of their own, instead of having a joint one with the Etruscans.

During the subsequent short reign of the emperor Julian there was complete toleration for the *haruspices,* and in fact they were consulted by the emperor, and accompanied him on his campaigns. Even the emperors Valentinian I, Valens, and Gratian permitted hepatoscopy. Theodosius, however, in two decrees, of A.D. 385 and 392, imposed severe penalties on any kind of haruspicy. Anyone who sacrificed an animal and consulted the entrails for the purpose of divination incurred the same punishment as for high treason, and might be burned alive. Under Theodosius's youngest son and successor Honorius, the Vandal Stilicho, the boy emperor's protector, burned the Sibylline Books, and possibly also the Etruscan Vegoian books which were kept with them in the temple of Apollo on the Palatine.

But in 408, when the Gothic army under Alaric was approaching Rome, Etruscan priests were suddenly in the forefront again. *Haruspices* offered their help to Pope Innocent I, claiming that they could bring down lightning on the enemy and thus save the city. But nothing came of it. The soothsayers insisted that their ritual must be held in public, and that the old pagan sacrifices should be performed by the magistrates on the Capitol, but the senate was not prepared to sanction this. However, the fact that the offer was made and discussed with the pope shows how seriously the Etruscan doctrine was still taken in the fifth century.

But thereafter the Etruscan discipline faded away. Not a single section of the ancient doctrine was preserved. It disappeared for good, along with all the copies and extracts, commentaries and translations. Only tiny fragments of the Latin version have survived.

There were no half-measures in the church's fight against paganism. Tuscany and its people, with their mysterious cults and rites at the gates of Rome, had long been on the blacklist. "The originator and mother of superstitions"—that is what Arnobius called Etruria near the end of the third century A.D., when, as a new Christian convert, he wrote his seven-volume work against the pagans, *Adversus nationes.*

But did the new doctrine of salvation really succeed in cleansing its own churches of the ancient, deeply rooted superstitions and belief in miracles? The Romans, like the Etruscans before them, never managed to shake off the constraining outlook of an archaic age and to take the great liberating step into new, modern ways of thinking.

The opportunity seemed to have come when Rome, after five centuries of unceasing wars and conquests, had become master of the world. By then the Greeks had succeeded the Etruscans as Rome's teachers. As late as 161 B.C., Greek philosophers and rhetoricians were expelled from Rome, but a change began in the first century when Cicero made Greek philosophy known among the Romans. With a sudden rush, the enlightenment of Greek knowledge and teaching poured into the country. For a little while it seemed as though the Hellenic spirit would spark the tramping soldiery of Rome into throwing off the primitive and superstitious ways of thinking and feeling inherited from a remote, archaic past. Caesar himself and Sallust had already declared their skepticism about the prodigies, the heavenly signs which were supposed to indicate the will of the gods. And Strabo classed thunderbolts and other portents among the fables and bugbears used to frighten "the great mass of women and common people."

In his philosophical poem, *The Nature of the Universe,* Lucretius proclaimed a new vision. He expounded the philosophy of his idolized master Epicurus, which was based on the atomist theory of Democritus. For Lucretius everything in the world is born and dies according to eternal laws; there is no intervention by supernatural powers and no survival after death. Lucretius wanted to free mankind at last from illusory fears of the gods and the terror of death. Livy said that portents were the mark of historical writing in the past, but not of that in his own time. And Tacitus, under the spell of the new knowledge from Greece, criticized the mania for marvels of earlier uneducated times, and frequently dismissed supernatural explanations of historical events as delusion, as a reflection of mere psychological dispositions and mass suggestion.

There were many such efforts at making known the innovative thought of the Greeks in philosophy and science, in bringing it home to the Romans. But the great stride forward was never taken. The number of those who felt and thought in a modern way remained small. It was only among a limited circle of cultured people that they made any impression. The new ideas never got through to wider circles. Rome could not change its ways. A way of thinking that was skeptical and questioning, that cherished independent individual opinions, was bound to remain alien to the people of a conquering, military state who had had obedience to orders bred in the bone for generations.

Rome, from its emperor to the mass of its people, remained fundamentally what it had always been, narrow-minded and uninterested in anything that was not material. Certainly Rome had become immensely rich, had decked itself out in marble, and was practically suffocated under the excessively lavish splendor of its palaces, *fora,* and baths. But within its walls there were no academies. No one cared about cultivating the sciences. No one was interested in art and culture.

The people of Rome were not interested in music, still less in the theater. What they liked was crude, vulgar farces, and it was these that were staged, not the great dramas of Hellas. What would have been the point? The city already had "spectacles" of the kind it liked, in the shape of the bloodthirsty animal baitings and gladiatorial butchery of the amphitheater. It was not only the plebs, but also the most respected citizens who flocked to these barbarous displays.

At Augustus's command 3,500 beasts from Africa were slaughtered in the amphitheater. In one single display given by Pompey, five hundred lions were killed. At the triumphal games of Trajan in A.D. 107 ten thousand gladiators fought in pairs, armed with net and trident against sword and buckler. For centuries people had been accustomed to murderous scenes on the battlefields, and they were loath to do without them in the peaceful age of the emperors.

Rome never took up the legacy of Etruria. It never created any industry within its walls. Even the wide acres at its gates were never cultivated. The desolate latifundia extended over land that Etruscan hard work had once made fertile.

> **The unique, intellectual heritage of Greece that fell into Rome's lap was wasted, as was the civilizing inheritance from the Etruscans.**

The unique, intellectual heritage of Greece that fell into Rome's lap was wasted, as was the civilizing inheritance from the Etruscans. Rome did not equal the achievements of Hellas in philosophy, the natural sciences, nor even in the art of history. What Greece gave the world Rome watered down; much that was greatest and most seminal was not even preserved and handed on to posterity, despite Rome's achievements in law and in technology.

Rome was not capable of doing that. In this sphere it had no stimulating model in its own past, for its first teachers had failed it. The Etruscans, despite the progress made by their highly developed civilization, paid no heed to the tremendous intellectual breakthrough of the Greeks. They never made the leap from thought rooted in mysticism, belief, and emotion to reason and scientific investigation. They remained fast in their world of myth, stubbornly and fearfully closed to reason. And the Romans followed them in this attitude. In this respect they took up the Etruscan legacy, with disastrous consequences for the intellectual life of Europe in the centuries to come.

Apart from Tacitus, no Roman historian can match Herodotus or Thucydides. None of them brings a genuinely scientific, objective mind to the task of discovering the facts.

In the natural sciences Rome was uncreative. It is not the Romans that the world can thank for new knowledge. They were content to reproduce what was already known, to digest traditional material assembled from all over the world, in vast collections that gathered dust in imperial libraries.

The typical works were compilations and abstracts, in which the authors merely endeavored to present their material as conveniently as possible for the use of their contemporaries. The enormous *Natural History* of Pliny the Elder, dedicated to Titus in A.D. 77, while a work of immense industriousness, dispenses with clarity of thought and independent judgment. The author, an old cavalry officer and one-time commander of the fleet, simply assembles extracts from hundreds of books without any kind of discrimination, regardless of whether they are good or bad.

In contrast to the precise evaluation of Aristotle, for instance, Pliny sets down the most infantile marvels and old wives' tales. He refers to a race of people who have only one leg, to others who can wrap themselves up in their ears. He cites King Pyrrhus's big toe, which had the property of curing certain diseases, and mentions alleged eyewitnesses of satyrs and tritons. The superstitious chatter of ignorant people, "marvels" and "paradoxes" as they were called, often aroused more interest than the laws of nature.

It seems incredible, but it is true that this compilation, replete with the unscientific misinformation of a scribble-happy Roman military man, was treated by late antiquity as the supreme reference book. All through the Middle Ages and down to the beginning of modern times Pliny was considered in Europe as *the* authority. He was only finally dislodged from this position by the discoveries of empirical research. And even as late as 1830 Pliny was still read and taught in secondary schools in Germany; they had no other teaching material for the natural sciences.

And Pliny was no exception. It was the same with the *Natural Questions* concocted by the philosopher Seneca. And the bearer of another famous name, the Roman physician Galen, never bothered with research in the interests of new knowledge. All he did was put together existing material and report on it. Even a man of science like Claudius Ptolemaeus, who lived in the second century A.D. in Alexandria, did not recognize the importance of one of the greatest and most revolutionary discoveries of the Greeks, and yet his textbooks on astronomy, mathematics, and geography were considered the last word down to the beginning of modern times and obstructed all progress. His compilations were no advance on early Greek thinkers. He did not accept what Aristarchus of Samos had discovered four centuries earlier, namely, that the sun does not revolve around the earth, but the earth around the sun. In his main work, the *Almagest,* he asserted the long-outdated, retrograde view that the earth and man were the center of the cosmos.

He thus provided the pseudo-scientific equipment for the disastrous, anthropocentric delusions of medieval scholastic philosophy, which penalized any progress. So things remained, until Copernicus, on the basis of ancient sources, laboriously rediscovered the old Greek heliocentric system.

In philosophy, too, thought became increasingly shallow. It lacked the wide-ranging view and capacity to pose new problems, to generate new ideas. The old masters were canonized and the old theories rehashed, in particular those of Platonism and the Stoa. To dress up old ideas and circulate popular, undemanding philosophic commonplaces was considered enough. Throughout the Roman empire there began an unparalleled intellectual retrogression, a process of decay and atrophy in that scientific thought which centuries earlier had made a breakthrough among the Greeks and could lay claim to immortal triumphs. Philosophical speculation abandoned the main road of pure investigation, of the critical approach, and took to the sidetrack of emotional and religious fantasy.

The Stoics began to intensify belief in all kinds of "revelations" through portents and dreams, inspirations and visions, and through the course of the heavenly bodies, as well as belief in oracles and prophecies. Elements of a magic faith in fate and the stars were mixed up with the ideas of genuine Greek science. During the first century of the Imperial Age neo-Pythagorean doctrines gained currency. Falsely attributed to Pythagoras and his followers, these were a faked mass of pseudo-philosophical writing that attempted to smuggle demons and magic into philosophy. And the scientist Ptolemaeus wrote a book on astrology.

These developments were the beginning of intellectual decay. The mind lost its powers of resistance to belief in authority, to the incursions of mysticism and mythology. In place of progress through reason, man was once again entangled in the web of supernatural relationships that theology and superstition cast over earthly existence.

The line Thucydides drew between truth and hearsay was blurred. The saying of Epicharmus of Crastus, in the fifth century B.C., that doubt makes the mind supple, which inspired ancient thought to its highest achievements, was forgotten. Beginning with philosophy the same decadence appeared in all intellectual disciplines.

The belief in signs and wonders flourished once again, and not only in Suetonius's *Lives of the Caesars*. Even so cultivated a man as Plutarch thinks that one should not reject out of hand stories about images of the gods sweating and sighing, speaking and closing their eyes. Even he submits, "if history with many valid testimonies obliges us to believe."

From such an attitude among the most cultured pagans it was only a step to the miracles wrought by relics which Christianity used for the defense and glorification of the new religion. Even St. Augustine did not disdain to include in his famous work *De civitate Dei* as attested historical fact the most improbable stories of miraculous cures effected by relics, indeed, even of the resurrection of the dead.

The course was set which culminated in the stultification, the darkness of the Middle Ages. The intellectual "development" that was laid down was to be the fate of the christianized inhabitants of Europe for more than fifteen hundred years.

Rome proved unable to follow in Greece's footsteps and to complete what she had begun. She had neither the needed ability and greatness nor the will and the power. Etruria, which cast a religious spell for centuries over the Romans, thus in the end, long after it had been vanquished, proved to be more powerful than Hellas. The conquered triumphed over the world's conqueror.

And when the teaching of Jesus was officially recognized, its representatives made that same city which the Etruscans once founded, which was the heart of the Roman empire, into the base of their own, Roman Catholic empire. On the Tiber a new priestly hierarchy, whose teaching was directed to the poor and humble, forgot the exemplary simplicity of its founder, donned splendid, elaborate vestments and appropriated the insignia of an archaic, orientalized age—insignia which the Romans had taken over from Etruscan kings and priests more than a thousand years earlier. The purple of Etruscan kings, which for centuries adorned Rome's victorious generals in their triumphs, became the color of the cardinals. The *lituus,* the curved staff of Etruscan *haruspices,* became the bishops' crozier. However differ-

> *And when the teaching of Jesus was officially recognized, its representatives made that same city which the Etruscans once founded, which was the heart of the Roman empire, into the base of their own, Roman Catholic empire.*

ent the doctrines, the new and the old were nevertheless closely alike, in their external forms and their claim to infallibility.

"A power admitting no rival, all-ruling, all-regulating, all-requiring." Thus Dennis describes the religion of the Etruscans. "Such was its sway, that it moulded the national character, and gave the Etruscans a pre-eminently religious reputation among the people of antiquity. Like the Roman Catholic in after-times, it was a religion of mysteries, of marvels, of ceremonial pomp and observances."

He adds: "Yet it was her system of spiritual tyranny that rendered Etruria inferior to Greece. She had the same arts—an equal amount of scientific knowledge—a more extended commerce. In every field had the Etruscan mind liberty to expand, save in that wherein lies man's highest delight and glory. Before the gate of that paradise where the intellect revels unfettered among speculations on its own nature, on its origin, existence and final destiny, on its relation to the First Cause, to other minds, and to society in general—stood the sacerdotal Lucumo, brandishing in one hand the double-edged sword of secular and ecclesiastical authority, and holding forth in the other the books of Tages, exclaiming, to his awe-struck subjects, 'Believe and obey!' Liberty of thought and action was as incompatible with the assumption of infallibility in the governing power in the days of Tarchon or Porsena, as in those of Pius IX."

"With such shackles as were imposed on it, it was impossible for the Etruscan mind, individually or collectively, to reach the highest degree of culture"—such as that of Hellas—"to which society, even in those early ages, attained."

It was to be no different for the Christian peoples of Europe for more than a thousand years. They remained in fetters, were confined by a theological doctrine that would suffer no rival, that presented a topography of heaven, earth, paradise, and hell which, even before it was invented, was already outdated by Greek science.

The Etruscan discipline was destroyed. It is impossible to say to what extent it may have had an influence on alchemy, gnosticism, and the mystery religions, on the intellectual life of late antiquity, and hence on the teaching of the church. Nor do we know anything about the conversion to Christianity of the former Etruscan lands. All we know is that many of the old city-states became episcopal sees, among them Roselle, Volterra, Arezzo, and Orvieto.

In the places where the Etruscan priest-kings once ruled, thenceforth resided the spiritual princes of the new priestly hierarchy, with their pomp and ceremony. Within the cyclopean walls where once the Etruscan temples crowned the heights, there now arose the churches of the new religion. They were often built on exactly the same site, on the old foundations. And inside them the bronze censers were swung to and fro, just as had been done at the religious ceremonies of the Etruscans, to diffuse the sweet perfume of incense.

We can only guess at what other ancient relics of the Etruscans still lie buried under the churches and cathedrals of Tuscany. There have been no comprehensive systematic explorations of these places. Even the very walls of the churches may contain, under the plaster, many interesting fragments, incorporated in the masonry.

Etruscologists have so far barely glanced at these still untouched archeological sources. And yet anyone who goes about Etruria with an observant eye can hardly fail to notice everywhere unmistakable evidence of the interconnections between the archaic Etruscan age and medieval Christianity.

To the east of Lake Bolsena, on a steep hill continually threatened by landslides, is Bagnoregio which, in the sixth century, was chosen as an episcopal see. Stone lions mount guard at the gate. They hold human heads in their paws, a common Etruscan motif. In the dusky interior of S. Donato hang broad, brightly colored ribbons—reminiscent perhaps of the festoons, looped from tree to tree, that are to be seen in Etruscan tomb paintings.

At Tuscania, halfway between Tarquinia and Viterbo, stands the cathedral of S. Pietro, now severely damaged after an earthquake in the spring of 1971. The church is believed to have been built on the site of an Etruscan citadel. Incorporated in the facade is a rectangular slab carved in relief, depicting an Etruscan dancer with upraised arms. On the right of the facade a devil with a trifacial head looks out. Like the demons and the Charun of Etruscan tombs he holds a snake in his hands.

At the time when Christian churches were being built amid the ruined and rebuilt cities of the Etruscans, knowledge of their history and achievements was already largely lost. But the countryside was still permeated by their ancient cults, rites, and customs, and the evidence of them was on all sides. Within sight of the city walls stretched the vast cemeteries, tomb after tomb along the proces-

Etruscan sculpture of a dancer inserted into the facade of the twelfth-century cathedral of San Pietro, Toscanella

sional ways, often extending over several miles. The tombs, so carefully hewn out of the rock, painted with frescoes and packed with gifts, preserved a faithful reflection of the religious ritual and the daily life of the civilization which the Roman legionaries had destroyed. The living were haunted by the inescapable, if shadowy, remembrance of a great and ancient people. And this past, which was still so mysteriously present and tangible, continued to exercise its powerful influence. The descendants of the Etruscan artists who painted the walls of the subterranean tombs, who cast the bronze temple doors and carved the sides and covers of sarcophagi with reliefs, were now at work creating the images of the new Christian religion.

It is hardly surprising that the sinister representation of the underworld which we found in Etruscan times reappears in the church art of Tuscany, in central and northern Italy. Or that the terrifying demons reemerge along with the winged beings who accompanied the dead on their last journey. The figures with which Etruria peopled the world of the dead migrated into the new churches. They lived on in the plastic images, just as we find among the medieval mystics symbols and figures from the Etruscan world of shadows.

The conception of Hell with all its terrors, which came with Christianity and was unknown to the Old Testament, found its first expression on the soil of ancient Etruria, and was more sinister and more powerful there than elsewhere. The images which were first created in tombs during the decline and death struggle of the Etruscan nation reappeared from the depths and, transposed and reshaped, expressed the gloomy and macabre visions of the new faith. Amid the tortures and fears of the Christian Purgatory and Hell sits enthroned the commanding figure of Satan.

Romanesque and Gothic church art revived the ancient cult symbols, fabulous creatures, and wild beasts of the Orient, some of which the Etruscans were the first to introduce in the West and which they acclimatized in their empire.

Does he not recall the grim demons who inhabit the sepulchers of late Etruria? Surely the monstrous Charun with vulturine nose and pointed ears is his prototype.

Even the symbol of the heavy hammer with which he delivers the stroke of death lived on in the ritual that surrounds the death of the Pontifex Maximus. In the treasury of St. Peter's in Rome is a silver hammer with which the cardinal *camerlengo,* or chamberlain, strikes three times the temples of the dead pope.

Along with Charun as Satan, other figures of the Etruscan underworld to be seen in the reliefs and frescoes of tombs and sarcophagi made their reappearance. The winged beings who accompany the dead on their last journey came back, with other duties, and no longer armed with serpents.

Romanesque and Gothic church art revived the ancient cult symbols, fabulous creatures, and wild beasts of the Orient, some of which the Etruscans were the first to introduce in the West and which they acclimatized in their empire. Such were the six-headed Scylla, the lions, serpents, and griffins, the winged horses, the dragons, and chimeras. These weird creatures, spawned in an archaic world, made their way into the new churches. They squat on capitals and cornices. Engaged in murderous combat with one another, they appear on pulpits and porches.

The Etruscan chimera can be seen in the floor mosaic of Aosta cathedral, as also at Milan in the pulpit of S. Ambrogio. The dread figures that sculptors carved in stone were likewise depicted by painters on altarpieces, and in their visions of Hell on church and cemetery walls. In the Strozzi chapel of S. Maria Novella, Florence, Nardo di Cione painted a Last Judgment and Hell; Orcagna and assistants painted them and a Triumph of Death in S. Croce; in the Campo Santo, Pisa, an artist who cannot be securely identified, painted the same subjects. At the end of the fifteenth century, in Orvieto, on its tufa plateau surrounded by Etruscan burials in the valley, Luca Signorelli painted the end of the world on the walls of a chapel in the cathedral. And Dante in his *Divine Comedy* described the terror, torment, and pain of souls in Purgatory and Hell, outside which prowl the mysterious beasts of prey, the leopard, the lion, and the she-wolf.

But with Dante, born in 1265 at Florence, we are on the eve of events which were to influence all Europe and open the way to a new freedom. They were to usher in a new age, to lead out of the medieval centuries of superstition and ignorance dominated by papal Rome, in which every independent mind was suppressed.

Now at last the liberation was to begin from the after-effects of that world which the Etruscans brought into Italy, a world imbued with myth and magic.

In many places, especially in the north toward the Apennines, life went on, despite temporary setbacks after the collapse of the Roman empire, much as it had always done. Once more, towns big and small flourished in the very same places as at the time of the Etruscan League of Twelve; some of them actually enjoyed a considerable prosperity. A new splendor brightened ancient names like Arezzo, Perugia, Volterra, and Cortona, as well as Siena and Florence on the Arno, at the foot of ancient Fiesole. They too created city-states, each following its own policy and maintaining its individuality, in fact each displaying just that particularism which was so marked among the Etruscans.

The pioneer spirit and the talents of former times must have survived in the descendants of the ancient masters of the land between the Arno and the Tiber, despite the intermixture of Roman colonists. The genius of the Etruscan element in the population seems to have been inherited through generation after generation. For how else are we to explain that the great new start came in precisely those cities, and not in Rome or Byzantium? It was Tuscany, of all places, whose very name preserves that of its former inhabitants, which became the scene of the new awakening. Here and nowhere else the spark was struck which lit a clear, radiant light in the darkness of the times. It was as though it had been granted to the descendants of the Etruscans to make good what the latter had never achieved, to make the leap from myth to reason, from an archaic age to a modern one. In their cities and villages those great men were born whose names are still linked with the dawn of modern times.

The great rebirth came in the heart of the Italian peninsula, despite Rome's muzzling of science and religion, despite her tutelage. The ancient land of the Etruscans became the cradle of humanism and the *Rinascimento,* the Renaissance.

It is to Francesco Petrarca, the Father of Humanism, that we owe the rediscovery of classical literature, which in the early Middle Ages had almost fallen into oblivion. He was born in 1304 at Arezzo, the Tuscan city which was probably the birthplace of Maecenas, whose patronage contributed much to the first efflorescence of Roman poetry. Petrarch, Dante Alighieri of Florence, and his countryman Giovanni Boccaccio, of a Tuscan family, constitute the great triumvirate. Machiavelli, who two centuries later represented the political side of humanism, was also a Florentine.

From Tuscany, too, came the new beginning in the plastic arts. "It was on the Etruscan soil," says Dennis, "that the seeds of culture, dormant through the long winter of barbarism, broke forth anew when a genial spring smiled on the human intellect: it was in Etruria that immortality was first bestowed on the lyre, the canvas, the marble, the literature, the science of modern Europe."

But the new movement took its inspiration not from the Roman model, nor even from that of classical Greece. The great stimulus came from the ancient creations of Etruria, still visible above and below ground. What had been begun and was then interrupted when the Etruscan people were subjugated by the Roman legions, was resumed and developed in a new and better shape. Suddenly the soil of Etruria gave birth to a whole series of creative geniuses.

The finest triumphs of the Renaissance were concentrated in Florence. It was here that the great, immortal masters worked in architecture, painting, and sculpture. Leonardo, born at the little village of Vinci near Florence, and Michelangelo, from the Tuscan township Caprese, both worked there. So did Filippo Brunelleschi, born in Florence, the architect and real founder of Renaissance architecture, and Giotto, from Colle di Vespignano, near Florence, the founder of Italian painting and master of the Tuscan art of fresco.

It was then that final perfection was given to the ancient, circular form which first appeared in the West with the tumuli of the great Etruscan tombs. Florence saw the first dome of modern times when Brunelleschi in 1420–34 built the wonderful cupola of the cathedral S. Maria del Fiore. This was the model for Michelangelo's mighty dome at St. Peter's, Rome. And on the Piazza S. Pietro, one of the finest squares in the world, the Tuscan column was reborn. Bernini used for his masterpiece the two great colonnades, the simple and severe Tuscan form, developed from the Doric, which had once graced the temples of the Etruscans.

In the cloister of the Museo Civico at Viterbo are to be seen slabs with inscriptions in which the citizens of Renaissance times proudly describe themselves as descendants of the Etruscans. Such deliberate acknowledgment is rare. But the productions of the age are unthinkable without the great models of the country's past. Tracing connections and relationships between Etruscan art and works of the Renaissance has led to the most surprising discoveries.

Nicola Pisano, the sculptor of the pulpits at Pisa and Siena and one of the greatest medieval Italian artists, is said by Vasari to have spent some time at Volterra where he doubtless studied the Etruscan carved alabaster funerary urns, large numbers of which still exist. In any case, his pulpit in the Baptistery at Pisa shows Etruscan influence. "The reclining figure of the Virgin," says John Pope-Hennessy, "is related to Etruscan grave figures." Jacopo della Quercia and Michelangelo were also admirers of Etruscan sarcophagi and their miniature models, the ash-chests.

Michelangelo's works seem to reveal echoes of Etruscan art. His relief of the battle of the Titans recalls scenes on Volterra urns, as does his *Pietà* in the Florence cathedral. One of his drawings shows Aita, the god of the Etruscan underworld, with his head covered by a wolf's snout, just as he appears in Etruscan tomb frescoes. Michelangelo's figure of Christ, with right arm upraised, in the Sistine Chapel *Last Judgment,* has been held to show a resemblance to the Etruscan Aita depicted in the Tomba dell'Orco at Tarquinia, with left arm raised and right outstretched.

> **Michelangelo's works seem to reveal echoes of Etruscan art.**

The reclining figures on Etruscan sarcophagi, a motif that was adopted by the Romans, were also used in Romanesque art. And Etruscan architectural forms were revived in Florentine Renaissance palaces. A terra-cotta funerary urn from Chiusi looks like a model for the Palazzo Strozzi. Painted coffered ceilings recall the underground chamber tombs hewn out of the tufa rock.

There is a striking affinity, as Raymond Bloch points out, between the head of Donatello's St. George and the Etruscan head of a young man found at Veii, and now in the Villa Giulia Museum in Rome, despite the difference of material, the former being in marble and the latter in terra-cotta.

There are innumerable parallels. Those given above are merely a selection, chosen more or less at random. Hitherto there has been no systematic investigation of the connections and relationships stretching over two thousand years, fascinating and full of surprises though they are.

Historically, one thing is certain. When the Etruscans spread their advanced civilization and culture in Italy, at a time when all else there was still prehistoric, they set in motion the emergence and ascendance of western Europe. Fifteen hundred years after the decline of that gifted people in the lands they had once inhabited, humanism and the Renaissance started another momentous epoch for the West, an epoch in which the gate was flung wide open from the darkness of the Middle Ages into modern times.

Appendixes

Chronology

Etruria	Rome	Greece and the rest of the world
8th century B.C.		
Around 750: First evidence of Etruscan culture.	Hut settlements on the Tiber.	Homer in Ionia, Asia Minor. Greek colonies in south Italy and Sicily. Foundation of Cumae. Carthage dominates western seas. 745–727: Tiglath-pileser III, founder of second Assyrian empire. 738–696: Midas, king of Phrygia. 725–711: Syrian states annexed by Assyria. 721: Fall of Samaria, capital of the northern Kingdom of Israel. 720: Assyrian conquest of Urartu.

Etruria	Rome	Greece and the rest of the world

	7th century B.C.	
Tumuli, painted tomb chambers, sumptuous graves of princes. Etruscan coastal towns with mining, industry, crafts, and international trade. Etruscan sea power.	Etruscan expansion in Latium. c.625: Beginning of the Tarquins' sway on the Tiber. Drainage of valleys. 607–569: Tarquinius Priscus.	Around 700: Hesiod speaks of Tyrsenians. 671: Assyria conquers Egypt. 624–546: Thales of Miletus. Beginning of Ionian natural philosophy. 612: Fall of Nineveh, end of Assyrian empire. 612–538: Neo-Babylonian empire. c.610: Lydian empire in Asia Minor.

	6th century B.C.	
Greatest extent of Etruscan empire. Leagues of Twelve in the Po valley and in Campania. First trade with northern Europe, especially with Celts. Revolt of the brothers Vibenna against priest monarchy. c.545: Etruscan-Carthaginian alliance against Greece. 535: Etruscan-Carthaginian naval victory at Alalia. c.508: Porsena takes Rome. Land route to Campania interrupted.	575: Pebbling of the Forum, foundation of Rome as city. Jupiter temple begun. Construction of Circus Maximus. Etruscan triumph and insignia adopted. 569–525: Servius Tullius, 2nd Etruscan king. Centuriate order. 525–509: Tarquinius Superbus, 3rd Etruscan king. Builder of Jupiter temple and Cloaca Maxima. 509: Fall of Tarquin dynasty. Republic proclaimed by Etruscan nobles.	600: Phocaeans found Marseilles. 594: Solon's code of law. 586: Destruction of Jerusalem. c.560–547: Croesus, king of Lydia. 547: Persians conquer Lydia. 525: Cambyses conquers Egypt. 521–486: Darius I, king of Persia.

Etruria	Rome	Greece and the rest of the world
5th century B.C.		
483–474: Early wars of Veii with Rome.	494: Rising of the plebeians.	499–494: Ionian revolt.
474: Etruscan fleet defeated at Cumae by Syracusans.	477: Fabians annihilated. Fighting with Etruscans, Sabines, Aequi, and Volsci.	494: Sack of Miletus.
453: Syracusan fleet raids Etruscan coastal towns, Elba, Corsica.	450: Law of the Twelve Tables.	490–449: Persian Wars.
438–425: Veii's second major war with Rome.	449: End of wars against the Sabines.	486–465: Xerxes.
428: Death of Veii's king L. Tolumnius.		480: Greeks defeat Persian fleet at Salamis, and Carthaginians at Himera.
c.425: Fall of Capua. Samnites take Etruscan cities in Campania.		?484–?419: Herodotus.
414–413: Etruscan sea and land forces fight with Athens against Syracuse.		478–467: Hieron I of Syracuse.
406: Beginning of the Roman siege of Veii.		447–432: Construction of the Parthenon in Athens.
		446–429: Periclean Age in Athens.
		431–404: Peloponnesian War.
		c.429–347: Plato.
		415–413: Athenian campaign against Sicily.
		c.400: Dionysius I, tyrant of Syracuse.
4th century B.C.		
396: Fall of Veii and Melpum. Gauls invade Po valley. Fighting for Sutri and Nepi in south Etruria.	390: Battle on the Allia. Gauls under Brennus capture and sack Rome.	399: Death of Socrates.
384: Dionysius I of Syracuse raids Pyrgi. End of Etruscan mastery of Tyrrhenian Sea.		385: Plato founds Academy.
358: Tarquinii and Faliscans make war on Rome.		384–322: Aristotle.
351: Tarquinii granted forty-year truce.	343–341: First Samnite War.	Mid-century: Heraclides Ponticus

Etruria	Rome	Greece and the rest of the world
323: Etruscan embassy to Alexander the Great at Babylon. 308: Tarquinii granted second forty-year truce. 302: Social unrest at Arezzo.	340–338: War against Latins. 326–304: Second Samnite War. 310: Romans cross Ciminian forest. 306: Rome's treaty with Carthage.	teaches earth's axial rotation. 336–323: Conquests of Alexander the Great. 323–281: Macedonian generals fight for Alexander's succession.

3rd century B.C.

Etruria	Rome	Greece and the rest of the world
295: Alliance of Etruscans, Gauls, Samnites, and Umbrians defeated at Sentinum. 283: Etruscans and Gauls defeated at Lake Vadimo. 280: Fall of Vulci and Volsinii. 273: Roman colony at Cosa. 264: Sack of Volsinii. 247: Roman colony at Alsium. 245: Roman colony at Fregenae. 225: Gauls invade Etruria. Battle of Telamon. Etruscans welcome Hannibal, sabotage acts against Rome. 209: Unrest at Arezzo. Etruscan volunteers join Hasdrubal and Mago. Treason trials in Etruria. 205: Etruscan cities' contributions for Scipio's war.	298–290: Third Samnite War. 282: King Pyrrhus in Italy. 264–241: First Punic War. 264: Etruscan gladiatorial combat introduced in Rome. 218–201: Second Punic War. Hannibal in Italy. 216: Battle of Cannae. 202: Battle of Zama.	270–100: Great age of Hellenistic civilization.

Etruria	Rome	Greece and the rest of the world
2nd century B.C.		
183: Roman colony at Saturnia. 181: Roman colony at Graviscae.	149–146: Third Punic War. 146: Destruction of Carthage. 133: Agrarian Law of Tiberius Gracchus.	
1st century B.C.		
88: Beginning of 9th saeculum. 82: Sulla's bloodbath in Etruria. 80: Volterra capitulates. 44: Beginning of 10th saeculum. 40: War for Perugia. Etruria becomes Seventh Region. Maecenas, friend and adviser of Augustus.	91–88: Social War. 88: Sulla against Marius. 83: Jupiter temple burns down. 44: Death of Caesar. 42: Battle of Philippi.	
1st century A.D.		
	Claudius writes *Tyrrhenica*. 54: Death of Claudius.	

The Etruscan Alphabet

Comparison with other ancient forms of the alphabet
reproduced from the work of Professor M. Lopes Pegna

Phoenician	Hebrew	Early Greek	Etruscan	Latin
𐤀	𐤀	A	A	A
𐤁	𐤁	B	>	B
𐤂	𐤂	Λ		C
𐤃	𐤃	Δ		D
𐤄	𐤄	E	∃	E
𐤅	𐤅	F	Ⅎ 8	F
𐤆	𐤆	I	I	Z
𐤇	𐤇	𐌇	𐌇	H
𐤈	𐤈	⊕	⊗	
𐤉	𐤉	I	I	I
𐤊	𐤊	K	𐌊	K
𐤋	𐤋	𐌋	𐌋	L
𐤌	𐤌	M	𐌌	M
𐤍	𐤍	N	𐌍	N
𐤎	𐤎	Ⱶ		
𐤏	𐤏	O		O
𐤐	𐤐	P	ꟼ	P
𐤑	𐤑	Ϙ	Ϙ	Q
𐤒	𐤒	P	𐌓	R
𐤓	𐤓	M	M	
𐤔	𐤔	Ϲ	3	S
𐤕	𐤕	Y	Y	V
		X	X ↓	X

423

Etruscan Sites and Museums in Italy

Abbreviations

A: Autostrada   Prov.: Province
SS: National Highway (Strada Statale)

Adria (Prov. Rovigo).   SS 16 or A 13 to Rovigo, then 23 km. due E. Museo Civico: local Etruscan finds.

Arezzo (Arretium).   Autostrada del Sole Florence–Rome. Museo Archeologico Mecenate: *Bucchero,* bronzes, Arretine vases. Remains of possibly Etruscan wall in N.E. of the city.

Bieda (Blera) (Prov. Viterbo).   SS 2 (Via Cassia) Viterbo–Rome, W. at Cura, about 3 km. S. of Vetralla. Necropolis, rock tombs with architectural facades. Etruscan bridge across Biedano. Remains of walls.

Bologna (Felsina).   Autostrada del Sole. Museo Civico: finds from Felsina cemeteries, bronze situla from Certosa.

Bolsena (Volsinii) (Prov. Viterbo).   SS 2 (Via Cassia) Viterbo–Chianciano. Tombs, walls, temple ruins.

Bomarzo (Prov. Viterbo).   SS 204 Viterbo–Orte, N. at km. 16.1. Remains of walls and drainage canals. Tombs: Grotta dipinta, Grotta della Colonna.

Brescia. A 4 Milan–Venice. Museo Archeologico: Etruscan vases, finds from Arezzo and Orvieto.

Capua (Prov. Caserta). A 2 Rome–Naples, exit Caserta or S. Maria Capua Vetere. Museo Campano: terra-cottas.

Cerveteri (Cisra, Caere) (Prov. Rome). SS 1 (Via Aurelia) or A 16. Banditaccia necropolis: chamber tombs and tumuli, Regolini–Galassi tomb. Museum in castle.

Chiusi (Camars, Clusium) (Prov. Siena). SS 71 Orvieto–Cortona, or Autostrada del Sole, exit Chianciano. Museo Archeologico Nazionale: *Bucchero,* painted vases, bronzes. Tombs: of the Monkey, del Granduca, del Colle. 5 km. N.E. at Poggio Gaiella: supposed tomb of Lars Porsena.

Civita Castellana (Falerii) (Prov. Viterbo). SS 3 (Via Flaminia), turn off W. at 53 km. from Rome. Cemeteries, temple ruins.

Corchiano (Prov. Viterbo). SS 3 (Via Flaminia) to Civita Castellana, take road N.W. to Carbognano, turn right after about 11 km. Tombs with inscriptions. Drainage canals.

Cortona (Curtun) (Prov. Arezzo). SS 71 Arezzo–Orvieto, 29 km. S. of Arezzo. Museo dell'Accademia Etrusca: bronze lamp. Tombs: di Pitagora, del Sodo, Sergardi (Melone di Camuscia).

Ferrara. SS 16 (Via Adriatica) or A 13 Padua–Bologna. Museo Archeologico Nazionale: finds from Spina.

Fiesole (Faesulae), above Florence. Remains of Etruscan temple. Museum: Etruscan and Roman finds.

Florence. Autostrada del Sole. Museo Archeologico: Etruscan pottery, including François vase, bronzes (*Chimera, Orator*), gold and silver work, coins. Tomb reconstructions.

Grosseto. SS 1 (Via Aurelia), 183 km. from Rome. Museo Archeologico: finds from Roselle and Vetulonia.

Mantua. A 22 Verona–Modena. Museo Archeologico in the Palazzo Ducale: Etruscan antiquities.

Marsiliana d'Albegna (prov. Grosseto). SS 1 (Via Aurelia), SS 74 inland at Stazione di Albinia 32 km. S. of Grosseto, turn right at about 12 km. Cemeteries: Poggio Macchiabuia and Banditella.

Marzabotto (Misa) (near Bologna). Autostrada del Sole Bologna–Florence, exit Sasso Marconi, SS 64 (Via Porrettana) for about 8 km. Two cemeteries, town and temple ruins; local finds in the Museo Pompeo Aria.

Massa Marittima (Prov. Grosseto). SS 1 (Via Aurelia), SS 439 at Follonica for about 18 km. Etruscan ruins.

Milan. Civico Museo Archeologico: Etruscan coin collection.

Montepulciano (Prov. Siena). Autostrada del Sole Florence–Rome, exit Chianciano to SS 146, 9 km. N.W. of Chianciano. Urns with inscriptions on the facade of Palazzo Bucelli, Etruscan collection in Palazzo Tarugi.

Nepi (Nepet) (Prov. Rome). SS 2 (Via Cassia) Rome–Viterbo, SS 311 at Bivio di Monterosi. After 6 km. walls and tombs on the right.

Norchia (Prov. Viterbo). SS 2 (Via Cassia) Rome–Viterbo as far as Vetralla, N.W. to Casalone. Necropolis, rock tombs with temple facades.

Orvieto. Autostrada del Sole Florence–Rome. Necropolis at Crocifisso del Tufa. Painted tombs in vicinity (Castel Rubello, Settecamini). Museo Civico in the Palazzo Faina: sculptures, fine vases, bronzes from the vicinity.

Palermo (Sicily). Museo Archeologico: Etruscan collection with finds from Chiusi.

Pavia. A 7 Milan–Genoa. Istituto Archeologico dell'Università: Etruscan bronzes from the Po valley.

Perugia (Perusia). Autostrada del Sole Florence–Rome, exit Betolle. Museo Archeologico Nazionale dell'Umbria: Etruscan urns. Two Etruscan gates: Arco d'Augusto and Porta Marzia. Tombs in vicinity: Ipogeo dei Volumni, Tomba di S. Manno.

Piacenza (Placentia). Autostrada del Sole Milan–Bologna. Museo Civico: Bronze liver.

Populonia (Pupluna) (Prov. Livorno). SS 1 (Via Aurelia) Livorno–Grosseto to San Vicenzo, due S. along the coast in direction Piombino, right after 12.3 km. Acropolis walls. Porto Baratti necropolis; tumulus graves.

Porto Clementino (Graviscae) (Prov. Viterbo). SS 1 (Via Aurelia) Rome–Orbetello to Tarquinia, branch off to the coast. Remains of the old harbor of Tarquinii.

Rome. (1) Museo Capitolino: bronze she-wolf, finds from Caere. (2) Museo Baracco: tomb reliefs from Chiusi. (3) Museo Etrusco Gregoriano (Vatican): Regolini–Galassi tomb, Mars of Todi. (4) Villa Giulia (Museo Nazionale delle Antichità del Lazio): contents of the Barberini and Bernardini tombs from Palestrina (Praeneste); finds from Cerveteri: Ficorini cista, terra-cotta sarcophagus; from Veii: Apollo and head of Hermes. Tomb groups from most of Latium and southern Etruria. (5) Museo di Villa Albani: frescoes from Vulci. Not usually open to public.

Roselle (Rusellae) (near Grosseto). SS 223 (Via Rosellana) for about 8 km. to signpost "Rovine di Roselle." Walls, remains of gates.

Santa Maria Capua Vetere (Capua) (Prov. Caserta). A 2 Rome–Naples. Antiquarium: finds from Capua.

Santa Severa (Pyrgi) (Prov. Rome). SS 1 (Via Aurelia) from Rome, about 20 km. before Civitavecchia. Vestiges of Caere's port. Foundations of two temples recently excavated by Pallottino and Colonna.

Siena. SS 2 (Via Cassia) or direct road from Florence. Museo Etrusco Senese: *Bucchero,* vases, sculptures, bronzes.

Sovana (Suana) (Prov. Grosseto). SS 1 (Via Aurelia) to Orbetello turnoff, SS 74 to Pitigliano, N. on unmetaled road for 8 km. Rock tombs with architectural facades, chamber tombs.

Sutri (Sutrium) (Prov. Viterbo). SS 2 (Via Cassia) Rome–Viterbo. Chamber tombs, traces of defenses and drainage canals. Etrusco–Roman amphitheater.

Talamonaccio (Telamon) (Prov. Grosseto). SS 1 (Via Aurelia) Grosseto–Rome, at Fonteblanda W. to Talamone. Soon after Fonteblanda, on the right of the road, hill and excavation site, remains of fortifications.

Tarquinia (Tarquinii) (Prov. Viterbo). SS 1 (Via Aurelia) Rome–Orbetello. Museo Nazionale Tarquiniense: sarcophagi, detached tomb frescoes. Necropolis: famous painted tombs. Remains of old city walls.

Todi (Prov. Perugia). SS 3, at 47 km. S. of Perugia turn right into SS 79. Museo Civico: gold and iron objects, bronzes, terra-cottas, Etruscan coin collection.

Turin. A 4. Museo Archeologico in the Palazzo dell'Accademia delle Scienze: Etruscan urns and vases.

Tuscania (Prov. Viterbo). SS 1 (Via Aurelia), just N. of Tarquinia turn inland for 24 km.; or SS 2 (Via Cassia), just N. of Vetralla turn left for 21 km. Tombs: Tomba Grotta della Regina with several stories of subterranean passages, Tomba del Carcarello, Tomba della Televisione. Small museum with sarcophagi.

Veii (near Rome). SS 2 (Via Cassia), about 17 km. from Rome to La Storta, turn off E. to Isola Farnese: ruins of temples, subterranean passages and water conduits. Ponte Sodo, tunnel for river Valchetta (Cremera). Two painted tombs: Campana and Tomba delle Anatre.

Vetulonia (Vetluna) (Prov. Grosseto). SS 1 (Via Aurelia) Grosseto–Folonica, at Grilli turn S. on a side road signposted Castiglione della Pescaia, and then almost immediately left. Remains of city walls. Tumulus tombs: della Pietrera, del Diavolino.

Viterbo (Surina). SS 2 (Via Cassia). Museo Civico: sarcophagi, inscriptions. Etruscan bridge: Ponte del Castello.

Volterra (Velathri, Volaterrae) (Prov. Pisa). SS 1 (Via Aurelia) Grosseto–Livorno, turn E. at Cecina into SS 68 for about 40 km.

Walls and gates: Porta all'Arco and Porta di Diana. Museo Etrusco Guarnacci: Villanovan pottery, Etruscan alabaster urns and sarcophagi, bronzes, terra-cottas, etc.

Vulci (Prov. Viterbo) (ruins). SS 1 (Via Aurelia), 16 km. N. of Tarquinia turn E. at Montalto di Castro on SS 312, turn left after about 13.5 km. Necropolis: tumuli (Cucumella and Cucumelletta) and the famous painted François tomb. Ponte della Badia. City ruins. Small antiquarium in the castle by the Ponte della Badia.

Suggestions for Further Reading

Classical Works

Sources of English version
LCL: Loeb Classical Library   Bohn: Bohn's Classical Library

Aelian. *De natura animalium*. Translated by A. F. Scholfield. LCL, 1959.
Appian. *Roman History*. Translated by Horace White. LCL, 1912–13.
   Vols. 1, 3, 4.
Aristotle. *The Politics*. Translated by T. A. Sinclair. Penguin, 1962.
Arrian. *The Campaigns of Alexander*. Translated by Aubrey de Sélin-
   court. Penguin, rev. ed., 1971.
Caesar. *The Civil War*. Translated by Jane F. Mitchell. Penguin, 1967.
Cicero. *The Speeches*. LCL, 1923–61.
   De lege agraria. Translated by John Henry Freese. 1961.
   Pro Caecina. Translated by H. Grose Hodge. 1927.
   In Catilinam, Pro Murena. Translated by Louis E. Lord. 1937.
   De re publica, De legibus. Translated by Clinton Walker Keyes.
   1928.
————. *De divinatione*, in *De senectute, de amicitia, de divinatione*.
   Translated by William Armistead Falconer. LCL, 1923.

————. *Letters to Atticus*. Translated by E. O. Winstedt. 3 vols. LCL, 1913–19.

Diodorus Siculus. *The Library of History*. Translated by C. H. Oldfather, C. L. Sherman, C. Bradford Welles, Russel M. Geer, F. R. Walton. LCL, 1939–63. Vols. 3, 4, 6, 10.

Dionysius of Halicarnassus. *Roman Antiquities*. Translated by Ernest Cary. LCL, 1937–45. Vols. 1, 2, 3, 4.

Florus. *Epitome of Roman History*. Translated by Edward Seymour Forster. LCL, 1929.

Herodotus. *The Histories*. Translated by Aubrey de Sélincourt. Penguin, 1954.

Horace. *Satires,* in *Satires, Epistles and Ars Poetica*. Translated by H. Rushton Fairclough. LCL, 1926.

Juvenal. *The Sixteen Satires*. Translated by Peter Green. Penguin, 1967.

Livy. *History of Rome*. Translated by B. O. Foster, F. G. Moore, Evan T. Sage, Alfred C. Schlesinger. LCL, 1919–59. Vols. 3, 4, 9, 11, 13.

————. *The Early History of Rome* (Books I–V). Translated by Aubrey de Sélincourt. Penguin, 1960.

————. *The War with Hannibal* (Books XXI–XXX). Translated by Aubrey de Sélincourt. Penguin, 1965.

Lucretius. *On the Nature of the Universe*. Translated by Ronald Latham. Penguin, 1951.

Pindar. *The Odes of Pindar*. Translated by Richmond Lattimore. University of Chicago Press, 1947.

Pliny the Elder. *Natural History*. Translated by H. Rackham. Books III–VII, LCL, 1942. Vol. 2.

————. *Natural History*. Translated by John Bostock and H. T. Riley. Books VI–XXIII, XXXII–XXXVII, Bohn, 1890–8. Vols. 2, 3, 4, 6.

Pliny the Younger. *The Letters of the Younger Pliny*. Translated by Betty Radice. Penguin, 1963.

Plutarch. *The Lives of the Noble Grecians and Romans*. Translated by John Dryden and revised by Arthur Hugh Clough. London: John Lane, the Bodley Head, n.d. (reprint of 1864 edition).

————. *Fall of the Roman Republic. Six Lives by Plutarch*. Translated by Rex Warner. Penguin, 1958.

Polybius. *The Histories*. Translated by W. R. Paton. Books I–II, V–VIII, LCL, 1922–7. Vols. 1, 2, 3, 5.

Propertius. *The Poems of Propertius*. Translated by A. E. Watts. Penguin, rev. ed., 1966.

432

Sallust. *The Jugurthine War. The Conspiracy of Catiline.* Translated by
S. A. Handford. Penguin, 1963.

Seneca. *Moral Essays.* Translated by John W. Basore. Vol. 2, De con-
solatione ad Helviam, LCL, 1927.

Strabo. *The Geography.* Translated by H. C. Hamilton and W. Falconer.
Bohn, 1887. Vol. 1. *The Geography.* Translated by Horace L.
Jones. LCL, 1917–32. Vol. 2.

Suetonius. *The Twelve Caesars.* Translated by Robert Graves. Penguin,
1957.

Tacitus. *The Annals of Imperial Rome.* Translated by Michael Grant.
Penguin, rev. ed., 1959.

———. *The Histories.* Translated by Kenneth Wellesley. Penguin, 1964.

Thucydides. *The History of the Peloponnesian War.* Edited in translation by Sir Richard Livingstone. World's Classics, 1943.

———. *History of the Peloponnesian War.* Translated by Rex Warner.
Penguin, 1954.

Varro. *On the Latin Language.* Translated by Roland G. Kent. LCL,
1951. Vol. 1.

Virgil. *The Eclogues, Georgics and Aeneid of Virgil.* Translated by
C. Day Lewis. London: Oxford University Press, 1966.

———. *The Aeneid.* Translated by W. F. Jackson Knight. Penguin,
1956.

Modern Works

Alföldi, Andrew. *Early Rome and the Latins.* Ann Arbor: University of
Michigan Press, 1965.

Altheim, Franz. *Italien und Rom.* Amsterdam, 1937.

———. *Der Ursprung der Etrusker.* Baden-Baden, 1950.

———. *Römische Geschichte.* Frankfurt am Main, 1953.

Banti, Luisa. *Il Mondo degli Etruschi.* Rome: Primata, 1960.

Bloch, Raymond. *The Etruscans.* Translated by Stuart Hood. London:
Thames & Hudson, 1958.

———. *The Origins of Rome.* Translated by Margaret Shenfield. London: Thames & Hudson, 1960.

———. *Etruscan Art.* London: Barrie & Rockliff in association with
Cory, Adams & Mackay, 1966.

Boëthius, Axel. *The Golden House of Nero: Some Aspects of Roman
Architecture.* Ann Arbor: University of Michigan Press, 1960.

Boëthius, Axel, and Ward-Perkins, J. B. *Etruscan and Roman Architecture*. Penguin, Pelican History of Art, 1970.

Boni, Giacomo. *Scavi nel Foro Romano*. Rome, 1902.

Clemen, Carl. *Die Religion der Etrusker*. Bonn: Röhrscheid, 1936.

Cles-Reden, Sibylle von. *Das versunkene Volk*. Frankfurt am Main, 1956.

Colonna, G. "The Sanctuary at Pyrgi in Etruria." *Archaeology* 19, 1966.

Dennis, George. *The Cities and Cemeteries of Etruria*, 2 vols. London: John Murray, 3rd edn., 1883.

Ducati, Pericle. *Etruria antica*, 2 vols. Turin, 1927.

Ducati, Pericle, and Giglioli, Giulio Q. *Arte Etrusca*. Rome, 1927.

Etruscan Culture. New York: Columbia University Press, 1962.

Finley, M. I. *Aspects of Antiquity*. London: Chatto & Windus, 1968.

Freeman, Edward A. *The History of Sicily from the Earliest Times*, 4 vols. Oxford: Clarendon Press, 1891–4.

Gjerstad, Ejnar. *Legends and Facts of Early Roman History*. Lund: Gleerup, 1962.

———. *Early Rome*, III. Lund: Acta Inst. Romani Regni Sueviae, 1960.

Grimal, Pierre. *A la recherche de l'Italie antique*. Paris: Hachette, 1961.

Harris, W. V. *Rome in Etruria and Umbria*. Oxford: Clarendon Press, 1971.

Haynes, Sibylle. *Etruscan Bronze Utensils*. London: British Museum, 1965.

Hencken, H. O'N. *Tarquinia, Villanovans and Early Etruscans*, 2 vols. Cambridge, Mass., 1968. American School of Prehistoric Research, Peabody Museum, Harvard University, Bulletin 23.

———. *Tarquinia and Etruscan Origins*. New York: Praeger, and London: Thames & Hudson, 1968.

Herbig, R. *Götter und Dämonen der Etrusker*. Mainz: Zabern, 2nd edn., 1965.

Heurgon, Jacques. *Daily Life of the Etruscans*. Translated by James Kirkup. London: Weidenfeld & Nicolson, 1964.

———. "The Inscriptions of Pyrgi." *Journal of Roman Studies* 56, 1966.

Heuss, Alfred. *Römische Geschichte*. Braunschweig, 1960.

Judson, Sheldon, and Kahane, Anne. "Underground Drainageways in Southern Etruria and Northern Latium." *Papers of the British School at Rome*, Vol. XXXI (New Series, Vol. XVIII), 1963.

Lanciani, Rodolfo. *The Ruins and Excavations of Ancient Rome*. London: Macmillan, 1897.

———. *New Tales of Old Rome*. London: Macmillan, 1901.

Lawrence, D. H. *Etruscan Places*. London: Secker & Warburg, 1932.
Lopes Pegna, Mario. *Storia del popolo etrusco*. Florence, 1959.
Lukan, K. *Land der Etrusker*. Vienna, 1861.
Mansuelli, Guido A. *The Art of Etruria and Early Rome*. New York: Crown, 1964.
Mommsen, Theodor. *Romische Geschichte*. Berlin, 3rd edn., 1861.
Moretti, Mario. *La tomba delle Olimpiadi*. Milan, 1960.
———. *New Monuments of Etruscan Painting*. Pennsylvania State University Press, 1971.
Moretti, Mario, and Maetzke, G., with photographs by Leonard von Matt. *The Art of the Etruscans*. London: Thames & Hudson, 1970.
Mostra dell'Etruria Padana e della Città di Spina. Catalogue. Bologna, 1960.
Pallottino, Massimo. *Etruscan Painting*. Translated by M. E. Stanley and Stuart Gilbert. Geneva: Skira, 1952.
———. *The Etruscans*. Translated by J. Cremona. Penguin, 1955.
Pallottino, Massimo, and Jucker, H. and I. *Art of the Etruscans*. London: Thames & Hudson, 1955.
Pfiffig, Ambros Josef. *Die Ausbreitung des römischen Stadtwesens in Etrurien*. Florence, 1966.
———. "Die Haltung Etruriens im 2. Punischen Krieg." *Historia* XV, 1966.
———. "Das Verhalten Etruriens im Samnitenkrieg und bis zum I. Punischen Krieg." *Historia* XVII, 1968.
Picard, Gilbert Charles and Colette. *The Life and Death of Carthage*. Translated by Dominique Collon. London: Sidgwick & Jackson, 1968.
Randall-MacIver, D. *Villanovans and Early Etruscans*. Oxford, 1924.
———. *The Etruscans*. Oxford, 1927.
———. *Italy before the Romans*. Oxford, 1928.
Richardson, Emeline. *The Etruscans: Their Art and Civilization*. University of Chicago Press, 1964.
Riis, P. J. *Tyrrenika*. Copenhagen: Munksgaard, 1941.
———. *An Introduction to Etruscan Art*. Copenhagen, 1953.
Romanelli, Pietro. *Tarquinia: La necropoli e il museo*. Rome: Istituto Poligrafico dello Stato, 1957.
Scullard, H. H. *From the Gracchi to Nero: A History of Rome from 133 B.C. to 68 A.D.* New York: Praeger, 1959.
———. *A History of the Roman World from 753 B.C. to 146 B.C.* London: Methuen, 3rd edn., 1961.
———. *The Etruscan Cities and Rome*. London: Thames & Hudson, 1967.

Teitz, R. S. *Masterpieces of Etruscan Art*. Worcester, Mass.: Worcester Art Museum, 1967 (exhibition catalogue).

Trachtenberg, Marvin. "An Antique Model for Donatello's *David*." *Art Bulletin* 50, September 1968.

Vacano, Otto-Wilhelm von. *The Etruscans in the Ancient World*. Translated by Sheila Ann Ogilvie. London: Edward Arnold, 1960.

Ward-Perkins, J. B. "Etruscan and Roman Roads in Southern Etruria." *Journal of Roman Studies* 47, 1957.

————. "Veii. The Historical Topography of the Ancient City." *Papers of the British School at Rome*, Vol. XXIX (New Series Vol. XVI), 1961.

————. *Landscape and History in Central Italy*. The Second J. L. Myres Memorial Lecture. Oxford: Blackwell, n.d. (1964).

Index

ii

iv

A NOTE ABOUT THE AUTHOR

WERNER KELLER is one of Germany's best-selling authors. Born in 1909 in the Anhalt region of Germany, he was educated in Germany and Switzerland, and received an LL.D. from the University of Jena. His other books include *The Bible as History* (1956), which was translated into twenty-two languages and sold over six million copies throughout the world; *East Minus West = Zero* (1962), a study of Russian influences in Western culture; and *Diaspora* (1969), a history of the Jewish people from post-biblical times to the present. For the past nineteen years, Dr. Keller has lived in Switzerland with his family.

A NOTE ON THE TYPE

THE TEXT OF THIS BOOK was set on the Linotype in a face called TIMES ROMAN, designed by STANLEY MORISON for *The Times* (London), and first introduced by that newspaper in 1932.

Among typographers and designers of the twentieth century, Stanley Morison has been a strong forming influence, as typographical adviser to the English Monotype Corporation, as a director of two distinguished English publishing houses, and as a writer of sensibility, erudition, and keen practical sense.

In 1930 Morison wrote: "Type design moves at the pace of the most conservative reader. The good type-designer therefore realises that, for a new fount to be successful, it has to be so good that only very few recognise its novelty. If readers do not notice the consummate reticence and rare discipline of a new type, it is probably a good letter." It is now generally recognized that in the creation of *Times Roman* Morison successfully met the qualifications of this theoretical doctrine.

Composed by American Book–Stratford Press,
Brattleboro, Vt.
Printed and bound by Halliday Lithograph
Corporation, West Hanover, Mass.
Typography and binding design by
Clint Anglin